FrontPage® 2002
Virtual Classroom

C0-EDX-714

FrontPage® 2002

Virtual Classroom

David Karlins

Osborne / McGraw-Hill

New York   Chicago   San Francisco
Lisbon   London   Madrid   Mexico City
Milan   New Delhi   San Juan
Seoul   Singapore   Sydney   Toronto

Osborne/**McGraw-Hill**
2600 Tenth Street
Berkeley, California 94710
U.S.A.

To arrange bulk purchase discounts for sales promotions, premiums, or fund-raisers, please contact Osborne/**McGraw-Hill** at the above address. For information on translations or book distributors outside the U.S.A., please see the International Contact Information page immediately following the index of this book.

FrontPage® 2002 Virtual Classroom

Copyright © 2001 by The McGraw-Hill Companies. All rights reserved. Printed in the United States of America. Except as permitted under the Copyright Act of 1976, no part of this publication may be reproduced or distributed in any form or by any means, or stored in a database or retrieval system, without the prior written permission of the publisher, with the exception that the program listings may be entered, stored, and executed in a computer system, but they may not be reproduced for publication.

Brainsville.com™
The better way to learn.

CD-ROM Portions Copyright © 2001 The McGraw-Hill Companies, Inc. and Portions Copyright © 2001 Brainsville.com. The exact portions of the Work owned by each of the parties has been recorded with the U.S. Copyright Office.

1234567890 QPD QPD 01987654321

Book p/n 0-07-219173-2 and CD p/n 0-07-219174-0
parts of
ISBN 0-07-219172-4

Publisher
Brandon A. Nordin

Vice President & Associate Publisher
Scott Rogers

Acquisitions Editor
Gretchen Ganser

Project Editor
Pamela Woolf

Acquisitions Coordinators
Alissa Larson
Emma Acker

Technical Editor
Jody Cline

Proofreader
Sossity Smith

Indexer
Karin Arrigoni

Illustrator
Michael Mueller

Production Manager
epic/Eric Houts

Computer & Series Designer
epic/Andrea Reider

Cover Design
Ted Holladay

This book was composed with QuarkXPress™.

Information has been obtained by Osborne/**McGraw-Hill** from sources believed to be reliable. However, because of the possibility of human or mechanical error by our sources, Osborne/**McGraw-Hill**, or others, Osborne/**McGraw-Hill** does not guarantee the accuracy, adequacy, or completeness of any information and is not responsible for any errors or omissions or the results obtained from use of such information.

Dedication

For everyone in the world with a message that needs to be heard on the Internet.

About the Author

David Karlins is an acclaimed Web designer, Web design instructor, and author of a dozen books on Web design and graphics. His Web design clients range from the Himalayan Fair to insurance companies, and from cutting-edge music producers to literary agencies.

In addition to the *FrontPage 2002 Virtual Classroom*, David's previous FrontPage books include *Create FrontPage Web Pages in a Weekend*, *Wild Web Graphics with Microsoft Image Composer*, *MCSD: Designing and Implementing Web Sites Using Microsoft FrontPage*, *Teach Yourself FrontPage in a Week*, and the *FrontPage Bible* (co-author). Other recent Web design and graphics book by David Karlins include the *Teach Yourself CorelDRAW in 24 Hours* and the *Complete Idiot's Guide to Flash*. David is a Microsoft Certified Professional in FrontPage, and he runs the FrontPage Forum at ppinet.com.

Contents at a Glance

   Introduction   xxv
1 FrontPage Web Sites—A Running Start   1
2 Getting Around in FrontPage   21
3 Editing and Formatting Web Pages   33
4 Working with Pictures   55
5 Designing with Tables, Photo Galleries, and Positioning   77
6 Many Ways to Navigate Your Site   93
7 Page Design with Shared Borders   113
8 Using Frames   127
9 Creating Your Own Themes   145
10 Using Web Components   163
11 Creating Input Forms   187
12 Managing Form Data   203
13 Animating with Dynamic HTML   221
14 Adding Sound and Video   235
15 Creating Complex Webs with Web Templates   251
16 FrontPage and Web Servers   271
17 Managing Your Web Site   283
A Installing FrontPage 2002   309
B FrontPage Add-In Programs   315
   Index   321

Contents

Introduction XXV

1 FrontPage Web Sites—A Running Start 1

Start with a FrontPage Web 2
Choosing a Location for Your Web 3
Working with Web Templates 5

Adding Global Web Design Elements 7
Instant Formatting with Themes 7
Formatting Shared Borders 8
Formatting Link Bars 9

Testing and Publishing a Web 14
Using the Preview Tab 14
Interested in HTML? 15
Previewing in a Browser 16
Publishing Your Site to the World Wide Web 17
Saving a Disk-Based Web 17
Publishing to a FrontPage Web Server 17

Contents

WHAT'S NEXT? 19

On the Virtual Classroom CD-ROM: Lesson 1, "Creating a FrontPage Web" 19

2 Getting Around in FrontPage 21

LOOKING AT YOUR WEB SITE 22
EXPLORING IN FOLDERS VIEW 23
   WHAT'S WHERE? 23
   STRUCTURING FILES IN FOLDERS 24
   RENAMING PAGE FILES AND TITLES 25
AVOIDING THE MISSING LINK 26
SCOPING OUT YOUR SITE WITH REPORTS 27
MANY WAYS TO EDIT A PAGE 28
   NORMAL PAGE VIEW 29
   HTML PAGE VIEW 29
   PREVIEW PAGE VIEW 31
   VIEWING A PAGE IN A BROWSER 31
READY TO EDIT PAGE CONTENT? 32

3 Editing and Formatting Web Pages 33

CHECKING OUT THE TOOLBARS 34
   CREATING PAGES—USING THE STANDARD TOOLBAR 34
   MAKING YOUR PAGE LOOK GOOD—THE FORMATTING TOOLBAR 36
EDITING TEXT 37
DEFINING LINKS 38
   AUTOMATIC LINKS 38
   ASSIGNING LINKS TO SELECTED TEXT 38
USING BOOKMARKS 41
FORMATTING TEXT 42
   FORMATTING SELECTED TEXT 43
   FORMATTING PARAGRAPHS 44
   FORMATTING BORDERS AND SHADING 46

Formatting Pages 48
Defining Page Backgrounds 49
Adding Background Sounds 51
Defining Page Margins 52
Other Page Properties 53
What's Next? 54

> On the Virtual Classroom CD-ROM: Lesson 2, "Formatting Page Text" 54

4 Working with Pictures 55

Getting Pictures into FrontPage 56
Copying Pictures into FrontPage 56
Inserting Picture Files 56
Adding Clip Art 57
Saving Picture Files 58
Sizing and Locating Images 60
Resizing Images 60
Aligning and Locating Pictures 62
Editing Pictures in FrontPage 65
Picture Links and Image Maps 67
Creating a Picture Link 67
Creating an Image Map 68
More Picture Properties 69
Exploring the Picture Properties Dialog Box 70
Horizontal and Vertical Spacing 71
Border Size (or No Border) 71
Alternative Representation 72
Interlacing/Progressive Passes 73
A Quick Look at FrontPage's Drawing Tools 74
Next Up... Tables 75

> On the Virtual Classroom CD-ROM: Lesson 3, "Working with Pictures" 75

5 Designing with Tables, Photo Galleries, and Positioning 77

- **CREATING A TABLE** 78
- **USING TABLES TO PRESENT DATA** 79
  - ENTERING DATA 79
  - USING TABLE AUTOFORMATS 80
- **USING TABLES AS A LAYOUT TOOL** 81
  - BORDERLESS TABLES FOR LAYOUT 81
  - FORMATTING TABLE CELLS 82
  - MORE TABLE LAYOUT OPTIONS 84
- **USING THE PHOTO GALLERY** 86
- **USING ABSOLUTELY POSITIONED TEXT AND PICTURES** 89
- **EVERYTHING IN POSITION?** 91

> ON THE VIRTUAL CLASSROOM CD-ROM: LESSON 4, "DESIGNING WITH TABLES" 91

6 Many Ways to Navigate Your Site 93

- **TEXT AND GRAPHIC LINK PROPERTIES** 94
  - DEFINING SCREENTIPS 94
  - OPENING A LINK IN A NEW WINDOW 95
- **CREATING LINK BARS** 97
  - CREATING A LINK BAR FROM NAVIGATION STRUCTURE 97
  - DEFINING CUSTOM LINK BARS 101
  - LINK BARS WITH BACK AND NEXT LINKS 103
- **GENERATING A TABLE OF CONTENTS** 105
  - CREATING A TABLE OF CONTENTS BASED ON YOUR SITE 106
  - TABLE OF CONTENTS BASED ON CATEGORIES 107
- **ADDING INTERNET SEARCH BOXES** 108
  - SEARCH BOXES 108
  - STOCK QUOTES 109
  - FORMATTING STOCK AND INTERNET LOOKUP BOXES 110
- **NAVIGATE AWAY** 110

> ON THE VIRTUAL CLASSROOM CD-ROM: LESSON 5, "DEFINING LINKS" 111

7 Page Design with Shared Borders 113

Using Shared Borders 114
- Why Use Shared Borders? 114
- Shared Borders vs. Frames 115
- Avoiding Shared Border Confusion 115

Creating Shared Borders 116

Editing Shared Borders 118
- Wrestling with Shared Border Width 119
- Formatting Shared Borders 120
- Advanced Formatting for Shared Borders 121

Controlling Link Bars in Shared Borders 123

Customizing Shared Borders for Individual Pages 123

Shared Border Design Tips 124

8 Using Frames 127

Using Frames in Web Sites 128
- Frames as Navigation Tools 128
- Frames Can Be Flexible 129
- Frames Are Made Up of HTML Pages 130

Building Framed Pages in FrontPage 130
- Creating a Frameset from a Template 131
- Adding Frame Content 132
- Editing Framed Page Content 137

Changing Frame Properties 138
- Resizing a Frame 138
- Defining Frameset Margins 139
- Making a Framed Page Resizable 140

Splitting or Deleting Frames 141

Providing No Frame Options 141

Frames and Links 142

INLINE FRAMES	143
SIZING UP FRAMES	144
ON THE VIRTUAL CLASSROOM CD-ROM: LESSON 6, "WORKING WITH FRAMES"	144

9 Creating Your Own Themes — 145

USING FRONTPAGE THEMES	146
ASSIGNING A THEME TO A WEB SITE	147
USING A THEME ON JUST ONE PAGE	148
LOOKING AT FRONTPAGE THEME FILES	149
TWEAKING FRONTPAGE THEMES WITH CHECK BOXES	150
CREATING YOUR OWN FRONTPAGE THEMES	151
CHANGING THEME COLORS	152
CREATING YOUR OWN THEME GRAPHICS	156
FORMATTING THEME TEXT	158
CUSTOM THEMES CREATE UNIQUE SITES	160
ON THE VIRTUAL CLASSROOM CD-ROM: LESSON 7, "CREATING CUSTOM THEMES"	161

10 Using Web Components — 163

AN OVERVIEW OF FRONTPAGE COMPONENTS	164
HOW DO COMPONENTS WORK?	164
INSERTING COMMENTS AND DATES	165
UPDATING A PAGE WITH TIMESTAMPS	166
ADDING INVISIBLE COMMENTS	167
DYNAMIC EFFECTS	168
HOVER BUTTONS	168
MOVING TEXT IN MARQUEES	171
BANNER ADS	173
WEB SEARCH	174
COUNTING HITS	176
DISPLAYING PICTURES IN A PHOTO GALLERY	178

Using Included Content 179
Inserting Link Bars 181
Generating an Automatic Table of
Contents 181
bCentral, Expedia, MSN, and MSNBC
Web Components 182
Advanced Controls 184
Components Add Dynamism to Your Site 184

11 Creating Input Forms 187

Creating a Form 188
   First Step: Define a Form 189
   Adding Buttons 190
Adding Form Fields 191
   Creating Text Boxes 192
   Adding Text Areas 193
   Allowing for File Uploads 194
   Including Check Boxes 195
   Adding Option Buttons 196
   Adding Drop-Down Boxes 197
Adding Form Extras 199
Formatting Forms 199
Validating Input Data 200
Testing Input Forms 202
Moving On to Collect Data 202

    On the Virtual Classroom CD-ROM: Lesson 8,
    "Designing Input Forms" 202

12 Managing Form Data 203

Four Ways to Collect Form Data 204
How Data Gets Managed 205
Collecting Form Data Through E-mails 206
Collecting Form Data in Text Files 208

Contents

SENDING FORM DATA TO A WEB PAGE 212
    CREATING A WEB PAGE TO DISPLAY FORM DATA 212
    POSTING FORM DATA TO A WEB PAGE 212
USING THE DATABASE INTERFACE WIZARD TO
CREATE A LIVE DATABASE CONNECTION 214
MANY OPTIONS FOR COLLECTING DATA 218

    ON THE VIRTUAL CLASSROOM CD-ROM: LESSON 9,
    "COLLECTING DATA ONLINE" 219

13 Animating with Dynamic HTML 221

BEFORE YOU USE DHTML... READ THIS! 222
CREATING PAGE AND SITE TRANSITIONS 223
APPLYING DHTML TO PICTURES AND TEXT 224
SWAPPING PICTURES 225
ADDING DHTML TO TEXT 228
    USING ROLLOVER EFFECTS ON TEXT 228
    USING PAGE LOAD EFFECTS ON TEXT 229
    ASSIGNING DHTML TO TEXT 230
REMOVING DHTML EFFECTS 231
DHTML EVERYWHERE... 231
DHTML—TECHIE STUFF 232
INTERACTIVITY, ANIMATION... AND MEDIA 232

    ON THE VIRTUAL CLASSROOM CD-ROM: LESSON 10,
    "USING DYNAMIC HTML EFFECTS" 233

14 Adding Sound and Video 235

SOUND AND VIDEO—THE COMING WAVE 236
    HOW DO VISITORS SEE AND HEAR MEDIA FILES? 236
    A QUICK SURVEY OF MEDIA FILE TYPES 237
    HOW DO YOU GET VIDEO AND SOUND FILES? 241
IMPORTING MEDIA FILES INTO FRONTPAGE 241
THE EASY WAY TO EMBED SOUND AND VIDEO 242

EMBEDDING MEDIA FILES IN YOUR PAGE	244
ADDING A PLUG-IN	244
EMBEDDING VIDEO AS PICTURES	247
ALIGNING, SIZING, AND CREATING SPACE FOR EMBEDDED VIDEOS	248
ADDING BACKGROUND AUDIO TO PAGES	249
HAVE FUN WITH MEDIA	250
ON THE VIRTUAL CLASSROOM CD-ROM: LESSON 11, "EMBEDDING MEDIA IN YOUR WEB SITE"	250

15 Creating Complex Webs with Web Templates 251

SAVING TIME WITH WEB TEMPLATES	252
INCLUDING A DISCUSSION FORUM	255
SETTING UP A DISCUSSION FORUM	255
USING A DISCUSSION FORUM	258
USING THE SHAREPOINT-BASED TEAM WEB SITE	260
SHAREPOINT—DO YOU NEED IT?	260
SHAREPOINT PORTALS—EDITED BY VISITORS	261
CREATING A SHAREPOINT PORTAL	263
FORMATTING AND EDITING A SHAREPOINT PORTAL	263
LIST AND LIBRARY WEB COMPONENTS	264
USING A SHAREPOINT PORTAL	267
WORKING WITH SERVERS	269

16 FrontPage and Web Servers 271

REMOTE WEB SITES—LET SOMEONE ELSE SWEAT THE SERVER STUFF	272
SHOPPING FOR A WEB PRESENCE PROVIDER	272
CONNECTING TO A REMOTE SERVER	273
PUBLISHING YOUR SITE TO A LOCAL SERVER	274
INSTALLING INTERNET INFORMATION SERVER (IIS) 6.0	275
ADDING FRONTPAGE 2002 EXTENSIONS TO IIS 6.0	276

Contents

- Administering Your Server 277
- Defining Server Permissions 278
  - Assigning Unique Permissions for Your Site 279
  - Adding Roles 280
  - Defining Users 281
- Server Administration and Site Management 281

17 Managing Your Web Site 283

- Looking at Files 284
  - Analyzing Your Site Summary Report 284
  - Finding 285
- Identifying Problems in Your Site 290
  - Finding and Fixing Unlinked 290
  - Identifying Slow Pages 291
  - Finding and Fixing Broken Links 294
  - Finding and Fixing Component Errors 297
- Managing Workgroups 298
  - Assigning Work 299
  - Tracking Work 300
  - Checking In and Checking Out 300
  - The Publish Status Report 303
- Tracking Site Usage 304
  - Summarizing Site Hits 304
  - Who Is Coming to Your Site? 304
- Assigning and Managing Tasks 306
  - Adding Tasks 306
  - Editing Tasks 306
- Where to From Here? 307

A Installing FrontPage 2002 309

WHICH OPERATING SYSTEM IS BEST FOR FRONTPAGE 2002? 310

    DO YOU NEED TO INSTALL SERVER EXTENSIONS? 310

    DIFFERENT SERVER EXTENSIONS ARE AVAILABLE FOR DIFFERENT OPERATING SYSTEMS 311

INSTALLING FRONTPAGE 311

    WHICH INSTALLATION IS BEST? 312

    CHOOSING FEATURES TO INSTALL 313

B FrontPage Add-In Programs 315

INSTALLING FRONTPAGE ADD-INS 316

    INSTALLING MICROSOFT ADD-INS 316

    REMOVING ADD-INS 318

A QUICK LOOK AT FRONTLOOK 318

JAVASCRIPTING WITH J-BOTS PLUS 2002 319

OTHER ADD-INS 320

Index 321

Acknowledgments

First and foremost, I need to credit the thousands of readers, students, and fellow FrontPage developers who have shared their questions, frustrations, discoveries, and insights with me over the last five years. I've learned a tremendous amount from all of you. Hopefully I've done a decent job of pulling together our collective experiences and using them to present FrontPage in a fun, accessible, and candid book.

For those astute readers who recognize that the editing, layout, design, and promotion of this book are way above par, please take careful note of the list of editors and other folks at Osborne who made this book happen. I can't list them all here, but each one went all out to make this a quality book. Ditto for the video crew at Brainsville.com.

Thanks also to my agent Lisa Swayne.

Finally, Hi Sam! This one's for you.

Introduction

WHO WILL ENJOY THIS BOOK?

You will, if you want to create attractive, feature-packed, and easy-to-use Web sites with FrontPage. Because of its Microsoft Office-like interface, FrontPage is a very accessible Web design tool. But beneath the surface, you'll find powerful features that allow you to edit pictures, generate JavaScripts, and collect input data—features not available in any other Web design package. My goal with this book is to make those features accessible to both brand new Web designers, as well as veteran FrontPage designers who would like to add advanced features to their sites.

I've been teaching folks like yourself to use FrontPage for five years now. I've written Microsoft authorized books on how to pass the Microsoft FrontPage MCSD exam (and I've passed the Microsoft FrontPage Certified Professional exam myself). But I've also taught people FrontPage who have never created a Web site before. Perhaps most importantly, I use FrontPage almost every day to create Web sites. I've learned through trial and error the best ways to create Web sites with FrontPage, and also the best ways to learn FrontPage.

Beginning level, intermediate, and many advanced FrontPage designers will all find important resources in this book. Many chapters approach concepts like tables, frames, and input forms on different levels. At first, new FrontPage users might want to try the more basic step-by-step sections early in the chapter, while more advanced developers will push the envelope using all the features covered in a chapter.

And, this book is much more than a *book*. The accompanying CD-ROM, which is discussed in detail in the remainder of this introduction, has more than an hour of videos with demonstrations, tips, and candid advice.

FrontPage 2002 Virtual Classroom CD

This CD contains an exciting new kind of video-based instruction to help you learn FrontPage faster. We believe this learning tool is a unique development in the area of computer-based training. The author actually talks to you, right from your computer screen, demonstrating topics he wrote about in the book. Moving "screencams" and slides accompany the presentation, reinforcing what you're learning.

The technology and design of the presentation were developed by Brainsville.com. The content on the CD-ROM was developed by Osborne/McGraw-Hill, David Karlins, and Brainsville.com. Patents (pending), copyright, and trademark protections apply to this technology and the name Brainsville.com.

To ensure that the lessons play as smoothly as possible, please read the following directions for usage of the CD-ROM.

Getting Started

The CD-ROM is optimized to run under Windows 95/98/ME/NT/2000 using the QuickTime player version 5 (or greater), from Apple. This CD-ROM is not designed to run on a Mac. If you don't have the QuickTime 5 player installed, you must install it either by downloading it from the Internet at http://www.quicktime.com, or running the Setup program from the CD-ROM. If you install from the Web, it's fine to use the free version of the QuickTime player. You don't need to purchase the full version.

To install the QuickTime player from the CD-ROM on a Windows PC:

1. Insert the CD-ROM in the drive.
2. Use Explorer or My Computer to browse to the CD-ROM.
3. Open the QuickTime folder.
4. Double-click the setup program there.
5. Follow the setup instructions on screen.

Running the CD in Windows 95/98/ME/NT/2000

Minimum Requirements:

- QuickTime 5 player
- Pentium II P300 (or equivalent)
- 64MB of RAM
- 8X CD-ROM
- Windows 95, Windows 98, Windows 2000, Windows ME, or Windows NT 4.0 with at least Service Pack 4
- 16-bit sound card and speakers

FrontPage 2002 Virtual Classroom CD-ROM can run directly from the CD (see the following for running it from the hard drive for better performance if necessary) and should start automatically when you insert the CD in the drive. If the program does not start automatically, your system might not be set up to automatically detect CDs.

To change this, you can do the following:

1. Choose Settings | Control Panel, and click the System icon.
2. Click the Device Manager tab in the System Properties dialog box.
3. Double-click the Disk drives icon and locate your CD-ROM drive.
4. Double-click the CD-ROM drive icon, and then click the Settings tab in the CD-ROM Properties dialog box. Make sure the Auto Insert Notification box is checked. This specifies that Windows will be notified when you insert a compact disc into the drive.

If you don't care about the auto-start setting for your CD-ROM, and don't mind the manual approach, you can start the lessons manually. Here's how:

1. Insert the CD-ROM.
2. Double-click the My Computer icon on your Windows desktop.
3. Open the CD-ROM folder.
4. Double-click the startnow.exe icon in the folder.
5. Follow the instructions on screen to start.

THE OPENING SCREEN

When the program autostarts, you'll see a small window in the middle of your screen with an image of the book; click that image to launch the QuickTime player and start the lessons.

The QuickTime player window should open and the *Virtual Classroom* introduction should begin running. On some computers, after the lesson loads you must click the Play button to begin. The Play button is the big round button with an arrow on it at the bottom center of the QuickTime player window. It looks like the play button on a VCR. You can click the links in the lower-left region of the QuickTime window to jump to a given lesson. The author will explain how to use the interface.

The QuickTime player will completely fill a screen that is running at 800 × 600 resolution. (This is the minimum resolution required to play the lessons.) For screens with higher resolution, you can adjust the position of the player on screen, as you like.

If you are online, you can click the Brainsville.com logo under the index marks to jump directly to the Brainsville.com Web site for information about additional video lessons from Brainsville.com. (See the description in the back of this book about the *Web Design CD Extra* for more details.)

Improving Playback

Your *Virtual Classroom* CD-ROM employs some cutting-edge technologies, requiring that your computer be pretty fast to run the lessons smoothly. Many variables determine a computer's video performance, so we can't give you specific requirements for running the lessons. CPU speed, internal bus speed, amount of RAM, CD-ROM drive transfer rate, video display performance, CD-ROM cache settings and other variables will determine how well the lessons play. Our advice is to simply try the CD. The disk has been tested on laptops and desktops of various speeds, and in general, you'll need at least a Pentium II-class computer running in excess of 300Mhz for decent performance. (If you're doing serious Web-design work, it's likely your machine is at least this fast.)

Close Other Programs

For best performance, make sure you are not running other programs in the background while viewing the CD-based lessons. Rendering the video onscreen takes a lot of computing power, and background programs such as automatic e-mail checking, Web-site updating, or Active Desktop applets (such as scrolling stock tickers) can tax the CPU to the point of slowing the videos.

Adjust the Screen Color Depth to Speed Up Performance

It's possible that the author's lips will be out of synch with his voice, just like Web-based videos often look. There are a couple solutions: Lowering the color depth to 16-bit color makes a world of difference with many computers, laptops included. Rarely do people need 24-bit or 32-bit color for their work anyway, and it makes scrolling your screen (in any program) that much slower when running in those higher color depths. Try this:

1. Right-click the desktop and choose Properties.
2. Click the Settings tab.
3. In the Colors section, open the drop-down list box and choose a lower setting. If you are currently running at 24-bit (True Color) color, for example, try 16-bit (High Color). Don't use 256 colors, because video will appear very funky if you do.
4. OK the box. With most computers these days, you don't have to restart the computer after making this change. The video should run more smoothly now, because your computer's CPU doesn't have to work as hard to paint the video pictures on your screen.

If adjusting the color depth didn't help the synch problem, see the following section about copying the CD's files to your hard disk.

Turn Off Screen Savers, Screen Blankers, and Standby Options

When lessons are playing you're likely to not interact with the keyboard or mouse. Because of this, your computer screen might blank, and in some cases (such as with laptops) the computer might even go into a standby mode. You'll want to prevent these annoyances by turning off your screen saver and checking the power options settings to ensure they don't kick in while you're viewing the lessons. You make settings for both of these parameters from the Control Panel.

1. Open Control Panel, choose Display, and click the Screen Saver tab. Choose None for the screen saver.
2. Open Control Panel, choose Power Management, and set System Standby, Turn off Monitor, and Turn off Hard Disks to Never. Then click Save As and save this power setting as Brainsville Courses. You can return your power settings to their previous state, if you like, after you are finished viewing the lessons. Just use the Power Schemes drop-down list and choose one of the factory-supplied settings, such as Home/Office Desk.

Copy the CD Files to the Hard Disk to Speed Up Performance

The CD-ROM drive will whir quite a bit when running the lessons from the CD. If your computer or CD-ROM drive is a bit slow, it's possible the author's lips will be out of synch with his voice, just like Web-based videos often look. The video might freeze or slow down occasionally, though the audio will typically keep going along just fine. If you don't like the CD constantly whirring, or you are annoyed by out-of-synch video, you might be able to solve either or both problems by copying the CD-ROM's contents to your hard disk and running the lessons from there.

To move CD content to your hard disk:

1. Using My Computer or Explorer, check to see that you have at least 650M free space on your hard disk.
2. Create a new folder on your hard disk (the name doesn't matter) and copy all the contents of the CD-ROM to the new folder. (You must preserve the sub-folder names and folder organization as it is on the CD-ROM).
3. Start the program by opening the new folder and double-clicking the file startnow.exe. This will automatically start the lessons and run them from the hard disk.
4. (Optional) For convenience, you can create a shortcut to the startnow.exe file and place it on your desktop. You will then be able to start the program by clicking the shortcut.

Update Your QuickTime Player

The QuickTime software is updated frequently and posted on the Apple QuickTime Web site (www.quicktime.com). You can update your software by clicking Update Existing Software, from the Help menu in the QuickTime player. We strongly suggest you do this from time to time.

Make Sure Your CD-ROM Drive Is Set for Optimum Performance

CD-ROM drives on IBM PCs can be set to transfer data using the DMA (Direct Memory Access) mode, assuming the drive supports this faster mode. If you are experiencing slow performance and out-of-synch problems, check this setting.

These steps are for Windows 98 and Windows ME:

1. Choose Control Panel | System.
2. Click the Device Manager tab.
3. Click the plus (+) sign to the left of the CD-ROM drive.
4. Right-click the CD-ROM drive.
5. Choose Properties.
6. Click the Settings tab.
7. Look to see if the DMA check box is turned on (has a check mark in it). If selected, this increases the CD-ROM drive access speed. Some drives do not support this option. If the DMA check box remains selected after you restart Windows, this option is supported by the device.

In Windows 2000, the approach is a little different. You access the drive's settings via Device Manager as above, but click IDE/ATAPI Controllers. Right-click the IDE channel that your CD-ROM drive is on, choose Properties, and make the settings as appropriate. (Choose the device number, 0 or 1, and check the settings.) Typically it's set to DMA If Available, which is fine. It's not recommended that you change these settings unless you know what you are doing!

Troubleshooting

This section offers solutions to common problems. Check www.quicktime.com for much more information about the QuickTime player, which is the software the *Virtual Classroom* CD uses to play.

The CD Will Not Run

If you have followed the instructions above and the program will not work, you might have a defective drive or CD. Be sure the CD is inserted properly in the drive. Test the drive with other CDs to see if they run.

The Screencam Movie in a Lesson Hangs

If the author continues to talk, but the accompanying screencam seems to be stuck, just click the lesson index in the lower-left region of the QuickTime window to begin your specific lesson again. If this doesn't help, close the QuickTime window; then start the *Virtual Classroom* CD again.

Volume Is Too Low or Totally Silent

1. Check your system volume first. Click the speaker icon next to the clock, in the lower-right corner of the screen. A little slider pops up. Adjust the slider, and make sure the Mute check box is *not* checked.
2. Next, if you have external speakers on your computer, make sure your speakers are turned on, plugged in, wired up properly, and the volume control on the speakers themselves is turned up.
3. Note that the QuickTime player also has a volume control setting. The setting is a slider control in the lower-left of the QuickTime player window.
4. The next place to look if you're still having trouble is in the Windows volume controls. Double-click the speaker next to the clock and it will bring up the Windows Volume Control sliders. Make sure the slider for Wave is not muted, and make sure it's positioned near the top.

For Technical Support

- Phone Hudson Software at (800) 217-0059
- Visit www.quicktime.com
- Visit www.brainsville.com

© 2001 The McGraw-Hill Companies

© 2001 Brainsville.com Patents pending

1

FrontPage Web Sites— A Running Start

One of the coolest things about FrontPage is how quickly and easily you can create a high-powered Web site. Even if you are brand new to Web design, with FrontPage and this book, you can create a large, attractive, easy-to-navigate Web site. *Within hours* your site can include formatted text and paragraphs, images with text wrapping around them, links to pages in and outside your site, and even site-wide color coordinated "themes" that assign graphic design elements, navigation bars, and animated links throughout your Web site.

CHAPTER 1
FrontPage Web Sites—A Running Start

One of the *myths* about FrontPage is that it is easy to use but not too robust. The easy-to-use part is true. You can create nice Web sites quickly with FrontPage. But you can also load up a site with input forms, animated graphics, multimedia sound and video, and the latest in page design techniques. All these features are covered in this book.

As we dive into FrontPage, we'll take the approach of starting with the *big picture*—the organization, content, and style of your *entire Web site*. That's the way FrontPage "thinks," and it's helpful for any Web designer to start from an overview of what is to be accomplished.

Start with a FrontPage Web

FrontPage *Webs* are what FrontPage calls *folders* that organize all the files in your Web site. As long as all your files are created (or imported) while working in a FrontPage Web, FrontPage will make sure that embedded picture files are saved with your Web; links between pages work; and that when you publish (upload) your files to a server, all your files are sent in a way that enables them to work together.

In short, FrontPage Webs do a heck of a lot of work for you. FrontPage is a *page* design tool, but that's not what makes it so valuable. You can get page design programs for free on the Internet (like at Geocities, or Netscape's Composer). FrontPage's value lies in its capability to organize your files and add features usually not available in Web pages.

> **Why Start With Web Design?** An architect starts designing a building before calling in an interior decorator. A painter starts with a sketch before filling in detail, and a FrontPage Web designer starts by creating a *structure* of Web pages.
>
> Why? Well, for one thing, almost all Web sites include more than one page. Which means you have to decide what content to put on each page. Web design gurus generally concur that Web site content should be broken down into digestible bites rather than crammed into an overwhelming page. By organizing your content into

many pages, and *planning how a visitor will move from page to page,* you can create a friendly, accessible Web site.

In addition to the aesthetic side of Web design, it's important to take into consideration that even a small Web site can have dozens, or hundreds of files. A Web page with a dozen pictures requires at least 13 files—both HTML (HyperText Markup Language) files for Web pages and graphic files (usually in GIF or JPEG format). Throw in some sound files, maybe a JavaScript object, and your Web site requires a virtual filing cabinet to organize all your files. Which brings up the second reason to organize your Web site.

Choosing a Location for Your Web

Eventually, you probably want to make your Web site available to others. You might want to publish your site to a server available on the Internet, or you might want to publish your site to an internal intranet for your company or organization.

We'll return to these issues at the end of this chapter—after we've explored how to create a site. FrontPage forces you to decide where you want your Web to reside at the *very beginning* of the process of creating Web site files. This is so FrontPage can organize your files and ensure that all the elements you create are saved.

If you already have a Web server, you need the following information to publish your FrontPage Web to that server:

▶ URL (or, in the case of an intranet, an IP address)
▶ User name
▶ Password

These three things are required to publish your site to an intranet or Internet Web site; they are provided by your server administrator. That's not quite as mysterious as it sounds—it's just like when your phone company issues you a phone number or a Web server administrator issues you a URL (or an IP address), user name, and password. If your company or organization has an intranet site or Internet site, find out who the server administrator is, and get these three items of information from him or her.

CHAPTER 1
FrontPage Web Sites—A Running Start

"Wait," some of you are saying, "I don't have a *server*, let alone a *server administrator*." That's cool. Relax. You can still create a FrontPage Web. You'll just save that Web to a folder on your local computer. The downside of this is that nobody will see it. And, many advanced FrontPage features (like the ability to easily collect input form data, for example) don't work until your site is published to a server that has special files called *FrontPage server extensions* (sometimes called FrontPage extensions for short). But we'll worry about those issues later—at the end of this chapter, and as they confront us in creating Webs. For now, if you're just getting started with FrontPage, decide that you'll save your site to a local folder—what FrontPage calls a *disk-based Web*. If you have already created a Web, FrontPage will, by default, open your last worked-on Web site. You can choose File | Close Web to get rid of that site if you want.

To Begin TO CREATE A FRONTPAGE WEB:

1 Launch FrontPage from Windows.

2 Choose File | New | Page or Web. The New Page or Web Task Pane opens, as shown on the right:

3 Click the Web Site Templates link in the New Page or Web task pane. You'll see a selection of Web site template options, like below:

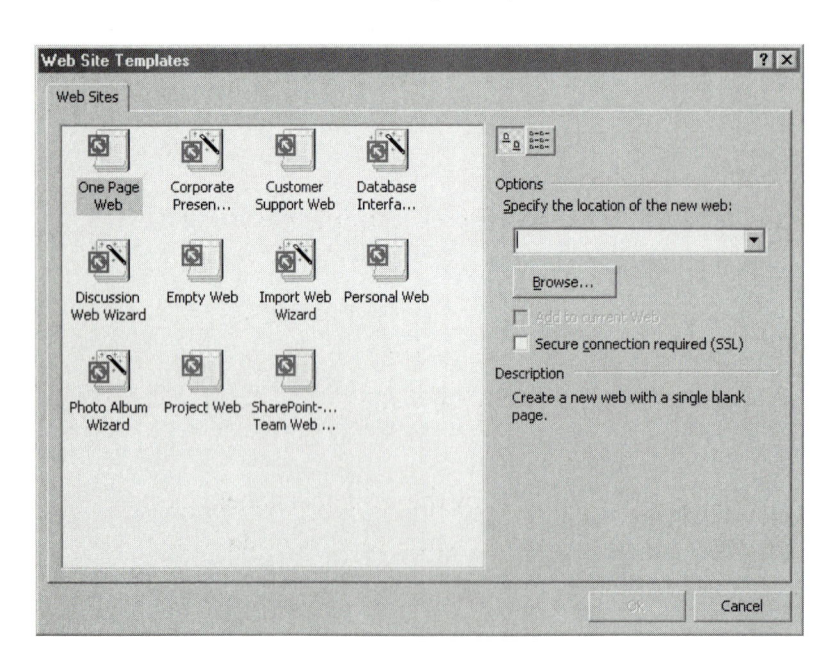

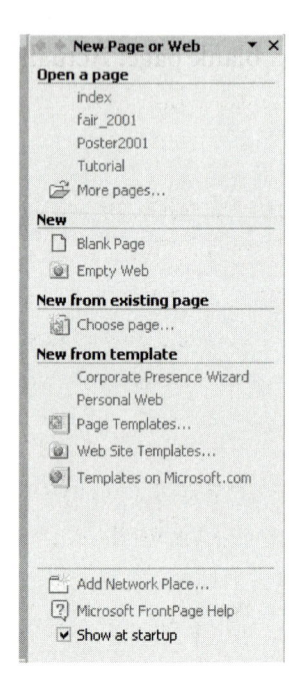

4 For now, don't worry about the template options. First, you need to define a location for your Web. If you have a URL (or IP address) for a server location on an intranet or the Internet, enter that information in the Specify the Location of the New Web box in the Web Site Templates dialog box. If you don't have a server location (yet), use the Browse button to browse to a folder on your local computer, and click OK. Then, type a name for your site after the folder location, as shown in this illustration.

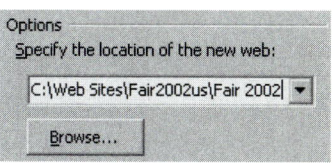

5 When you have entered a location for your site, you're halfway to creating a FrontPage Web. The next step is to choose a template.

Working with Web Templates

All FrontPage Webs are created from templates. That might seem strange if you've worked with other programs (like Microsoft Word, for example), where most of the time you simply start with a blank page. Actually, FrontPage has a *blank* template, which you can think of as using no template at all.

As you click on different Web templates in the Web Site Templates dialog box, brief descriptions appear in the Descriptions area of the dialog box. Here are a few notes to supplement the descriptions provided in FrontPage:

> **NOTE** If you are defining a location on a Web URL, you should enter http://*xxx*, where *xxx* is the URL for your Web site. If your site administrator tells you that you have *permission*—a technical term that means your server setup allows it—to create a *subweb*, you can enter a Web name after the URL. For example, if your URL is http://www.ppinet.com, and you have permission to create a subweb, you can name your Web http://www.ppinet.com/newsite.

▶ **One Page Web** A new Web with a single blank page. A good place to start, because this template automatically generates a blank home page for your site.

▶ **Corporate Presence Web** An instant corporate Web site. However, you still need to edit the many generated pages to add real content!

▶ **Consumer Support Web** Handy—this template creates input forms for questions and feedback.

▶ **Database Interface Web** For serious database folks, this template generates an online database with input forms to collect data, queries to present data, and forms to allow visitors to edit the database content.

- **Discussion Web Wizard** A wizard to help you create a Web site in which visitors can post questions and get answers.
- **Empty Web** This template does the work of creating the necessary folders for a FrontPage Web without creating any pages.
- **Import Web Wizard** Helps you integrate an existing Web site, or folder of files, into a FrontPage Web.
- **Personal Web** A cute four-page Web site for sharing your interests, photos, and favorite sites.
- **Photo Album Wizard** Creates a variety of animated displays for pictures. You supply the scanned pix, FrontPage organizes them into a presentation.
- **Project Web** A specialized Web site template for project management data.
- **SharePoint Team Web** This Web only works with intranets (or, Internet sites—although the design is better suited to intranets) that have Office XP's SharePoint technology installed. If you've got that, you can use this template to create a site for sharing files, announcements, and schedules.

To get started on your Web site, choose one of the templates, and click OK. Your Web will open in Folders view, which looks something like the Windows Explorer and allows you to see the folders and files in your Web site. Folders view for a single page Web is shown in Figure 1-1.

If you choose a template that generates any pages at all, at least one of these pages will be named either index.htm or default.htm. These pages are your site's *home page*—the page to that visitors will go to automatically when they visit your Web site.

> **NOTE** Every Web site must have a home page.

> **TURN THIS CHAPTER INTO A TUTORIAL...** If you want to experiment with creating a Web site as you read this chapter, a good way to go is to generate a Personal Web using the Personal Web template. Choose File | New | Page or Web. When the New Page or Web pane appears on the right side of your screen, click the Web Site Templates link. In the Web Site Templates dialog box, double-click the Personal Web icon. That will create a four-page Web that you can use to test the different Web features explored in the rest of this chapter.

FIGURE 1-1
Folders view shows the directory/folder structure of your site. The Index.htm file in this view is the site's home page

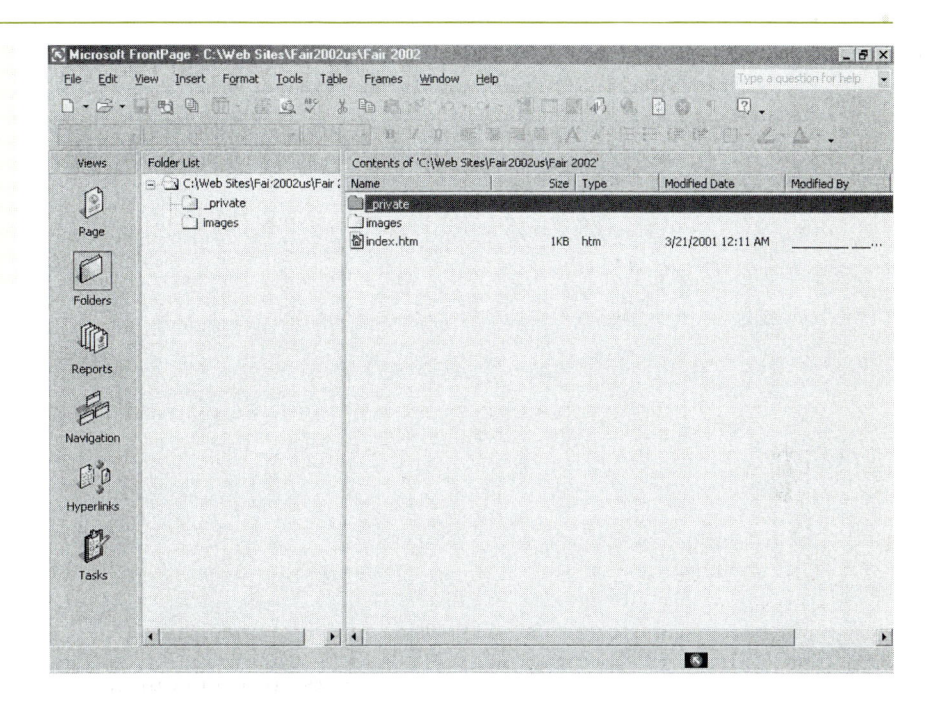

Adding Global Web Design Elements

FrontPage has three powerful ways of formatting and organizing your entire Web site: themes, shared borders, and link bars. Themes add global formatting elements like page background colors, text font and color, and icons (like navigation buttons). Shared borders are embedded Web pages that attach to the top, bottom, right, and/or left side of your pages. They attach to *every* page in your Web site—thus the *shared* border terminology. Shared borders are often used to display navigation links.

FrontPage has a number of ways to embed *automatically generated* navigation links in your Web site pages. The advantage: You can instantly apply navigational links to hundreds of Web pages at a time. The drawback: Because these links are automatically generated, you might still need to manually add navigational links to some pages in your Web site.

Instant Formatting with Themes

Few features of FrontPage provide as much instant impact as a theme. When you apply a theme to a Web site, you generate all kinds of global look-and-feel elements, including the following list.

Chapter 1
FrontPage Web Sites—A Running Start

- A color scheme that is applied to page backgrounds and text
- A set of icons including graphical navigation buttons, horizontal lines, bullet list icons, and page background graphics
- Text fonts, colors, and styles

> **NOTE** While FrontPage provides dozens of themes, advanced designers will probably want to customize their own themes. You explore that in Chapter 9.

Themes can be applied to every page in a Web site, or just some.

To Assign a theme, follow these steps:

1. Select Format | Theme from the menu.

2. To apply your theme to all pages in your site, click the All Pages radio button.

3. Click one of the themes in the list on the left side of the Themes dialog box. You will see a preview of how the theme will look in the Sample of Theme area of the dialog box. Use the check boxes to experiment with vivid colors and active graphics.

> **NOTE** The Active Graphics option generates navigation buttons that change their appearance when visitors interact with them by hovering over them or clicking them.

4. Click OK to apply the theme to your Web site.

Because themes create and format elements used in shared borders and navigation bars, we'll look at and format these additional global site elements before we check out the impact of the theme assignment.

Formatting Shared Borders

Shared borders are formattable embedded pages attached to the side, bottom, or top of every (or many) page in a Web. Since they can appear on *every page* in your Web site, you can save time by creating a set of shared borders, and then attaching them to many pages within your site. Shared borders often are used to display navigation links.

FrontPage 2002 allows you to format shared pages by changing their background color. For a full exploration of shared borders, see Chapter 7.

To Apply SHARED BORDERS:

1 Select Format | Shared Borders from the menu.

2 Select the All Pages radio button to apply the shared borders to the entire Web, or select the Selected Pages radio button to apply shared borders only to selected pages.

3 Select any combination of shared borders. In this illustration, the left and top borders have been selected.

4 After you select shared borders, click OK.

> **NOTE** If you select top and/or left shared borders, you can select the Include Navigation Buttons check boxes for one or both of these shared borders.

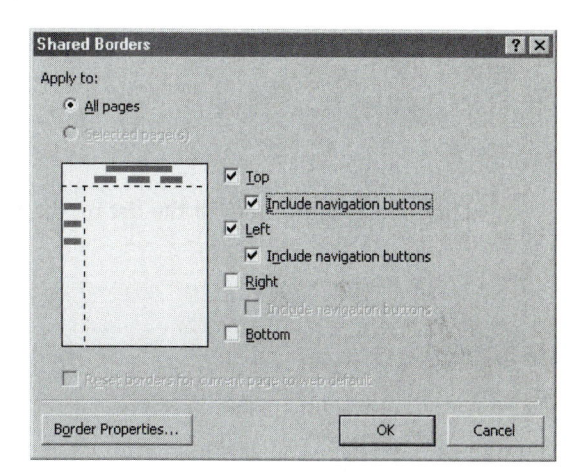

FORMATTING LINK BARS

When you attach top or left shared borders to pages in your site, you are given the option of generating Navigation buttons in those shared borders. Navigation buttons are link buttons that FrontPage *creates for you* based on a navigation structure you define in your Web.

All kinds of options for generated link bars are explored in Chapter 7. But here, we'll take a quick look at how to control the links FrontPage creates for you in shared borders.

A QUICK PREVIEW OF NAVIGATION VIEW

Navigation view is used to define link relationships between pages in your Web. It's also a good place to create *new* (blank) pages for your Web. To see your Web site in Navigation view, click the Navigation icon in the Views bar on the left of your FrontPage window.

> **NOTE** If you don't see the Views bar, choose View from the menu, and click Views Bar.

CHAPTER 1
FrontPage Web Sites—A Running Start

> **FRONTPAGE FAMILY VALUES** FrontPage uses a "family" analogy in defining relationships between pages. A page at the top of the pecking order is the "parent" page, whereas the page under that page in Navigation view is a "child" page. Child pages can, in turn, have child pages of their own. And so it goes, reproducing an infinite number of generations of FrontPage Web pages.

To create a new page in Navigation view, start by choosing the page that you want your new page to be a *child* of—the page that will link to your new page in the Web site navigation bars. Click the Create a New Normal Page button at the far-left edge of the Standard toolbar. If you have a page selected when you create a new page, the new page is inserted into the navigation flowchart as a child page of the selected page. For example, in this illustration on the right, New Page 1 is a child page of the Home Page. When you create a new page in Navigation view, the new page becomes a child page of the page that was selected when you created the new page.

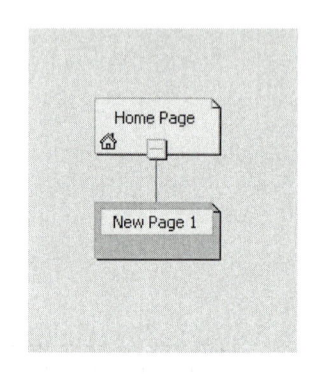

Once you create a page in Navigation view, you can assign a new *page title* to that page by clicking (once) to select the page, and pressing the F2 function key. Or, right-click the page and choose Rename from the context menu. Enter the new filename, and press ENTER to change the page title.

You can click and drag pages to move them around in your navigation structure. For example, in Figure 1-2, the Dug-less page is being dragged underneath the New CDs page.

What's the big deal with the links you define in Navigation view? They don't do anything in and of themselves. But they define page relationships that FrontPage uses to generate links in your navigation bars—a process we'll check out next.

> **NOTE** We'll return to Navigation view in Chapter 2, and explore some of the file management features available.

If you have pages in you Web that you didn't create in Navigation view, you can drag a page from the folder list into Navigation view, as shown in Figure 1-3.

FIGURE 1-2

You can change navigational structure by clicking and dragging on pages in Navigation view

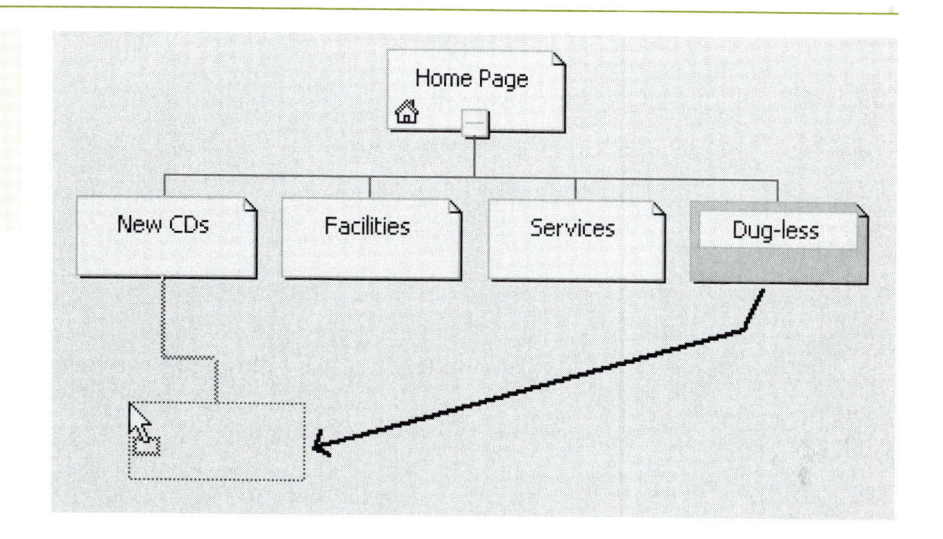

Defining Link Bars Based on Navigation Structure

Once you have established a navigation structure, it becomes the basis for you to define what kinds of links you want FrontPage to generate in a navigation bar. For example, you can tell FrontPage: "I want links to the respective child page(s) from every page in my site." And FrontPage will comply.

To define the logic of a navigation bar, we'll jump to Page view. In Page view, you look at the content of one page at a time.

FIGURE 1-3

Dragging a Web page into the Navigation structure

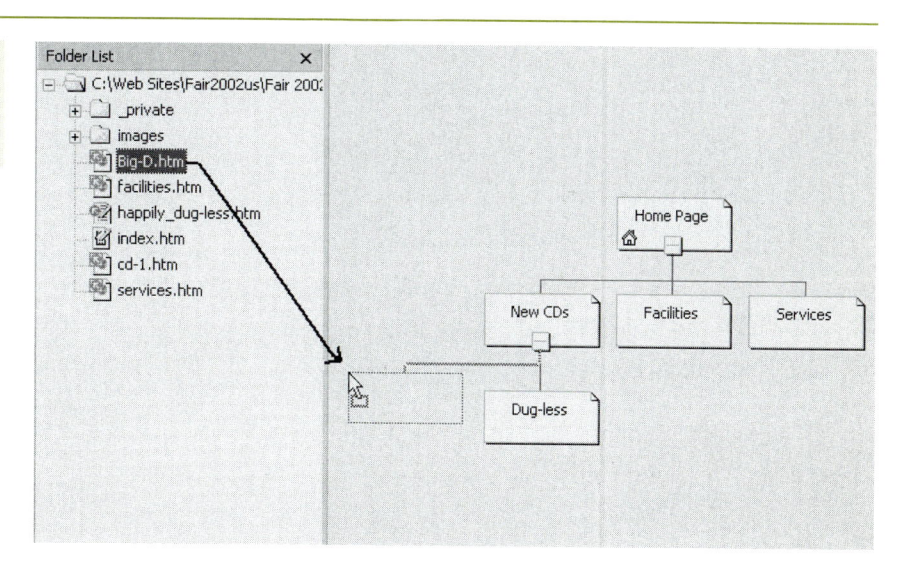

CHAPTER 1
FrontPage Web Sites—A Running Start

The best way to open a Web page in Page view is to double-click the page in Navigation view. As you do, FrontPage switches to Page view, with your page open. Even if you don't have any content on your Web page yet, you *will* see shared borders with whatever navigation links were generated by default, based on your Navigation structure. For example, in Figure 1-4, the left-shared border has a navigation bar that includes child pages of the home page.

> **WHEN DO YOU DEFINE WEB PAGE CONTENT?** Page view is where you add, edit, and format the content of your Web pages. If you're doing your page design right in FrontPage (and why not?), you'll spend much of your Web design time in Page view. In fact, most of the remaining chapters in this book focus on *page* design features, and you'll spend most of the rest of your learning time in Page view. We're digging into the nuts and bolts of *Web* design first, so that's when we zero in on page design, the basic architecture of your site will already be in place.

FIGURE 1-4
FrontPage automatically generates navigation links when you include a navigation bar in a shared border

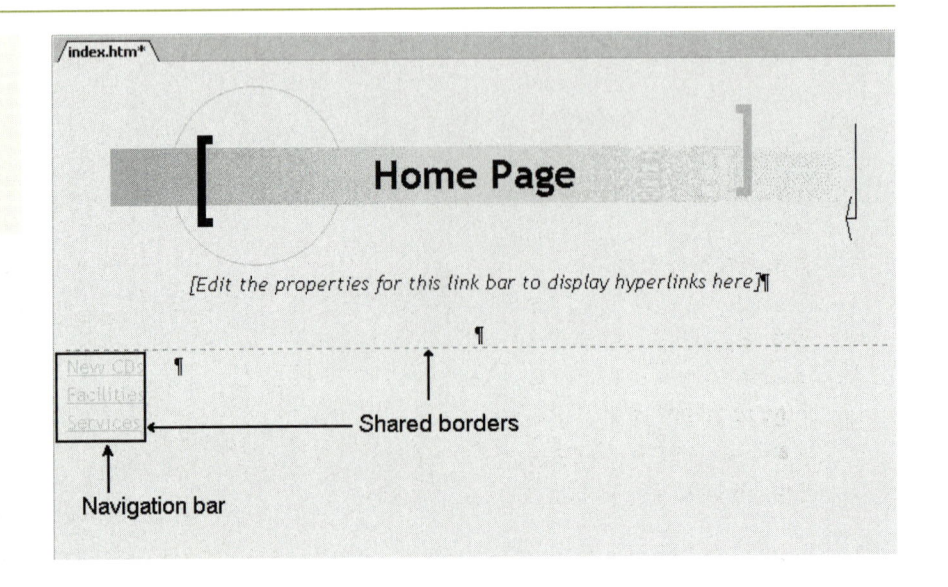

To Change THE NAVIGATION LOGIC OF A NAVIGATION BAR:

1 Click a navigation bar to select it.

2 Right-click your selected Link bar, and choose Link Bar Properties from the context menu. The Link Bar properties dialog box opens, as shown next. This is where you define which links are displayed in a Link bar.

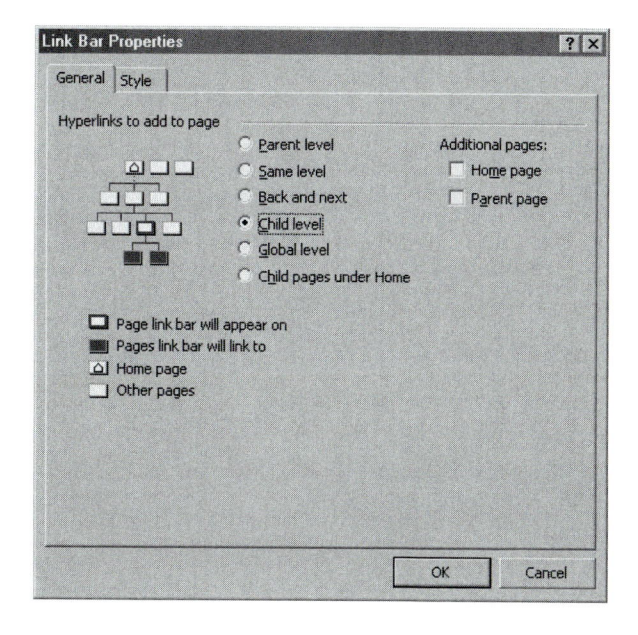

3 Choose one (and only one) of the Hyperlinks to Add to Page option buttons. As you do, the graphical display in the dialog box illustrates the links that will be generated.

4 You can add a link to the home page, and/or the parent page of any page by selecting the Home Page or Parent Page check boxes. Here, too, the graphical diagram changes to display the links you are generating.

5 You can use the Style tab in the Link Bar Properties dialog box to choose a format for your navigation links. Select from the list of styles, and then choose either Horizontal or Vertical to define how the set of links will display.

> **NOTE** As you move your cursor over a navigation bar, your cursor will change into an icon cursor. When you click and select a navigation bar, the bar will display in reverse colors. *Sometimes navigation bars will not display any links (yet),* but instead will display a message saying, "Edit the Properties of this Link Bar to Display Hyperlinks Here." That means that the current navigational logic applied to the Link bar is not generating any links yet.

CHAPTER 1
FrontPage Web Sites—A Running Start

6 After you define your navigation links in the Link Bar Properties dialog box, click OK. FrontPage will generate new links for each page to conform with the navigation logic you defined for the Link bar.

> **LINK BAR STRATEGIES** If you have more than one Link bar on a page, you can repeat this process to define links for each bar. Sometimes it's useful to use *different* navigational logic for different Link bars on a page. For example, a Link bar in the left-shared border might have links to child pages, whereas a Link bar in the top-shared border might just have links to Child Pages Under Home, which would allow visitors to quickly jump to pages at the second level in your Navigation hierarchy.

Testing and Publishing a Web

Time to see what you've created! Even though you have focused your attention on generating *site* structure, and left pages blank, you still have created quite a bit in this chapter. You've learned to generate a FrontPage Web with pages, a graphical theme, navigation icons, page titles (they come with the theme), and a navigation structure that is reflected in generated Link bars. In short, everything's in place for you to start adding content to your pages.

Before you explore editing individual pages, let's explore ways to look at the work you've done.

Using the Preview Tab

The Preview tab in Page view allows you to see *some* of your page features. Just click the word Preview underneath your page in Page view to see how your page will look in a *browser*. Personally, I prefer to preview my pages in a Web browser to see how they will look. But I'll admit that the Preview tab is faster than opening a page in a Web browser—and for many features, it's a quick and dirty way to see how pages will look.

> **NOTE** By browser, I mean the software that allows you to view a Web page. The two dominant browsers today are Internet Explorer and Netscape Navigator. These programs translate the information on Web pages, which is encoded in a language called HyperText Markup Language—HTML.

In Preview mode, non-visible page elements like the dashed lines that define shared borders and the hidden (from visitors) comments that describe navigation bars without links are invisible. You see the page pretty much the way a visitor will see your page in a Web browser.

Interested in HTML?

HyperText Markup Language (HTML) is the code that is interpreted by browsers. This is the way browsers know how to display the content and formatting on your page. FrontPage 2002 *translates* the page elements and formatting you add into HTML. You can see this HTML by clicking the HTML tab in Page view.

Even if you haven't placed any content on your page, elements like borders and themes display in the HTML generated for your page, as shown in Figure 1-5.

If you know HTML, you can add your own in HTML view, or edit the HTML generated by FrontPage. If not, HTML view is a painless way to introduce yourself to some HTML code.

FIGURE 1-5

FrontPage generates HTML as you format and add content to your page; this HTML can be edited directly

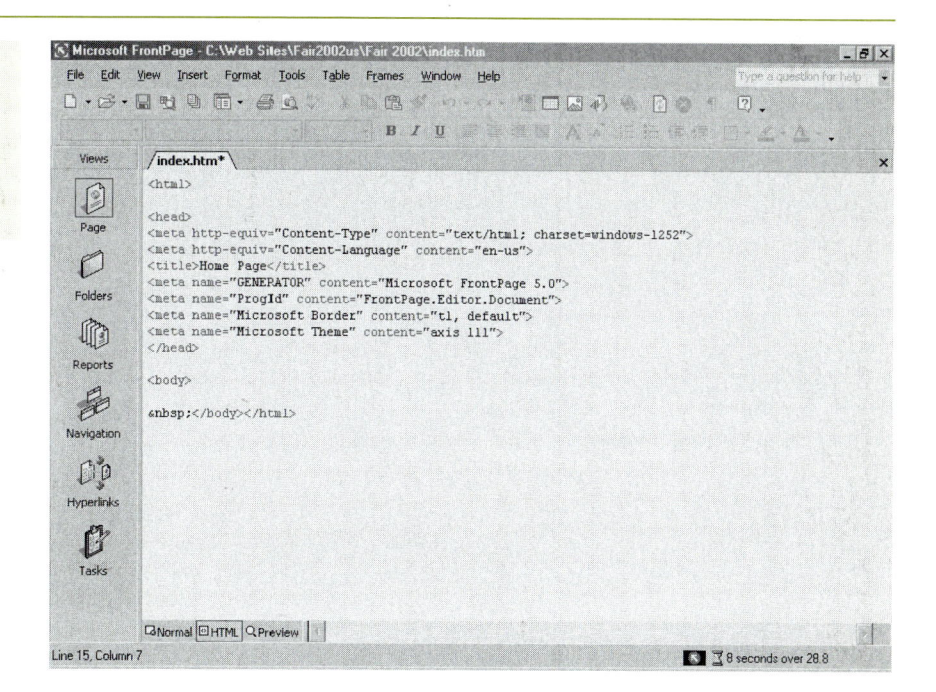

CHAPTER 1
FrontPage Web Sites—A Running Start

Previewing in a Browser

While the Preview tab in Page view gives you an approximate picture of how your page looks in a browser, there's no substitute for actually seeing your page in a browser itself. FrontPage allows you to preview your page in a browser by choosing File | Preview in Browser. If you have more than one browser installed, you can choose between them in the Preview in Browser dialog box, as shown here.

Use the Add button in the Preview in Browser dialog box to add additional browsers (you must have them installed on your system to do this). Or, click the Preview button to open your page in the selected browser.

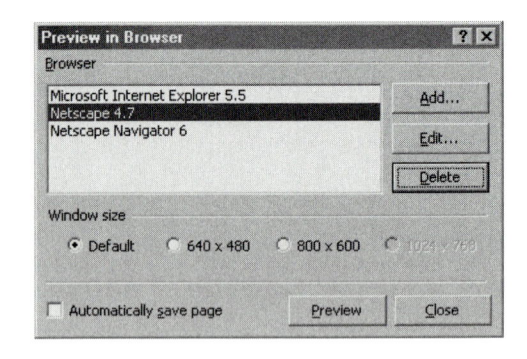

> **NOTE** If you haven't saved your page before you try to preview it, FrontPage will prompt you to save your changes first.

When you preview your page in a browser, you can test the links generated in Link bars. In Figure 1-6, we are using generated links to surf around the (still contentless) Web site.

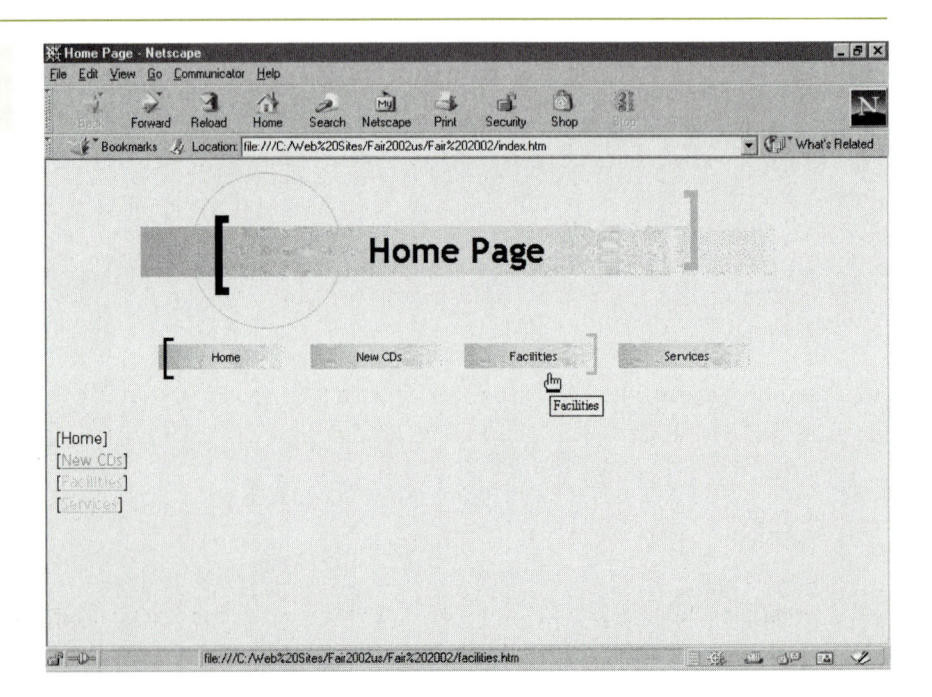

FIGURE 1-6
Testing links in a browser

PUBLISHING YOUR SITE TO THE WORLD WIDE WEB

If you developed your site using a disk-based Web (you saved it on your hard drive), you might be thinking about how to get your site on the World Wide Web (WWW). That's easy. All it takes is a little money.

> **NOTE** As of this writing, the era of free, FrontPage-ready Web site providers seems to be biting the dust. However, as we go to press, tripod.com is still offering free FrontPage Web sites.

Microsoft provides a list of FrontPage Web site providers at http://www.microsoftwpp.com/wppsearch/. A short list of reliable, cheap site providers is available at www.ppinet.com. Or, you can simply keep saving your Web to your disk for now.

SAVING A DISK-BASED WEB

If you created a disk-based Web, each time you save a page, you not only save that page, but you save all the links, graphics, and formatting attached to that page. Later, when you begin to add images and other files to your pages, you'll notice that FrontPage prompts you to save those embedded objects along with your page. When you choose File | Close Web, FrontPage prompts you to save any unsaved and open pages in your Web.

PUBLISHING TO A FRONTPAGE WEB SERVER

If you started out with a disk-based Web, and you're ready to publish to an intranet or Internet site, remember the three magic things you need:

▶ URL or IP address
▶ User name
▶ Password

In addition to this information, some Web hosting servers require a domain name as well; so, check with your Web server administrator to see if you need that.

To Publish YOUR SITE TO A WEB SERVER:

1 Choose File | Publish Web from the FrontPage menu. The Publish Destination dialog box appears, as shown on the next page.

2 In the Enter Publish Destination area, type the URL or IP address of your site (include http:// if that is part of your URL).

3 Click OK in the Publish Destination dialog box. You'll be prompted for your user name and password (remember, this is info you need to get from your Web service provider). Enter your user name, password, and (if prompted) domain name.

4 After your password is accepted, the Publish Web dialog box appears, as shown next. The Publish Web dialog box allows you to select which files to upload to your server. Index.htm has a question mark (?) next to it to warn you that uploading this file will replace any existing home page at the target site.

5 You can right-click files in the Publish Web dialog box, and choose Don't Publish from the context menu if you do not want to upload specific files. Once you have chosen files to upload (or just accepted the default—all files), click Publish. A cute animated icon will simulate your files being sent to your server.

6 After your files are uploaded, you'll see a dialog box with a link allowing you to open your newly published Web site in a server.

Congratulations! You're on the Web.

What's with FrontPage Server Extensions?

Some features in FrontPage require that the Web server to which you publish your Web have FrontPage server extensions—special files that reside on the Web server itself. If your site provider doesn't have FrontPage extensions, some features of your site might not work. Because hundreds if not thousands of site providers *do*

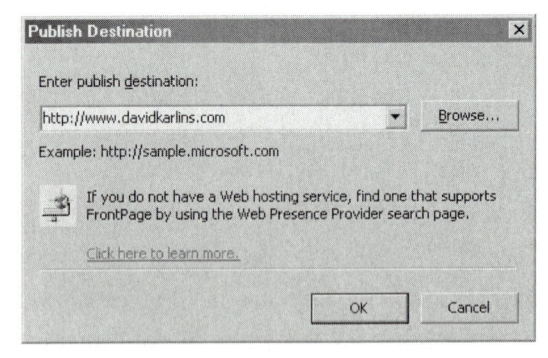

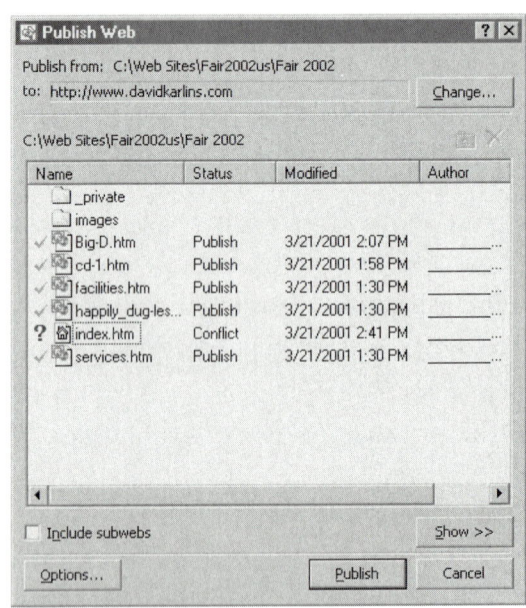

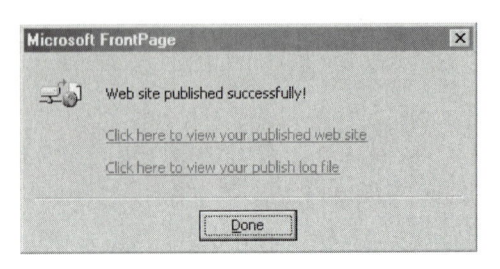

have FrontPage extensions, you're better off finding a site provider that supports these features.

Where Can I Get a FrontPage Web Server?

Creating a FrontPage Web server yourself is beyond the scope of this book, and beyond the scope of a FrontPage book in general. Server administrators are experts at configuring and maintaining software that shares files on server computers. FrontPage *used to* provide a relatively simple to install server that you could put on your own computer called the *Personal Web Server* (PWS). However, as of FrontPage 2002, Microsoft made the unfortunate decision to no longer enable the PWS to support FrontPage 2002 extensions.

> **NOTE** FrontPage will look at the server to which you are publishing and determine if it supports all the features on your Web site. If not, you'll see a friendly warning that your server is not equipped with a full set of files called FrontPage server extensions.

If you are on an intranet using Microsoft Windows 2000 or NT, your server administrator can—as an option—install FrontPage extensions, allowing full FrontPage Web hosting functionality on your intranet. Chapter 16 provides a basic explanation of how to use the Web server software in Windows 2000 and Windows XP with FrontPage 2002.

What's Next?

At this point, you've constructed a Web site with stylish graphics and an integrated navigational system. You've also assigned a unified and rather complex color scheme and set of icons to all your pages with a theme. Nice work! The general structure of your Web site is now in place, and you've only completed Chapter 1. Like a builder who had laid the foundation for a building and put up the frame and scaffolding, you have done much of the dirty work of creating a site. You're ready to add page content. In the next chapter, you'll prepare for that by fully exploring the FrontPage interface.

> **ON THE VIRTUAL CLASSROOM CD** Follow along with me in Lesson 1, "Creating a FrontPage Web," as I guide you through the process of creating a Web site, defining a navigation structure, and assigning a theme in FrontPage 2002.

2

Getting Around in FrontPage

One of FrontPage's most powerful features is its capability to keep track of and help organize all the files in your Web site. As you generate Web sites in FrontPage, you pile up a large number of files. FrontPage generates files for the HTML Web pages you create, for images you save, as well as folders for files used in themes, shared borders, and other FrontPage objects.

When you design a site in FrontPage, you will want to keep track of these files. Why? Well, besides the general concept of knowing what's "under the hood" at your Web site, you will want to have an idea of what is in your site for a number of specific reasons, including

▶ How big is your site? Size matters when you save your site to a local folder or when you contract for Web server space.

▶ Is your site loaded up with old files that aren't in use?

▶ Are the links in your Web site valid?

▶ Which pages in your site are linked to other pages?

These and other questions can be easily answered by using FrontPage's different views.

Looking at Your Web Site

You can easily switch to any view in FrontPage by selecting that view in the Views bar—on the left side of the FrontPage window. If the Views menu disappears, you can make it reappear by choosing View from the FrontPage menu bar, and selecting Views Bar.

NOTE Some of the site management features explored in this chapter will become more useful as your site grows in size and complexity. In some cases, you'll want to note site features that are available to you, and return to this chapter when you need those features to manage your growing Web site.

Let's take a quick tour of the views in FrontPage 2002:

▶ **Page view** Where you design your Web pages.

▶ **Folders view** Displays a list of the files that you create in FrontPage.

▶ **Reports view** Displays reports that update you on your Web site. When you click Reports in the View bar, you'll see a summary of the different reports available. You can view any particular report by double-clicking it in the Site Summary spreadsheet, or by selecting a report from the View Reports submenu.

NOTE FrontPage creates two empty folders (_private and images) when you open a new Web site. The _private folder holds data submitted by input forms (see Chapters 11 and 12). The Images folder holds images generated as part of your theme.

- ▶ **Navigation view** Defines navigational links between pages in your Web site.
- ▶ **Hyperlinks view** Shows you if you have corrupted or out-of-date links in your site.
- ▶ **Tasks view** Coordinates work between more than one developer on a Web site. Tasks can be assigned to different developers, and progress can be marked here as well.

Exploring in Folders View

You can use Folders view to see the files in your site, but you can also use Folders view to organize those files by moving them into new folders, renaming them, copying them, or deleting them as you perform "housekeeping" tasks on your site.

What's Where?

The Folders view is divided into six columns that give you useful information about every file in your site. The columns are listed here:

- ▶ **Name** Tells you the filename of the file.
- ▶ **Size** Tells you how many bytes of memory are taken up by the file.
- ▶ **Type** Tells you what kind of file this is—HTML (Web page), GIF (image), JPEG (another image file type), etc.
- ▶ **Modified Date** Tells you when the file was last changed and saved.
- ▶ **Modified by** Tells you who last worked on the file—this information is collected automatically by FrontPage based on the system user name assigned to a computer.
- ▶ **Comments** Displays comments assigned to a page. You can assign a comment to a file by right-clicking the file in a Folder list, and choosing Properties from the context menu. Assigning comments to files can help you keep track of what's what in your site. In the Summary tab, you can enter comment text, as shown on the next page.

Lists of files can be sorted by any column heading. So, for example, if you want to see your files organized by when they were last worked on (perhaps you are looking for an elusive file you edited just yesterday), you can click the Modified date column heading to sort your files chronologically.

Any file can be opened in Folder view by double-clicking it. If the file is an HTML file, it will open in FrontPage's Page view—ready for editing. If it is another file type (like a GIF or JPEG image file), it will open in the application you assign to that file type. To assign or change an application associated with a file type, choose Tools | Options, and then select the Configure Editors tab in the Options dialog box. Here you can add, modify, or remove filename extensions and associated editors. (Chapter 4 explores working with image files.)

Structuring Files in Folders

Not only can you view, sort, find, and open files in Folders view, you can also organize your files. This becomes handy when your file count heads up into the hundreds, and you find yourself spending too much time looking for a page file.

To create a new folder in Folders view, just click the root folder (or the folder in which you want to create a new subfolder), and choose File | New | Folder. A new folder appears right away in Folders view. By

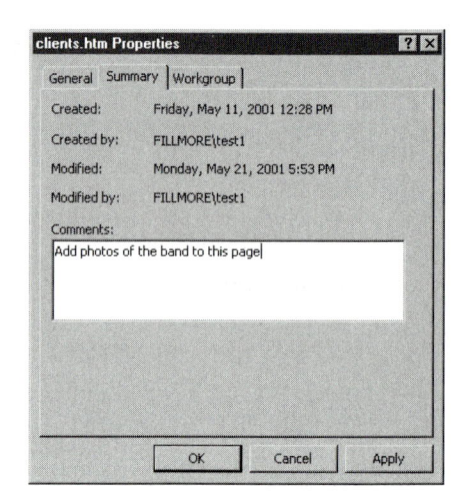

NOTE Let's say, for example, that you do your image editing in Microsoft Image Composer. You can associate GIF and JPEG files with PhotoShop by clicking the Add button in the Options dialog box and using the Browser button to navigate to the program file for Microsoft Image Composer, as shown in Figure 2-1. After you add or modify associated file editors, click OK to close the Options dialog box.

FIGURE 2-1
Assigning an image editor to the GIF and JPEG file formats

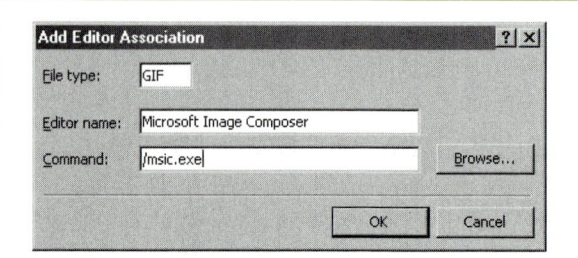

default, the folder is named something like New_Folder, but you can rename it by typing in a new name.

Any folder or file can be renamed by clicking it *once* in Folder view, and then clicking a second time. Careful, because if you double-click you'll open the file. Or, you can right-click a file, choose Rename in the context menu, and type a new folder (or file) name.

Once you have all the folders you need, you can click and drag files from one folder to another to keep them organized. When necessary, FrontPage will make changes to your Web pages to adjust for moved files. For example, if you drag a picture file from one folder to another, FrontPage will update the HTML code on your page so that Web browsers will still show your picture on your page.

Renaming Page Files and Titles

Web pages have two "names,"—a filename, like index.htm, and a page *title*, such as Home Page. Page filenames must use one of the special filename extensions required for browsers to interpret them. FrontPage will assign an appropriate filename extension to your pages as you create them in Navigation view (or in Page view, Folder view, or anywhere else). Usually FrontPage will assign an *.htm filename extension to your page filenames. Other times, if pages include special features, FrontPage may assign other filename extensions like *.asp (for Active Server Pages files used in FrontPage databases), or *.shtml for pages with special scripts.

Because FrontPage assigns filename extensions automatically, you don't need to be overly concerned with memorizing file naming rules, except to understand what's going on when FrontPage assigns a filename. *And*, if you rename a page file, be sure to keep the filename extension the same as the original name.

To change a filename, right-click a file in Folder view, and choose Rename from the context menu. Type a new filename and press ENTER. If you forget to end your filename with an appropriate filename extension (usually *.htm), FrontPage will warn you with a message like the one you see here:

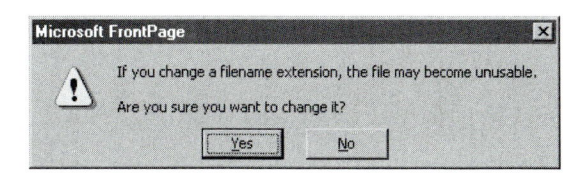

Web page *titles* are the name that displays in the title bar of a browser when you visit a Web site. For that reason, it's important that a title be assigned to each page, otherwise, visitors will see the dreaded Untitled Page heading in their browser title bar, which makes your page look a bit tacky. Web page titles are also displayed when a visitor saves a page in a browser's Favorites or Bookmarks list.

FrontPage automatically assigns a title to pages you create. You can change these titles by right-clicking a page in Folders view, and choosing Properties. In the General tab of the Properties dialog box, you can enter a new page title.

> **NOTE** In Navigation view, you can change a page title by clicking once on a page or by right-clicking on a page *in the navigation flowchart,* and choosing Rename from the context menu. Don't be deceived—you're not changing the page *filename* here, you're changing the page title.

Avoiding the Missing Link

As your Web site grows, links that you generate may grow old and out of date. FrontPage will perform the tedious and valuable task of checking all your internal (within your Web site) and external (outside of your site) links.

To check your links, choose View | Reports | Problems | Broken Hyperlinks from the FrontPage menu bar. A new toolbar appears, along with a list of all hyperlinks. If you have external links on your pages (leading outside of your Web site), you can also have FrontPage check those links: In the new toolbar, click the Verifies Hyperlinks in the Current Web button, as shown in Figure 2-2.

After you click the Verifies Hyperlinks in the Current Web button, you'll be prompted with a dialog box asking if you want to check just unknown links, or all links. Check *all* links if you want to *recheck* links that have already been tested. That's often a good choice, as yesterday's valid link is today's dot-com-gone-bad. After FrontPage tests your links, the Status column tells you if any of your links are broken. If so, you can double-click the page in the In Page column to edit the bad link.

FIGURE 2-2

Identifying bad links

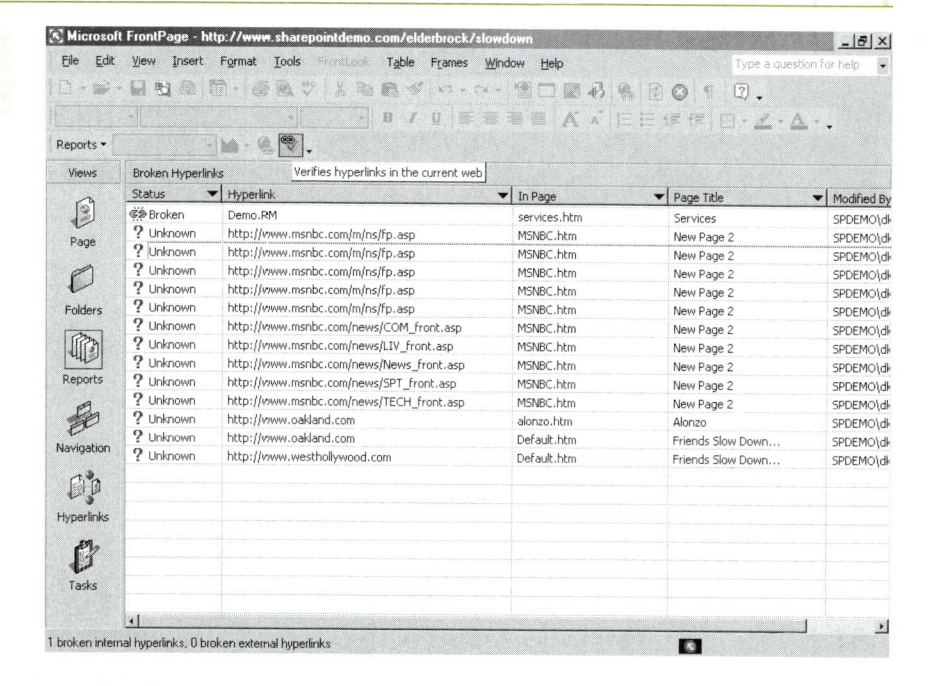

Scoping Out Your Site with Reports

FrontPage creates many handy reports that update you on the size and status of your site. As shown in Figure 2-3, when you click the Reports icon in the Views bar you'll see a summary of the different reports available. If you don't see the summary, choose Reports and Site Summary from the drop-down list above the View bar.

A quick look at Reports view will give you the basic facts about your site. Among the information you can glean from this report is

- ▶ **Usage Data** Tells you how many hits your site has gotten. This information is only available if your site has been published to a Web server that supports FrontPage server extensions.
- ▶ **All Files (Size column)** Tells you how large your site is—useful info when calculating how much Web server space you have to purchase or how much disk space your site is using.

> **NOTE** If you're familiar with earlier versions of FrontPage, you'll be impressed by new and improved reports available in FrontPage 2002. These new reports include Usage Analysis reports to identify where your visitors are coming from and which browsers they are using.

CHAPTER 2
GETTING AROUND IN FRONTPAGE

FIGURE 2-3

The main Reports view provides a comprehensive picture of your site content

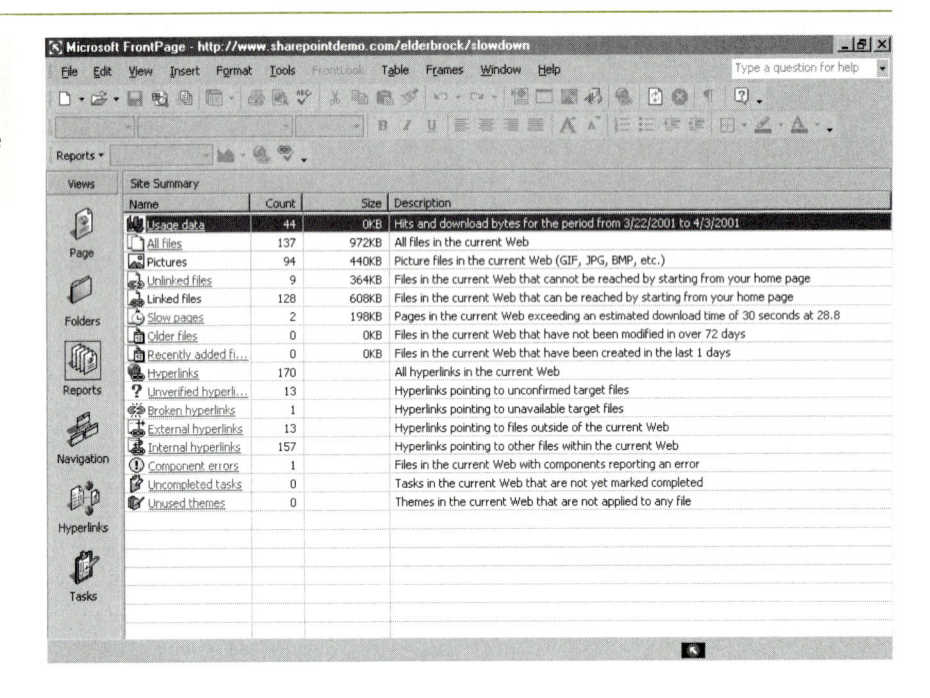

- **Pictures** Tells you how many pictures are in your site and how much disk space they are using.
- **Unlinked Files** Tells you how many pages in your site are not linked to any other page in your site. These *might* be pages that are no longer in use but wasting disk space.

You can view any of these reports, or any of the other reports available, by double-clicking a report in the Site Summary grid.

MANY WAYS TO EDIT A PAGE

Having stepped back to focus on FrontPage's *site* management tools, let's zoom in on page editing. After all, most of the work of creating and maintaining a Web site involves editing the content of specific Web pages.

There are almost too many ways to open a Web page in FrontPage. You can choose File | Open (from any view). Or you can double-click a filename or title in a Report view. I strongly recommend opening files from Navigation view if you are using Navigation view to organize your site. I find that opening files from Navigation view makes it easier to keep track of what files are in your site, and how they are linked together. This technique works as a guard against creating unlinked files.

Normal Page View

Normal Page view is the name for the *What You See Is What You Get* (WYSIWYG) HTML editor that comes with FrontPage. As you type and format text, add pictures, and so on in normal Page view, FrontPage "translates" your content and formatting into HTML code.

Many of us are blissfully ignorant of the HTML code that is getting generated. Who cares? FrontPage generates it, browsers interpret it, it works, and that's all we need to know. But some of us want to at least take a look at the HTML code that is generated or even make changes to that code. Either way, FrontPage's Page view is the feature you need—Normal Page view is the WYSIYG editor, and HTML view is a full-fledged HTML editing program.

Editing in Page View

Most of this book is dedicated to creating, formatting, and editing page content in Page view. But the basic rule is *type away*. You can enter text, use the Insert | Picture menu command to add pictures, and use the Microsoft Office user-friendly formatting toolbar to add attributes such as boldface, fonts, font sizes, and font colors to text.

Viewing HTML Tags

If you're curious about what HTML coding (tags) are being applied as you enter and format text and pictures, you can choose View | Reveal Tags to see the HTML with tags revealed. In Figure 2-4, you can see which HTML codes are applied to text.

HTML Page View

While you can *view* HMTL tags in Normal Page view, you can *edit* HTML by clicking the HTML tab at the bottom of Page view. If you right-click anywhere in the Page/HTML view, a context menu appears that allows you to control formatting, XML rules (for an enhanced coding language called Extensible Markup Language), and to search for coding, as shown in Figure 2-5.

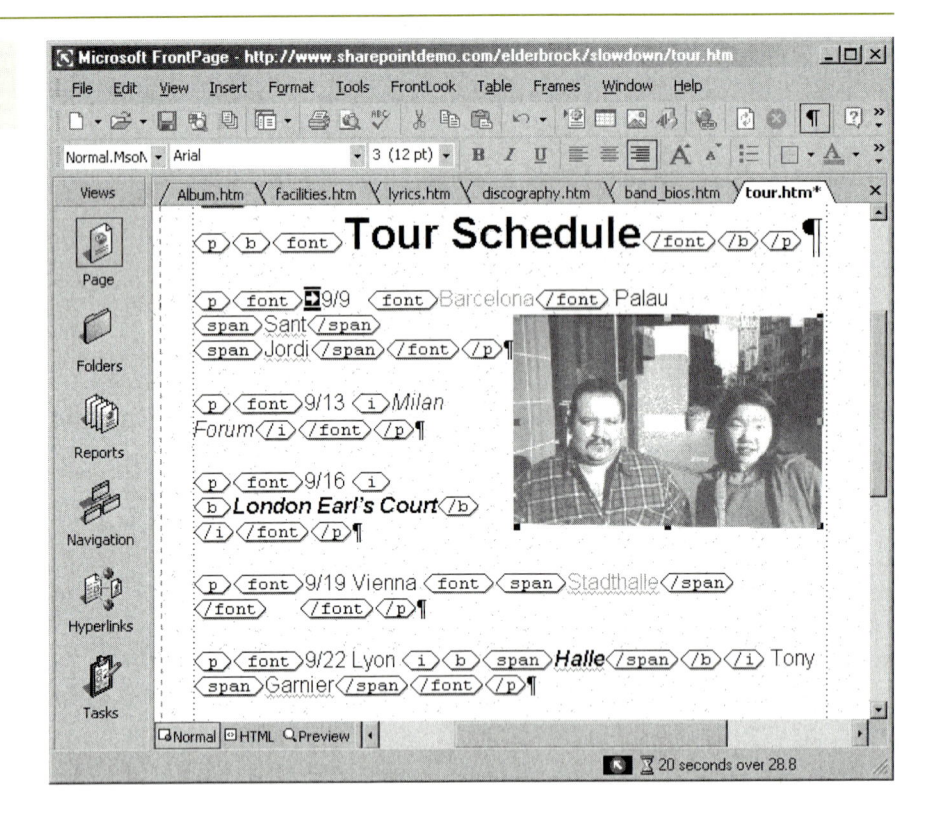

FIGURE 2-4
Viewing HTML tags

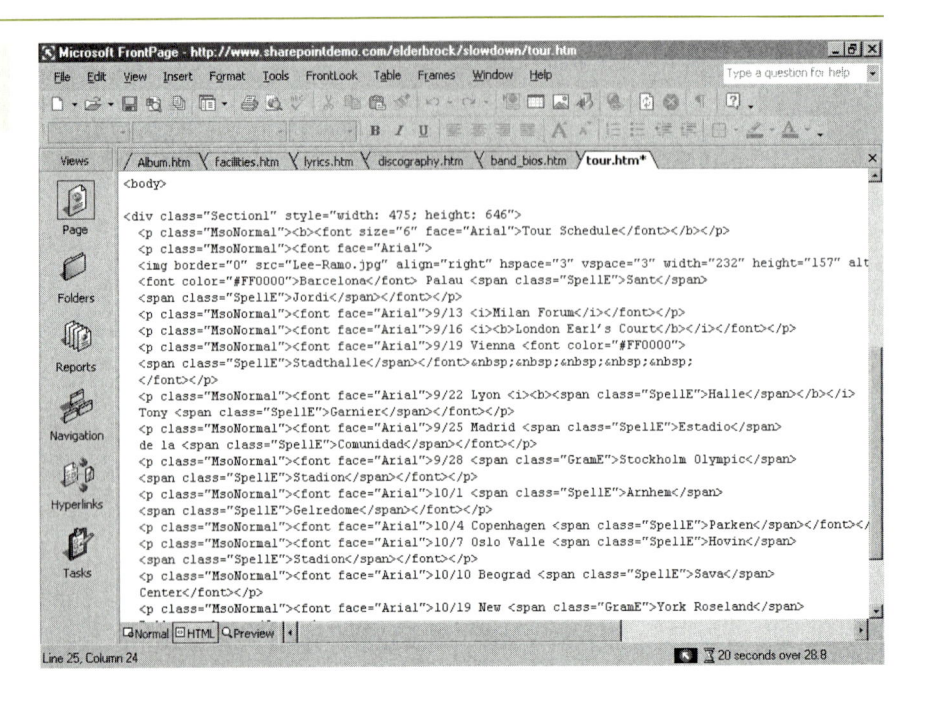

FIGURE 2-5
HTML view

Preview Page View

In addition to viewing your pages in WYSIWYG and HTML views, you can also *preview* your page by clicking the Preview tab at the bottom of Page view. Why do you need a preview of your page when Normal Page view is WYSIWYG anyway? The answer is that Normal Page view includes formatting marks, like dotted lines identifying shared borders, paragraph marks (turned on and off by clicking the Show All button on the Formatting toolbar), and other markup elements that aren't visible when someone sees your page in a Web site.

When you click the Preview tab, you'll see your page *more* like it will appear in a Web browser. However, you can't edit in the Preview tab.

Viewing a Page in a Browser

While Preview tab shows your page *more* like it will appear in a browser than Normal Page view, there are still elements of a page that are distorted in Preview view. For one thing, the View bar, FrontPage menu bar, toolbars, and other parts of the FrontPage interface show up in Preview mode, but aren't visible (of course) in a Web browser. And, some formatting elements—like tables—look different in Preview mode than in a real Web browser. (You'll explore creating and formatting tables in Chapter 5.)

For these reasons, the most reliable way to see what your page will look like in a browser is to choose File | Preview in Browser from the menu. When you do, the Preview in Browser dialog box will appear, as shown in this illustration. You can use the Preview in Browser dialog box to choose which of your installed Web browsers you want to use to view your page.

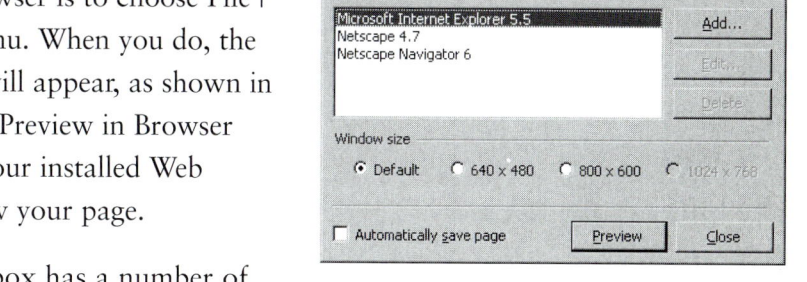

The Preview in Browser dialog box has a number of valuable options. You can use the Add button to add additional browsers to your list. The Window size options buttons allow you to check out your site in various browser window sizes—always a good idea because a page that looks good in an 800-pixel–wide window sometimes loses its looks in a 640-pixel–wide window.

The Automatically Save Page check box in the Preview in Browser window saves changes to your page each time you preview it in a browser window. If you don't choose this option, you'll be prompted to save any unchanged editing before previewing your page.

Ready to Edit Page Content?

With this overview of how FrontPage organizes Web sites, files, and pages, you have now looked "under the hood" at how FrontPage works. Each Web site can have many folders, and each folder can contain many files. Files can include HTML Web pages, as well as picture files, and other files (including small programs) that FrontPage uses to manage your Web site.

With all this under your belt, you can move on to create nice-looking Web pages with formatted text, defined page properties (like background colors), and paragraph formatting. You'll explore all that and more in the next chapter.

3

Editing and Formatting Web Pages

Having examined how FrontPage manages Web *sites*, it's time to get down to the nitty-gritty of designing Web *pages*. FrontPage Page view (Normal tab) looks much like Microsoft Word. And if you've used Microsoft Word, or other Microsoft Office products, the FrontPage Standard and Formatting toolbars will be familiar, comforting, helpful, and... a bit confusing. That's because many formatting features are applied in FrontPage just as they are in Word, while other formatting tools in FrontPage act differently than their Word cousins.

Chapter 3
Editing and Formatting Web Pages

We'll start this chapter by looking at the Standard and Formatting toolbars in FrontPage, paying special attention to tools that work differently from those in other Office applications. Then, you'll look at text, paragraph, and page formatting techniques that are unique to FrontPage.

Checking Out the Toolbars

You define which toolbars are displayed by choosing View | Toolbars from the FrontPage menu bar. These toolbars are detachable and can be moved off the top of the window by clicking and dragging the toolbar (but not a button).

Detached toolbars can be re-anchored at the top of the window by dragging them back to the top of the screen. It's worth taking a close look at the Standard and Formatting toolbars because so many of FrontPage's features are found there.

> **NOTE** Your cursor will turn into a four-sided arrow when you have placed it in just the right spot to click and drag on a toolbar.

Creating Pages—Using the Standard Toolbar

As you peruse the Standard toolbar, note some of the big differences from other Office toolbars. The New button can create *many* new things—pages, Webs, even task lists. Similarly, the Open button is really a drop-down list that opens either pages or Webs.

Other Standard toolbar options will be old friends to Office users—like Cut, Copy, Paste, and Save. The Standard toolbar is shown here:

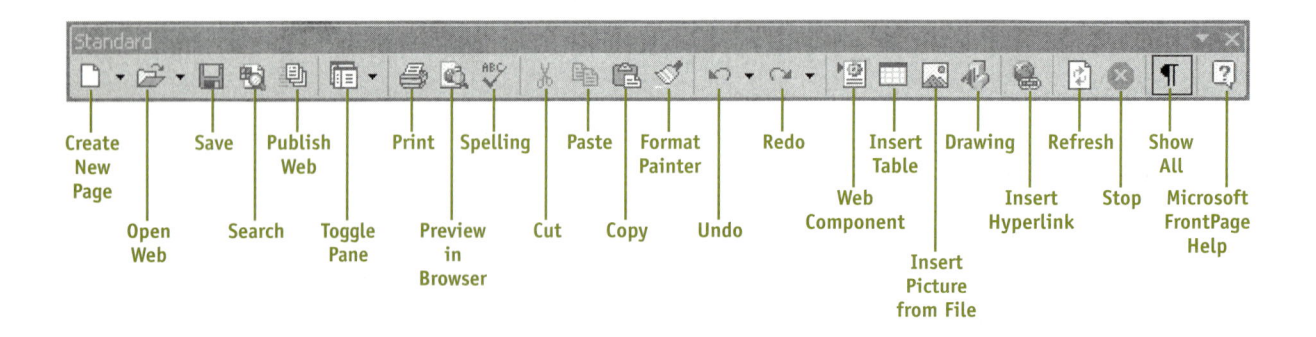

Standard toolbar labels: Create New Page, Open Web, Save, Search, Publish Web, Toggle Pane, Print, Preview in Browser, Spelling, Cut, Paste, Copy, Format Painter, Undo, Redo, Insert Web Component, Insert Table, Insert Picture from File, Drawing, Insert Hyperlink, Refresh, Stop, Show All, Microsoft FrontPage Help

Your Web page editing and formatting will flow much more smoothly if you take a moment to familiarize yourself with what the tools in the Standard toolbar are used for:

▶ **Create New** This drop-down list allows you to create a new page, Web site, task, folder, a document library, list, or survey (these last three are rather obscure applications used for intranets on specially designed Microsoft Web servers).

▶ **Open** This drop-down list lets you open a new Web page or site.

▶ **Save** Saves your Web page and any images on your open page.

▶ **Search** Looks for files in your Web site.

▶ **Publish Web** Transfers your site files to another drive or server. (More on that in Chapter 16.)

▶ **Toggle Pane** Displays panes (get it—window *panes*) that show navigational structure or file folder structure.

▶ **Print** Prints your Web page.

▶ **Preview in Browser** Displays your page in a browser. Use File | Preview in Browser to choose which browser to use.

▶ **Spelling** Spel-cheksx your current page. No professional would ever publish a page without spel chicing furst!

▶ **Cut** Cuts selected text (or other objects) to the Clipboard.

▶ **Paste** A fast, but inexact way to drop in content from the Clipboard. Instead, use Edit | Paste Special to choose different ways to handle the formatting of copied content.

▶ **Copy** Sends anything you select to the Clipboard, ready for pasting.

▶ **Format Painter** Works as it does in other Office app's—select formatted text, click this tool, and then use the New Brush icon to transfer the formatting of the initial text onto the newly "painted" text.

▶ **Undo** This button has saved many a Web designer's butt! Click it after you accidentally delete 10 hours of work.

▶ **Redo** Cancels the last Undo action.

▶ **Web Component** This omni-powerful button opens the Web Component dialog box—accessing powerful features you'll explore in Chapter 10 of this book.

CHAPTER 3
EDITING AND FORMATTING WEB PAGES

- ▶ **Insert Table** Creates tables.
- ▶ **Insert Picture from File** Opens the dialog box that allows you to navigate around to find a picture to place on your page.
- ▶ **Drawing** Activates the Drawing toolbar—just like the drawing tools in Word or PowerPoint.
- ▶ **Insert Hyperlink** Use this button to define a link for selected text or a selected picture.
- ▶ **Refresh** Reverts your page to the last saved version.
- ▶ **Stop** Breaks the connection between a page and a remote server.
- ▶ **Show All** Reveals formatting elements like forced line breaks (create them with SHIFT+ENTER) and paragraph marks.
- ▶ **Microsoft FrontPage Help** Activates a help window to the right of the FrontPage window that provides access to online help.
- ▶ **Add or Remove** Use these buttons to customize the toolbar.

MAKING YOUR PAGE LOOK GOOD— THE FORMATTING TOOLBAR

Probably 90 percent of the formatting you apply to pages can be done from the versatile Formatting toolbar. That toolbar, shown here, has many formatting features that you'll recognize if you use Word, PowerPoint, or Excel. At the same time, a couple of the formatting tools in FrontPage *look like* formatting tools in Word or other applications, but *act* a little *differently*. The Styles drop-down list is used to assign a limited set of Web compatible styles, as opposed to the more flexible and easily definable styles in Microsoft Word. And, you'll notice that the Font Size drop-down menu offers only a select number of font sizes—these are the font sizes supported by Web browsers.

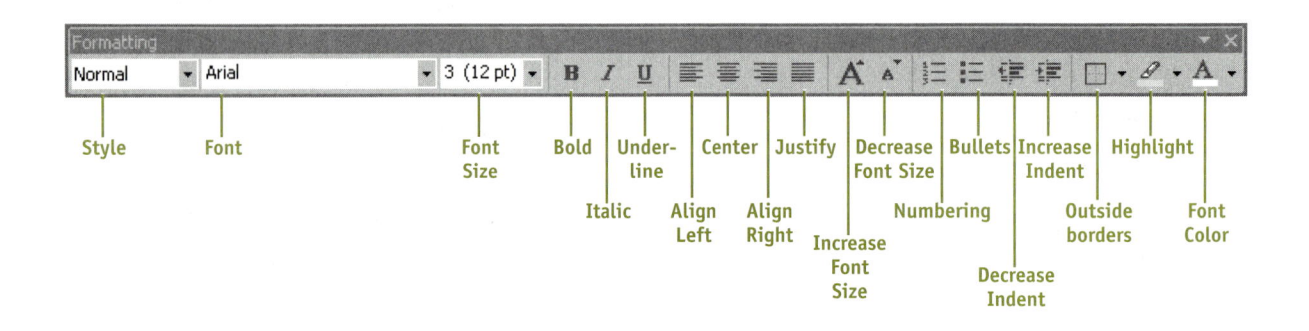

As you walk through the buttons on the Formatting toolbar, you'll also discover how to apply formatting to Web pages:

▶ **Style** Use this drop-down list to choose from global (in the sense of every one in the world uses 'em) formatting styles.

▶ **Font** Let's you choose which font to apply to selected text. However, unlike printed output, font display in Web pages is dependent on the fonts installed on your visitor's system. For that reason, the most reliable fonts are Arial, Times Roman, and Courier.

▶ **Font Size** Assigns a size to selected text. Want to assign 11.5 points? Forget it—the font options here reflect those supported by a wide variety of browsers, so your size choices are limited.

▶ **Bold, Italic, and Underline** These buttons work just as they do in Word, applying the respective attributes to selected text. Or... removing those attributes from selected text.

▶ **Align Left, Center, Align Right, and yes, a Justify** Defines paragraph alignment.

▶ **Numbering and Bullets** Applies automatic numbering or bullet formatting to selected paragraphs.

▶ **Increase Indent** and **Decrease Indent** Moves paragraph margins in or out.

▶ **Highlight Color** Applies a selected background color to selected text.

▶ **Font Color** Applies a selected color to selected text.

▶ **Add or Remove** Use these buttons to customize the toolbar.

Editing Text

You'll find text editing in Page view to be intuitive and easy. Simply click to insert your cursor and type away. Or, copy text from other programs like Word.

Most of the text editing techniques you use in Word will work with text in Page view. You can

> **NOTE** As noted earlier in the overview of the Standard toolbar, you're best off using the Edit | Paste Special menu choice instead of the Paste button in the toolbar. That way you give yourself more options over *how* text is pasted into FrontPage. My experience is that more often than not, I want to use the Normal Paragraphs option in the Convert Text dialog box shown in the illustration on the next page. That way, I can apply formatting in FrontPage without inheriting unpredictably interpreted formatting from the original application.

CHAPTER 3
EDITING AND FORMATTING WEB PAGES

click and drag to move text, or hold down your CTRL key as you click and drag to *copy* text. Navigation keystrokes, like up, down, right and left arrows work the same. Holding down the CTRL key as you click a right or left arrow button moves the insertion point forward and backward by word, and CTRL+ the up and down arrows moves the insertion point by paragraph.

Once you've entered (or pasted) text into a FrontPage Web page, basic Microsoft Office editing tools like cut, copy, and paste work just as they do in Word. So do Edit | Find and Edit | Replace.

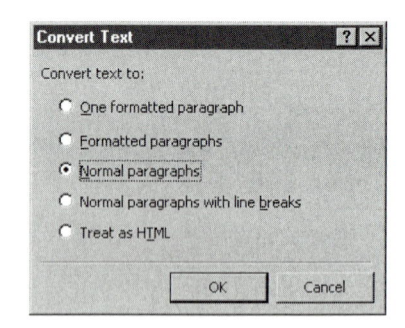

DEFINING LINKS

One of the distinguishing features of Web site text is that, unlike its duller printed version, it can be dynamically linked to other Web text. Visitors will expect your pages to include plenty of useful links leading to relevant, related content.

Links can be assigned to pictures or text. You'll explore links and pictures in Chapter 4. Here, you'll look at how links are associated with text, as well as some ways you can enhance text links. For example, you can define a link *target* as a *new browser window*, and you can define *ScreenTips* that appear when a visitor hovers his or her mouse cursor over linked text.

AUTOMATIC LINKS

FrontPage will generate a link for you if you type a link target. For example, anything you type that starts with **www**, and ends with **.com**, **.org**, **.net**, or another Web site file extension will automatically be converted to a link; the same goes for typed e-mail addresses.

Links are marked by an underline, and color is defined by your selected theme. Figure 3-1 shows text that has been converted into links.

ASSIGNING LINKS TO SELECTED TEXT

In addition to letting FrontPage turn your Web addresses (and e-mail addresses) into links, you can also assign links to *any* text. Article titles, product names,

FIGURE 3-1

Typed e-mail addresses and Web site addresses are automatically converted into links

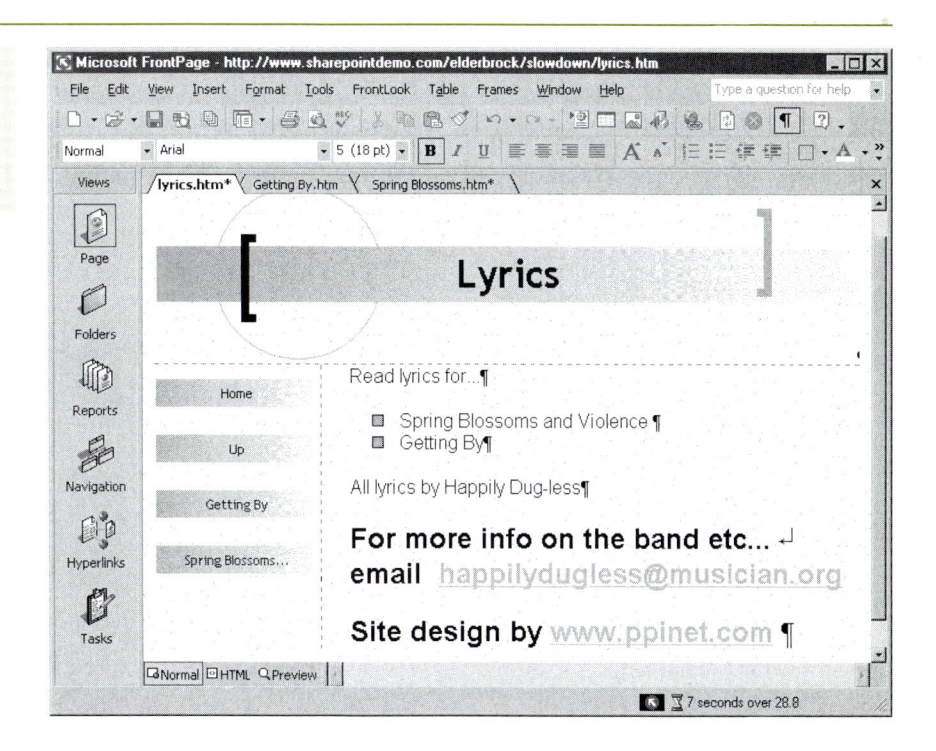

people... all can be linked to relevant content inside our outside your site or to an e-mail address.

To define a link, first select the text that will serve as the link. Then click the Insert Hyperlink button on the toolbar. (*Hyperlink* is FrontPage's extra-intense term for what most folks call a link.)

The Insert Hyperlink dialog box allows you to define a target for your link, as well as other attributes. To choose a target for your link, you can either enter a Web site address (or e-mail address) in the Address box, or you can click a page in your own Web site. Your own site pages are displayed in the Current Folder area. You can use the Up One Folder icon to move to a parent folder in your site. You can use the Browse the Web icon to find a link on the Internet, or you can use the Browse for File icon to link to a file on your local computer.

All this basically boils down to two choices: You can link to a page in your own site, or you can link to a page outside your site. If you want a page in your site, you'll find it in the set of listed files. If you want a link outside your site, the easiest way to define that link is to type the URL (*uniform resource locator*—the name of the site starting with **www**....) in the Address box.

Defining Link Target Frames

Think about this question for every link you create: Do you want visitors who follow this link to leave your Web site? If you are creating a link from one page in your site to another, this isn't much of an issue. But if you are creating a link to an external site, you have to decide if you want visitors who follow that link to zoom out of your site.

You can define links to open in a *new browser window* so that even if they follow a link out of your site, *your site will remain open in the original browser window*. To have a link open in a *new* browser window, click the Target Frame button in the Create Hyperlinks dialog box, and select New Window, as shown here:

After you define a link target, click OK to close the Target Frame dialog box. Return to the Create Hyperlink dialog box but don't close that dialog box just yet—you have other choices to make.

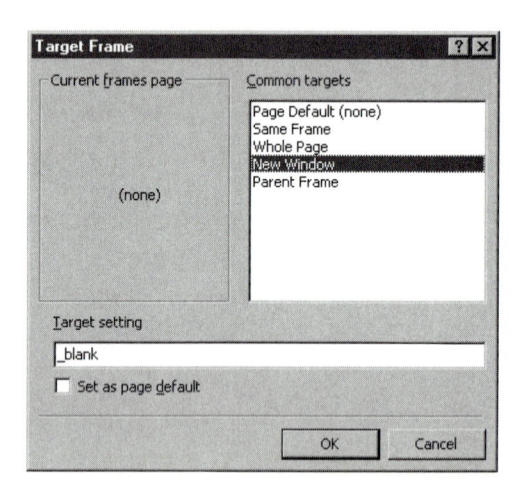

Adding ScreenTip text

You can also define pop-up text that will appear when a visitor hovers over your link. For example, in Figure 3-2, the pop-up text explains that clicking the link will send an e-mail. ScreenTip text allows you to add content to a text link, making it clear that text is, indeed, a *link*. And ScreenTip text makes your page more dynamic and fun, as text *pops up* when a visitor hovers over a link.

NOTE You should keep the ScreenTip text relatively short so that it can be easily read in a browser window.

To add a ScreenTip to your link, click the ScreenTip button in the Create Hyperlinks dialog box, and enter the ScreenTip text you want, as shown here:

After you have defined a link target for your text, along with (optional) ScreenTip text, and/or a Target Frame, click OK to close the Create Hyperlink dialog box. Links can be tested in the Preview tab or in a browser (choose File | Preview in Browser).

FIGURE 3-2

A link with ScreenTip text

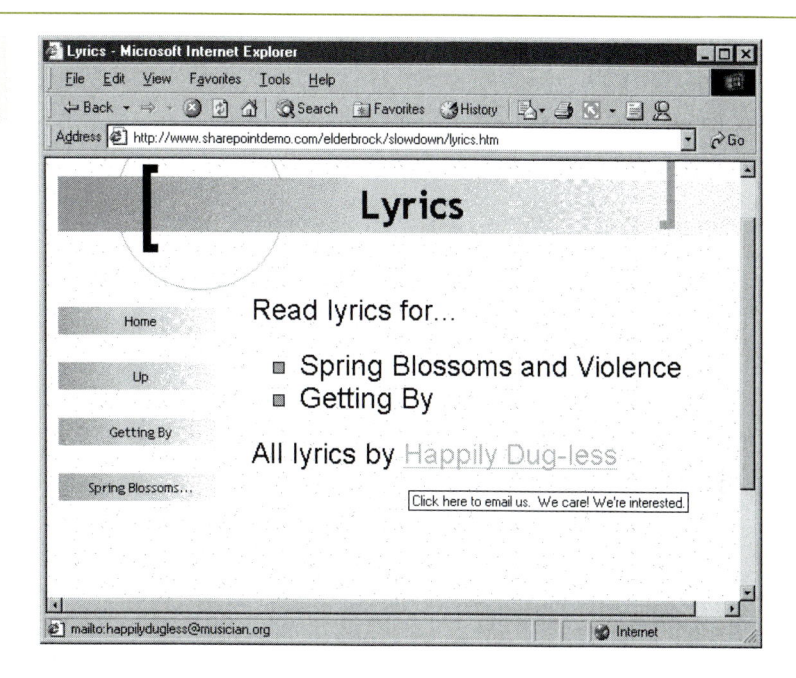

Using Bookmarks

Bookmarks are link targets within Web pages. They are especially helpful for large or long Web pages because they enable a visitor to jump right to a section of a page. Before you can create links to bookmarks, you have to create bookmarks on your page.

To Create a bookmark:

1 Click at the spot on your page that will be the bookmark target link.

2 Choose Insert | Bookmark.

3 Enter a bookmark name (the default name is determined by what text you selected—if any—to create the bookmark).

4 Click OK in the Bookmark dialog box.

Bookmarks appear as a small flag or text underlined with a dotted line. You can define links to any bookmark from other locations on your page (or other pages).

CHAPTER 3
EDITING AND FORMATTING WEB PAGES

To Define LINKS:

1 Select text (or you can also use a picture). This text (or picture) will be the link to a bookmark.

2 Click the Create Hyperlink tool in the Standard toolbar.

3 In the Create Hyperlink dialog box, click the Place in This Document icon on the left side of the dialog box.

4 Select your bookmark from the Bookmark list, as shown here:

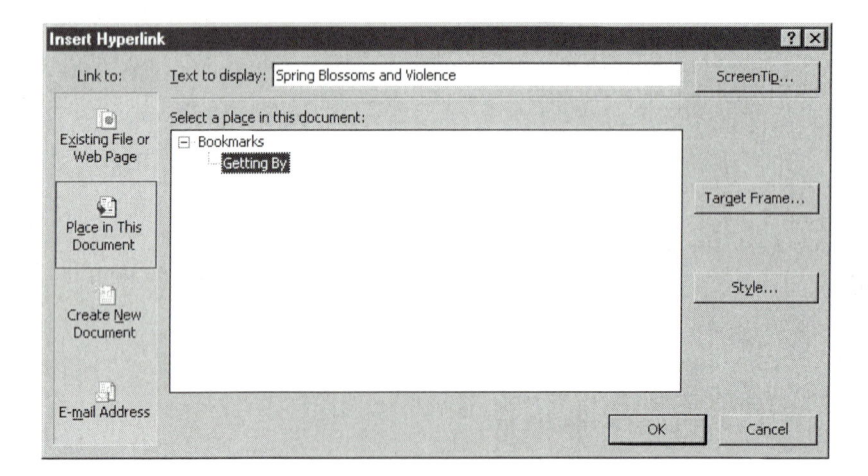

5 Click OK to close the dialog box.

6 Test your bookmark in Preview tab of FrontPage Page view.

FORMATTING TEXT

FrontPage allows you to assign font types, colors, sizes, and attributes such as boldface to selected text. You can also apply paragraph formatting—like alignment, spacing, and indenting. And you can even apply borders and shading to text. Keep reading to find out how.

Formatting Selected Text

To apply formatting to text, the first step is to select it. You can use the same techniques to select text in FrontPage Page view that you would use in Word. For example, you can double-click to select a word and triple-click (within a paragraph) to select the paragraph. To select an entire page of text, click CTRL+A. Once text is selected, you can format it.

To Assign formatting to text:

1. Select the text.

2. Use the Font drop-down list to choose a font.

3. Use the Font Size drop-down list to choose from the available (Web-supported) font sizes. (Another way to change font size is to use the Increase Font Size or the Decrease Font Size buttons.)

4. Use the Bold, Italic and/or Underline buttons to assign (or remove) those attributes.

5. You can highlight selected text by choosing a color from the Highlight drop-down list/button. Then, click the button to assign the highlight color to the text you selected.

6. Use the Font Color drop-down list to choose a color for your text, and click the Font Color button to apply that color to selected text.

> **NOTE** The first drop-down list in the Formatting toolbar is the Styles list. Styles apply preset formatting including font color, size, spacing, and alignment. Styles are associated with themes, so choosing a different theme causes the attributes of preset styles to change. For more on themes, see Chapter 9.

> **TIP** Whether a visitor to your Web site can see the font you assign depends on whether he or she has that font on their operating system. It's safest to stick with Arial, Times Roman, or Courier fonts as almost every computer system supports these fonts.

In addition to the set of text formatting buttons available in the Formatting toolbar, you can assign attributes to selected text by choosing Format | Font from the menu bar. This opens the Font dialog box, shown in Figure 3-3.

In the bottom half of the Font dialog box, you'll see a bunch of check boxes for formatting attributes. These check boxes can be used to apply additional font attributes such as Small Caps, All Caps, or Strikethrough formatting. Some of

FIGURE 3-3

You can apply formatting to text in the Font dialog box

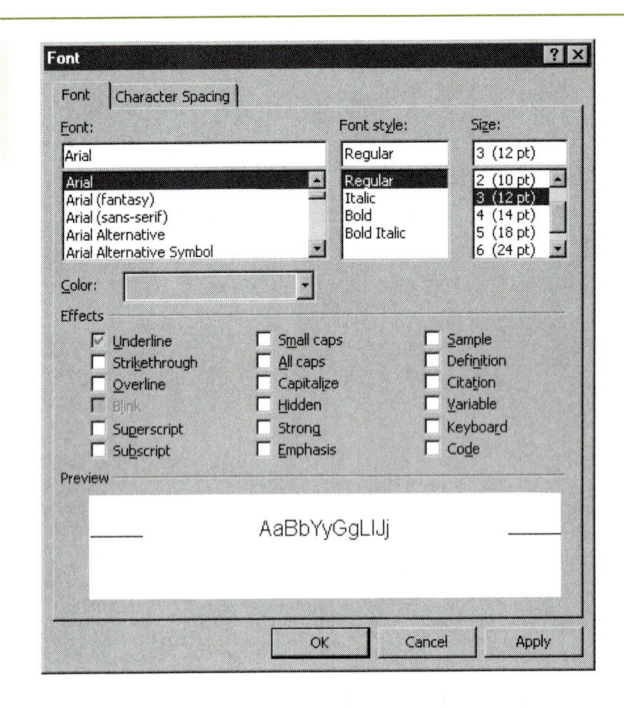

these check boxes (like those in the third column) apply text attributes used in the olden days of Web page formatting that don't have a practical use anymore.

In addition to the text formatting available in the Formatting toolbar, the Font dialog box has a Character Spacing tab that allows you to define spacing between letters (the Spacing drop-down list and the By spin box), and also subscript or superscript (the Position drop-down list).

Formatting Paragraphs

Modern Web browsers—meaning Netscape Navigator 4.7 and 6.0 and Internet Explorer 5.5—support all kinds of paragraph formatting. They can display line spacing, indenting, and—in the case of IE 5.5 and Netscape 6.0—borders and shading. So when you apply these features, most of your visitors will see them. As you apply paragraph formatting, keep in mind that some visitors with older browsers will not see these paragraph attributes.

You can use the Line Numbering or Bullets buttons to assign sequential numbering or bullets to selected text. You can align paragraphs using the Align Left, Center, Align Right, or Justify buttons.

More Paragraph Formatting Options

In addition to the paragraph formatting options available from the Formatting toolbar, FrontPage allows additional paragraph formatting, including line spacing, indentation, and even word spacing. The current generation of Web browsers, including Netscape Navigator 4.7 and newer and Internet Explorer 5 and newer, support most or all of these formatting options.

To Apply more paragraph formatting options to selected text:

1 Select a paragraph.

2 Choose Format | Paragraph from the menu bar.

3 Assign indentation before text (on the left), after text (on the right), or to the first line only.

4 Assign vertical spacing by entering numbers in the Before or After spin boxes.

5 Assign word spacing by entering numbers in the Word spin box. In the Line Spacing drop-down menu, the options are Single Spacing, 1.5 Spacing, or Double-Spacing.

More Bullet and Numbering Options

You can quickly and easily assign either bullets or numbering using the buttons in the Formatting toolbar. If you want more control over bullet and numbering format, select the paragraphs to be bulleted or numbered, and then select Format | Bullets and Numbering. The List Properties dialog box opens, as shown in Figure 3-4.

If you have your own graphics that you want to use as bullet icons, use the Picture Bullets tab to select a picture for your bullets. Use the Browse button to navigate to a picture file on your computer.

Use the Numbers tab to define bullet and numbering options similar to those in Word—you can assign automatic numbering as Roman Numerals or Letters (A, B, C...), and you can define a starting number for a list.

Use the Enable Collapsible Outlines check box if you want your visitors to be able to expand or collapse outlines. If you want to use the Enable Collapsible Outlines option, first assign it to your outline. Then, after you click OK in the

FIGURE 3-4

The List Properties dialog box is where you control bullet and numbering details

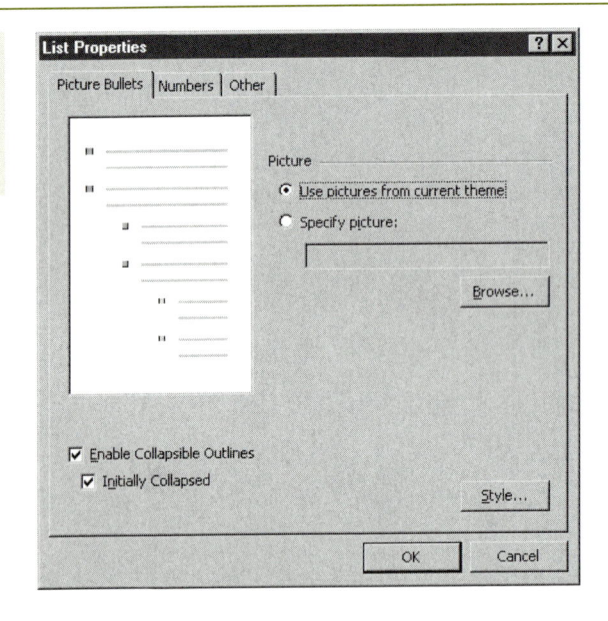

List Properties dialog box, go back and indent lower-level bullets or numbering by selecting paragraphs in a bullet (or numbered) list, and click the Increase Indent button in the Formatting toolbar twice. Figure 3-5 shows what a collapsible outline looks like in a Web browser.

> **NOTE** Visitors using older browsers will just see the entire outline and won't have the option of collapsing sections of it.

Formatting Borders and Shading

Borders and shading can be used to emphasize text. However, borders and shading are *not* supported uniformly by Web browsers, and most border and shading attributes are not supported by Netscape 4.7.

When you apply borders and shading, take browser compatibility issues into consideration. For example, *avoid* using a dark shading color combined with white text. Visitors to your site using Netscape Navigator 4.7 will "see" only white text on a white background because their browsers don't support shading. In other words, they won't be able to see the text at all.

It's okay, however, to use borders and shading as a formatting technique, as long as you don't rely on visitors being able to see the shading.

FIGURE 3-5

In this collapsible outline, tour stops in London and Lyon have been expanded, whereas other cities' schedules are collapsed

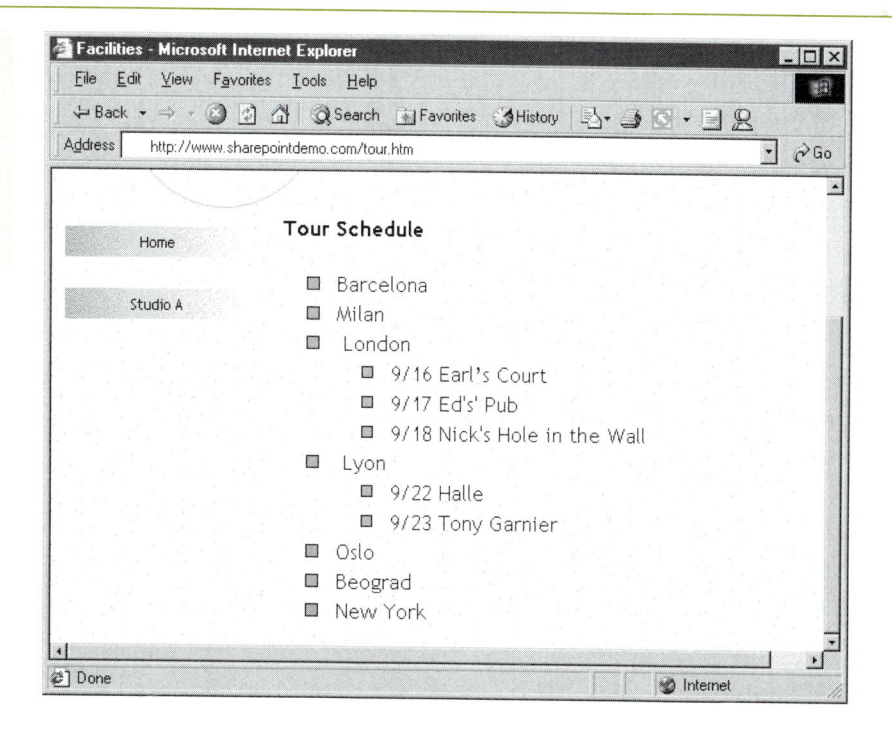

To Assign BORDERS OR SHADING:

Select text and then choose Format | Borders and Shading. The Borders and Shading dialog box opens, as shown here, allows you to apply borders around paragraphs.

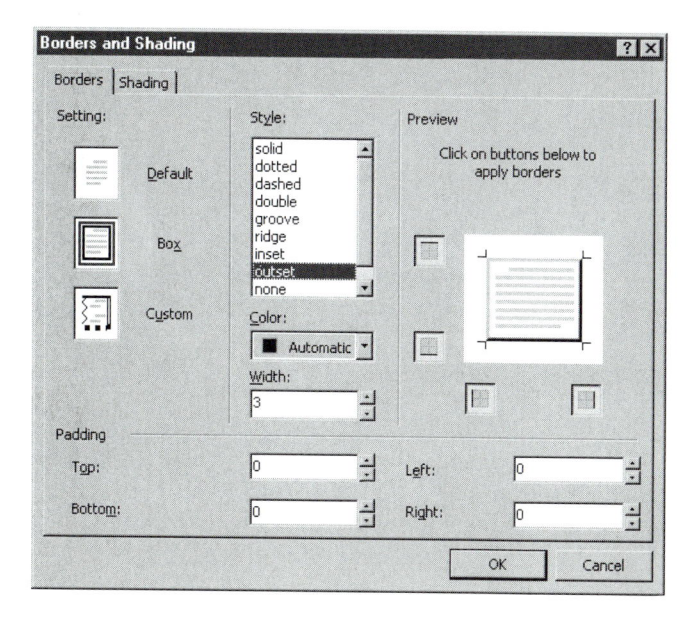

2 Choose line Style, Color, and Width, and then apply these attributes by clicking any of the border buttons in the Preview area of the dialog box. You can also define spacing using the Padding spin boxes. (*Spacing* is the "air" in between the text and the surrounding border.)

3 Use the Shading tab in the Borders and Shading dialog box to assign a background color for a paragraph. You can also define the color of text inside your border by using the Foreground color drop-down list.

This illustration shows a border with shading (and a generous spacing setting of 12 all around) to set off text.

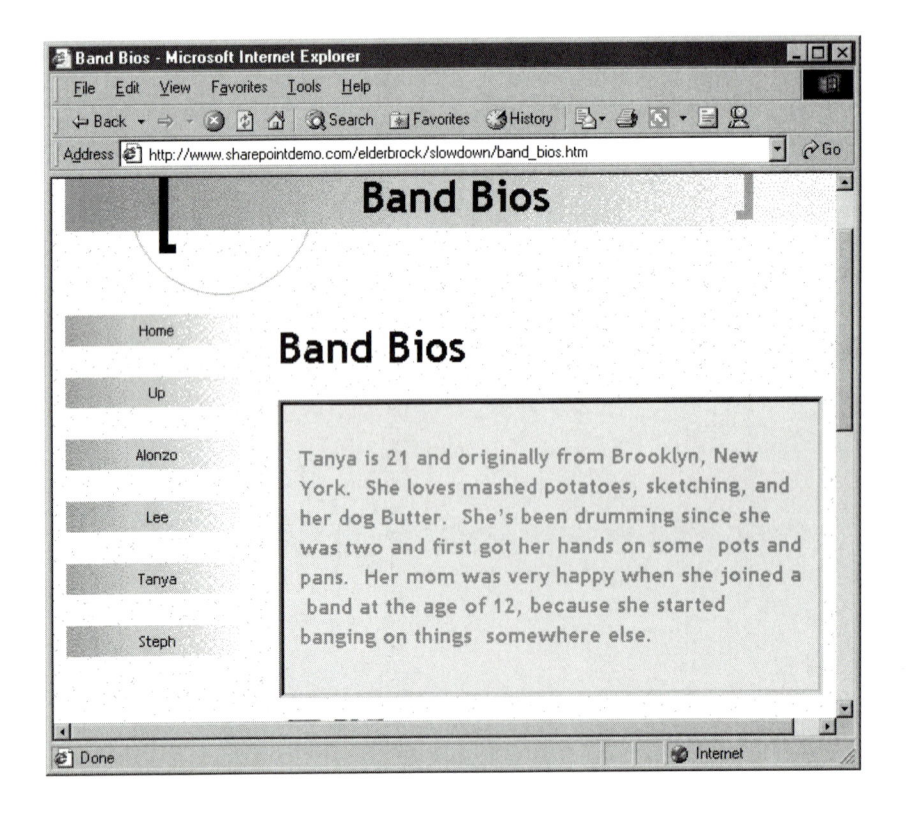

Formatting Pages

Page format attributes include the background color (or background image) for a page, a background sound, and page margins. Other page properties include default colors for your page text, links, and page title.

You control page properties in the Page Properties dialog box. To open it, right-click an open page in Page view, and choose Page Properties from the context menu.

Some page formatting features, like background color and text color, are automatically defined for you if you apply a theme to your page. In that case, these options won't be available until you remove any assigned theme from the page.

To Remove A THEME FROM AN OPEN PAGE:

1 Choose Format | Theme.

2 Choose the Selected Page(s) option button, as shown here, to apply your choice to only the open page.

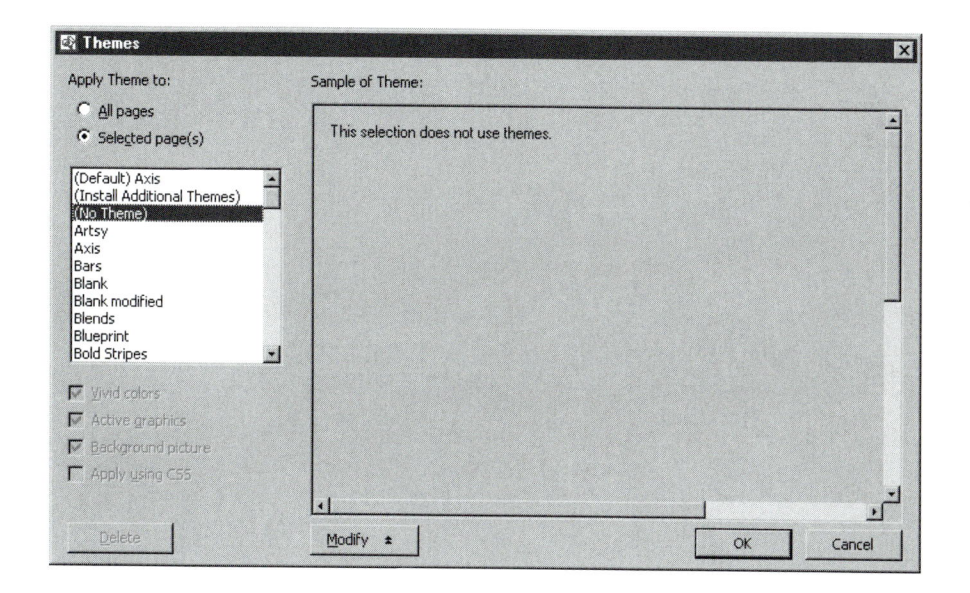

3 Select No Theme from the list of themes on the left side of the Themes dialog box.

4 Click OK in the Themes dialog box.

DEFINING PAGE BACKGROUNDS

The Background tab in the Page Properties dialog box lets you define both the page background and default text colors. You can use the Background tab, for

Chapter 3
Editing and Formatting Web Pages

example, to define a black page background with white text. Page backgrounds are supported by all current and recent browsers (as opposed to shading, which is not supported by Netscape Navigator 4.7).

The *default* text colors you define in the Page Properties dialog box are *overruled* by formatting you apply directly to text. So, for example, if you set the default page text as black, but assign green to selected text, the locally assigned color will take precedence over the default page color.

The following illustration shows the Background tab.

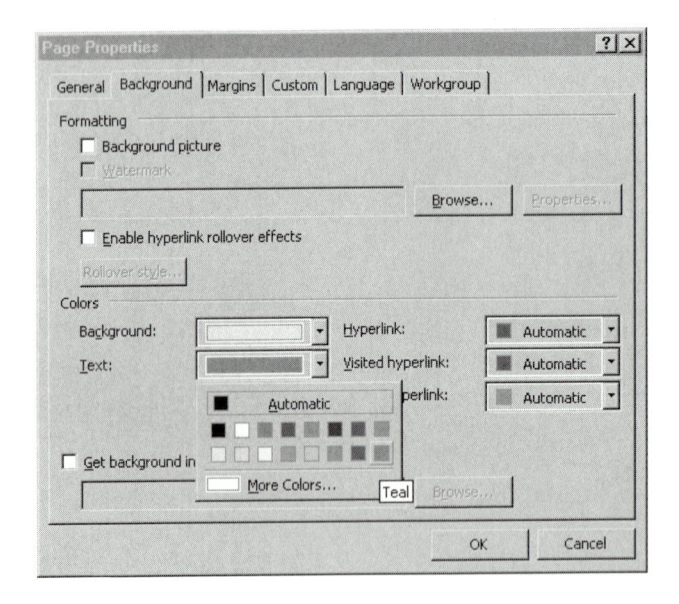

To find your way around the Page Properties dialog box, read through the following list:

▶ **Background Picture** Use this check box if you have a picture you want to use as a background for your page. Background images *til*—that is, they repeat themselves over and over to fill up the available browser window space.

▶ **Browse** Use this button to navigate to a background image.

▶ **Watermark** This check box freezes a background image on the browser screen, so when people scroll up and down, the background picture doesn't move.

▶ **Enable Hyperlink Rollover Effects** Use this check box to define font changes when someone moves his or her mouse over a link on your page.

▶ **Background** Use this drop-down list to choose a color for your Web page background.

▶ **Text** This drop-down menu allows you to choose a color for text on your page. This color will be applied to any text where you have not assigned a color.

▶ **Get Background and Colors from Page** This check box allows you to base the background and text colors on your page on another page background and colors.

▶ **Hyperlink** Use this drop-down box to choose colors for links on your page.

Adding Background Sounds

A Web page can have background sounds that play when your page is opened. These files can play just once or over and over. One drawback to adding background sound files is that sound files tend to be large. And a background sound can dramatically increase the time it takes for a Web page to download. Another drawback is that not everyone *likes* hearing sound files when they open a Web page. But if you think your visitors will appreciate a background sound, FrontPage makes it easy to include one.

FrontPage 2002 let's you stick just about any file format of sound file into your page as a background sound. The allowed file formats are listed here:

▶ **WAV** A file format used by many Windows application.
▶ **MID** Also known as "MIDI;" a very space-efficient file format used for Web audio.
▶ **RAM or RA** Audio file formats used by the popular Real Audio system.
▶ **AIF** A standard, high-quality sound file format for Macintosh computers.
▶ **AU** A sound file format native to the UNIX operating system.
▶ **SND** A file format used by Amiga, NeXT, and other operating systems.

Once you get a sound file in *any* of these formats, you can use it as a background sound for your page.

> **TIP** One way to find sound files is to search the Internet for sounds using your favorite search engine. Microsoft Office XP includes some sound files in its clip-art collection. To find them, look in the Clipart folder of Microsoft Office (located in your Program Files folder).

CHAPTER 3
EDITING AND FORMATTING WEB PAGES

To Insert a sound file into your page as a background sound:

1 With your page open, right-click anywhere on the page and choose Page Properties from the context menu.

2 Select the General tab in the Page Properties dialog box.

3 Use the Browse button to navigate to a sound file.

4 Select the Forever check box to play the sound over and over while the page is open. Or, deselect the check box, and use the Loop spin box to set the number of times the sound will play.

5 Click OK to close the Page Properties dialog box, and then save your page. FrontPage will prompt you to save the sound file (unless you have already saved the sound file as part of your Web site).

DEFINING PAGE MARGINS

If you look closely at most Web pages in a browser, you will see that they have spacing on the top and left side that creates a little buffer space between the page content and the browser window. The normal spacing for page top and left margins is 10 *pixels*—tiny dots that make up the picture on your monitor's screen. You can change the default margins in the Margins tab of the Page Properties dialog box.

To Change margins:

1 Right-click an open page and choose Page Properties from the context menu.

2 Select the Margins tab of the Page Properties dialog box, and select either the Top or Left margin check boxes.

3 You can enter custom margins (including a margin of zero) in either of the spin boxes, as shown in Figure 3-6.

FIGURE 3-6

Defining a top and left margin of zero

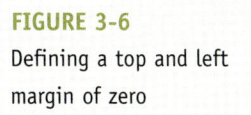

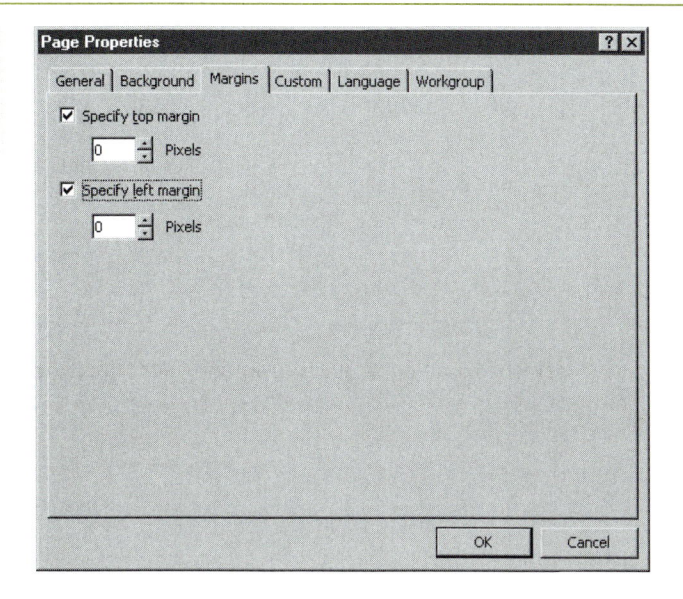

Other Page Properties

Several other page property options are available in the Page Properties dialog box. Some of them are beyond the scope of this beginner level FrontPage book. Others have some useful features. Take a quick look at them so you know what they are:

▶ **General** This tab of the Page Properties dialog box, including the Design-Time Control Scripting options are for folks who create HTML themselves rather than have FrontPage define their HTML code.

▶ **Custom** This tab allows you to define what are called *meta tags*. The keywords "meta tag" are used by search engines to find and list your page, and the description meta tag is used by search engines to provide a description of your page. To define keywords, click the Add button in the Custom tab of the Page Properties dialog box. This opens the System Meta Variable dialog box. Type **keywords** in the Name area. In the Value section type a list of words you want to connect to your site in search engines. Separate different descriptive words or phrases with commas, as shown here:

Chapter 3
Editing and Formatting Web Pages

Keyword meta tags are used by search engines to find your site. Description meta tags are often *displayed* by search engines along with a listing of your site. Adding a description meta tag is similar to adding a keyword meta tag.

To Enter a description meta tag:

1 Click Add, and enter a description in the Name area of the System Meta Variable dialog box.

2 Type a description of your site in the Value area.

3 After you define meta tags, click OK in the Page Properties dialog box. The keywords and description you define will be picked up by browsers and search engines.

What's Next?

In this chapter, you've explored many facets of page layout—ranging from formatting text to defining page properties. *Text* formatting controls the size, font, color, shading, and even spacing of text. *Page* formatting controls page background color (or image) and page background sounds, and can also be used to assign a *default* text color to a page. If there is a conflict between the text color assigned as a page property and text color assigned using formatting tools (such as the Font Color tool on the Formatting toolbar), formatting tools take precedence.

You also looked at text links, and learned how to control the target of a link and open links in new browser windows. In the following chapter, you'll look at how FrontPage handles Web graphics. You'll be pleasantly surprised at *how much* you can do with graphics in FrontPage.

> **ON THE VIRTUAL CLASSROOM CD** In Lesson 2, "Formatting Page Text," I demonstrate how to assign colors, fonts, and font size to Web page text in FrontPage. The lesson also demonstrates how to format paragraph alignment, indentation and spacing, as well as applying automatic numbering and bullet lists.

4

Working with Pictures

FrontPage not only seamlessly imports and integrates images into Web pages, it also gives you a nice set of tools for editing images. This chapter explores how to bring pictures into FrontPage Web sites and how to align them with page text. In the course of this chapter you'll also learn to assign links, ToolTip text, and even clickable image map areas that provide more than one link in a single graphic. You'll explore pictures in six bite-sized steps: getting pictures into your Web site, saving pictures as part of your Web site, sizing pictures and locating them on your page, editing pictures, adding links and image maps to pictures, and defining picture properties.

You'll also briefly look at the drawing tools that have been added to FrontPage 2002 and take a sober look at the limitations of using those tools in Web page design.

Getting Pictures into FrontPage

If you can see a picture on your computer screen, you can put it in a FrontPage Web site. It's that simple. Those of you who are a bit Web-savvy may know that the only globally recognized graphic file formats on the Web are GIF or JPEG. True. But FrontPage happily converts any image you paste onto a page into either GIF or JPEG format.

FrontPage can handle the process of converting any image to a Web-compatible GIF file, and it will save the image file so that it will be seamlessly embedded in your Web page. We'll explore that process in detail later in this chapter, but the short explanation is that when you save a page with a picture on it, FrontPage converts that picture into a GIF or JPEG file if necessary, and saves it for you in your Web site folder.

Copying Pictures into FrontPage

The most basic way to get a picture into a FrontPage Web is to open it in any application on your computer, right-click the picture and choose Copy from the context menu to put the picture on the Clipboard. Then, click anywhere in an open FrontPage Web page and choose Edit Paste from the menu. That's it!

Inserting Picture Files

FrontPage will insert image files from many formats, including the Web-compatible JPEG and GIF formats, the TIFF file format used by most scanners, and Windows' own WMF Windows Metafile format.

If your pictures are coming from a program that uses a file format not supported by FrontPage, you can always export graphics from PhotoShop, Adobe Illustrator, Macromedia Flash or almost any graphics program into a GIF or JPEG file.

FrontPage 2002
Virtual Classroom

To Place an imported file on your Web page:

1 Click to place your cursor insertion point where you want to place the picture.

2 Choose Insert | Picture | From File.

3 In the Picture dialog box, choose one of the sources for files from the Look In list on the left of the dialog box, and navigate to the folder with your picture file.

> **NOTE** In the Files of Type drop-down menu, select a desired picture file format (like GIF, or JPEG), or just leave the setting at the default All Image Files to show all picture files in a selected folder.

4 After you navigate to a picture, as shown here, click the Insert button to place the image in your Web page.

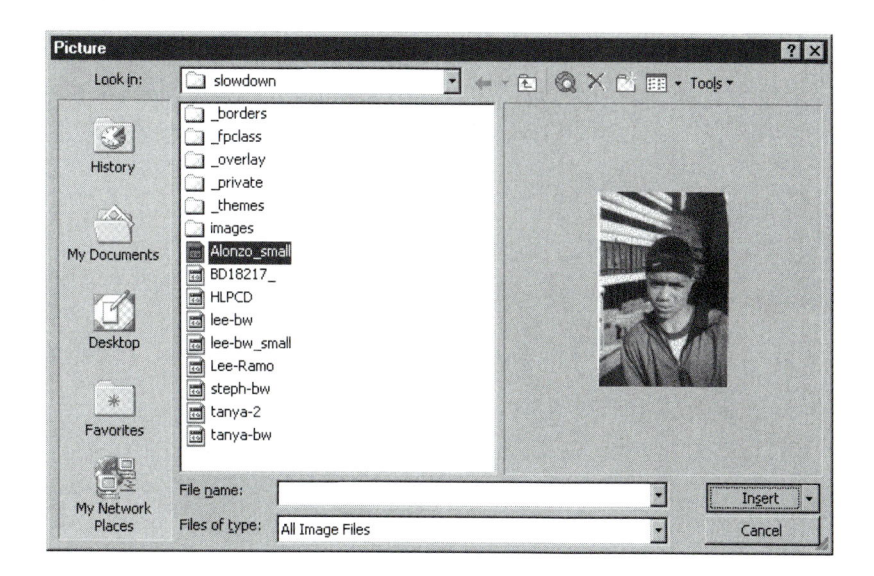

Adding Clip Art

Office XP (and previous versions) come with a variety of clip-art collections. Luckily, FrontPage helps organize the process of finding those sets of clip art on your computer.

CHAPTER 4
WORKING WITH PICTURES

To Find CLIP ART:

1 Click to place your insertion cursor point in an open page in Page view.

2 Select Insert | Picture | Clip Art from the menu bar.

3 To find clip art for a topic, type a word or phrase into the Search For box in the Insert Clip Art window, as shown on your right:

4 You can simply drag clip art onto your page, as shown below:

> **NOTE** The Insert Clip Art window pane opens on the right of your screen.

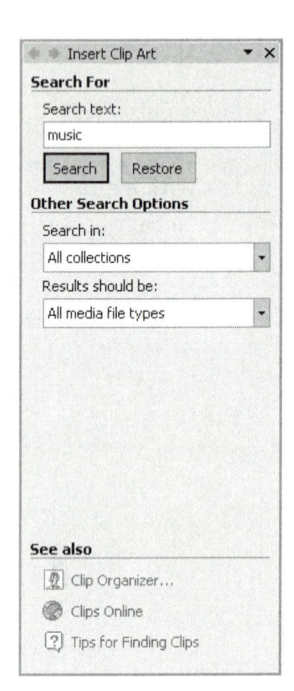

Sometimes when you drag clip art onto your page, the sizing is way out of scale. No worries—you can resize easily in FrontPage. You'll explore that process shortly, in the section "Sizing and Locating Images" later in this chapter.

SAVING PICTURE FILES

As promised, FrontPage handles the process of converting *any* copied, imported, or clip-art image into one of the two Web-compatible image formats: JPEG or GIF. Most Web graphics folks prefer the GIF format for drawings, line art, icons and other artwork that doesn't involve complex color processing. JPEG is the preferred format for photographs that usually require complex color management or shading.

FrontPage detects the type of image you are using and automatically saves it as either a GIF or JPEG file when you save your page.

To Save IMAGES AS PART OF SAVING A WEB PAGE:

1 With a page open that contains (unsaved) pictures, choose File | Save. The Save Embedded Files dialog box opens, as shown here:

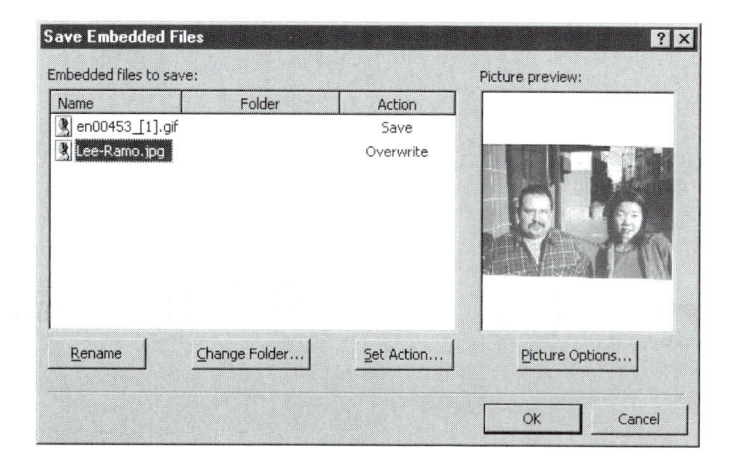

Two embedded pictures are being saved as files with this page—one is a photo that is being saved in JPG (JPEG) format and one is clip art that is being saved in GIF format

2 Four buttons in the Save Embedded Files dialog box allow you to change the properties of the picture being saved:

- **Rename** Use this to change the filename of a selected picture file.

- **Change Folder** Use this to select a folder other than the default folder in which to save your pictures.

- **Set Action** Use this if you want to revert to the previously saved version of your picture.

- **Picture Options** Use this if you want to change the decisions FrontPage made about what file format and file format settings to apply to your saved picture. Use this button only if you're already a graphic file format expert, and you want to overrule FrontPage's picture file saving process.

3 When you have examined and—if necessary changed—your picture file settings, click OK to close the Save Embedded Files dialog box and save pictures embedded in your Web page.

Sizing and Locating Images

Often images are the wrong size for your Web site. You can easily resize them in FrontPage. And, because smaller images can be resaved as smaller image *files*, which speeds-up the load time for your page, smaller is usually better when it comes to Web pictures.

You can also align images, so text flows around them. This allows you to create pages with text and pictures integrated together. For example, if you right-align a picture, text will flow to the left of the picture. Pictures are usually aligned either on the left or right side of the page.

You can also define a buffer space between a picture and the text that flows around it. This avoids the tacky look of text bumping up against a picture, allows you to add white space, and achieves a less "cramped" look to your page.

Resizing Images

FrontPage allows you to manually resize a picture to any size you want. Or, FrontPage automatically converts a picture into what is called a *thumbnail*—a small version of the picture that serves as an icon that provides a link to a full-sized version of the picture. We'll look at both ways of resizing pictures here.

Manually Resizing Pictures

You can change the size of a picture right in FrontPage. No need to spend $1,000 for the deluxe edition of PhotoShop for this task! When you select a picture, sizing *handles* appear—small square dots in the corners and on the sides of the picture. By clicking and dragging on these handles, you can easily resize a picture. When you drag a corner handle, you resize the picture while maintaining the original height-to-width ratio. If you drag on a side handle, you make the picture taller and skinnier or wider and fatter.

To Resize A PICTURE MANUALLY:

1. Select a picture by clicking it.

2. Resize the selected picture—making it larger or smaller—by clicking and dragging any corner or side handle. When you drag a corner handle, you resize the picture while maintaining the original height-to-width ratio. If you drag on a side handle, you make the picture taller and skinnier or wider and fatter. Figure 4-1 shows an image being resized using a corner handle.

3. When you have resized your picture, release the mouse button. Save your page to overwrite your old embedded image file with the new picture file.

> **NOTE** The eight black squares that appear on the corners and sides of a selected image are called *handles*.

CREATING THUMBNAILS

Because big pictures take a long time to download, and because browser window space is limited, it's often effective to convert large pictures into thumbnails. A visitor clicks the thumbnail and opens the full-sized picture.

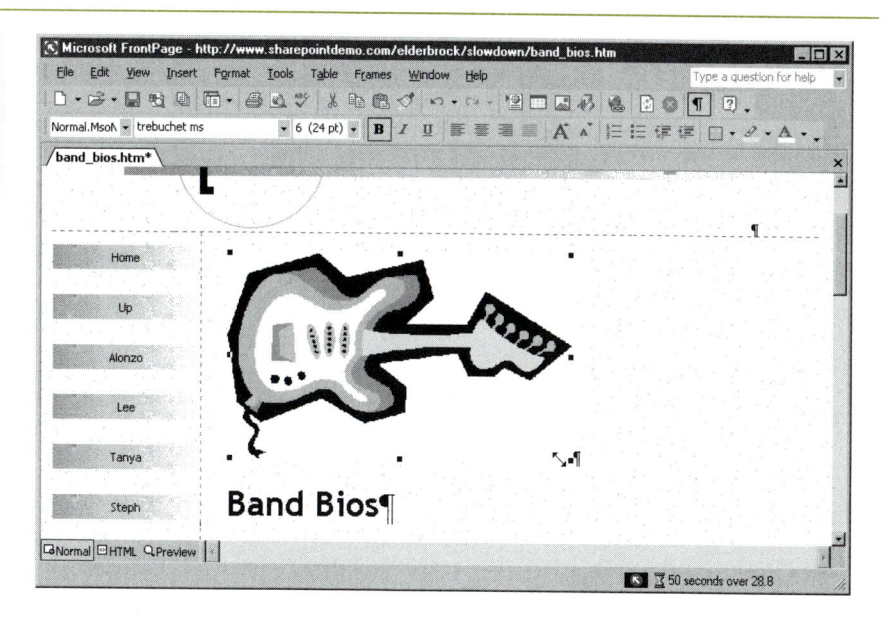

FIGURE 4-1

Resizing a picture while maintaining the original height-to-width size ratio

To Create A THUMBNAIL:

1 Click a large picture in your Web page.

2 Choose Tools | Auto Thumbnail.

3 Your image is automatically reduced to 100 pixels wide. The height will vary but will stay in proportion to the original size of the picture. The small picture is now a *link*. When it is clicked in a browser, the original full-sized photo opens.

4 If you want to change the size of automatically generated thumbnails, select Tools | Page Options, and click the Auto Thumbnail tab in the Page Options dialog box, as shown next. Here, you can redefine the size and features applied to automatic thumbnails.

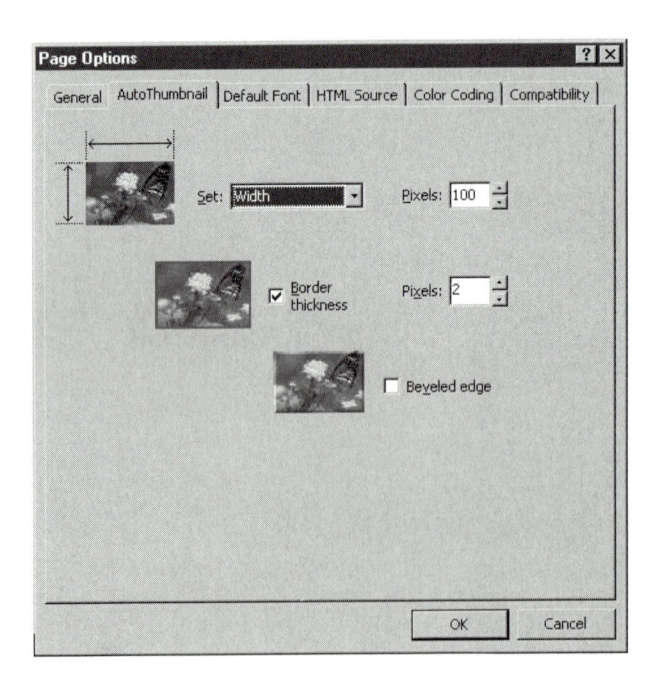

ALIGNING AND LOCATING PICTURES

You can move pictures around in FrontPage by clicking and dragging them. You'll notice that it's difficult to easily locate a picture in an *exact* spot on a page. Here, you'll explore how to flow text around pictures and position a picture at an exact spot on a page.

Aligning Pictures

Usually, when you combine text and pictures on a page, it's most effective to flow text *around* the pictures. This is done by *aligning* pictures on either the right or left side of the text. Figure 4-2 shows a page in Page view with pictures aligned both left and right.

To Align a picture:

1 Select a picture on a page in Page view.

2 Use the Align Left or Align Right icons in the Formatting toolbar to assign either left or right alignment to the picture.

3 After you align a picture, you can still move it around on a page by clicking and dragging the picture.

FIGURE 4-2

The small right and left arrow icons at the beginning of paragraphs mark the location of picture files, and indicate they are right and left aligned

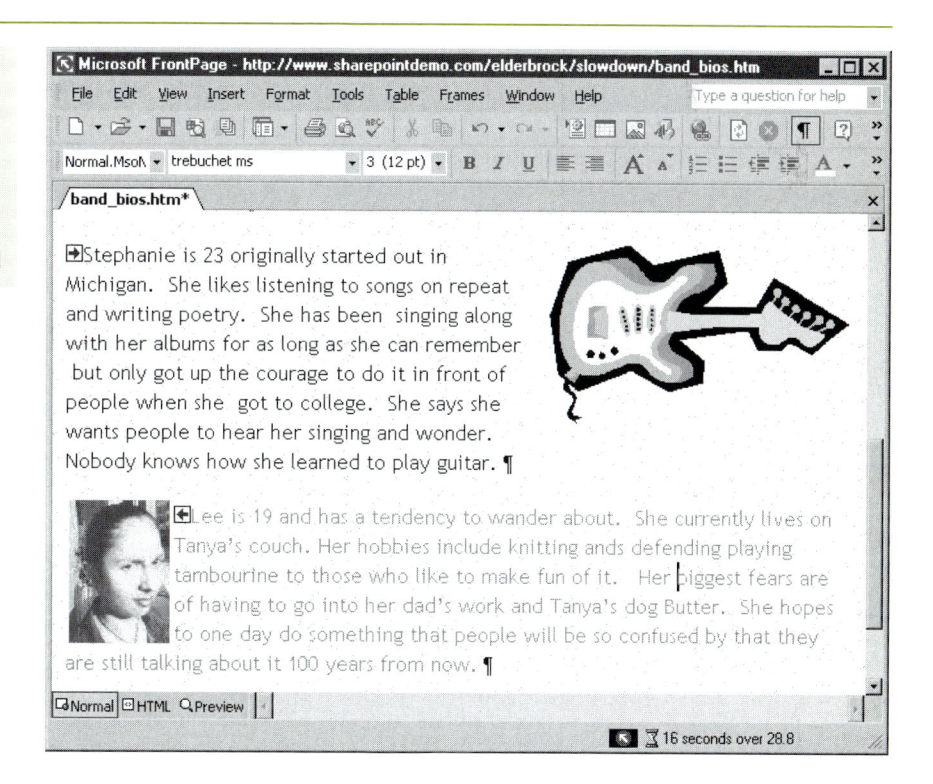

CHAPTER 4
Working with Pictures

Positioning Pictures Absolutely

You *can* position a picture at an exact spot on a Web page, but there are a couple drawbacks that will keep you from doing it except once in a while for special effects. The problems are

▶ Absolute positioning does *not* flow text around a picture the way aligning does, so your picture appears on top of or below your text.

▶ Absolute positioning is erratically interpreted by Web browsers.

That said, there are times and places to try absolute positioning. For example, in Figure 4-3, the piano clip art is positioned behind text. By combining a dark page background, light colored text, and the dark-colored clip art, it's possible to have the text visible "on top of" the piano.

To Define absolute positioning for a picture to an image:

1. Select it a picture on your page, and choose Format, Position from the menu.

FIGURE 4-3
The picture is absolutely positioned on the page underneath the text

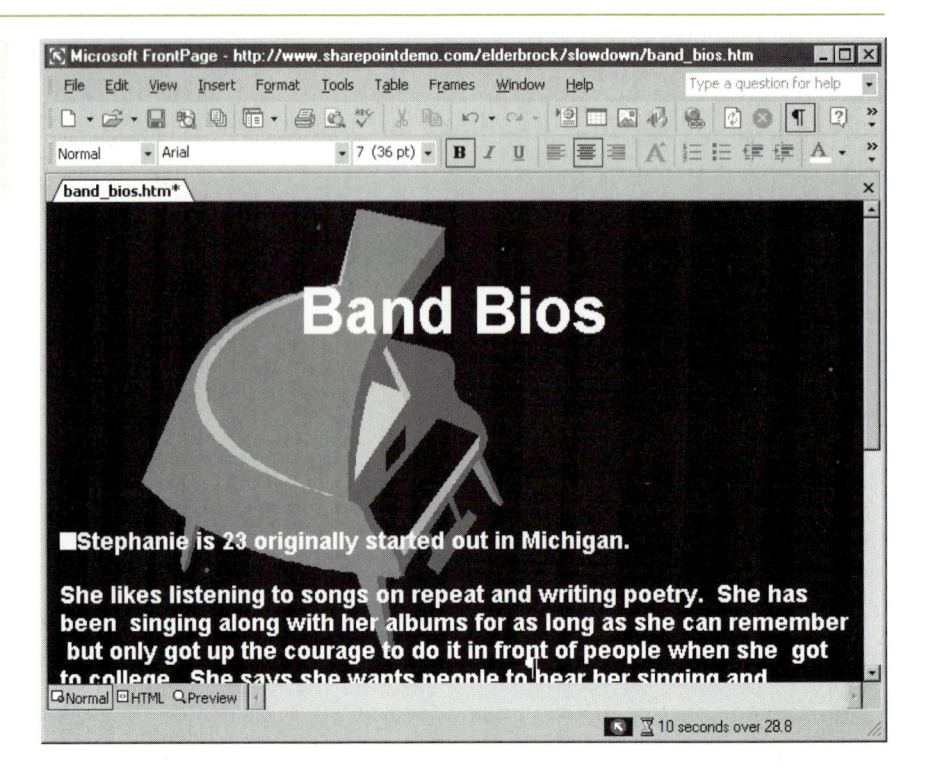

2 In the Position dialog box, select the Absolute button, as shown here:

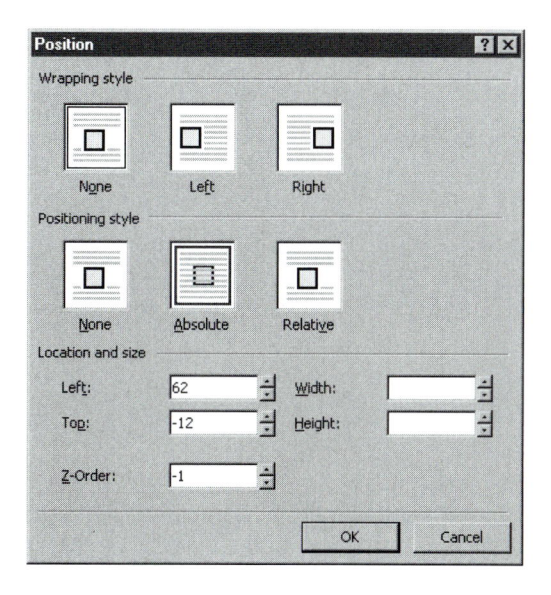

3 Use the Z-Order spin box to define how you want the absolutely positioned picture to intersect with other page content. The higher the Z value, the more the picture will appear on top of other objects (including page text). If you want the picture to appear *beneath* page text, set the Z value to a negative number—like –1)—as shown in the preceding illustration.

> **WARNING** The location you define for absolutely positioned pictures is not always accurately reflected in how a picture looks in a browser. Keep absolute positioning for simple pages with little text, and use sparingly for effect.

4 You can define location and size in the Position dialog box, but these attributes are easier to define by clicking and dragging on the picture. So click OK to close the Position dialog box now.

5 Click your picture and drag it to the desired location on the page.

6 Use the sizing handles that appear when you select a positioned picture to resize the picture if necessary.

Editing Pictures in FrontPage

FrontPage comes with it's own picture editor. It's is not going to put PhotoShop out of business, but it's picture editing tools allow you to lighten pictures, increase

CHAPTER 4
WORKING WITH PICTURES

contrast, resize and reshape pictures, and create transparent picture backgrounds—just what you need to fix up pictures for Web sites.

FrontPage's picture editing tools are best accessed on the Picture toolbar. To open that toolbar, select a picture. Sometimes the picture toolbar appears, sometimes it doesn't! If you don't see the picture toolbar when you select a picture, choose View | Toolbars | Pictures. The Picture toolbar tools are shown here:

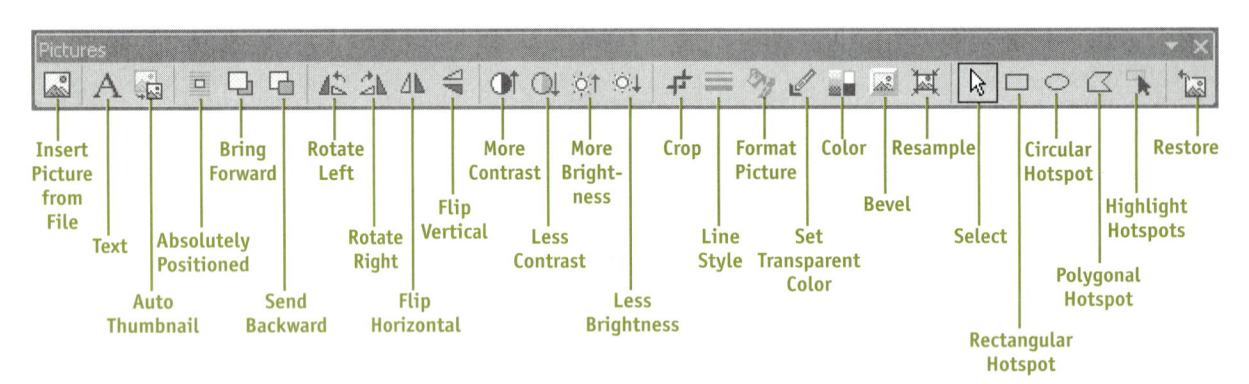

[Picture toolbar diagram with labeled buttons: Insert Picture from File, Text, Auto Thumbnail, Absolutely Positioned, Bring Forward, Send Backward, Rotate Left, Rotate Right, Flip Horizontal, Flip Vertical, More Contrast, Less Contrast, More Brightness, Less Brightness, Crop, Line Style, Format Picture, Set Transparent Color, Color, Bevel, Resample, Select, Rectangular Hotspot, Circular Hotspot, Polygonal Hotspot, Highlight Hotspots, Restore]

Here's how the Picture toolbar tools (buttons) work:

- ▶ **Insert Picture from File** Let's you navigate around and insert a picture.

- ▶ **Text** Creates a box for caption text that attaches to the selected picture.

- ▶ **Auto Thumbnail** Creates a thumbnail of the selected picture (see discussion of thumbnails earlier in this chapter).

- ▶ **Absolutely Positioned** Assigns absolute positioning to the selected picture (see discussion of absolute positioning earlier in this chapter).

- ▶ **Bring Forward** Works with absolutely positioned pictures—moving them in front of other objects on the page.

- ▶ **Send Backward** Also works with absolutely positioned pictures—moving them *behind* other objects on the page.

- ▶ **Rotate Left, Rotate Right, Flip Horizontal, and Flip Vertical** Rotates the picture.

- ▶ **More Contrast, Less Contrast, More Brightness, and Less Brightness** Changes the brightness and contrast of the picture. Very useful—especially since most images need some brightening when they are placed in Web sites.

- ▶ **Crop** Works like scissors—you can trim the edges off of a picture.

- **Line Style** Allows you to define outlines for *some* pictures. However, for *most* pictures, you'll define outlines in the Picture Properties dialog box, while is explored in the next section of this chapter.

- **Format Picture** Only works on pictures created with FrontPage's drawing tools, which are briefly addressed at the end of this chapter.

- **Set Transparent Color** Used to make *one* color in a picture invisible so that the page background shows through. When you click this tool an eraser cursor appears. Use it to point and click at a color in a picture to make that color disappear.

- **Color** Provides four color options (not all are available for every picture): Automatic (normal), Grayscale (shades of gray), Black and White (2 colors), and Washout (makes the picture colors fade).

- **Bevel** Applies a frame around a picture.

- **Resample** Overwrites your existing picture file with one that reflects the current size of the image. If you have made your picture smaller, this reduces file size.

- **Select** Deselects other tools.

- **Rectangular Hotspot, Circular Hotspot, and Polygonal Hotspot** Draws clickable links on a picture, transforming it into an *image map*. And to help out, the Highlight Hotspots button highlights those clickable areas.

- **Restore** Bails you out at times by undoing editing changes to your picture and converting back to the *last saved* version of your picture file.

Picture Links and Image Maps

You can assign a link to any image, or you can assign *many* links to a single image. Images with many links are called *image maps*. For example, you could literally take a picture of a map and draw different clickable link areas on it that corresponded to different countries, allowing visitors to jump to a link just by clicking a country on the map.

Creating a Picture Link

It's often effective to associate a link with a picture. The link can be to another Web page or even to another picture file. As visitors hover over a picture on your

Web page, the hand icon that appears will let them know there is a link assigned to the image.

To Assign A LINK TO A PICTURE:

1. Select the picture.

2. Click the Create Hyperlinks button in the Standard toolbar. The Create Hyperlink dialog box appears.

3. Use one of the folder options in the Look In list on the left side of the Insert Hyperlink dialog box to choose a source for the target Web page. Navigate to a page in the list of pages in the dialog box.

4. Use the Screen Tip button to define text that will appear when a visitor hovers over your picture with his or her mouse cursor.

5. Use the Target Frame button, and click New Window in the Target Frame dialog box if you want the link to open in a new window.

6. After you have defined the target for your picture link, click OK in the Insert Hyperlink dialog box.

Pictures with links automatically get borders placed around them, and the border color is the same as the color you assigned to link text. You'll explore how to get rid of a picture border later in this chapter.

Creating an Image Map

Image maps have many clickable areas that are defined using the Rectangular Hotspot, Circular Hotspot, or Polygonal Hotspot tools in the Picture toolbar.

To Create AN IMAGE MAP:

1. Select the picture that you want to convert into an image map.

2. If the picture toolbar isn't visible, choose View | Toolbars | Pictures.

3 In the Picture toolbar, click the Rectangular Hotspot button, and click and drag to draw a rectangle around an area that will be a hotspot, as shown here:

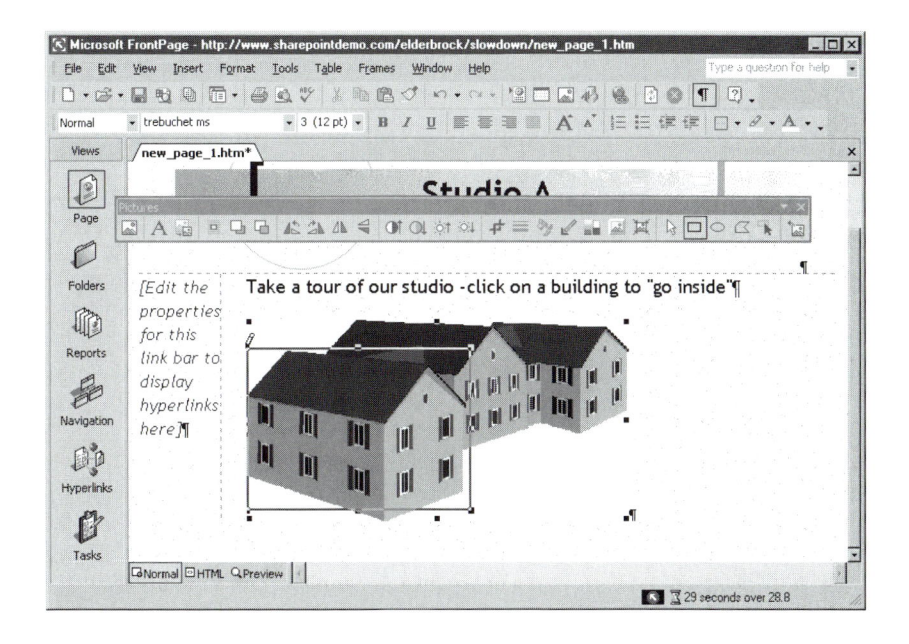

4 When you release your mouse button, the Insert Hyperlink dialog box appears. Navigate to a Web page to link the hotspot to, or enter an external URL (Web site) in the Address area of the dialog box, and then click OK.

5 You can add a circular hotspot by using the Circular Hotspot tool, or you can add an irregularly shaped hotspot by using the Polygonal Hotspot tool. To use the Polygonal tool, click several times to outline the hotspot, and double-click when you've completed the outline.

6 After you finish the image map, test your links in the Preview tab of Page view.

More Picture Properties

Most of the things you want to do to pictures are available from either the FrontPage Formatting toolbar (alignment), the Standard toolbar (links), or the Picture toolbar (contrast, coloring, transparency). And some picture editing—like sizing or moving a picture—is done just by clicking and dragging in Page view.

CHAPTER 4
WORKING WITH PICTURES

There are a few, additional picture-formatting features that are hidden in the Picture Properties dialog box. The most important additional picture formatting features are listed here:

- **Alternative representation** Define the text that appears as a ToolTip when a visitor hovers over a picture or when a picture is viewed in a browser that does not support pictures.

- **Horizontal and vertical spacing** Allow some "air" between your picture and the text that flows around it.

- **Border size** This is for the border around your picture or turning off the border all-together.

- **Interlacing** "Fades in" GIF images that take a long time to download.

- **Progressive passes** "Fades in" JPEG images that take a long time to download.

EXPLORING THE PICTURE PROPERTIES DIALOG BOX

The Picture Properties dialog box has some features not available on toolbars. It also let's you look at change just about all the settings you defined for a picture using toolbar buttons and on-page editing.

Open the Picture Properties dialog box by doing any of these things:

- Right-click the picture and choose Picture Properties from the context menu.
- Click (once) on the picture, and choose Format | Properties from the menu bar.
- Click once on the picture and press ALT+ENTER.

There are three tabs in the Image Properties dialog box: General, Video, and Appearance. For now, never mind the Video tab. Video is explored in Chapter 14.

The Appearance tab defines alignment—you can apply alignment using the Align Left and Align Right buttons in the Formatting toolbar, but you can *remove* alignment here. You can also use the Specify Size check box to activate the Width and Height spin boxes and define the size of a picture digitally—by entering either *pixels* (the tiny dots that make up a monitor screen) or percentage sizes. You also use the Appearance tab to define border thickness and spacing around a picture.

Horizontal and Vertical Spacing

You almost always want to define some buffering space between your pictures and content that surrounds them. For example, if you have text wrapping around an image, it's often unattractive to have that text bump right into the picture.

A good place to start is by assigning five pixels of horizontal spacing, and three pixels of vertical spacing around a picture. I "stole" those numbers from the way I observed images being laid out at Amazon.com, and figured the Web design folks there might know a thing or two about displaying pictures.

The following illustration shows Picture Properties dialog box, where horizontal and vertical spacing being are defined for a picture.

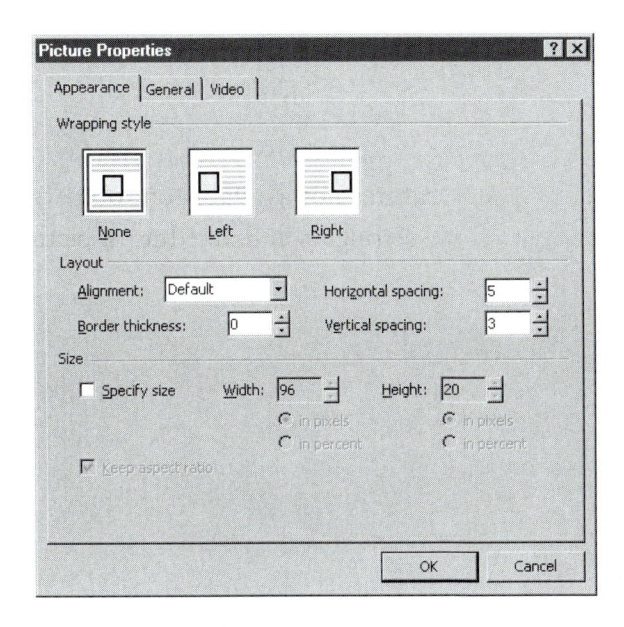

Border Size (or No Border)

Pictures that have links assigned to them are automatically formatted with a 1-pixel–wide border. By default, when you insert a picture that does *not* have a link assigned to it, FrontPage displays that picture with *no* border. Often, visitors will assume that a picture with a border is functioning as a link.

You can, however, delete or add a border to *any* picture. Sometimes a border will help set off an image. Other times, you might find a border unattractive, and even elect to *not* include a border on a picture that serves as a link.

To add a border to an image, enter a value in the Border Thickness spin box. (Borders are always measured in screen pixels.) To remove a border, enter 0 (zero) in the spin box.

Alternative Representation

Some more advance picture formatting options are found in the General tab of the Picture Properties dialog box. You can define a *low-resolution* alternative representation for your picture—a smaller file size version of your picture—although low-res alternatives are not normally needed with today's standardized browsers. You can also change the type of picture file from GIF to JPEG or vice versa. (You can also do that when you resave a picture in the Save Embedded Files dialog box.) And, the General tab is one more place (in addition to the more accessible Insert Hyperlink dialog box) where you can define picture links.

The most important feature in the General tab, that is *not* easily accessible anywhere else in FrontPage, is the ability to define alternate text. This is important because it is still the case that not all Web browsers display inline pictures. Plus, alternative text serves as a ScreenTip when a visitor moves his or her cursor over a picture in Internet Explorer.

Define alternative text by typing in the Text area of the General tab of the Picture Properties dialog box, as shown here:

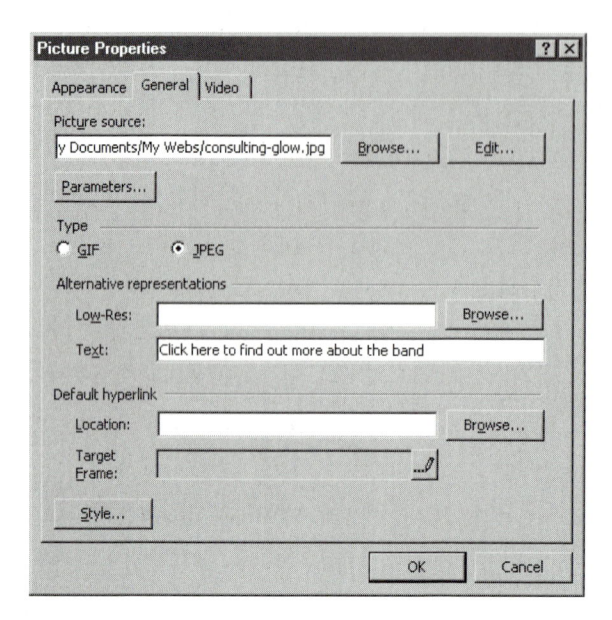

Interlacing/Progressive Passes

The Type option indicates the image format of the selected image. Click GIF, PNG, or JPEG to change the image format. GIF images have the advantage of allowing a *transparent* color, meaning you can hide one color in the picture. This technique is often used to make a picture appear to be set against the page background. However, JPEG images do a better job support complex colors found in photographs.

> **NOTE** PNG (pronounced *ping*) is a format similar to GIF but not as universally interpreted by Web browsers. Because GIF is much more widely accepted by browsers, most Web designers avoid the PNG file format.

Normally pictures download into a browser from the "top down." So, for example, a large picture downloading into a browser will display first the top section of the photo, and later the bottom section. FrontPage allows you to change the way pictures download, so that rather than appearing from "top to bottom," they "fade in" to a page. With GIF picture files, this effect is called *interlacing*, and with JPEG images, the effect is called *progressive passes*. In either case, the first version of the picture is low resolution, and subsequent versions get more and more clear until the entire picture is downloaded.

If the image is GIF format, two additional attributes of the image are indicated:

▶ **Transparent** This enables you to designate one color in the graphic, typically the background color, which can be rendered transparent, allowing any background on the Web page to show through. You cannot edit this property from the Image Properties dialog box. If the image contains a transparent color, the Transparent check box is checked. Otherwise, it is grayed out. (Controlling transparency on a GIF image is explained in Chapter 5.)

▶ **Interlaced** This refers to an alternative way of downloading GIF images, so that the picture "fades in" to a page as opposed to appearing line by line, starting at the top. Interlaced images can be displayed so that the entire image appears as the image is still downloading. The image at first appears blurry and becomes increasingly focused as more of its information is downloaded.

- **Quality** Adjusts the quality of the image as a percentage from 0–100. The higher the number, the higher the quality of the image and the larger the file size. See the earlier discussion of the JPEG format for more information on how JPEGs work.

CHAPTER 4
WORKING WITH PICTURES

- **Progressive passes** This is essentially the same as interlace for GIF images. You do, however, have one advantage: You can specify the number of steps required to go from the low-resolution version of your image to the full version. The number of steps can vary from 0–100.

A QUICK LOOK AT FRONTPAGE'S DRAWING TOOLS

FrontPage comes with a set of drawing tools that allow you to create drawings on your page—similar to drawing with the drawing tools that come with Word and PowerPoint. The drawings you create with FrontPage's drawing tools are *not* treated like other pictures in FrontPage. When you save your page, they are *not* converted into one of the two widely accepted image file types (JPEG or GIF). Instead, they are saved to a format that is *not* widely recognized or supported by Web browsers—except for Internet Explorer.

Further, you cannot flow text around pictures created with drawing tools (like you can with regular pictures). And when you view pages that include drawing tool pictures, the pictures tend to end up on top of text. With that as a warning, feel free to experiment with the drawing tools. You'll find them by choosing View | Toolbars | Drawing. Choose a tool from the Drawing toolbar (see the following illustration), which appears by default on the bottom of the FrontPage window, and draw away. You can use the drawing tools to create AutoShapes (a bunch of shapes like curves and arrows), Lines, Arrows, Rectangles, Ovals, Text Boxes, or you can insert WordArt—a little program for changing plain text into graphical text.

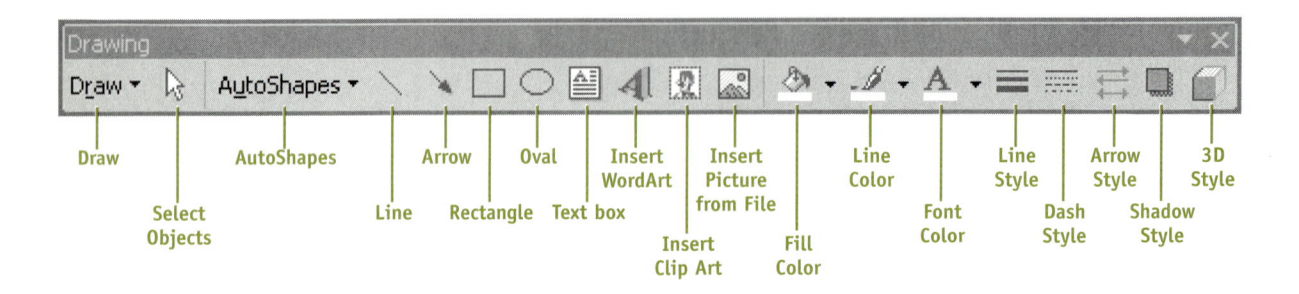

Other tools such as Fill Color, Line Color, Font Color, Line Style, Dash Style, Arrow Style, Shadow Style, and 3-D style tools are used to format text or drawing pictures. Is there ever a reason to use FrontPage's drawing tools? Perhaps... if you are creating a Web page that you plan on sharing with others using only Internet Explorer.

Next Up... Tables

In this chapter, you saw how easy it is to add pictures to FrontPage Web sites. If you can copy a picture into FrontPage, you can save it as a Web-compatible image. In fact, FrontPage senses whether a picture file should be saved in GIF or JPEG format and makes intelligent decisions for you on how to save embedded pictures.

In this, and previous chapters, you've learned to format pages, text, and pictures. The next challenge is to create more complex layouts where text and pictures are assigned to specific locations on a page. For that, you'll need to use *tables*. And you'll learn to do that in the next chapter.

> **ON THE VIRTUAL CLASSROOM CD** In Lesson 3, "Working with Pictures," I demonstrate how to insert pictures into a Web page, and how to edit pictures in FrontPage. The lesson demonstrates how to crop and resize pictures, how to edit picture brightness, contrast, and coloring, and how to restrict picture file size. You will also learn how to wrap text around pictures.

5

Designing with Tables, Photo Galleries, and Positioning

One of the challenges of laying out nice looking Web pages is how do you get your picture or text to position *just right* on your page? In the previous chapter, you learned how you can use left and right alignment to flow text around pictures. But sometimes, even that trick doesn't provide enough control over how your page is laid out.

The answer, then, is tables. If you're used to using tables in Word (or even Excel or Access), you might think of them as a way to display data in columns and rows. And that's *one* use for tables in Web sites. But mostly you use tables as a way to place objects (text, pictures, or even media) on a page.

The other option for locating objects in an exact spot on a page is absolute positioning—also referred to by Web designers as *layers* (because absolutely positioned objects can be *layered* on top of each other on a page). You took a quick look at absolute positioning in Chapter 4 when you examined working with pictures. Here, you'll return to absolute positioning as a way to place both text and pictures together on a page.

Creating a Table

As is sometimes the case in FrontPage, there are just too many ways to create a table. So let's do it the easiest and most reliable way—using the menu bar.

To Insert a table using the Table menu:

1 Choose Table | Insert Table. The Insert Table dialog box opens, as shown here:

2 Use the Rows and Columns spin boxes to define how many rows and columns to include in your table.

3 Use the Alignment drop-down list to define how you want the *entire table* aligned on your page. Choices are Left, Right, or Center alignment. (Default maintains the alignment of whatever objects are on your page just in front of the table.)

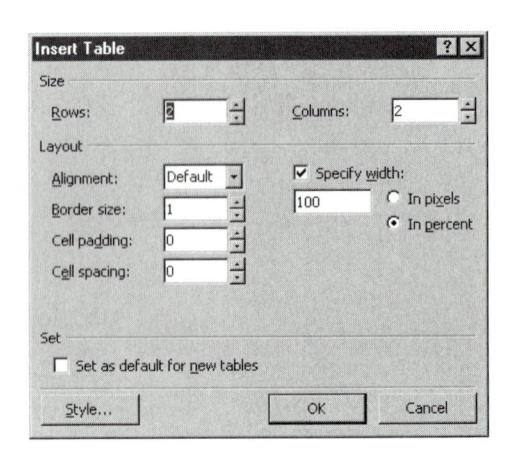

4 Use the Border Size spin box to define the thickness (in pixels) of lines around the outside of the table, and between cells.

5 Use the Spacing spin box to define space (in pixels) *in between cells*. Use the Padding spin box to define buffering space *within cells*—between the cell content and the edge of the cell.

6 Click the Specify Width check box to define how wide you want your table to be. You can define width in pixels or in percentage of the available browser window space.

> **NOTE** You can easily add or remove rows and columns later, if you need to.

7 If you plan to generate a whole bunch of identical tables (and you probably don't) you can check the Set As Default for New Tables check box in the Insert Table dialog box.

> **NOTE** If you *deselect* the Specify Width check box, FrontPage will create a table just large enough to display cell content.

8 Click OK to insert the table.

Using Tables to Present Data

While tables are *mainly* used in Web sites as a *design tool*—to lay out a page—they are also an effective way to display a bunch of information in rows and columns. A colorful, airy, nicely formatted table can do wonders for dry facts and figures. For example, you might want to present a budget summary or a brief financial statement with several rows and columns on a Web page. Or, you might want to include a list of products, with columns for price, description, a photo, and so on. Tables help make this kind of data easy to interpret and more attractive than just lines of text.

Entering Data

To enter data in a table, just click in a cell and begin typing. You can jump from cell to cell by pressing the TAB key. If you are in the *last* cell in a table, pressing the TAB key will create a new row, so you can keep entering data in new rows.

New rows are generated automatically by tabbing, but you can also create a new row or column by clicking in a cell and choosing Table | Insert | Rows or Columns, and adding either rows or columns using the Insert Rows or Columns dialog box, as shown to the right:

Of course you can also copy and paste data into a table from a FrontPage Web page or any Windows application. If you want to paste *an entire table* from Word, Excel, or another application, use Edit | Paste (not Paste Special) to paste your data as a table.

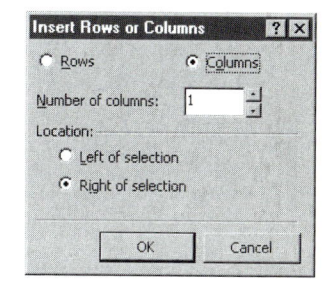

CHAPTER 5
Designing with Tables, Photo Galleries, and Positioning

You can *edit* or *format* table data just as you would any text. And you can apply any of the picture formatting (explored in Chapter 4) to a figure that is *inside* a cell. You'll explore these possibilities a bit later in this chapter when you look at tables as page layout tools.

Using Table AutoFormats

Because they were copped from Word and Excel, FrontPage's available table AutoFormats work well for presenting data. To assign an AutoFormat, click in a table and choose Table | Table AutoFormat. The Table AutoFormat dialog box opens, as shown here:

As you select from the available formats in the Formats list, and options available through check boxes, you can see how your table will look in the Preview area of the Table AutoFormat dialog box. When you're satisfied with the look of your table, click OK. Figure 5-1 shows a table displaying data with an automatic format applied. The only additional formatting is that I selected the text in the right column and right-aligned it.

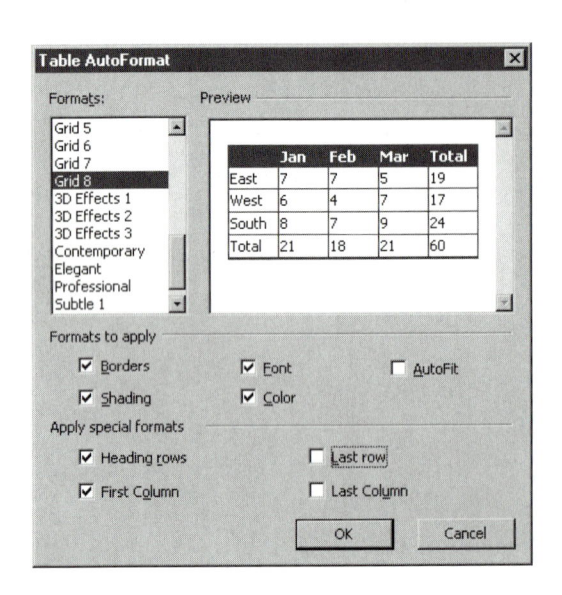

FIGURE 5-1

Using AutoFormat to display data in rows and columns

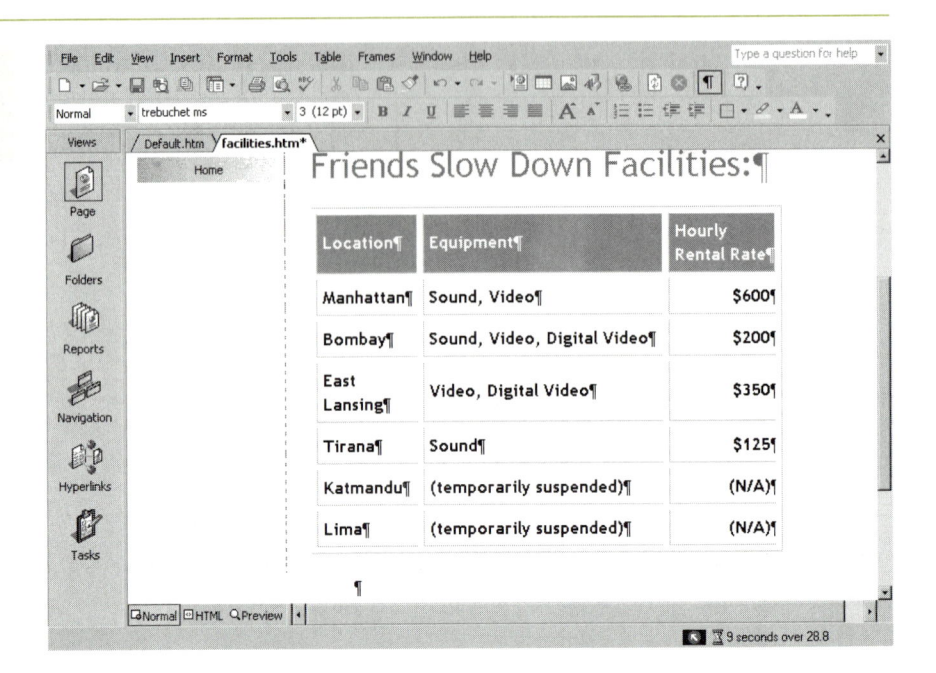

Using Tables as a Layout Tool

You can't (easily) place a block of text, or a picture, at a location on a page as you would in a desktop publishing program, for example. The solution is to use tables to locate objects on a page. Tables are the main tool used to layout Web pages.

One way to get a good sense of what you can do with tables as a layout tool is to check out the page templates that come with FrontPage. To do this, choose File | New | Page or Web. In the New Page or Web pane (that appears on the right side of the FrontPage window), choose the Page Templates link. You'll see many page templates that use columns:

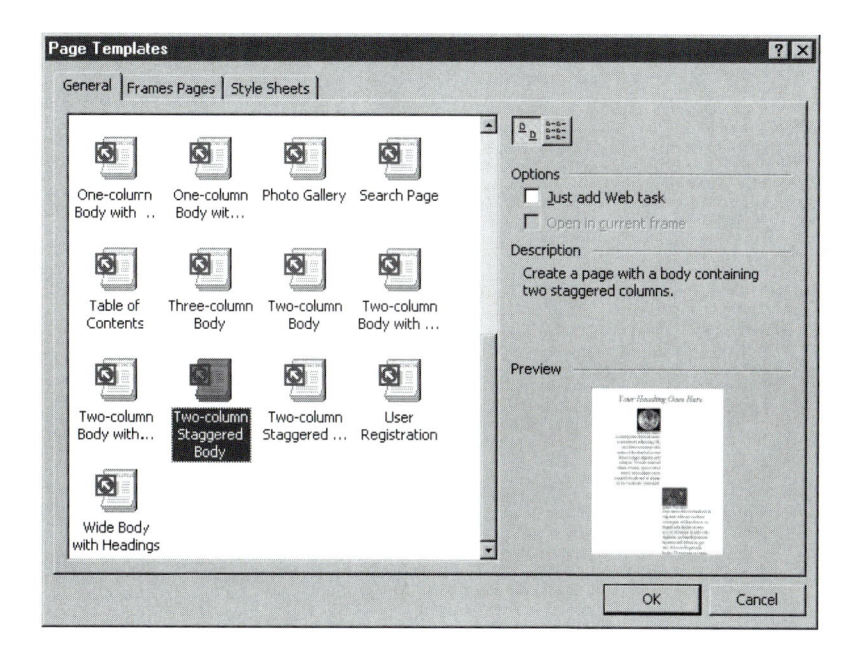

You can start with these page templates and substitute your own content in the table cells that come with them. Or, you can create your own page layouts from scratch using tables.

Borderless Tables for Layout

Usually, when you use tables as a layout tool, you want to hide the fact that your page objects are in table cells. Non-page designers among your visitors will see text and pictures floating on the page, and not be aware that these elements are actually located in table cells.

CHAPTER 5
DESIGNING WITH TABLES, PHOTO GALLERIES, AND POSITIONING

You can edit the properties of a table by right-clicking within it and choosing Table Properties from the context menu. To create this effect you generally want to assign the following settings to your table:

- **Border Size = 0** This way there are no lines to give away that you are using cells to locate objects
- **Cell Padding = 6** Start with this and experiment
- **Cell Spacing = 0** Creates the illusion that your objects are not in a table at all

Once your table properties are set, you'll find you need to complete your formatting by defining *cell* properties. Cell properties determine the vertical alignment for cell content, background color, and other features of your table.

FORMATTING TABLE CELLS

You can resize cells by clicking and dragging on their borders. Do this to make columns or rows wider or narrower. You can also change the vertical alignment for selected cell(s). Oddly enough, the default vertical formatting for table cells is *centered*, which means that if you have unequal amounts of content in different columns, the cell content will be centered top-to-bottom. To change this to top aligned, click (or click and drag) to select a cell (or cells), right-click and choose Cell Properties from the context menu. Change the cell Vertical alignment to Top, as shown here:

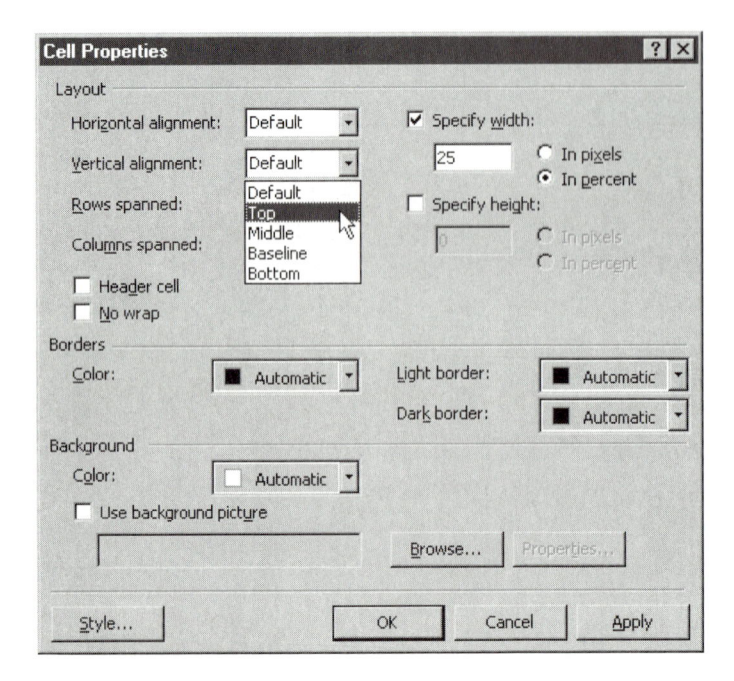

You can also define unique cell background colors for selected cells. To define a cell background color, right-click in the cell(s) and choose Cell Properties from the context menu. Then, use the Background Color drop-down menu in the Cell Properties dialog box to choose a background color for a cell.

By combining different text font colors and cell backgrounds, you can create what appear to be free-floating text blocks, as shown in Figure 5-2. How's it done? In Preview tab, the dotted lines that demarcate cell properties aren't visible, but this text is sitting in table cells with background colors. Cells with a white background color aren't apparent to the page visitor.

You can even use a picture as a cell background. This gets a little tricky, as any picture you use will *tile* (repeat itself) to fill the entire cell. But if you size your cell to match your picture, you can create the effect of text on top of a picture, as shown in Figure 5-3.

> **NOTE** In this example (Figure 5-2), the columns were defined by creating three wide columns and two narrow (empty) columns that act as spacers. In addition, each cell has padding defined to keep the text from running into the edge of the column.

FIGURE 5-2

Using a table to create the appearance of columns of text

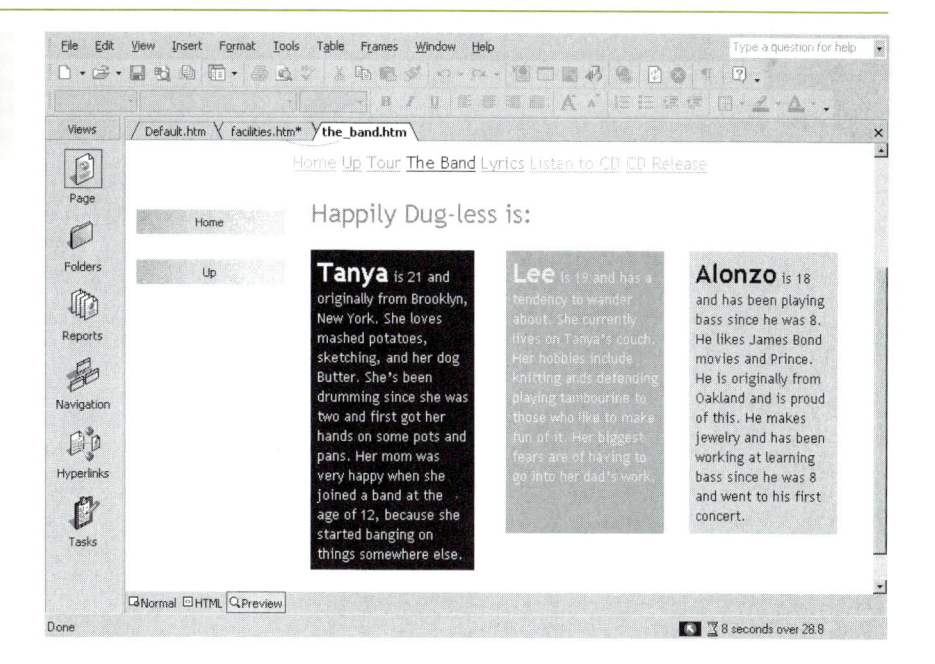

CHAPTER 5
Designing with Tables, Photo Galleries, and Positioning

FIGURE 5-3

Using a picture as a cell background

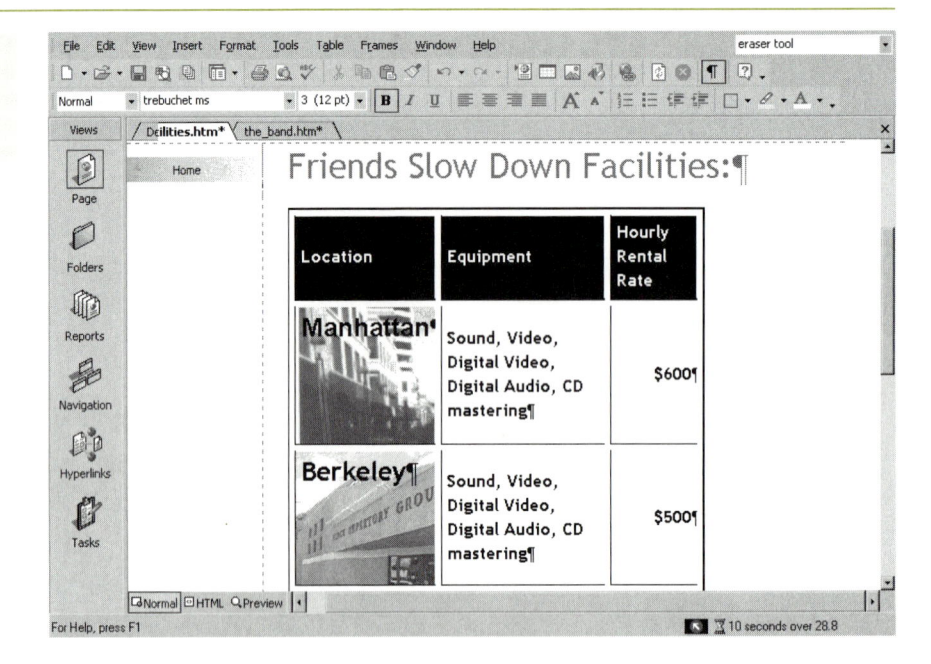

To Use A PICTURE AS A CELL BACKGROUND:

1 Click in a cell.

2 Right-click and choose Cell Properties from the context menu.

3 Click the Use Background Picture check box.

4 Use the Browse button to locate a picture.

5 Click Open in the Select Background Picture dialog box.

6 Click OK in the Cell Properties dialog box.

7 Resize your cell as needed to fit the background picture.

More Table Layout Options

Many table properties can be controlled with the Table toolbar. You can insert rows and columns, merge cells, and change cell alignment quickly using the Table toolbar, shown in Figure 5-4.

FrontPage 2002
Virtual Classroom

FIGURE 5-4
High-powered table design tools are available on the Table toolbar

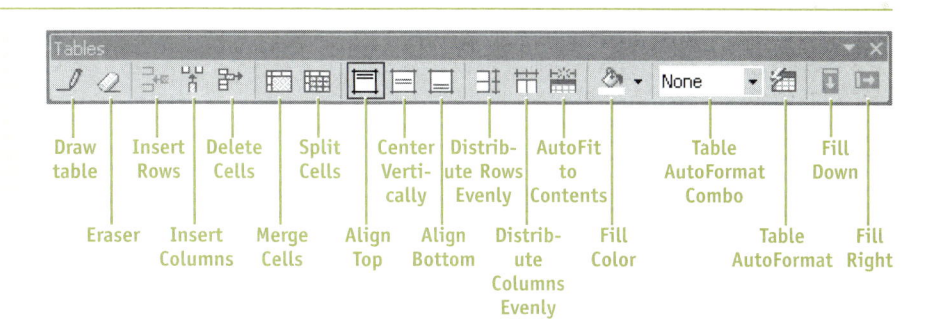

Top row labels (left to right): Draw table | Insert Rows | Delete Cells | Split Cells | Center Vertically | Distribute Rows Evenly | AutoFit to Contents | Table AutoFormat Combo | Fill Down

Bottom row labels (left to right): Eraser | Insert Columns | Merge Cells | Align Top | Align Bottom | Distribute Columns Evenly | Fill Color | Table AutoFormat | Fill Right

To view the Table toolbar, choose View | Toolbars | Tables. When you click *outside* a table, the toolbar will temporarily hide. It reappears when you select a table.

Let's look at the tools (buttons) on the Table toolbar, and quickly review how they can be used to control page layout (or data entry):

▶ **Draw Table** Changes your cursor into a somewhat tricky pencil that draws new cells in a table; make it go away by clicking the Draw Table tool again to regain normal cursor functioning.

▶ **Eraser** Removes rows or columns. Click and drag with it to wipe out borders between cells.

▶ **Insert Rows and Insert Columns** Inserts columns to the left of the selected column or inserts rows below the selected row.

▶ **Delete Cells** Deletes selected cells *and their content*. (If you want to delete a cell, but leave the content, choose Table | Convert | Table to Text from the menu bar.)

▶ **Merge Cells** Merges selected cells into a single cell.

▶ **Split Cells** Breaks cells apart.

▶ **Align Top, Center Vertically, and Align Bottom** Moves text up and down within a cell.

▶ **Distribute Rows Evenly and Distribute Columns Evenly** Makes all selected rows, or columns, the same size.

▶ **AutoFit to Contents** Resizes a table to accommodate cell content.

▶ **Fill Color** Applies a background color to selected cell(s).

▶ **Table AutoFormat Combo** Applies auto formats.

CHAPTER 5
DESIGNING WITH TABLES, PHOTO GALLERIES, AND POSITIONING

▶ **Table AutoFormat** Opens the Table AutoFormat dialog box.

▶ **Fill Down and Fill Right** Takes the left-most or top cell in a selected group of cells, and copies the content of that cell into the other selected cells.

> **NOTE** Available (active) tools depend on what elements in a table are selected. For example, you must select two adjacent cells before the Merge Cells button is active.

USING THE PHOTO GALLERY

A FrontPage Photo Gallery is an interactive area of a page that displays both *thumbnails* (small sized versions of a picture), and full-sized pictures. Photo Galleries are new to FrontPage with version 2002. You can see an example of a Photo Gallery in Figure 5-5.

There are four Photo Gallery layout options, and three of them (not the Slide Show option) automatically generate table layouts that place text and pictures on a page in a way similar to using tables. The technically inclined among us may be interested in the fact that Photo galleries are actually generated JavaScript. FrontPage creates a (hidden) folder in your Web where it stores both the photos you use in the gallery,

FIGURE 5-5
A FrontPage Photo Gallery—click a thumbnail and see the picture

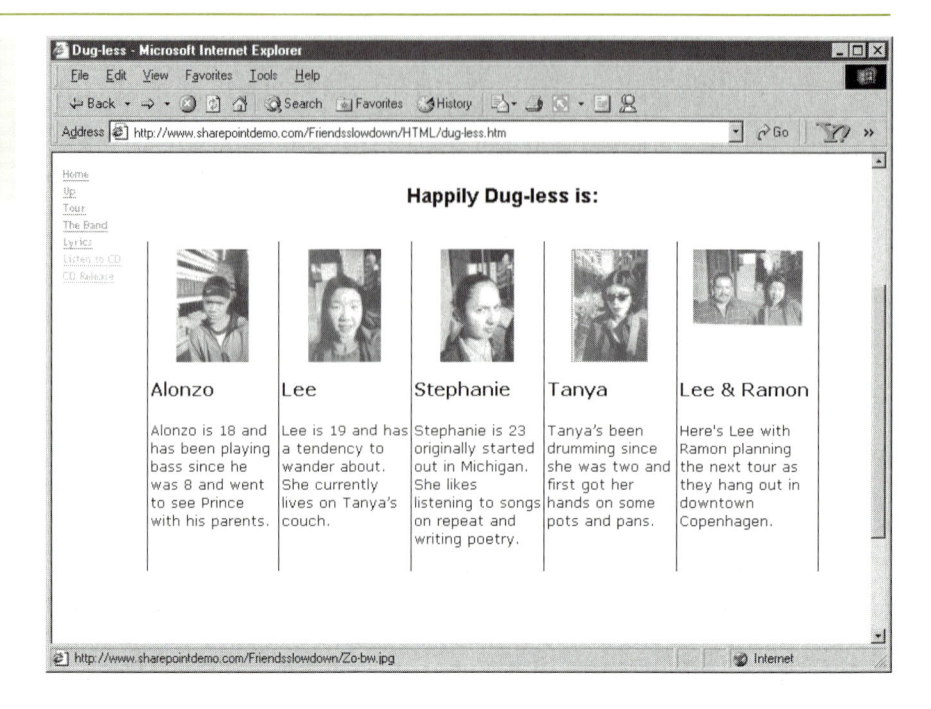

separate thumbnail pictures, and the JavaScript file (sldshow.js) used to make it all work.

To Create A Photo Gallery from picture files:

1 With a Web page open in Page view, choose Insert | Web Component.

2 Select Photo Gallery in the list of components in the Insert Web Component dialog box.

> **TIP** To view hidden folders in your Web site choose Tools | Web Settings, and click the Advanced tab in the Web Settings dialog box. Select the Show Hidden Files and Folders check box, and click OK. After you create a Photo Gallery, you'll be able to see the hidden Photo Gallery folder.

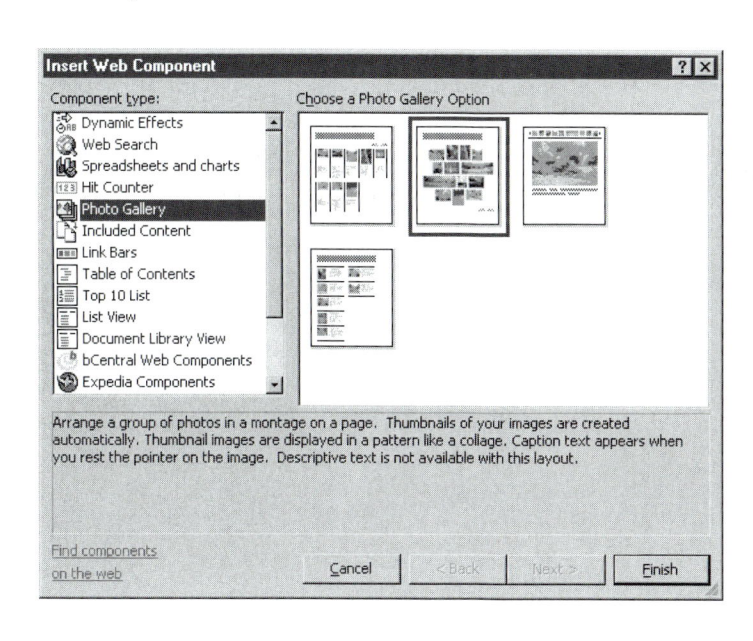

3 In the Choose a Photo Gallery option area of the Insert Web Component dialog box, click any of the options. A description of the type of Photo Gallery appears near the bottom of the dialog box:

4 With one of the Photo Gallery options selected, click Finish. This opens the Photo Gallery Properties dialog box, where you can add pictures and define text for your Photo Gallery.

5 In the Pictures tab of the Photo Gallery Properties dialog box, click the Add button to include photos in your gallery. When you click the Add button, you'll have the option of choosing pictures from a scanner or digital camera, or from a file. If you choose Pictures From Scanner or Camera, your connected devise will open and you can use it to

CHAPTER 5
DESIGNING WITH TABLES, PHOTO GALLERIES, AND POSITIONING

supply pictures. If you choose Pictures from Files, you can navigate to a picture file. With the picture selected, click Open in the Open File dialog box.

> **NOTE** You can also select several pictures at one time from one folder, which is handy.

6 After you add a photo, enter captions and descriptions in the boxes on the bottom of the dialog box, as shown in the following illustration. No description text is available in the Montage Layout. Captions display when a visitor points to your picture in a browser. Descriptions are incorporated into the layout of the different types of Photo Galleries.

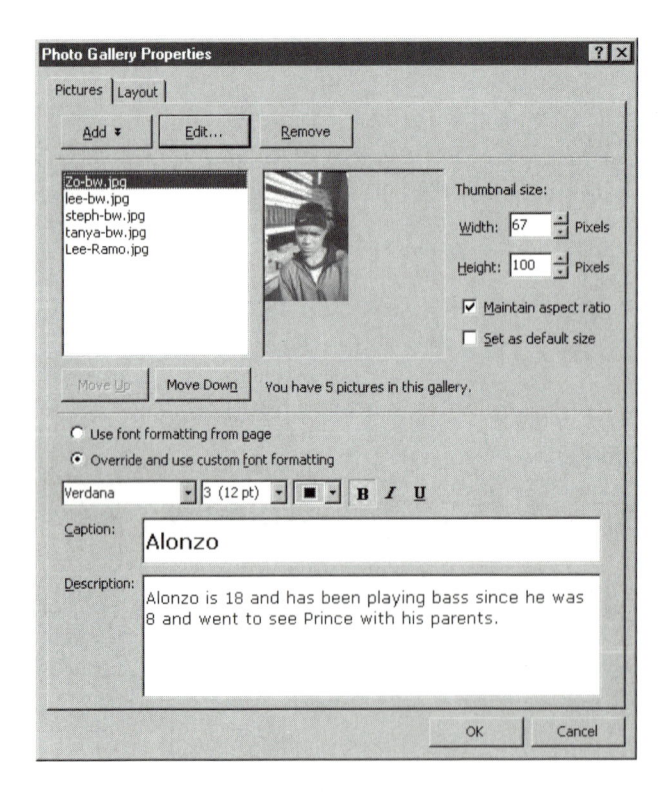

7 Continue to add additional pictures, as described in steps 5 and 6. You can use the Remove button to delete a selected photo.

8 Use the Edit button to change the photo by cropping, rotating, or resizing the original photo.

9 At any time, you can click the Layout tab in the Photo Gallery Properties dialog box to change the layout.

> **NOTE** If you click the Override and Use Custom Font Formatting options button in the dialog box, you can use the mini-toolbar in the dialog box to assign your own formatting to description text.

10 After you are done adding pictures (and defining captions and definitions) and changing the layout if necessary, click OK in the Photo Gallery Properties dialog box. The Photo Gallery

> **TIP** To edit your Photo Gallery, double-click it in FrontPage Page view.

is generated, and you can test it either with the Preview tab in Page view, or in a Web browser (choose File | Preview in Browser, and select one of your installed browsers).

Using Absolutely Positioned Text and Pictures

In Chapter 4, you used absolute positioning to locate a picture on a page. You can also position text blocks in an exact location on a page. This technique has the same drawbacks as positioning pictures: It doesn't work well in every browser, and the text blocks sit on top of other objects on your page.

Absolute positioned text works best for pages with very little text and pictures. You can create interesting effects by moving text over a picture, as shown in Figure 5-6.

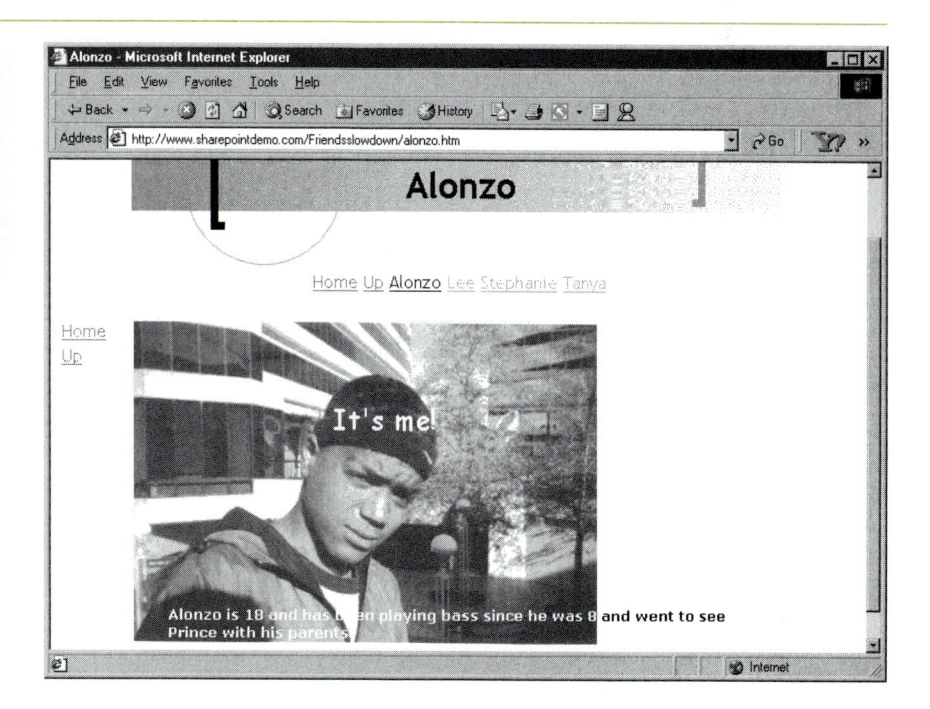

FIGURE 5-6

Absolute positioned text—in this case, the text over the picture has a light font color, while the text that sticks out beyond the picture is black

CHAPTER 5
DESIGNING WITH TABLES, PHOTO GALLERIES, AND POSITIONING

To Create ABSOLUTELY POSITIONED TEXT:

1 Click and drag to select all the text that will be positioned absolutely.

2 Choose Format | Position from the menu bar.

3 In the Position dialog box, click the Absolute icon.

4 If you want, you can use the Position and Size spin boxes to define position (from the left and the from top of the page) or size in pixels. Or, you can wait and do this in Page view.

5 Use the Z-Order spin box to define how you want the positioned text to *layer* (overlap) with other objects. Positioned objects with higher Z values will be on top of objects with lower Z values.

6 Click OK to convert your selected text into a block of text that can be moved around on the page.

7 Use the sizing handles that appear around the text block to resize the text if necessary.

8 Click the upper-left or right corner of the text block, and use the four-sided arrow cursor to move the text block anywhere on your page, as shown in Figure 5-7.

FIGURE 5-7
You can move absolutely positioned text by dragging on the upper-left or right corner of the text block

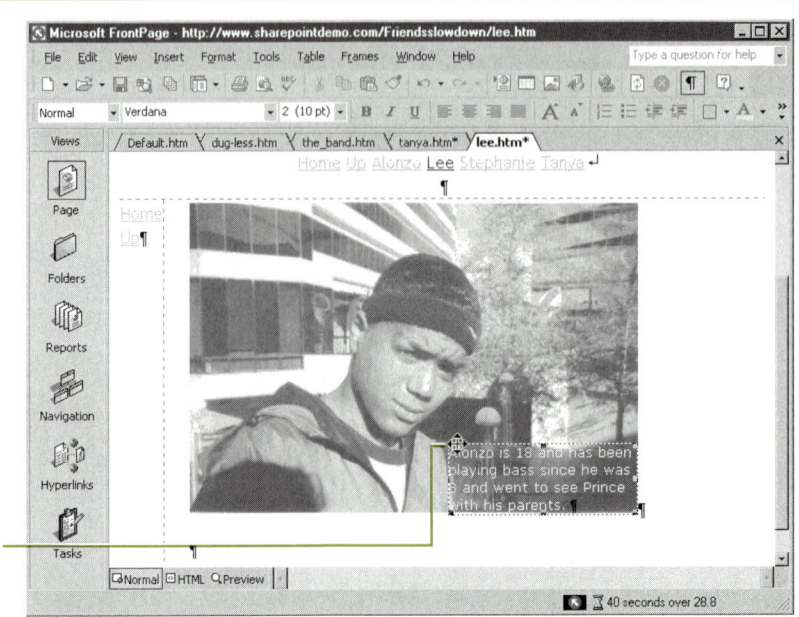

Moving a text block on top of a picture using the four-sided arrow

Everything in Position?

In this chapter, you explored the two ways to locate text and images in exact locations on a page. Tables are the most reliable way to position objects. They are interpreted by all browsers, and you can achieve quite a bit of control over object positioning if you are willing to spend some time fine-tuning table size and spacing.

Absolute positioning gives you more freedom in positioning objects than tables do. You can even use absolute positioning to place one object on top of another one. However, absolute positioning is not interpreted *reliably* by any browser. Use absolute positioning when you are willing to gamble with how your page will look to visitors.

In the next chapter, you'll return to links and look at ways to use FrontPage to generate complex navigation and link systems for your Web site.

> **ON THE VIRTUAL CLASSROOM CD** In Lesson 4, "Designing with Tables," I demonstrate how to use tables as a layout tool to control the location of objects on a Web page. The lesson demonstrates how to use tables to constrain page width, to place pictures and text on a page, and how to format table and cell background colors and pictures.

6

Many Ways to Navigate Your Site

One of the most important elements of a good Web site is providing visitors with easy-to-use ways to get from page to page. Allowing visitors to quickly *navigate* (get to) areas of your Web site keeps them happy, keeps them at your site, and allows you to get the most out of a Web site.

CHAPTER 6
Many Ways to Navigate Your Site

FrontPage provides a variety of ways to help visitors navigate your site. You can, of course, assign text and graphic links. You can also let FrontPage generate links of various types—including to what FrontPage calls *categories* of pages (groups of pages that you define).

Other navigation tools include search boxes that allow a visitor to enter a word or phrase and jump to relevant pages, or tables of contents that list all the pages in a site. This chapter explores all these techniques for making your site easy to navigate.

Text and Graphic Link Properties

In the first chapter of this book, you saw that simply typing a link (like www.ppinet.com or dkarlins@ppinet.com) automatically generated a link on your page. In addition, the Insert Hyperlink dialog box (opened by choosing Insert | Hyperlink) allows you to define a link for any selected picture or text.

There is more to links. You can assign pop-up ScreenTips that appear when a visitor hovers over a link, and you can control what window a link opens in. This is especially helpful when visitors follow a link to a location *outside* of your site. In that case, you often want that link to open in a *new browser window* so visitors will retain an open window with your Web site as well, even as they follow a link outside of your site.

Defining ScreenTips

ScreenTips can supplement text with additional information to make your Web page navigation-friendly. For example, in Figure 6-1, visitors get more information by simply pointing to a text link.

To Define a Text ScreenTip:

1. Select text.
2. Choose Insert | Hyperlink from the menu to open the Insert Hyperlink dialog box.
3. Choose a link in your site, or enter another Web page URL in the Address area of the dialog box.

> **NOTE** ScreenTips are not displayed in Netscape Navigator 4.7.

FIGURE 6-1

ScreenTips can be attached to text links

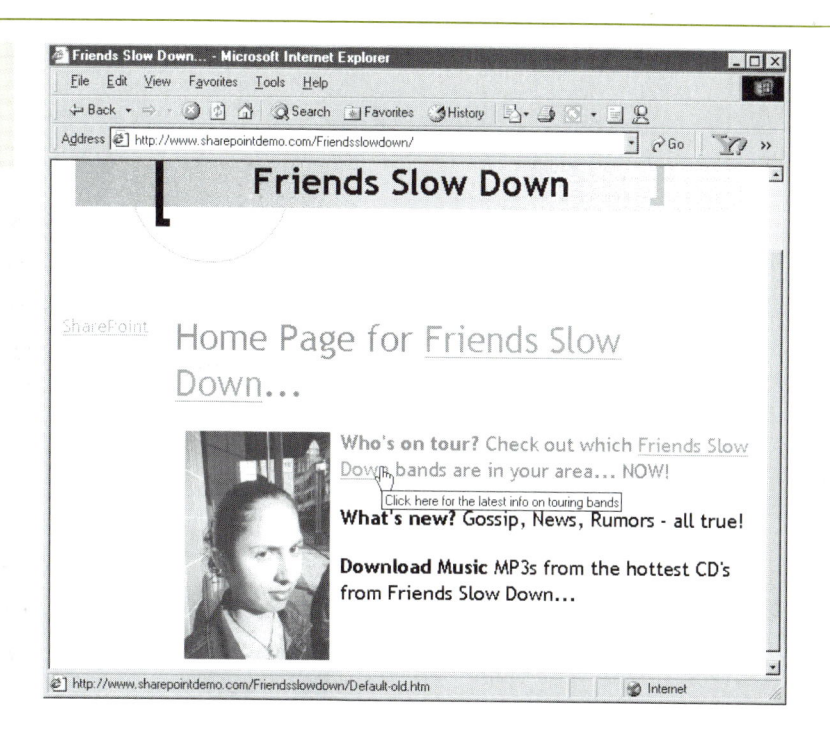

4. Click the ScreenTip button. In the Set Hyperlink ScreenTip box, type your text as shown here:

5. Click OK in the Set Hyperlink ScreenTip dialog box.

6. Click OK in the Insert Hyperlink dialog box.

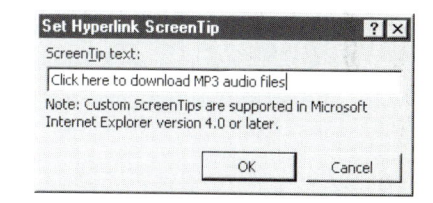

OPENING A LINK IN A NEW WINDOW

Rather than lose all connection with visitors who follow links off your site, you can define those external links to open in a new window.

To Define AN EXTERNAL LINK:

1. Select text or a picture.

2. Choose Insert | Hyperlink from the menu to open the Insert Hyperlink dialog box.

3. Choose a link in your site, or enter another Web page URL in the Address area of the dialog box.

4 Click the Target Frame button to open the Target Frame dialog box.

5 In the Common Targets area of the Target Frame dialog box, click New Window, as shown here:

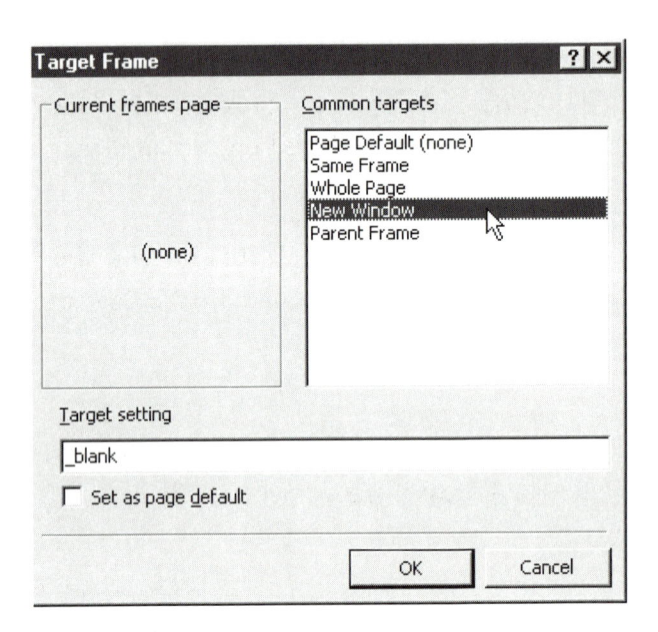

6 Click OK twice to close the Target Frame dialog box.

7 Click OK to close the Insert Hyperlink dialog boxes. You can test your link in a browser.

> **WARNING** There is a check box that allows you to set your target frame as the page default. Use this check box option with caution! It will apply the target default to *every* link on your page. The Page Default check box won't actually change hyperlinks that you previously defined on a page; it will just be the option for new links that are created. You don't always want links to open in *new* browser windows, and if all your site links open new browser windows, visitors will end up annoyed—with too many open windows.

Creating Link Bars

FrontPage 2002 has a somewhat bewildering set of options for generating link bars. But once mastered, these options allow you to include all kinds of groups of links anywhere in your site.

First, let's define a *link bar*—a defined set of links. You insert it anywhere in a page. Often link bars are placed in *shared borders* that appear on the side, top, or bottom of *every page* in your Web site. (Explore shared borders in detail in Chapter 7.)

How are link bars different than links you create using the Insert Hyperlink dialog box? They are *groups* of links that are *predefined*. Link bars can be generated two ways:

- **They can be based on a navigation structure that you define in Navigation view**   For example, you might include your home page in a generated navigation link. Or, you might include all "child" pages under the home page in your Navigation view flowchart.
- **They can be any group of pages that you define as a link bar**   For example, you could group a dozen pages associated with one department in your company as a link bar, and easily insert that group of links into any page.

The following sections look at both types of link bars.

Creating a Link Bar from Navigation Structure

FrontPage uses a family metaphor to describe navigation links. In Navigation view, a page at the top of the flowchart is a *parent* page, and pages under that page in the flowchart are *child* pages.

For example, in Figure 6-2, the home page has four child pages. The News page, in turn, has three child pages of its own. And the Bands page, which is a child page of the News page, is a *parent* page to the three band pages.

To add pages to Navigation view, drag them from Folder list, as shown in Figure 6-3.

CHAPTER 6
MANY WAYS TO NAVIGATE YOUR SITE

FIGURE 6-2

Child pages are beneath parent pages in the Navigation view flowchart

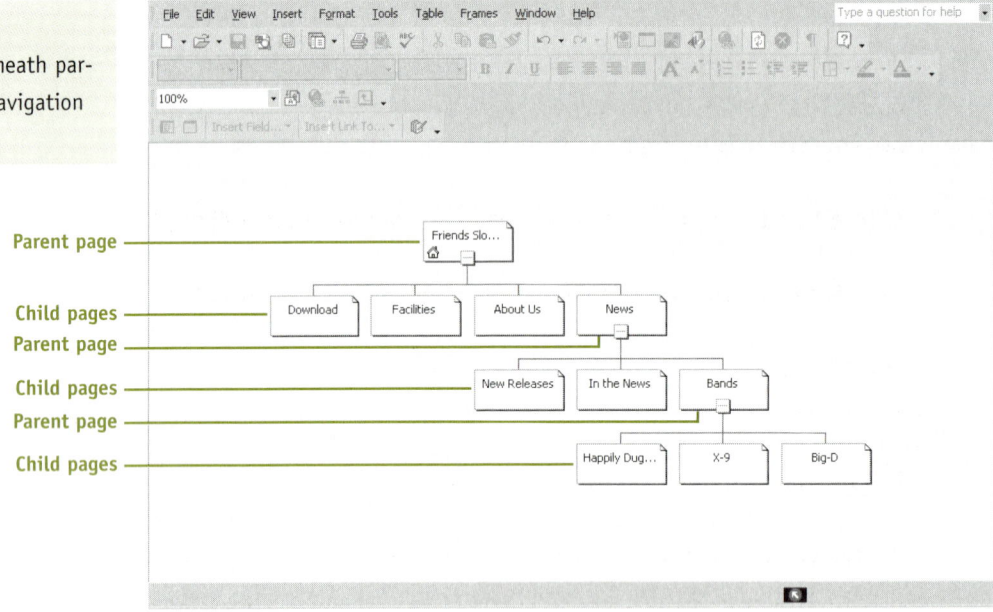

FIGURE 6-3

Dragging a page into Navigation view

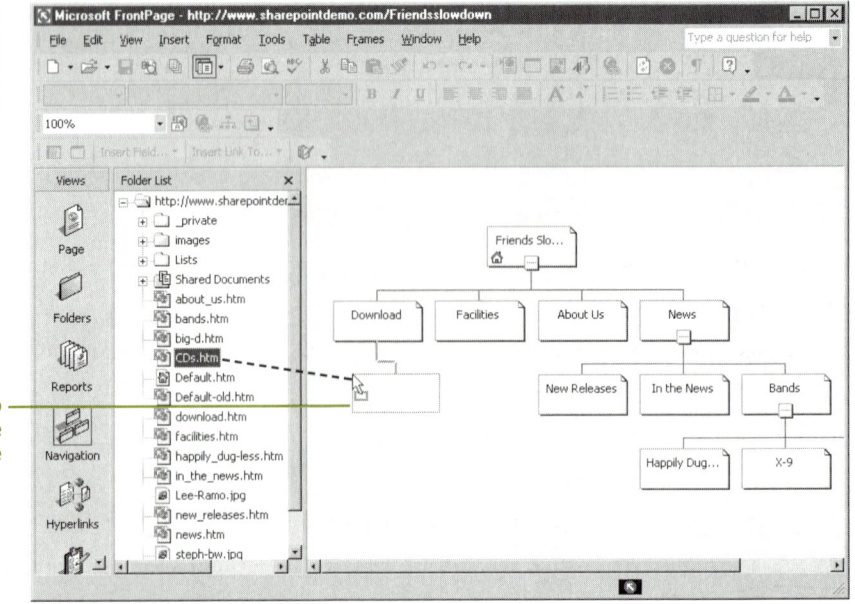

To Drag a page into Navigation view:

1 Click anywhere in a page. If you click in a shared border (marked in Page view by dotted lines), the link bar will appear in every page in which the shared border is displayed. (See Chapter 7 for more on shared borders.)

2 Choose Insert | Navigation to open the Insert Web Component dialog box.

3 Click Bar Based on Navigation Structure in the Choose a Bar Type list.

4 Click Finish (don't worry, you're not *really* finished) to open the Link Bar Properties dialog box.

> **TIP** By clicking Finish now, you are taking a "shortcut" past some repetitive wizard dialog boxes. You will define all your link bar properties in the next steps.

5 In the General tab of the Link Bar Properties dialog box, choose what kind of links to generate. As you do, the link structure you define will be illustrated in the dialog box, as shown in Figure 6-4.

6 Select the Style tab in the Link Bar Properties dialog box to choose a look for your links. To create link bars that use the theme assigned to your Web site, choose the default, Use Page's Theme option in the Choose a Style list. Or, choose a different theme or text. In Figure 6-5, a link bar is being created using text links.

7 The option buttons in the Style tab of the Link Bar Properties dialog box let you align links horizontally (across the page) or vertically (up and down).

> **NOTE** Parent Level will generate links that display a link to the parent page only. Same Level will generate links to any Web page on the same level of the Navigation view chart. The Back and Next options will generate links to Parent and Child Level pages. If you select Child Level links, you'll get links to just child pages. The Child Pages Under Home option creates links to pages that are child pages of the home page. Other options relate to custom link bars, which you'll explore later in this chapter. In addition to choosing one option for generating link bars, you can also use the check boxes in the Link Bar Properties dialog box to generate a link to the site home page to every page in the site, and/or to generate a link to the Parent page.

CHAPTER 6
MANY WAYS TO NAVIGATE YOUR SITE

FIGURE 6-4

Defining links for a link bar based on navigation structure

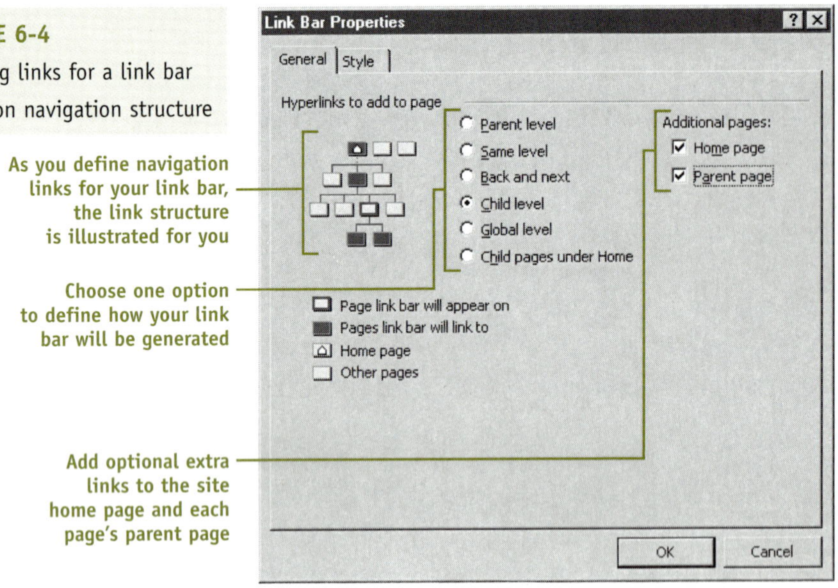

As you define navigation links for your link bar, the link structure is illustrated for you

Choose one option to define how your link bar will be generated

Add optional extra links to the site home page and each page's parent page

FIGURE 6-5

You can create link bars using graphics for link buttons or text links

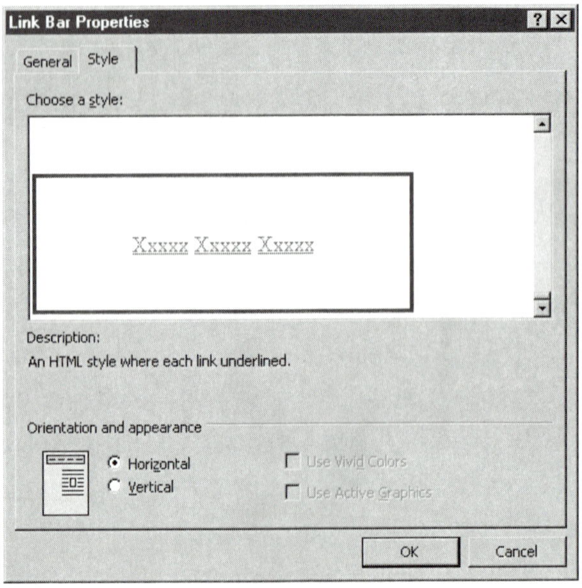

> **NOTE** Other options in the Style tab include orientation and colors check boxes. Horizontal orientation displays your links sideways across the page; vertical orientation displays them up and down (usually good for link bars in side shared borders). If you use a theme for your link bar, you can alter the colors using the Use Vivid Colors check box, and you can make graphics active—active buttons change color or style when a visitor moves his or her cursor over them or clicks them.

After you generate a navigation bar, you can test it in a Web browser (use File | Preview in Browser and select a browser in which to test your links).

Defining Custom Link Bars

Link bars based on navigation structure are often a handy way to create intuitive links on a Web page. The downside to navigation-based link bars is that you can't really customize them—they generate links based on your navigation structure and that's all.

The other option is to create link bars that have links to selected groups of pages. For example, you might create a custom link bar with links to all departments in your organization, or a custom link bar with five e-mail addresses that visitors are likely to need as they browse your site. Then, without having to create all these links individually, you can insert the group of links on any page.

Creating a Custom Link Bar

You can create as many custom link bars as you wish. Each custom link bar can include links to pages inside, or outside, your site. And each custom link bar is stored—library like—in the Link Bar Properties dialog box.

To Create a custom link bar:

1. In Page view, choose Insert | Navigation to open the Insert Web Component dialog box (with Link bars selected as the Component type).

2. In the Choose a Bar Type area of the Insert Web Component dialog box, select Bar with Custom Links.

Chapter 6
Many Ways to Navigate Your Site

3 Click Finish in the dialog box.

4 If you have not yet defined any custom link bars, the Create New Link Bar dialog box automatically appears. Name your link bar, as shown to the right.

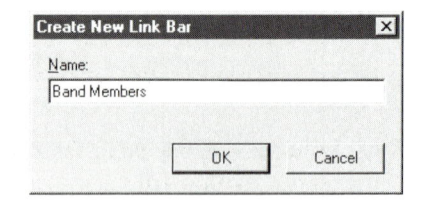

5 Click OK.

6 In the Link Bar Properties dialog box, you can either create a new link bar, or assign an existing one. If you didn't get prompted to create a new link bar in step 4, click the Create New button in the Link Bar Properties dialog box, and enter a name for your new link bar now; then click OK in the dialog box to return to the Link Bar Properties dialog box.

7 To add pages to your link bar, click the Add Link button.

8 In the Add to Link Bar dialog box, select a page, as shown here, and click OK.

NOTE We are again taking a "shortcut" past some repetitive wizard dialog boxes so that we can get right to the Link Bar Properties dialog box.

NOTE If you have already defined a link bar (or several), you won't see the Create New Link Bar dialog box. Instead, you'll go straight to the Link Bar Properties dialog box, and you'll pick you up in step 6 of these instructions.

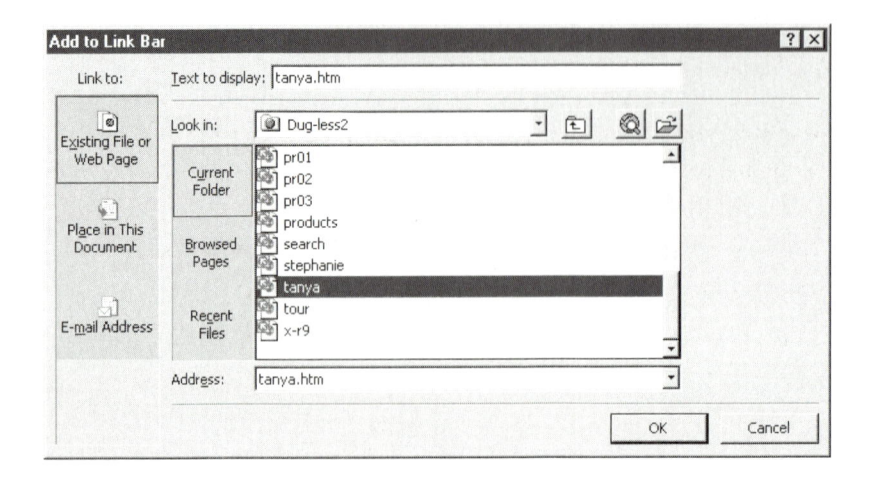

9 As you add links, they appear in the Links list of the Link Bar Properties dialog box. Use the check boxes to add links to the home page or parent page.

10 Use the Add Link, Remove Link, Modify Link, Move Up, and Move Down buttons to change your custom link bar.

11 After you've added all the pages you want included in the your link bar, use the Style tab to define the look of your custom link bar. Choose orientation (horizontal = sideways, vertical = up and down) by making a selection from the radio buttons in the Style tab. If you apply a theme to your link bar, you can elect to alter the colors using the Use Vivid Colors check box, and/or make your graphics *active*—so that they *react to visitors scrolling over them* by changing color or style.

12 When you've defined your link bar, click OK in the Link Bar Properties dialog box.

Inserting and Editing Custom Link Bars

After you define a custom link bar, you can use it anywhere in any page in your Web site. And, once you insert a custom link bar, you can add pages to that link bar right in Page view, without having to reopen the Link Bar Properties dialog box.

To Insert a custom link bar:

1 Choose Insert | Navigation.

2 Click on Bar with Custom Links in the Insert Web Component dialog box, and click Finish.

3 Select one of your custom link bars from the Choose Existing drop-down list in the Link Bar Properties dialog box, and click OK.

You can easily add links to a custom bar by clicking the Add Link link that displays in Page view at the end of your custom link bar, as shown in the illustration at the top of the next page.

Link Bars with Back and Next Links

Along with links based on navigation, and custom link bars, FrontPage allows you to create a third kind of link bar—link bars with Back and Next links. Back and Next link bars are used when you want to create a slide-show type Web site, where visitors click Back and Next buttons in the browsers to move from slide to slide.

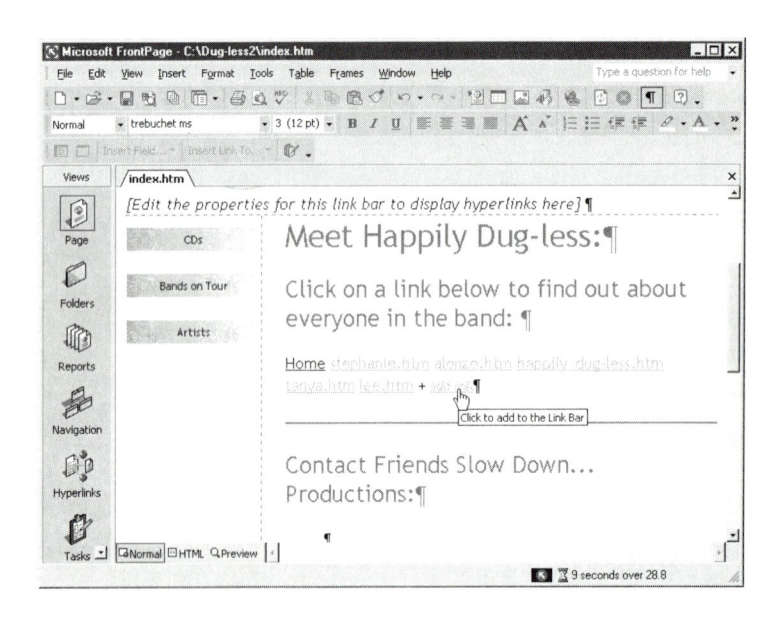

CHAPTER 6
MANY WAYS TO NAVIGATE YOUR SITE

Link bars with Back and Next links are just like custom link bars. In fact, they *are* custom link bars. The only difference is that instead of displaying *all* links, Back and Next link bars display links to the previous and following pages based on the list you define in the Link Bar Properties dialog box. Figure 6-6 shows a page with Back and Next links.

FIGURE 6-6

Back and next links are automatically generated based on custom link bars

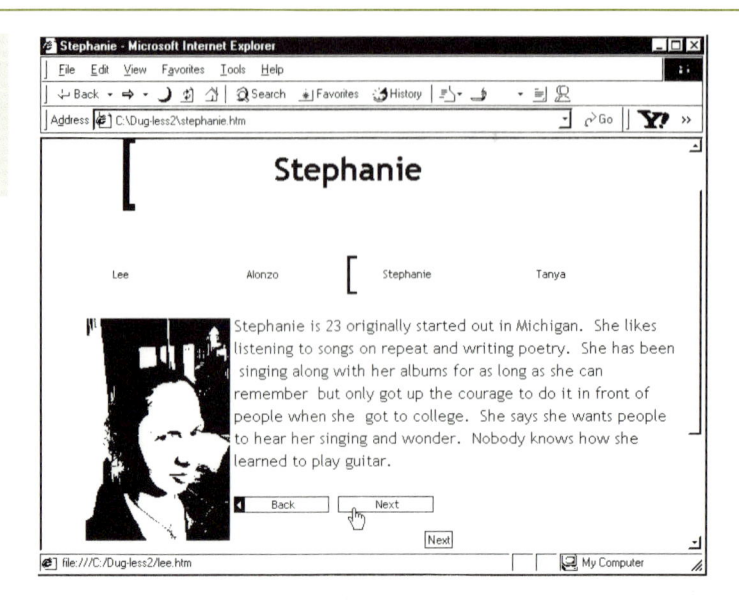

If you want to *change the order* of pages in the back/next sequence, use the Move Up or Move Down buttons in the Link Bar Properties dialog box. Be sure to include the current page in the list of pages in the back/next sequence.

Generating a Table of Contents

Another way to help visitors navigate your site is to create an all-inclusive table of contents that lists all (or most of) the pages in your Web site. Some visitors like to jump right to a page where they can see all their options, and find the page they're looking for that way. Kind of like the lists of tenants you see in the lobby of an office building. Figure 6-7 shows a table of contents for a Web site.

There are a couple ways to generate a table of contents:

▶ You can create one based on your entire site.

▶ You can base it only on specific types of pages.

FIGURE 6-7

The indented levels of this generated table of contents are based on links in the site's navigation structure

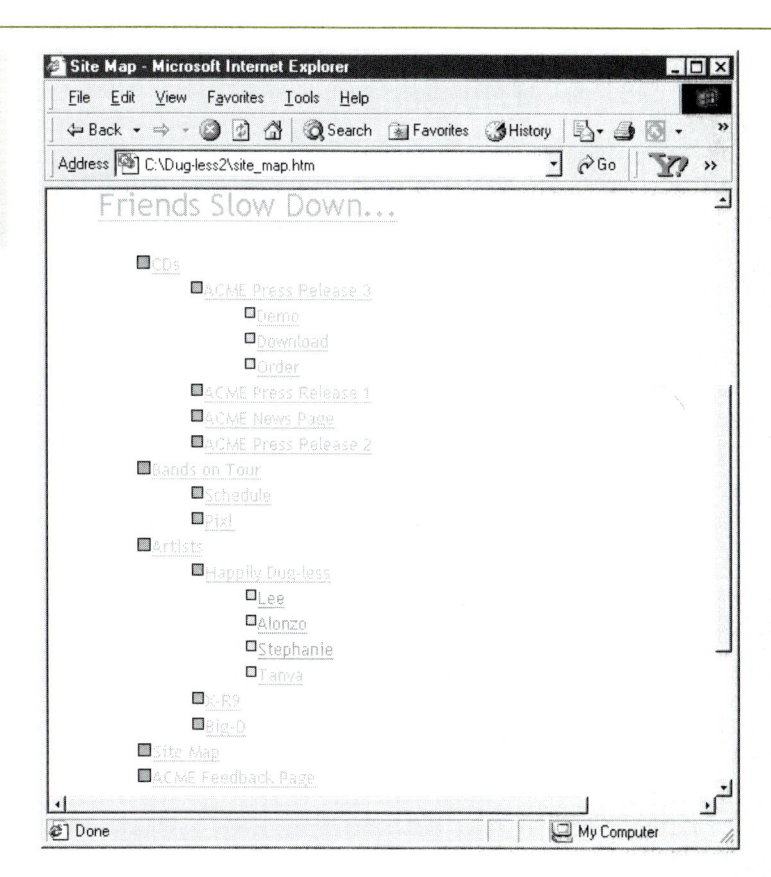

CHAPTER 6
MANY WAYS TO NAVIGATE YOUR SITE

CREATING A TABLE OF CONTENTS BASED ON YOUR SITE

When FrontPage generates a table of contents for your site, it includes all pages *except* those that are in folders that begin with an underscore—like _private or _themes. As you define a table of contents for your site, you can elect to include your whole site, or just part of the site. To include the whole site, you will define your Web site address (your URL) as the starting point for the table of contents. To include only some of your site, you can choose a "starting point" for your table of contents within the navigation structure to include in the contents.

To Create A TABLE OF CONTENTS BASED ON THE PAGES IN YOUR WEB SITE:

1 In Page view, choose Insert | Web Component.

2 Click Table of Contents in the list of Component types, and choose For This Web Site in the Choose a Table of Contents list.

3 Click Finish in the Insert Web Component dialog box to open the Table of Contents Properties dialog box.

4 Normally, you will want to leave the Page URL for Starting Point of Table area set to the site home page. This is the default setting. However, if you want to display just a section of your navigation structure, you can choose another page in your site, and have the TOC just display child pages of that page.

5 Use the Heading Font Size drop-down list to choose a size for your table of contents heading.

6 Use the Options check boxes to define whether to show each page just once (usually a good idea), or to show pages without incoming hyperlinks (careful—this might add pages you didn't want to be easily accessible—such as unfinished pages). Click the Recompute Table of Contents When Any Other Page is Edited to automatically update your TOC whenever you edit your site.

7 Click OK to place the table of contents on your page.

Table of Contents Based on Categories

FrontPage allows you to narrow the listings in a table of contents by including only specific categories of pages. In order to use this feature, you first have to assign categories to pages in your site.

To assign a category to a page, right-click in the page in Page view, and choose Page Properties from the context menu. In the Page Properties dialog box, click on the Workgroup tab. Use the Categories button to add your own categories, or use the preset ones listed in the Available Categories list. Click a category to include the open page in that category listing, as shown in here:

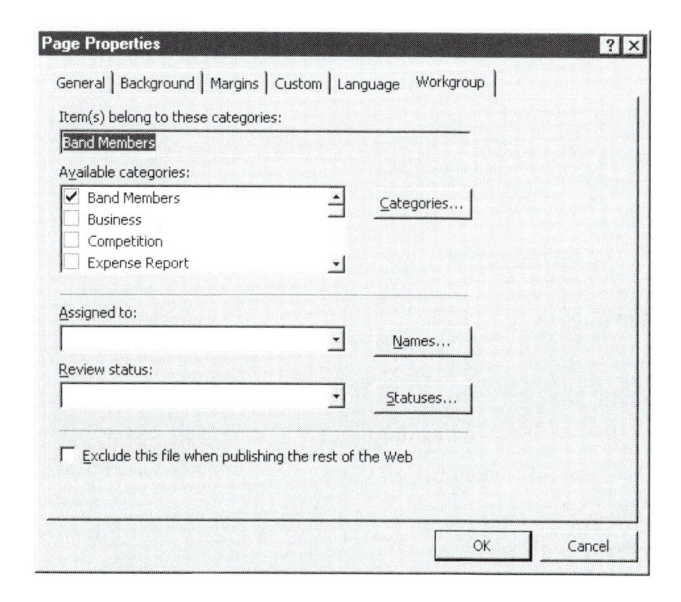

After you have assigned pages to categories, you can generate a table of contents that includes just one or a selected set of categories.

To Generate a table of contents with a selected set of categories:

1. In Page view, choose Insert | Web Component.

2. Click Table of Contents in the Component Type list, and choose Based on Page Category in the Choose a Table of Contents list.

> **TIP** To add a comment to a page, right-click a page in the Folder list. Choose Properties from the context menu, and click the Summary tab of the Properties dialog box. Enter comments in the Comments field, and click OK.

CHAPTER 6
MANY WAYS TO NAVIGATE YOUR SITE

3 Click Finish and the Categories Properties dialog box opens.

4 In the Categories Properties dialog box, select the categories(s) to include in the table of contents, as shown here:

5 Use the Sort Files By drop-down list to sort files either by page title or by when the file was last changed. Use the check boxes to include the date a page was last changed or any comments attached to a page. Then click OK to place the table of contents on a page.

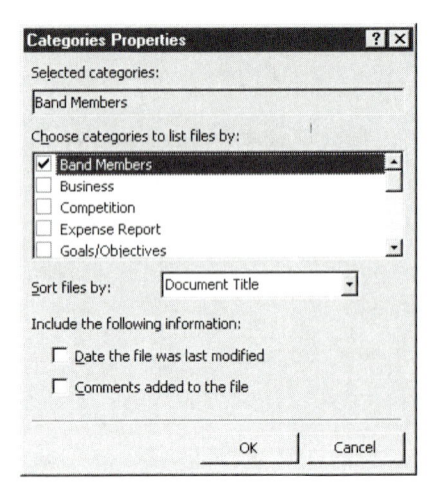

You can test and display your table of contents by previewing your page in a browser.

ADDING INTERNET SEARCH BOXES

FrontPage allows you to add an Internet search box to your page that connects visitors to the search engine provided by—you guessed it—Microsoft's MSN. You can also allow visitors to look up information on their stocks using MSN's Money Central.

SEARCH BOXES

By allowing visitors to your site to search the Internet, you are providing them with a service that might keep them coming back.

To Add AN INTERNET SEARCH BOX TO YOUR SITE:

1 In Page view, choose Insert | Web Component.

2 Click MSN Components in the Insert Web Component dialog box.

3 Select Search the Web with MSN in the Choose an MSN Component list.

4 Click Finish in the Insert Web Component dialog box.

The search box will appear in Page view like the one in Figure 6-8. It will work when you view your page in a browser.

FIGURE 6-8
Adding an Internet search box to a Web page

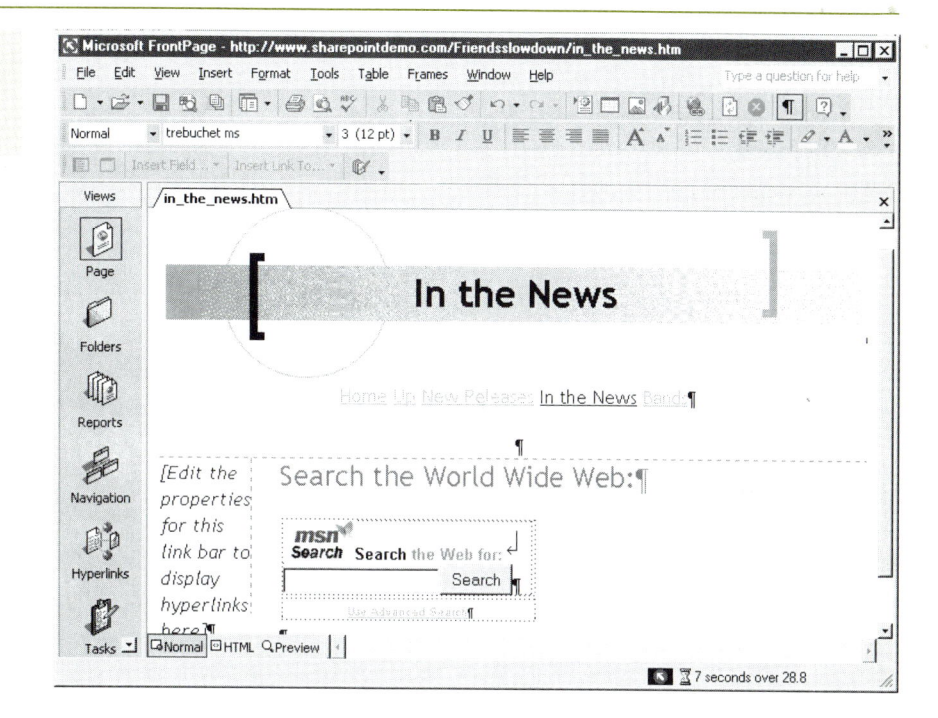

Stock Quotes

If your visitors are stock-obsessed, why make them leave your site to track their stocks? FrontPage 2002 offers a component that allows visitors to enter their stock name or symbol, and see how much they've made or lost that day.

To Add a stock look-up box:

1 In Page view, choose Insert | Web Component.

2 Click MSN Components in the Insert Web Component dialog box.

3 Click the Look Up a Stock Quote in the Choose an MSN Component list.

4 Click Finish.

Visitors who enter stock symbols or names will be transported to MSN's financial site where their stock will be featured.

Formatting Stock and Internet Lookup Boxes

Both the stock quote and Internet search components are formattable. They are laid out using tables, so you can use the table formatting features covered in Chapter 5 to widen columns, format cells, align tables, and so on. The stock and search boxes in Figure 6-9 were created by widening the tables, reformatting the text and cell background colors, and deleting a picture.

Navigate Away

In this chapter, you explored many ways to make it easy for visitors to find what they're looking for. Sometimes clearly marked links work best. Sometimes a search box is most helpful. In any case, FrontPage makes it easy to load up your pages with helpful navigation tools.

FIGURE 6-9

Feel free to format the Internet and stock search tables

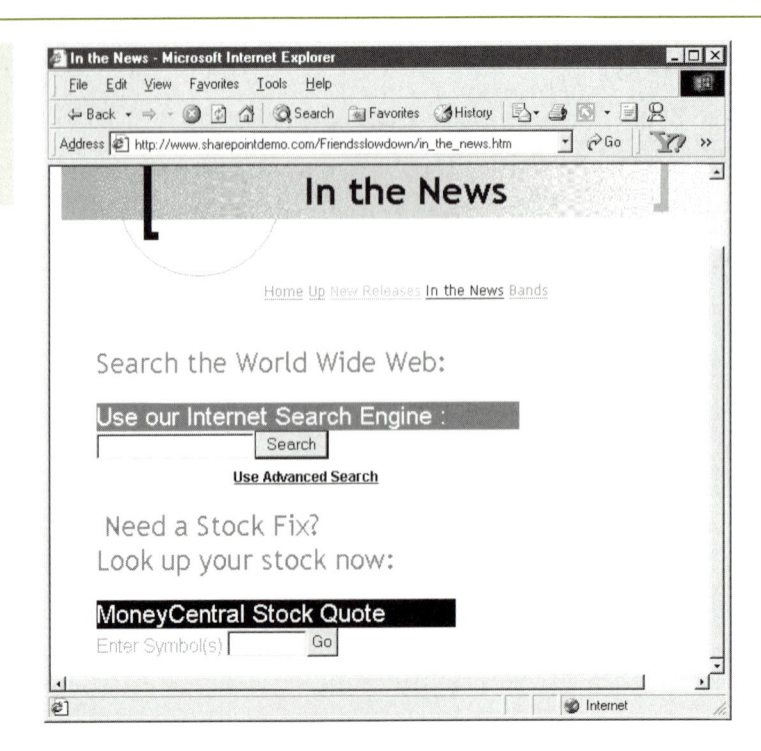

In the next chapter, you'll investigate one of FrontPage's most powerful, and sometimes most confusing, features: shared borders.

> **ON THE VIRTUAL CLASSROOM CD** In Lesson 5, "Defining Links," I demonstrate how to assign links to text and pictures, and how to open link targets in new browser windows. The lesson demonstrates how to use new features in FrontPage 2002 to add ScreenTip captions to links.

7

Page Design with Shared Borders

Shared borders can be attached to the top, left, bottom, or even the right side of your Web pages. In a Web browser, shared borders appear to be part of your Web page. These shared borders are used to display the same information on *every* page in your Web site. By modifying a shared border, you can therefore update how each page in your site appears to visitors.

Using Shared Borders

Shared borders are page borders that can be placed on every page in your Web site. Shared border content can include text or pictures. Or, it can include FrontPage Web components like link bars.

If you applied a theme to your FrontPage Web, you already have shared borders in your Web pages. In this chapter, you'll explore how to add and delete shared borders where they already exist, and how to create them for pages that don't have shared borders.

> **NOTE** Shared Borders sometimes display a message "Edit properties for this link bar to display hyperlinks here." This indicates that a shared border includes a link bar, and that can define the properties of that link bar to control what links appear in the shared border. Link bars are explored more in Chapter 6.

You can identify shared borders in your pages by the dashed lines that surround them in Page view. For example, in Figure 7-1, the shared border on the left has a link bar, and the shared border on top of the page has a page title.

Why Use Shared Borders?

Because shared borders can be assigned to *every* page in your site, they are a very convenient way to create and update content that you want to display with your

FIGURE 7-1
This page has two shared borders—the dotted lines on the top and left

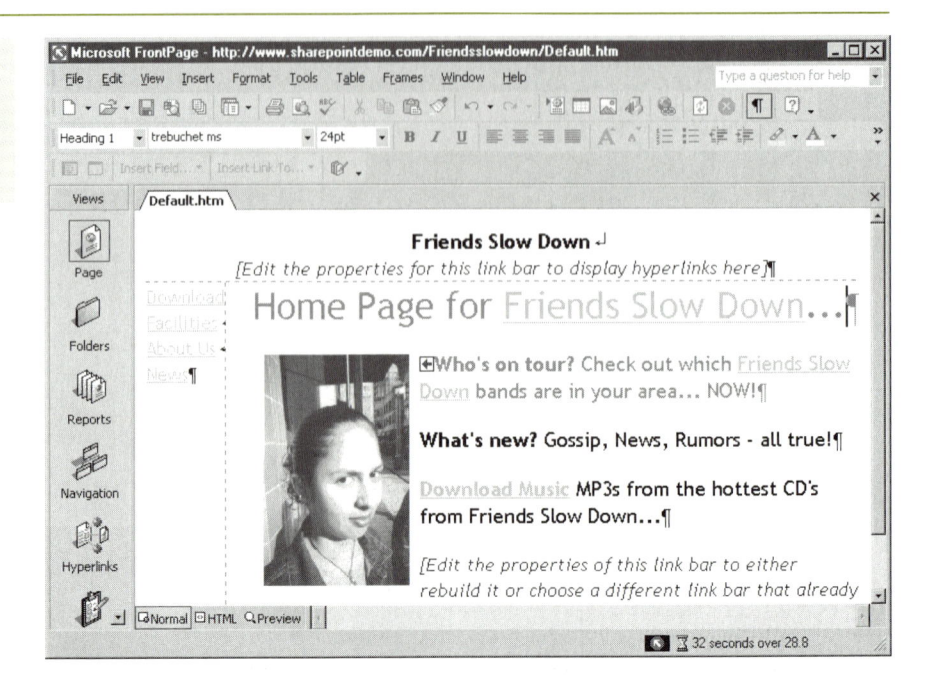

pages. For example, you might want to include contact information for your company or organization on the bottom of each page in your site. You can place this information in a bottom shared border and assign that bottom shared border to all pages in your site.

Shared borders are especially handy for navigation links. By placing link bars in shared borders, you can provide *dynamic* (changing) links on each page in your site. Since link bars are based on navigation structure or specially defined categories (see Chapter 6 for details), link bars in shared borders will change depending on which page is displayed.

Another use of shared borders is for content that you want to include in every page. For example, you might want to have a picture of yourself, your department, your staff, or your building appear on every page. By placing this content in a *shared border*, the content will appear with every page in your site. And in the case of pictures, there is another advantage to placing them in a shared border. Because shared borders download only once, the content on them does not need to reload when a visitor moves from page to page in your site.

Shared Borders vs. Frames

Some of you, if you are familiar with the use of *frames* in Web sites, might be asking: "Aren't shared borders like frames?" The answer is "yes;" they are *similar* to frames. The technical similarity is that both shared borders and frames are actually separate Web pages that are embedded in, or attached to, other pages. More significantly, shared borders and frames play a similar role—they both provide constant Web-wide content that displays in a browser window next to changing page content.

In Chapter 8, you'll look at how FrontPage can be used to easily create frames (or *framed pages* to be more technically correct). Here, simply note that because shared borders and frames do similar things, you will probably *not* want to use *both* in your site.

Avoiding Shared Border Confusion

When I teach FrontPage classes, invariably at least a few students get disoriented by the fact that when you edit a shared border, it changes on *every* page. We'll walk through the process of creating and editing shared borders in detail in this chapter. But as we do, keep in mind this concept: Shared border content appears

CHAPTER 7
PAGE DESIGN WITH SHARED BORDERS

on *every page* (or at least on many pages) in your site. And when you change it, you change how *every page* in your site looks.

In Page view shared borders are marked by dashed lines. You can edit the content of shared borders by clicking inside of the dashed lines. When you click inside a shared border, the dashed lines become solid lines, as shown in Figure 7-2.

Any changes you make to a shared border are, as I emphasized earlier, applied to *every page* in your site that has shared borders applied to it.

When visitors look at your page, it won't be obvious to them that you are using shared borders. The dashed lines that set off the shared borders in Figure 7-1 won't show up in a Web browser. Figure 7-3 shows the same page you looked at in Figure 7-1. But this time, viewed in a browser, the shared border content blends seamlessly into the page.

CREATING SHARED BORDERS

Since shared borders are usually defined for an *entire* Web site, you can apply them in Page view, or *any* view. (Later in this chapter, you'll explore how to exclude shared borders from selected pages, but the first step is to create shared borders.)

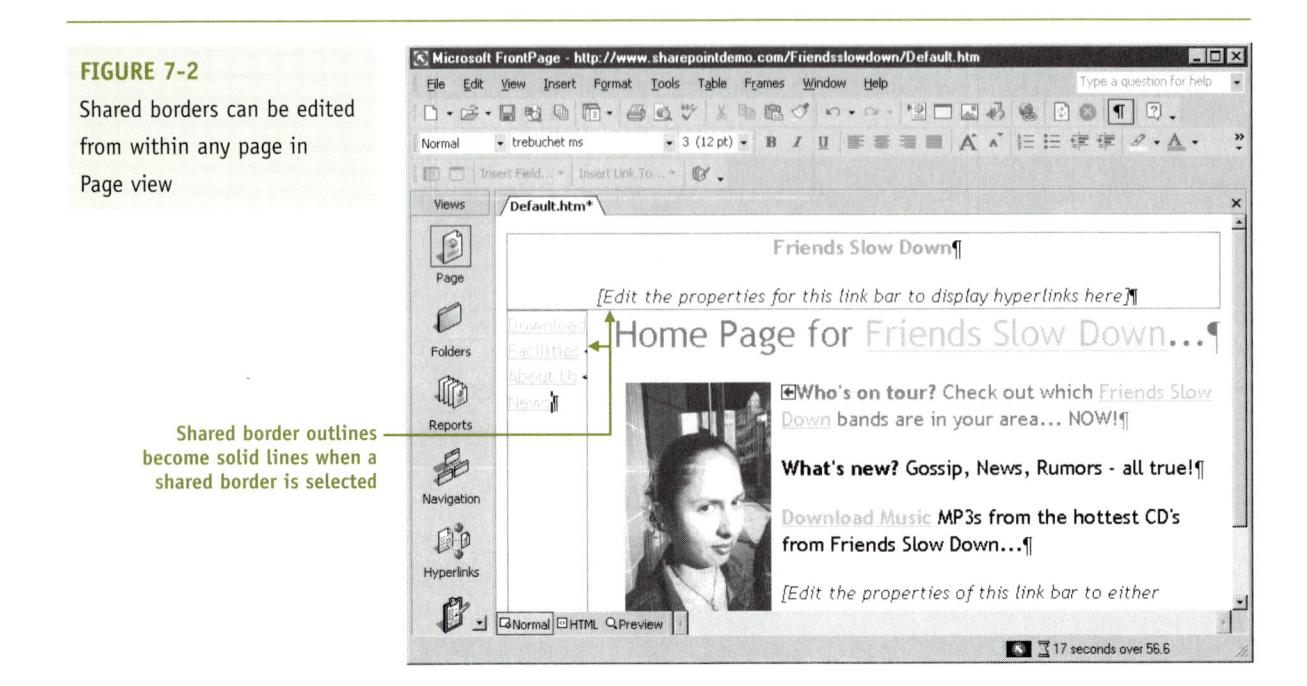

FIGURE 7-2

Shared borders can be edited from within any page in Page view

Shared border outlines become solid lines when a shared border is selected

FIGURE 7-3
Shared border content as viewed with a browser

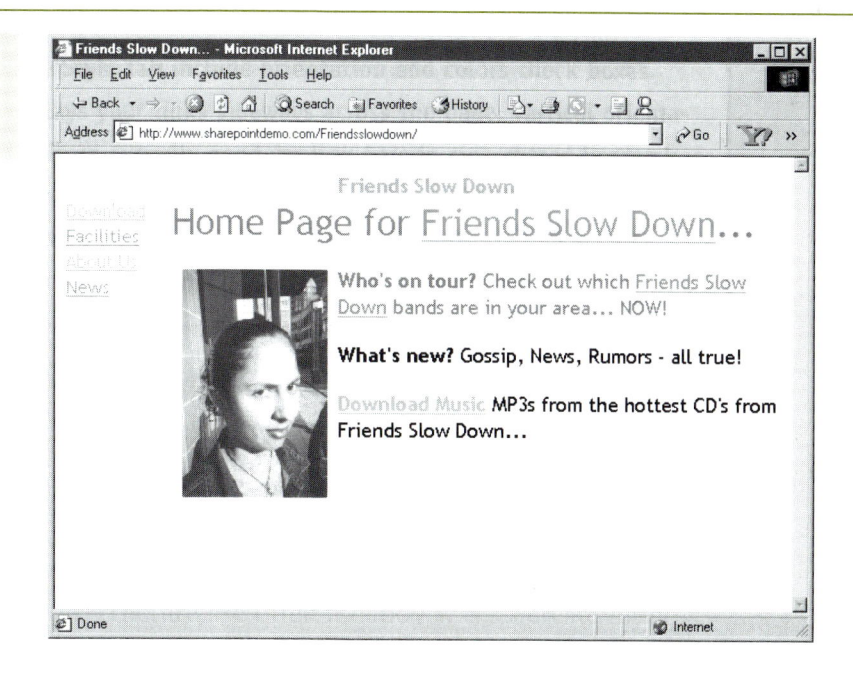

To Create SHARED BORDERS FOR A FRONTPAGE WEB SITE:

1 In any view, choose Format | Shared Borders from the FrontPage menu.

2 The Shared Borders dialog box, shown here, has four check boxes: Each one creates a shared border on the top, left, right, or bottom of every page.

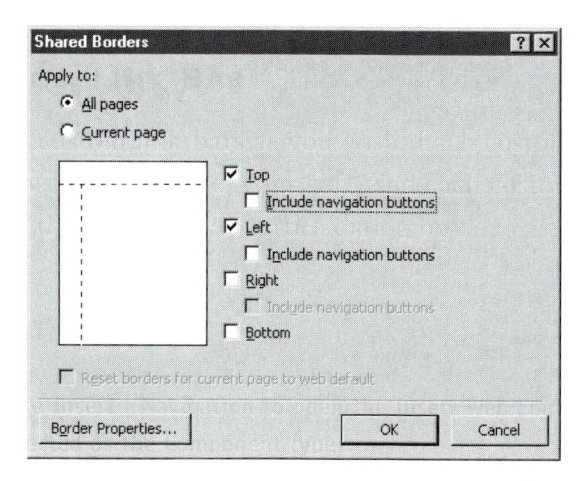

3. As you select shared borders, the illustration area on the left side of the dialog box displays how the shared borders will appear on your page.

4. If you apply a top and/or a left shared border, you can automatically include link bars in those borders by clicking the Include Navigation Buttons check boxes.

> **NOTE** If you opened the Shared Borders dialog box in Page view, the Current Page radio button is active. This radio button applies shared borders to only the current page. You'll explore that option later in this chapter.

5. To define separate colors (or background pictures) for shared borders, click the Properties button in the Shared Borders dialog box. From the Border drop-down menu that appears in the Border Properties dialog box, choose a border.

6. With a border selected, you can choose a distinct background color for that border using the Color check box and drop-down list.

7. After you define border color(s)—you can use the Picture check box and Browse button to assign a background picture—for one border, you can use the Border drop-down menu to define additional border background colors if you want.

8. Click OK to close the Border Properties dialog box.

9. Click OK to close the Shared Border Properties dialog box. Your shared borders will appear in Page view as dashed lines on the page.

Editing Shared Borders

To edit the content of a shared border, click inside it. Then, edit content just as you would any other page. When you save your page, the changed content of the shared border will be saved as well, and automatically applied to every page to which the shared border is attached.

Often shared borders will have link bars inside them. This can make editing content a little tricky, because when you select a shared border, you tend to select the link bar as well. If you want to add or edit content *outside* the link bar, an easy way to do that is to use your right or left cursor keys on your keyboard to move outside the selected link bar.

Shared borders can have text, pictures, and even audio or video content (more on that in Chapter 14). Insert, edit, and format text and pictures in a shared border just as you would any other kind of Web page content. Just remember—your changes will apply to *every* page in which the shared border is displayed.

Wrestling with Shared Border Width

FrontPage handles shared border width automatically. This is a real limitation for designers who want to control how wide their shared borders appear. Borders will force text to wrap in order to fit inside the border. However, borders won't hyphenate text. So one way to force a border to widen is to include some large text with no spaces. In. Figure 7-4, I'm assigning a large font to text in a shared border, and I've also added a few dots (without any spaces before or between them) to prevent the text from wrapping. In this way, I've widened the shared border to the desired width.

Another way to force a shared border to maintain a set width is to include a picture in the border. That way, the border is forced to be as wide as the picture. Yet a third trick for defining the width of a shared border is to place a one-cell table inside the border. If you define the table with a 0-pixel border, as shown in Figure 7-5, nobody will know that your table is being used to define border width.

FIGURE 7-4

Shared borders will be as wide as the largest word within them—here a large font-formatted word is being used to widen a shared border

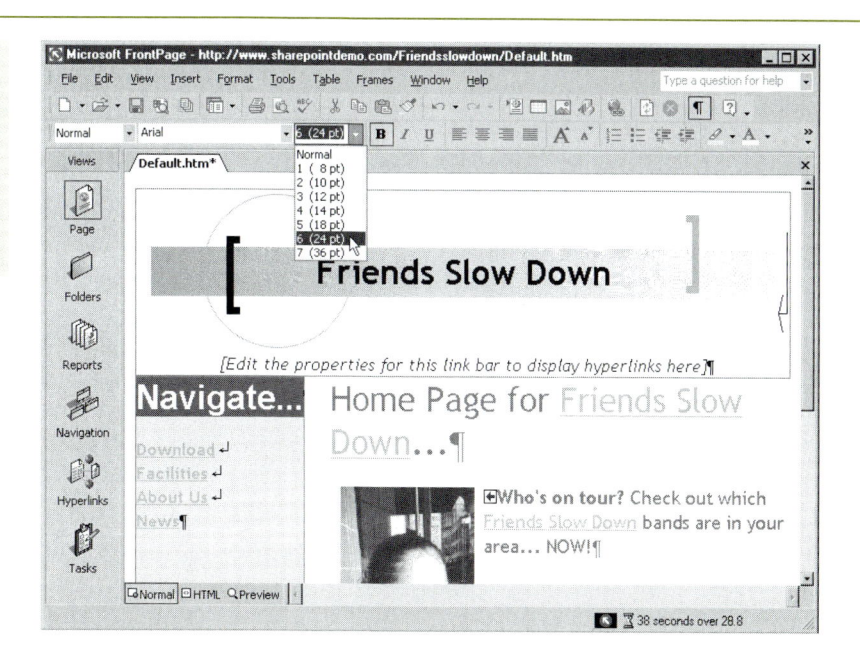

CHAPTER 7

PAGE DESIGN WITH SHARED BORDERS

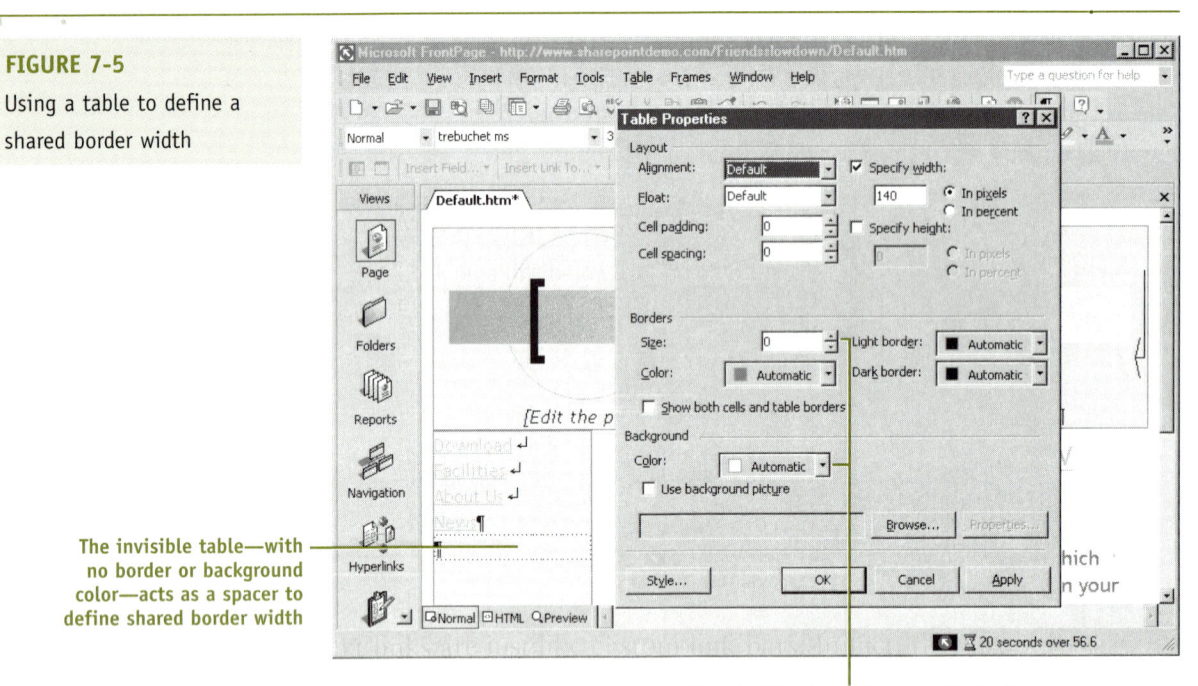

FIGURE 7-5

Using a table to define a shared border width

The invisible table—with no border or background color—acts as a spacer to define shared border width

A 0-pixel border and automatic (no) background color make the table invisible—it's just here as a spacer

Formatting Shared Borders

After you generate shared borders in the Shared Border dialog box, you can change the formatting (background color or picture) for a border. This can create a cool effect where visitors see a border with a different color than the rest of the page. (Of course, only FrontPage experts will know you've achieved this effect by formatting a shared border background.) The technical reason why this works is that shared borders are actually *distinct Web pages* that are embedded within every Web page to which they are assigned.

To Change the color of a shared border background:

1 In Page view, right-click in a border.

2 Choose Border Properties from the context menu.

3 Choose a border from the Borders drop-down menu.

4 Oddly enough, FrontPage can't sense what border you clicked in, you have to specifically select a border in the Border Properties dialog box. Change the color (or picture) settings for the selected border, as shown here:

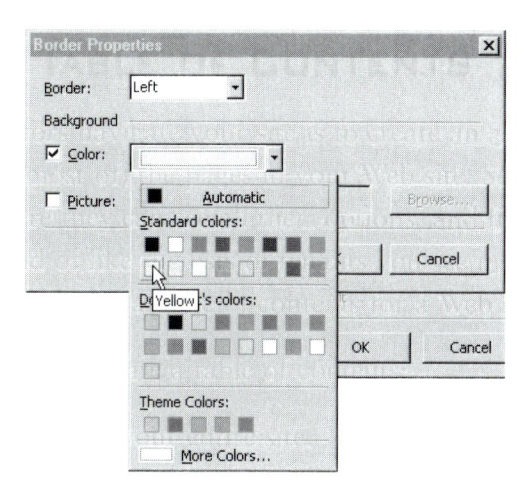

5 Change settings for other borders if you want.

6 Click OK to assign the new border formatting.

When you save a page, you automatically save any changes you made to embedded borders within that page. And, as I've emphasized again and again, those changes will apply to *every* page in which the border is embedded.

Advanced Formatting for Shared Borders

Borders are actually Web pages. You can open them *separately*, as Web pages, and edit them that way. Editing a border separately (in Page view) allows you to define additional page attributes like default text colors and link colors. The tricky part is that by default, FrontPage hides these border pages. So, before you can edit them, you have to display hidden pages and folders.

Unhiding Hidden Folders

FrontPage creates many Web pages that are normally hidden. These include files that are used for some FrontPage components (see Chapter 10), as well as files for border pages.

CHAPTER 7
Page Design with Shared Borders

To Display HIDDEN PAGES IN FRONTPAGE'S FOLDER VIEW:

1 Choose Tools | Web Settings to open the Web Settings dialog box.

2 Click the Advanced tab.

3 In the Advanced tab, select the Show Hidden Files and Folders check box, as shown here:

> **NOTE** Options available in the Advanced tab may vary depending on the server to which you are publishing your FrontPage Web.

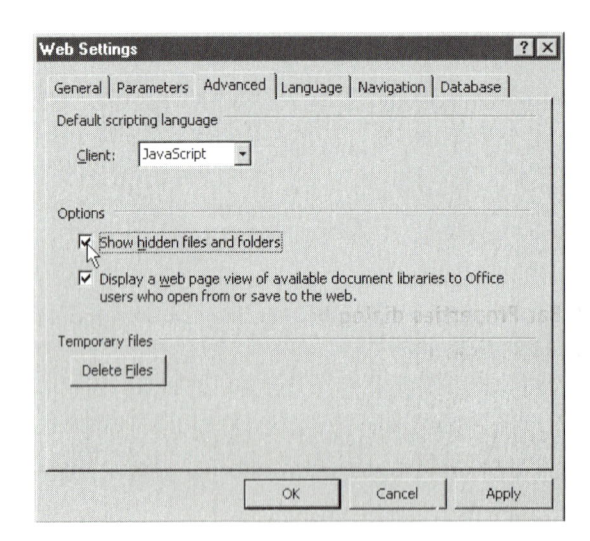

4 Click OK to close the Web Settings dialog box. As you do, you'll be prompted to OK a dialog box that will refresh your Web settings. When you do, FrontPage will display hidden files and folders in Folders view.

Editing Shared Border Pages

Once you have "unhidden" your shared border files, you can edit them. To open a shared border folder, double-click it in the _borders folder (in Folders view). With your shared border page open, choose File | Properties. The Page Properties dialog box opens. Use the Background tab in the Page Properties dialog box to define default text and link colors. Click OK to apply new formatting to your border page.

> **NOTE** The _borders folder includes files for borders used in the site. If you have a picture in a shared border, that image is saved in a shared border folder.

When you save the border page, any editing or formatting changes will be applied to the shared border, and appear in all pages in which the shared border is embedded.

Controlling Link Bars in Shared Borders

In Chapter 6, you learned about links and link bars. Here, you'll just take a quick look at how links and link bars are applied to shared borders.

To Place a link bar on a shared border:

1. In Page view, click *inside* a shared border.

2. Choose Insert | Navigation.

3. In the Insert Web Component dialog box, choose Bar Based on Navigation Structure.

4. Click on Finish. In the Link Bar Properties dialog box, define your link logic (this process is explored in detail in Chapter 6).

5. Click OK to place the link bar in the shared border.

Link bars in shared borders can be tested by previewing your page in a browser (choose File | Preview in Browser).

Customizing Shared Borders for Individual Pages

Sometimes, you might want to delete shared borders from one page or selected pages in a site. This will disrupt the consistent look and feel provided by navigation bars. And it will remove any links or link bars you placed in a shared border.

You might want to remove shared borders from a page that, for example, displayed a large graphic and nothing else. Or, you might want to remove shared borders from a page that has content you don't want to directly associate with your Web site (such as a legal disclaimer, for example).

To Remove SHARED BORDERS FROM A SPECIFIC PAGE:

1 In Page view, with the selected page open, choose Format | Shared Borders.

2 Since you opened the Shared Borders dialog box in Page view, the Current Page radio button will be active. Select the Current Page radio button.

3 Deselect any or all shared borders you don't want to display on the selected page, as shown here:

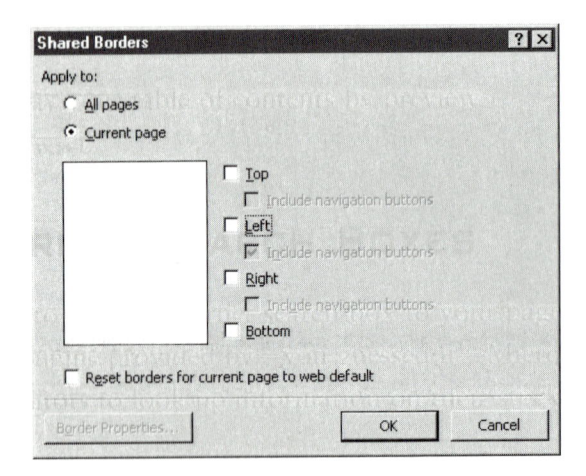

4 Click OK to close the Shared Borders dialog box. Changes will be applied *only* to the open page.

Shared Border Design Tips

Theoretically, you can have up to four shared borders on a page. But more than three shared borders create a cluttered look. Try to avoid right-side shared borders—visitors will usually not look to the right edge of a page for navigation links. Bottom borders are good for site information, like e-mail links to contact the Webmaster or contact info, copyright notices, and other site-related notices.

Themes place a component called a *page banner* in top shared borders. Page banners display the *title* of a page either in text or as a graphic. You can edit the display of these banners by right-clicking them and choosing Page Banner Properties from the context menu.

One technique you can experiment with is to have two or more shared borders with the same color background. This creates a framed look for your page, as shown in Figure 7-6.

Shared borders are a great way to provide *consistent* navigational elements on all (or most) of your Web pages. You do need to be careful when you edit the content of shared borders, because any change you make to a shared border *will affect all pages* to which that shared border is attached.

While shared borders are *actually* separate Web pages that are attached to other pages, they don't *look* like separate pages in a browser. I like that clean look—visitors don't feel like they are looking at more than one page.

If you want to display more than one page in a browser window, and allow *each page* to operate *independently*, you can use frames instead of shared borders. You'll explore frames in the next chapter.

FIGURE 7-6
This page has three shared borders, all with the same color background

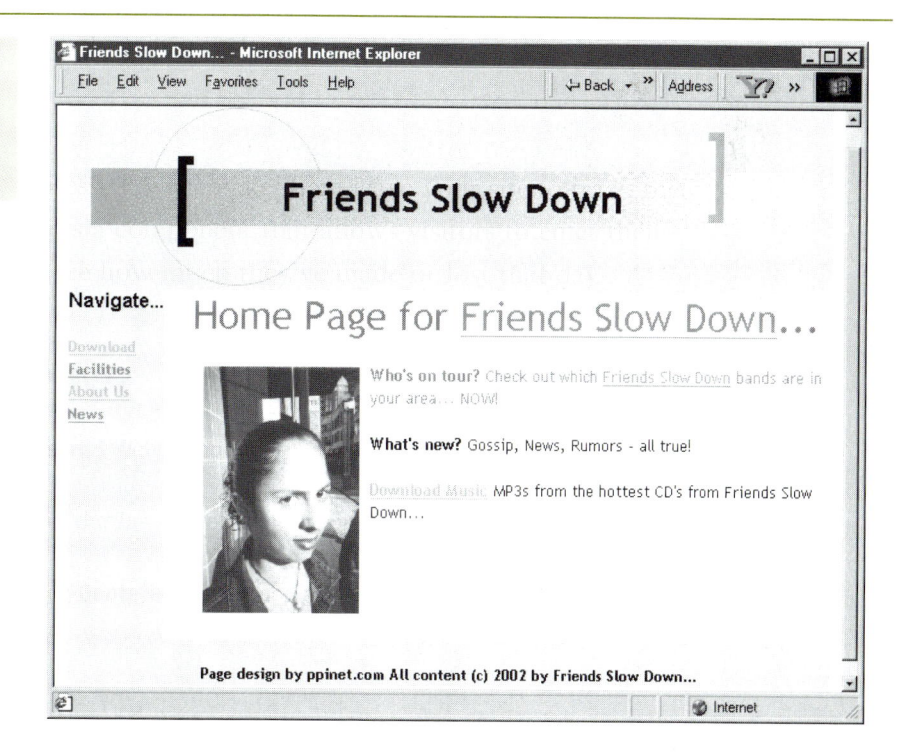

8

Using Frames

Frames combine two or more Web pages into a browser window. If you surf the Net much (and aspiring Web designers should!) you've seen Web sites with frames. A combination of Web pages that display together in a browser window is called a *frameset*. In this chapter, I'll refer to *frames*, and *framesets*—in both cases I mean the same thing: a combination of Web pages that display together in a window.

CHAPTER 8
USING FRAMES

USING FRAMES IN WEB SITES

Because frames *divide* the visitors screen into smaller.... well, *frames*, they can either help organize Web pages or clutter up Web pages. It's hard to imagine an attractive Web page that displays more than three frames—four gets awfully crowded on anyone's monitor. On the other hand, nicely done framesets can provide easy to find navigation links in one frame, and still leave plenty of room on today's larger monitors to display page content at the same time.

Frames also allow visitors to customize their browsing experience, since frames can be (depending on how they are set up) resized by a visitor right in his or her browser window.

And, because frames are *distinct Web pages*, you can apply different formatting (like different page backgrounds) to individual frames. This opens up more design options for Web developers. In short, used carefully, frames can often enhance a Web site.

FRAMES AS NAVIGATION TOOLS

More often than not, framesets combine a *navigation* frame with a *display* frame. The navigation frame acts like the controls on your VCR, while the display frame acts like your TV screen. For example, Figure 8-1 shows a framed Web site I use

FIGURE 8-1

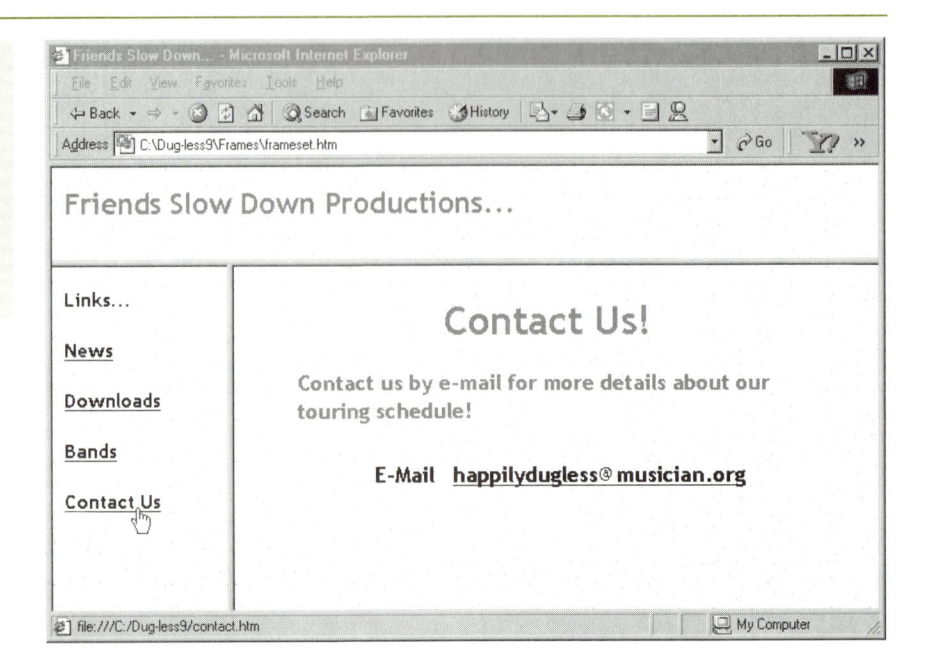

In this frameset, the top frame displays constant info on the company, the left frame provides navigation links, and the main (right) frame displays site content

for one of my Web design classes. The frame on the left has navigation links that, when selected, display content in the main frame on the right.

When you create frames in FrontPage, be careful to make good decisions about *which frame* a link should open within. The worst thing that can happen with a badly designed frameset is that links open pages in the wrong frame. Figure 8-2, in the spirit of the famous "Web Pages that Suck" guys (www.webpagesthatsuck.com) shows what can happen if frames open links in the wrong frame.

Frames Can Be Flexible

One of the cool things about frames is that visitors can resize frame windows themselves. What if you *don't want* visitors fussing with your carefully defined frame sizes? That can be arranged as well. In the next part of this chapter, you'll learn to create both resizable and rigidly sized frames.

Each frame in a frameset can also have its own scrollbars. Too many scrollbars on a page can get a bit cluttered. But the advantage is that visitors can scroll around *within* frames, as shown in Figure 8-3, where both the navigation (left) and main frame (right) have scrollbars.

FIGURE 8-2
Ooops! Learn to avoid having a link open in the wrong frame, like this one

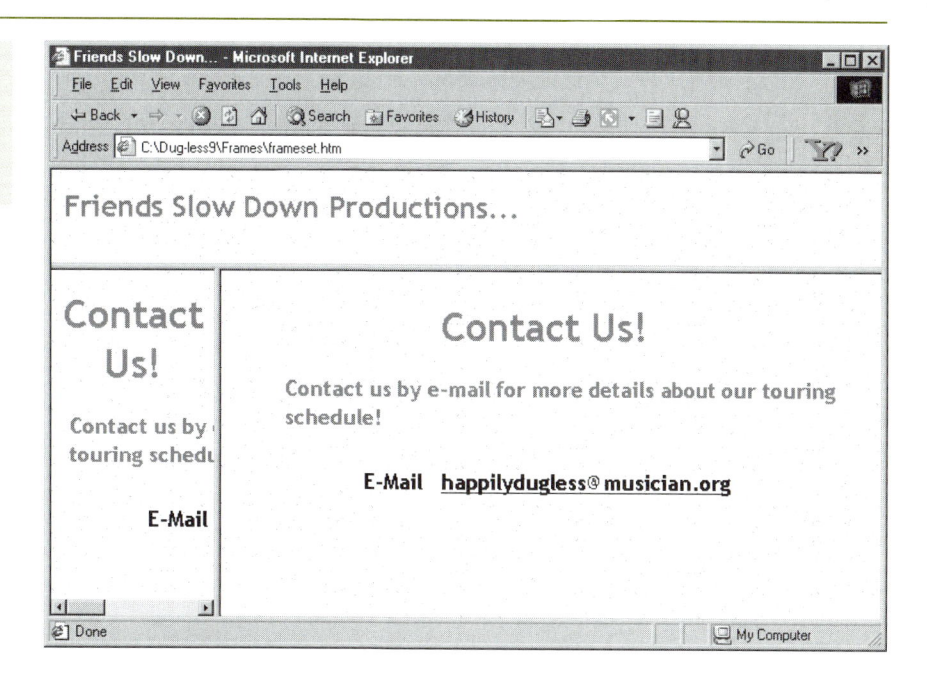

CHAPTER 8
USING FRAMES

FIGURE 8-3

Scrolling around in a frame

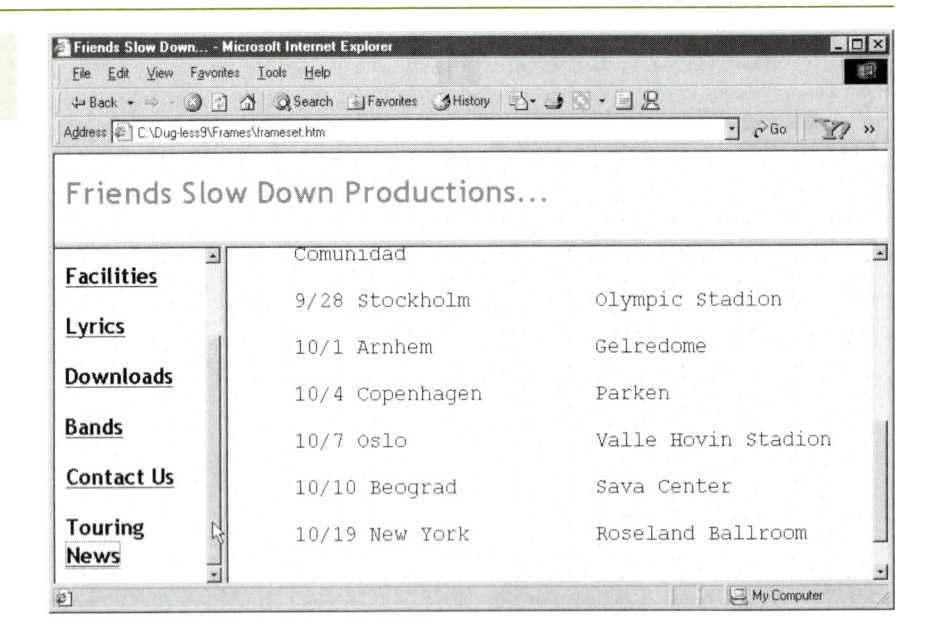

Frames Are Made Up of HTML Pages

Before we jump into the process of creating frames in FrontPage, it will be helpful to understand one more concept: Framesets are made up of at least three HTML pages. One HTML page is used to *define the frameset*. This page keeps track of how many frames are displayed, where, and how large each frame will be.

Additional HTML pages are used to define the framed pages *within* a frameset. As you begin to create frames in FrontPage, remember that you'll actually be working with several Web pages *at the same time*.

Building Framed Pages in FrontPage

FrontPage automates some of the work of creating frames by providing a full selection of frame page templates. Don't like *any* of the templates? That's fine, you can start with a template, and adopt it to your own desires.

However, in the real world there are only a handful of frameset configurations that really work well, so you'll probably find one that you want in FrontPage. And if you don't... think twice about your page design. It could be that you're heading in the dreaded direction of too many frames on a page.

Creating a Frameset from a Template

Creating a frameset means that *somebody* has to keep track of *at least* three HTML (Web page) files—one for each frame and one for the *frameset* that keeps the frames organized. Luckily for you, FrontPage will do that work—either by providing you with a pre-made template or by helping keep track of the files needed for frames.

There's two basic ways to go about creating a frameset in FrontPage:

▶ You can have all your content *already created* in pages, and then just plug those pages into a frameset.

▶ You can create your page content *as you go*—designing your frameset and your pages all at once.

In either case, the routine is similar. If you have a page that you want to display as part of a frameset, keep it handy. If not, no problem, you'll create pages as you design the frameset.

To Create framed pages in FrontPage:

1 In Page view, choose File | New | Page or Web from the menu bar. The New Page or Web pane appears, as shown to the right.

2 In the New Page or Web pane, click the Page Templates link, and the Page Templates dialog box opens.

3 In the Page templates dialog box, click the Frames tab. A set of framed page templates is displayed, as shown on the next page. These templates are just a starting point; you can make changes to any of the frame sets after you create the new page.

CHAPTER 8
USING FRAMES

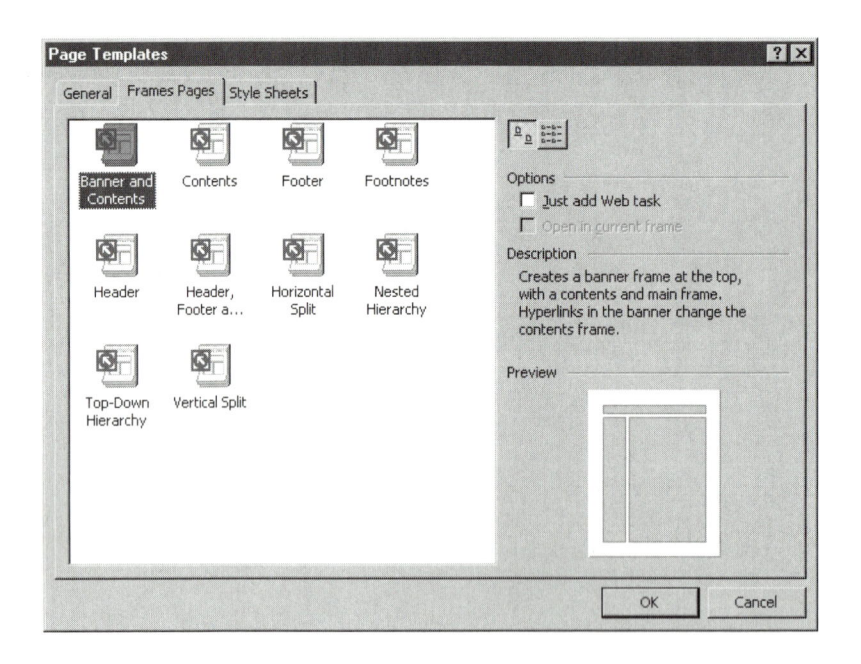

4 Click on a frame template icon in the area on the left side of the dialog box. Notice that a model of the frameset previews on the on the right side of the dialog box, along with a description of the frame template.

5 Choose a template from the set of icons on the left side of the Page Templates dialog box, and click OK.

FrontPage generates a blank frameset, ready for you to fill in—like the one shown in Figure 8-4.

> **NOTE** Make sure the Just Add Web Task check box is not selected, or FrontPage will not create a new frames page.

> **TIP** If you would like to work along with the book, and have your pages roughly match those in the book, choose the first frame template: the Banner and Contents template.

ADDING FRAME CONTENT

As soon as you've generated a frameset using one of FrontPage's frame templates, you'll see that each frame within your frameset has two buttons:

▶ Set Initial Page
▶ New Page

FIGURE 8-4

A blank frameset in FrontPage, ready to connect with page content

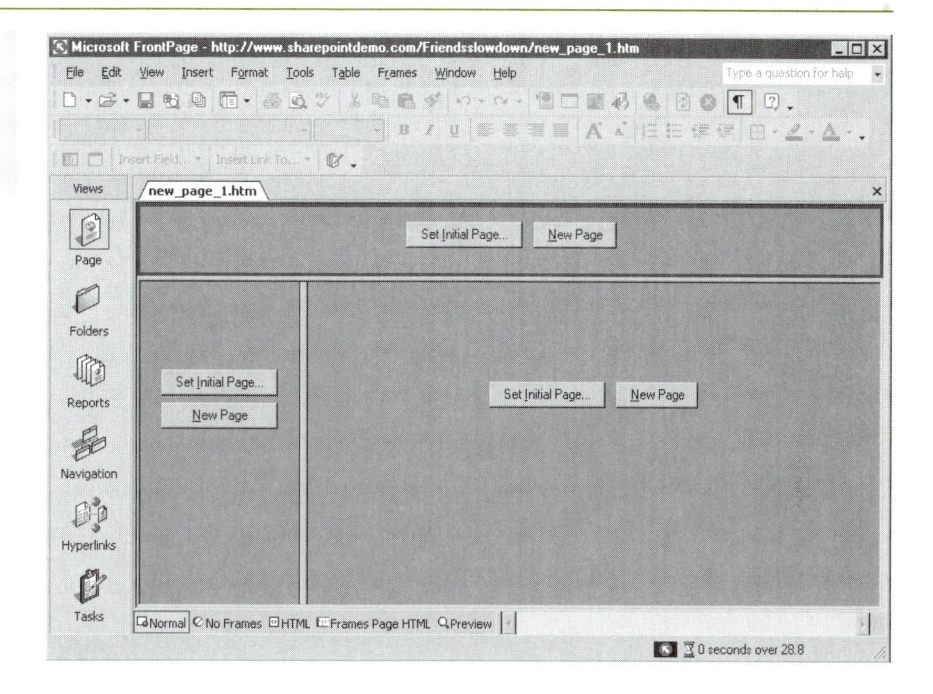

Here's what they mean: Set Initial Page means that you *already have a Web page* ready to go; you want to plug into your frameset. For example, you might have a home page that you already designed, and now you want to include it in a frameset. New Page means that you don't already have a page to plug into your frameset, and you want to create it right now.

FrontPage is happy to accommodate you either way. If you have pages you want to plug into a frameset, follow the next set of instructions. If you are creating a frameset and you want to use new content, skip to the section, "Creating Frame Content from Scratch."

Can you create *new* content in one frame, and plug an existing page into *another* frame in the *same* frameset. Sure, it just means you need to read *both* sets of directions that follow.

Embedding Existing Pages into a Frameset

To plug existing pages into a frameset, you'll use the Set Initial Page in a frame. This will enable you to browse around your Web site for a file to plug into the frame.

CHAPTER 8
USING FRAMES

To Add AN EXISTING PAGE TO YOUR FRAMESET:

1 Click the Set Initial Page button *in the frame in which you want to display an existing page*. The (oddly named—in this case) Insert Hyperlink dialog box opens, as shown here:

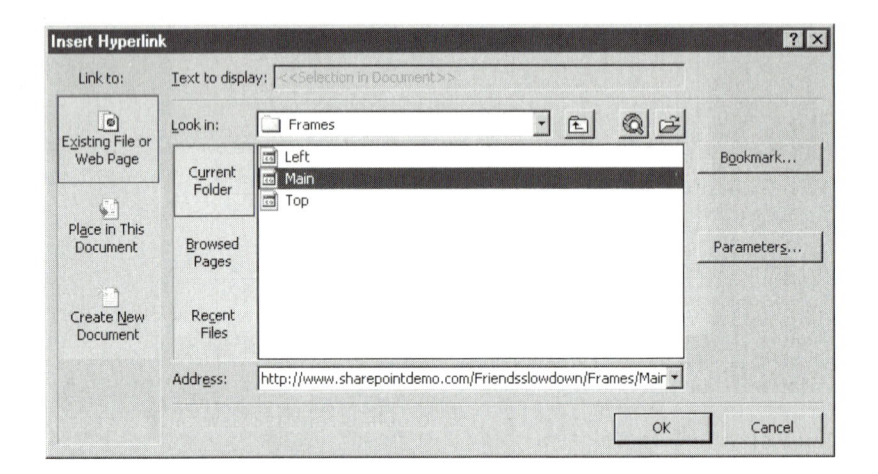

2 Click OK in the Insert Hyperlink dialog box. The selected page is embedded in your Frameset.

3 If you want to display a *different* page in the selected frame, right-click in the frame and choose Frame Properties from the context menu. Use the Browse button in the Frame Properties dialog box to locate and insert a *different* page in the frameset. Then click OK.

> **TIP** If the page you embed within a frameset already has *shared borders*, those borders aren't going to look very good in a framed page. Get rid of them by choosing Format | Shared Borders, and deselecting all shared borders for the selected page.

CREATING FRAME CONTENT FROM SCRATCH

Many times, you'll want to create a frameset and the embedded (framed) pages *all at once*. FrontPage will let you do that—you'll just save your framed pages along with the frameset. You'll explore that process in the next section of this chapter.

To Create NEW FRAMED PAGES DIRECTLY FROM A FRAME PAGE TEMPLATE:

1 Click the New Page button in the frame in which you want to display a new page, as shown in Figure 8-5.

FIGURE 8-5
Creating a new page within a Frameset template

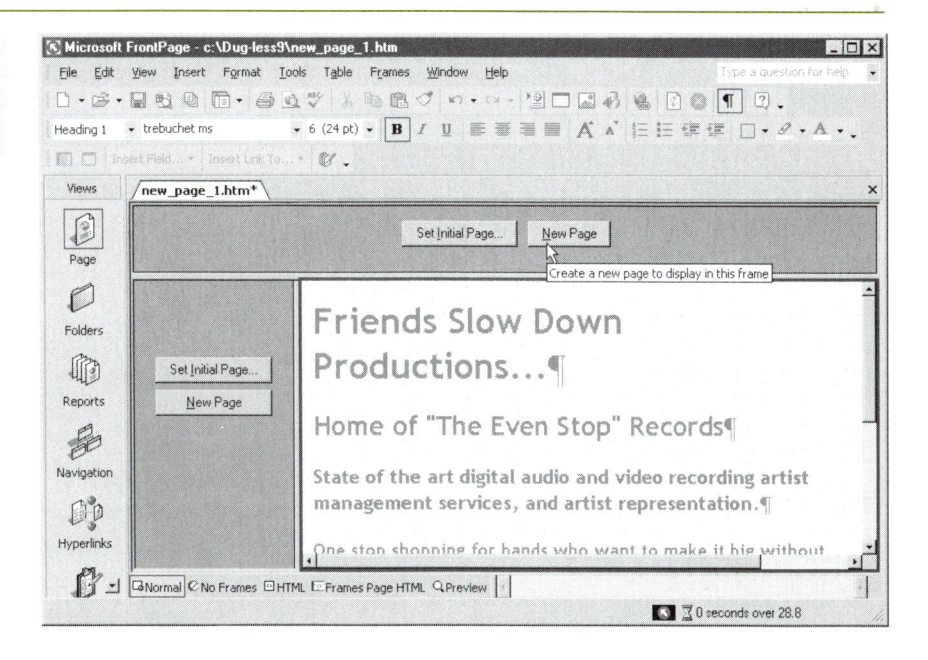

2. Enter content in the new page, just as you would any other page (except that your framed page will be *smaller* than a regular page).

3. You can click on any framed page within a frameset, and edit the contents.

SAVING A FRAMESET

Once you have created content in the frames within your frameset—either by embedding existing pages or creating new ones—it's time to save your frameset.

Since you're going to be saving a bunch of pages, it will be helpful to think of a naming system that will allow you keep them straight. For example, I usually name my top frame top.htm, my main frame main.htm, and my left frame left.htm. Creativity is not a virtue here—the object is to remember which page is which when you see these files in Folders view.

To save a frameset, click the Save button in Page view. One by one, you'll be prompted to save all the pages within your frameset. You can tell *which* page your are saving because FrontPage will highlight the page being saved in blue in the Save As dialog box, as shown in Figure 8-6.

Chapter 8
Using Frames

FIGURE 8-6
Saving the embedded page that forms the top part of a frameset

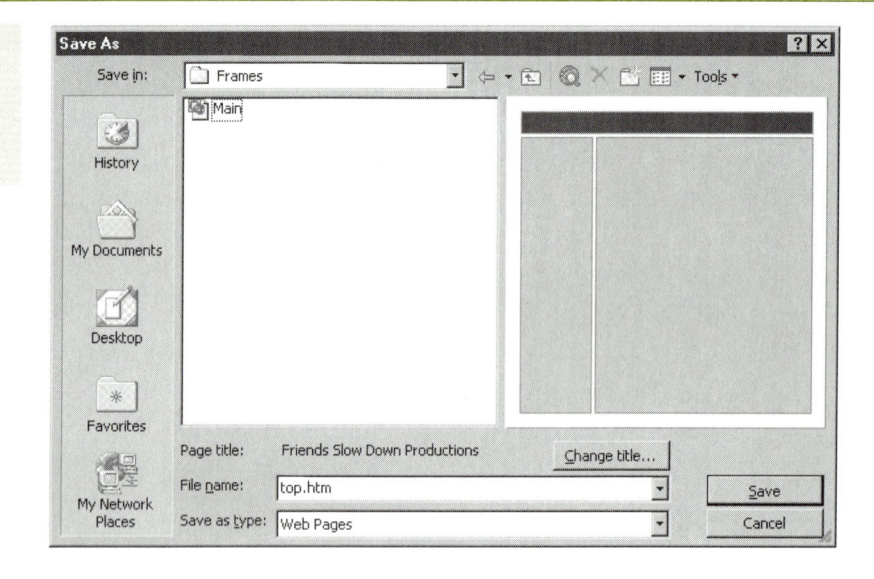

After saving all your embedded pages, FrontPage will prompt you to save the frameset itself. This Save As dialog looks a little different, because *none* of the individual embedded pages is shaded in blue. Instead, the entire frameset is outlined in the Save As dialog box, as shown here:

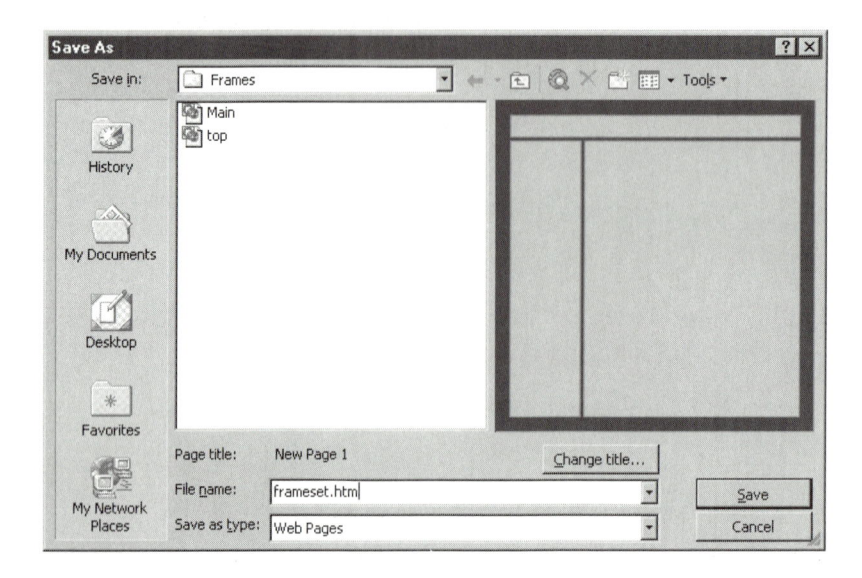

After you go through all this rigmarole once, you won't have to do it again for this frameset. From now on, when you click the Save button, FrontPage will automatically save changes to your frameset file and all your embedded pages.

Naming a Frameset

Web pages have *filenames* and they have titles. Page titles are important because they display in a browser window when a visitor comes to your Web site. FrontPage assigns the page title New Page1 (or New Page2, etc.) to pages as they are created. A sure sign of a novice Web designer (or one who has been up too late at night working on his or her site!) is a page named "Untitled Page."

Defining page titles can get a bit tricky when working with framed pages. That's because the page title that displays in a browser is the page title for the *frameset* page. So, you need to be sure to *define a title* for the frameset page. Here's how:

To Define a title for the frameset page:

1. In Page view, right-click in *any* frame within a frameset and choose Frame Properties from the context menu.

2. In the Frame Properties dialog box, click the Frames Page button. This opens the Page Properties dialog box for the *frameset* HTML page.

3. Click the General tab in the Page Properties dialog box, and enter a page title in the Title area. Then, click OK to return to the Frame Properties dialog box. Click OK once more.

4. Save your frameset (click the Save button) to save the frameset page with a title.

Editing Framed Page Content

After you create or add pages to your frame set, you can edit them just like you edit a page that isn't in a frameset. Enter or edit text, add pictures, format your page content, or add links. You can also define page properties separately for each page. To do this, right-click within the page, and choose Page Properties from the context menu.

The main thing to keep in mind when you add and format page content is that framed pages *aren't as big* as full-sized pages. So you should try to include *less* content in a framed page than you normally would.

CHANGING FRAME PROPERTIES

Frame properties include the relative size of each frame within the frameset. You can change the size of frames in FrontPage, *and*, you can allow *visitors* to resize frames right in their browser window.

You can define the kind of border that will be displayed between frames. You can go with the "borderless" frame look, creating a smooth, clean page appearance. Or, you can define a visible border. You can also elect to include or hide scrollbars in each particular frame.

RESIZING A FRAME

Even if you elect to allow visitors to resize frames in their browser window, you still need to decide how wide (or high) to make each frame when the frameset page *initially* opens. If one of your frames has navigation links, you'll want that frame to be smaller than the main frame that displays site content.

Because visitors will see your framed pages in different size browser windows, experiment by viewing your frameset in different sized browser windows yourself, before finalizing the size of your frames.

To change the relative size of frames within a frameset, click and drag on the border between frames, as shown in Figure 8-7.

A more exact way to define the size of frames is to use the Frame Properties dialog box. When you size a frame in the Frame Properties dialog box, you have three choices on how to define frame width or height:

- ▶ **Percent** Defines a frame as a percent of the total browser window. So, for example, if you elect to make a side navigational frame 15%, it would fill 15% of the browser window, leaving 85% for other windows.

- ▶ **Pixels** Defines frame height or width exactly and absolutely. (*Pixels* are the tiny dots that make up a monitor screen.)

- ▶ **Relative sizing** Defines frame height or width in relation to other frames in the same frameset. So, for example, if one framed page has a relative width of 2 and another framed page has a relative width of 3, the framed page with a relative width of 3 will be 50% wider than the framed page with a relative width of 2.

FIGURE 8-7
Resizing frames

Click and drag this double-headed arrow to resize frames

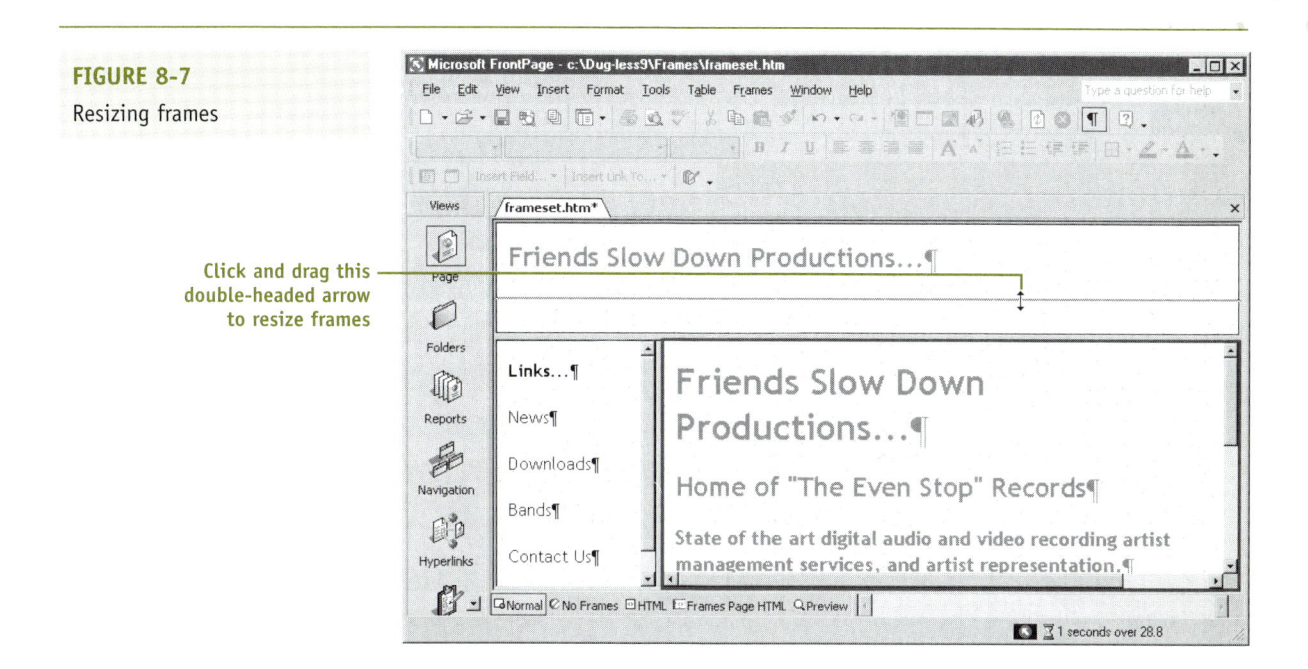

To Assign SIZING TO FRAMED PAGES:

1 Click inside the framed page that you want to resize.

2 From the menu bar, choose Frames | Frame Properties.

3 In the Frame Properties dialog box, choose Relative, Percent, or Pixels for the Width, and enter a value.

4 Choose Relative, Percent, or Pixels for the Height, and enter a value.

5 Click OK to close the Frame Properties dialog box and resize the framed page. You can define sizing for each frame in your frameset individually this way.

DEFINING FRAMESET MARGINS

The margins within each frame provide buffering between the contents of the frame and the edge of the frame. Frame content looks ugly when it bumps up against the edge of a frameset, so page designers usually create spacing of at least 3–6 pixels between content and the edge of the frame.

To Define MARGINS FOR A FRAMED PAGE:

1 Click inside the framed page that you want to resize.

2 From the menu bar, choose Frames | Frame Properties.

3 In the Frame Properties dialog box, enter values in the Height and Width margins spin boxes.

4 Click OK to close the Frame Properties dialog box.

MAKING A FRAMED PAGE RESIZABLE

If you want, you can allow visitors to resize frames in their browsers. In Figure 8-8, the divider between frames is being moved in Internet Explorer. You can also define whether to display a scrollbar in a frame.

FIGURE 8-8
Resizing a frame in a browser

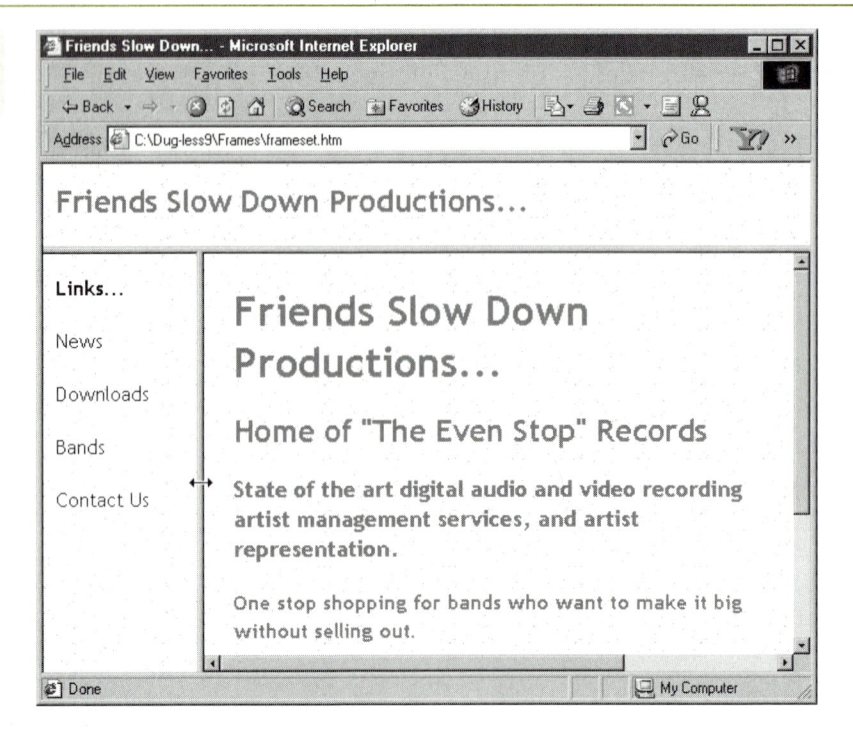

To Define a frame as resizable in a browser and define scrollbar properties:

1 Click inside the framed page that you want to resize.

2 From the menu bar, choose Frames | Frame Properties.

3 In the Frame Properties dialog box, select the Resizable in Browser check box to allow visitors to change the size of frames in their browsers.

4 From the Show Scrollbars drop-down list, choose Always to display a scrollbar always, Never to hide the scrollbar always, or If Needed to display a scrollbar only if the entire frame is not already visible in the browser window.

5 When you have defined resizing and scrollbars for your selected framed page, click OK.

Splitting or Deleting Frames

You can change the layout of a frameset by splitting an existing frame or deleting a frame. Splitting a frame creates a new frame. To split a frame, first click in the frame. Choose Frames | Split Frame from the menu bar to open the Split Frame dialog box. Then choose either the Split into Columns or Split into Rows radio button and click OK in the Split Frames dialog box.

To delete a framed page from a frameset, click in the page, and choose Frames | Delete Frame.

> **WARNING** There is no dialog box or "OK" message for deleting a frame from a frameset! Once you choose Frames | Delete Frame from the menu, the selected frame is a goner. You can, luckily, restore the framed page to the frameset by choosing Edit | Undo Delete Frame.

Providing No Frame Options

As the years rush past, the world changes: We add more candles to our cakes, throw away our bathroom scales, and get stronger eyeglasses. The good news is that while all this is going on, more and more Web browsers support frames.

In the olden days of Internet Explorer 3 and before, it was critical to design pages that could be interpreted by browsers with or without frame capability. Because browsers of version 4 and newer support frames, the need for a "no frames" option is less critical.

CHAPTER 8
USING FRAMES

Still, some new generation Web browsers, like the ones promised for cell phones and watches, may not support frames. So it's still important to provide a "no frames" option for your framed page.

Visitors who come to your page with a browser that doesn't support frames will see the content you create using the No Frames tab in Page view. Click on that tab, shown in Figure 8-9 and create a page that will be viewed by frameless browsers.

The content that displays in browsers that don't support frames is edited in the No Frames tab of Page view. This No Frames tab is only available when you are working on a frameset. Edit the No Frames page the same way you would as you would any page. When you save your frames page, the No Frames page will save as well.

FRAMES AND LINKS

Much of the point of creating framed pages is so one frame can link to another frame. This involves assigning not only a *link*, but a *target frame* for that link. FrontPage makes this easy. As long as you created your frameset using one of the many Frame page templates, default linking is assigned by FrontPage so that navigation frames (like the top or side frames) open links in the main frame (the larger frame).

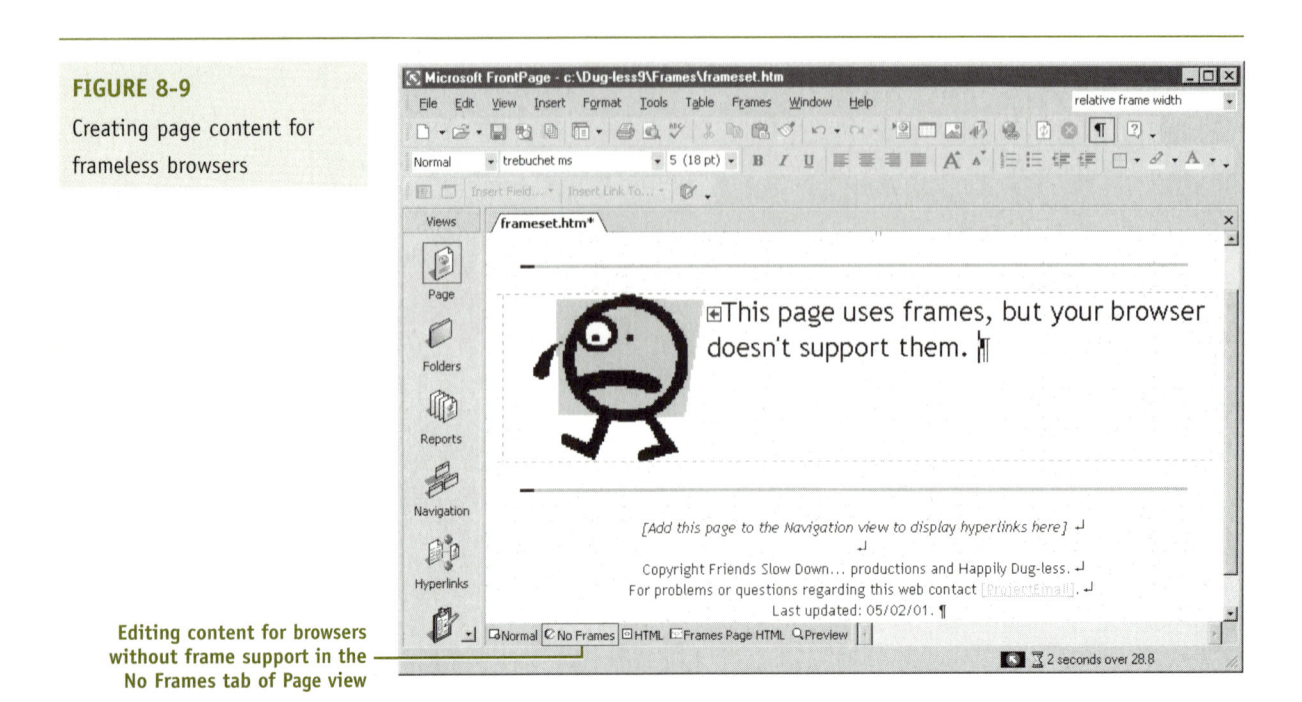

FIGURE 8-9

Creating page content for frameless browsers

Editing content for browsers without frame support in the No Frames tab of Page view

Normally, it is not necessary to define a target frame for framed page links—FrontPage handles this for you. However, for troubleshooting purposes, and in order to understand how links work in frames, follow these steps:

To Assign a link to text or a picture in a navigation (side or top) frame:

1. Select text or a picture in a navigation frame.

2. Click the Insert Hyperlink tool in the Standard toolbar to open the Insert Hyperlink dialog box.

3. In the Insert Hyperlink dialog box, choose a link for the selected text.

4. Click the Target Frame button.

5. The default target for frame links will be the main, or largest, frame within the frameset—this is defined by FrontPage. This illustration shows the Main frame as the target frame for the defined link.

6. You can change the target frame by clicking any section of figure in the Current Frames Page area of the Target Frame dialog box.

7. Click OK in the Target Frame dialog box when you have examined (or changed) the link target.

8. Click OK in the Insert Hyperlink dialog box.

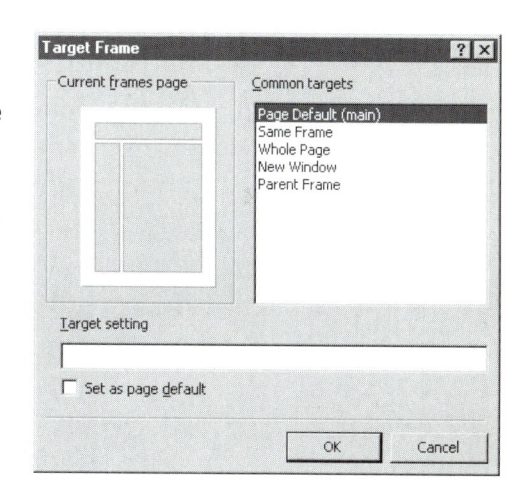

After you define framed page links, resave your frameset. This will update links in your saved page.

Inline Frames

Inline frames are a new feature of FrontPage 2002. They work like regular frames *except* they can be *right in the middle* of a regular page. Inline frames don't work too well in Internet Explorer, and they don't work at all in Netscape Navigator 4.7.

To create an inline frame *within a regular Web page*, choose Insert | Inline Frame from the menu bar. As with regular frames, use the Set an Initial Page or New Page buttons to define the content of the embedded frame.

Chapter 8
Using Frames

After you define frame content, click outside of your new inline frame. Select it again by clicking its border. You'll see side and corner handles that can be used to resize the inline frame. To move the inline frame, click and drag the frame from the *middle* of the inline frame.

Save your open Web page to save the embedded inline frame. Inline frames come with scrollbars when viewed in a browser window.

If you want to live dangerously, feel free to create an inline frame. Perhaps a next generation of browsers will interpret them more reliably than the current ones.

Sizing Up Frames

Frames are kind of a love 'em or hate 'em thing. They can be a useful and even attractive way to establish a consistent navigation interface in a small top or side frame, while presenting site content in a main frame. Or, they can clutter up a page with annoying scrollbars, borders, and chaos. Use your judgment, but try to apply the "less is more" principle when designing with frames. It's rare that a page with more than two framed pages looks good.

As noted in the previous chapter, shared borders and framed pages are *similar* ways to achieve the same effect. Therefore, you will almost always want to avoid *mixing* both frames and shared borders in a Web site.

In the next chapter, you'll look at another tool for establishing a global look and feel for Web sites—FrontPage themes. And you'll learn to create *your own* custom themes.

> **ON THE VIRTUAL CLASSROOM CD-ROM** In Lesson 6, "Working with Frames," I demonstrate how to create framed pages, including how to define links that open content in a main frame. The lesson demonstrates how to start with one of FrontPage's many Frame page templates, and modify it to create your own desired frame layout. The lesson includes "dos and don'ts" for frame use.

9

Creating Your Own Themes

FrontPage 2002 comes with a collection of a few dozen themes. Each theme applies its own distinctive set of colors, fonts, and graphical elements to your site. Themes are a great way to create a global look and feel to a *lot* of Web pages in a hurry. Within minutes, your site can change character from Bold Stripes to Poetic, or from Industrial to Nature.

CHAPTER 9
CREATING YOUR OWN THEMES

FIGURE 9-1

What a difference a theme makes...

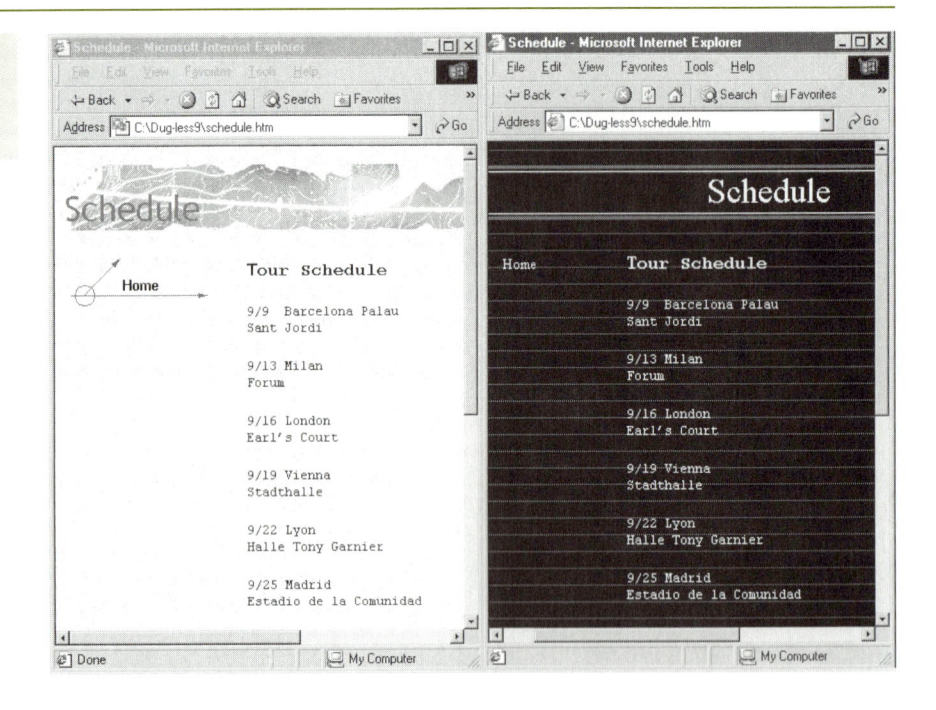

Figure 9-1 gives a sense of how much difference a theme can make. The exact same content makes a different "statement" depending on how it is presented. The page on the left has the Topo theme applied, whereas the page on the right has the Refined theme.

Note the differences between the two themes: Page backgrounds, text font, text color, navigation links, page titles, heading styles, and icons (like the title bar background and the navigation links) all contribute to create a different effect on each page.

USING FRONTPAGE THEMES

FrontPage themes include many different elements that can appear on every page in a Web site. Themes define what colors are applied to fonts in your Web site and what graphics files are used for horizontal rules and bullets

Themes define navigation icons like the graphic used for navigation buttons in link bars, the picture that goes behind a page title, and the image that can be tiled (repeated) as the page background. Themes also tell FrontPage how to

FIGURE 9-2

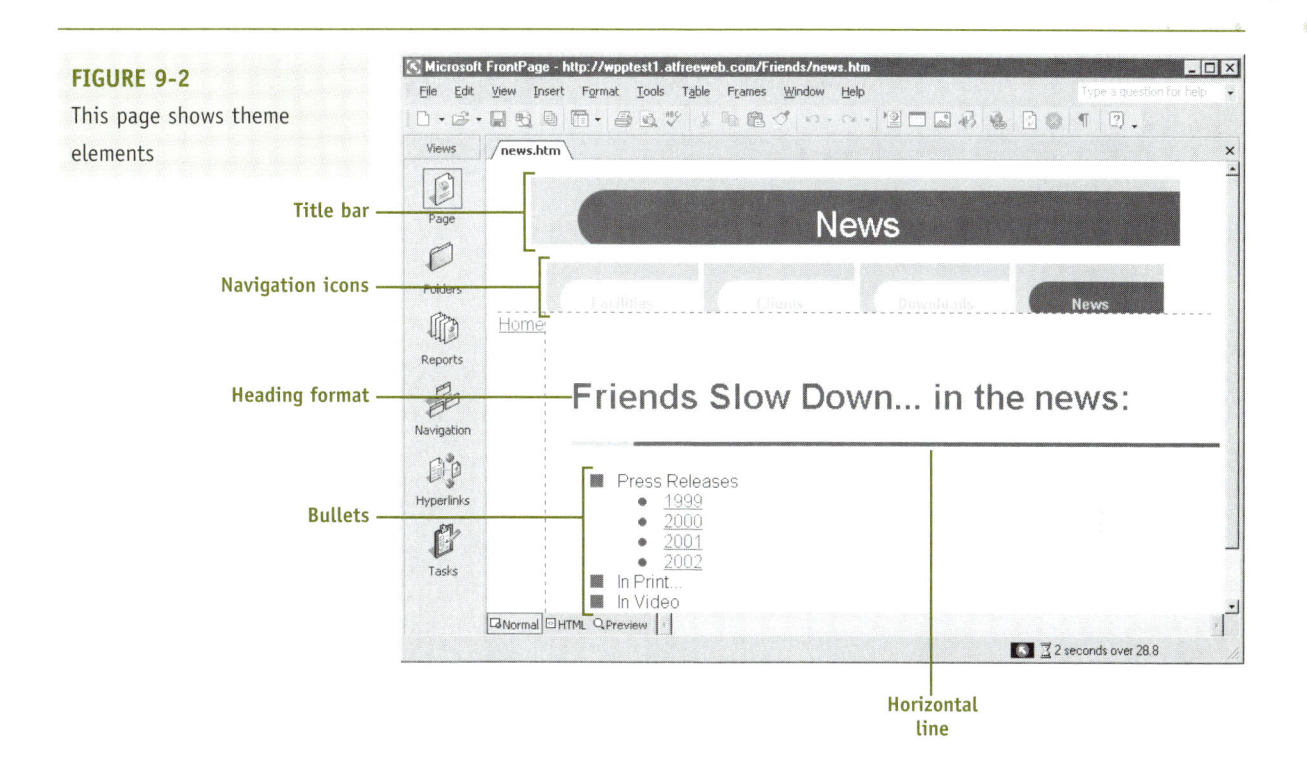

This page shows theme elements

Labels: Title bar, Navigation icons, Heading format, Bullets, Horizontal line

format text for headings (assigned in the Style drop-down list in the Format toolbar), text colors, and link colors. Figure 9-2 shows a page in Page view with many theme elements.

Assigning a Theme to a Web Site

In Chapter 1, you briefly explored how to attach a theme to your Web site. You'll walk through that process in a little more detail in this chapter. And, before you're done, you'll learn how to create your own *unique* themes.

You can assign a theme to either an entire Web site from anywhere in FrontPage. You just have to have your Web site open.

To Assign a Theme to a Web site:

1 From any view in FrontPage (with your site open), choose Format | Theme. The Themes dialog box appears, as shown on the next page.

CHAPTER 9
CREATING YOUR OWN THEMES

2 Because you are defining a theme for your entire Web site, click the All Pages options button.

3 Click a theme in the list on the left side of the Themes dialog box. As you do, the theme will preview in the large Sample of Theme area on the right side of the dialog box. Feel free to explore the entire set of themes.

4 When you find a Theme you like, click OK. Then, take a look in the left side of the FrontPage Status bar at the bottom of the page. After you choose a theme, you'll see FrontPage hard at work creating files. After files are created, you can see the effect of your chosen theme by opening a page in Page view.

> **NOTE** If you have a page open in Page view, or have a page or pages selected in Folders another view, you'll have the option of applying a theme to just the selected page(s). You'll explore this process in the next section of this chapter.

> **NOTE** The Themes dialog box also includes four check boxes that allow you to alter your theme. You'll take a look at how these check boxes operate in the section "Tweaking FrontPage Themes with Check Boxes" a bit later in this chapter.

USING A THEME ON JUST ONE PAGE

Usually you'll want to apply a theme to an entire Web site, because the point is to create a global look and feel for your site with common colors, fonts, navigation icons, page backgrounds and so on.

Sometimes I elect to remove a theme from just one page in the site. For example, if I have a page that displays a large photograph, I might want to strip away the page background and other features associated with the theme to create more freedom to design a custom page within my site. Or, sometimes I will have a page that for one reason or another I *don't* want to appear to be part of the Web site. In that case as well, I might remove the theme from a page or assign a separate theme to that one page.

To Apply a theme to just one page or to selected pages:

1. Either open a page in Page view, or use CTRL+click to choose several pages in the Folder List.

2. Choose Format | Theme. The Themes dialog box appears.

3. Since you are defining a theme for *just the selected page(s)*, click the Selected Pages options button.

4. Choose a theme in the list on the left side of the Themes dialog box. You can remove a theme from selected page(s) by choosing No Theme from the list.

5. Click OK in the Themes dialog box.

Looking at FrontPage Theme Files

When you assign a theme to your Web site, FrontPage creates many files on your Web site to add navigation graphics, background images, font formatting instructions, and other features. FrontPage stores these files in a folder called _themes.

These files *do* take up considerable Web site space! You can see them if you display hidden folders on your Web site.

To Display hidden folders and explore files in your FrontPage theme:

1. Choose Tools | Web Settings to open the Web Settings dialog box.

2. Click the Advanced tab in the Web Settings dialog box, and select the Show Hidden Files and Folders check box, as shown next.

CHAPTER 9
CREATING YOUR OWN THEMES

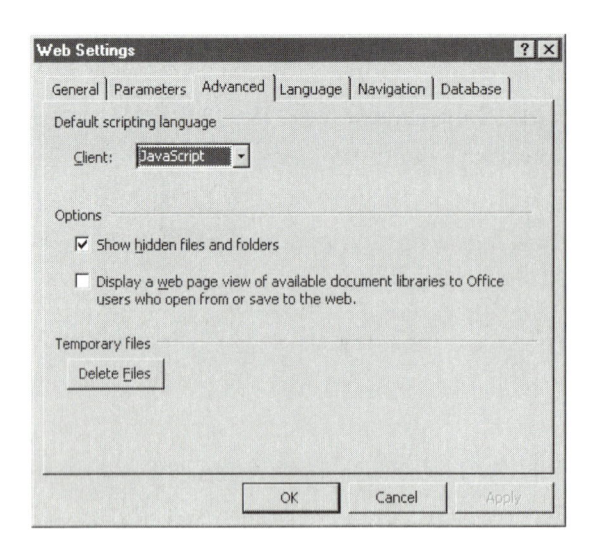

3 Click OK to close the Web Settings dialog box.

4 Choose Folders view from the Views bar.

5 Double-click the _themes folder to display sub-folders. Each theme you assign to a page creates it's own folder. If you have just one theme assigned to your site, you'll see one folder here.

6 To examine files in a Theme folder, double-click a subfolder for the theme.

> **TIP** If your View list is not available, choose View | Views bar.

> **NOTE** Theme folder names are similar to theme names. For example, if you assign the Bold Stripes theme, the folder name is boldstri. Folder names are constrained to eight characters to make them compatible with all Web servers.

You can examine the files created by your theme in Folders view. Files with a .gif or .jpg extension are picture files used in your pages. Files with .css filename extensions are called *Cascading Style Sheet* files in Web terminology and instruct your site on what fonts, sizes, and colors to assign to text in your pages.

TWEAKING FRONTPAGE THEMES WITH CHECK BOXES

Every FrontPage theme comes with three check boxes that allow you to *alter* how that theme looks, plus a check box that defines what kinds of files are generated for your theme.

To Change your theme:

1 Choose Format | Theme. The Theme dialog box appears, and you can elect to change the theme either for selected page(s), or for the whole Web site.

2 To apply a more extreme set of colors, with higher color contrast, click the Vivid Colors check box in the Themes dialog box.

3 To create navigation buttons that react to a visitor's actions, click the Active Graphics check box.

4 Use the Background Picture check box to attach a tiled background image to your theme.

5 As you apply Vivid colors, Active graphics, or a Background image, the changes display in the Sample of Theme area of the Theme dialog box. You can experiment with different combinations of features. The Sample of Theme area cannot fully display the effect of applying Active Graphics—you can only see all the Active Graphics effects when you test your page in a browser (or in the Preview tab of Page view). When you find a combination of features, click OK to apply the theme.

> **NOTE** Active graphics have three states: *Normal* (before a visitor points to or clicks on them), *Hovered* (that displays when a visitor points his or her mouse at a button), and *Selected* (that displays when the button is clicked).

> **NOTE** Background images *tile*—repeat themselves—so they fill all the available space in a browser window. Tiled pictures reduce download time because they are small, and they fill the *entire* page background because they repeat indefinitely as needed to fill the page.

In addition to the three check boxes that apply different effects to your theme, there is a fourth check box in the Themes dialog box. The Apply Theme Using CSS check box creates additional files for your theme that are supposed to make your theme compatible with a wider variety of browsers. My discussions with Microsoft and my own experiments have failed to convince me that this check box actually has any effect on how browsers interpret a theme.

Creating Your Own FrontPage Themes

If your goal is a truly unique Web site, customizing your theme with the three check boxes in the Themes dialog box won't really satisfy you. If you want to create a completely new theme, I'll show you how in this section of the book.

CHAPTER 9
CREATING YOUR OWN THEMES

Oddly enough, there is no Create a New Theme option in FrontPage. The process is that you modify an existing theme, and then resave it with a new name. From then on, that theme is yours, and you can create a truly custom look and feel for your site.

To Create AND SAVE A NEW THEME:

1 With your Web site open, choose Format | Theme to open the Theme dialog box.

2 With any theme selected in the list on the left side of the dialog box, click the Modify button in the Themes dialog box.

3 Click the Save As button that is now visible in the Themes dialog box. The Save Theme dialog box appears.

4 Enter a new name for your theme, as shown here:

5 Click OK in the Save Theme dialog box. You have a custom theme, but *don't stop now*. Before you click OK in the Themes dialog box, define the colors, text, and images for your custom theme. You'll walk through that process in the following sections.

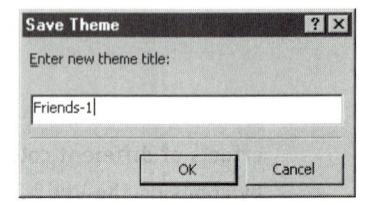

All the processes you explore in the following sections require that you use the Modify button in the Themes dialog box to display the Colors, Graphics, and Text buttons.

CHANGING THEME COLORS

The easiest way to change the look and feel of your custom theme is to change the color scheme. FrontPage lets you do this three different ways: You can choose from a large selection of color schemes, you can choose a custom color scheme, or you can assign specific colors to each element of your theme.

Changing theme colors does *not* change the coloring of the *graphics* used in your theme. Creating custom graphics is a separate process that you'll explore later in this chapter.

> **NOTE** An add-in product called *FrontLook* has a component called the Theme Chameleon that changes the colors of graphics that come with FrontPage themes. For more information on FrontLook and other FrontPage add-ins, check out the FrontPage Resources area of my Web site at www.ppinet.com.

Choosing a Color Scheme

You can create a distinctive look for your site by choosing from one of dozens of color schemes that come with FrontPage. These color schemes apply a set of five aesthetically matched colors to the text and page backgrounds in your site.

If you plan to apply a color scheme to your page background, you need to deselect the Background Picture check box in the Themes dialog box. Otherwise the tiled background picture will overwrite your page background color.

To Change the color scheme in your custom theme:

1. If you aren't already in the Theme dialog box, choose Format | Theme to open the Themes dialog box. Select the theme you are customizing, and click the Modify button in the Themes dialog box.

2. Click the Colors button to display the Modify Themes dialog box.

3. In the Color Schemes tab of the Modify Theme dialog box, experiment with the effects of different color schemes. These sets of colors can be applied differently by choosing the Vivid Colors options button.

4. After you apply a color scheme, click OK to close the Modify Theme dialog box. This returns you to the Themes dialog box.

5. Click the Save button in the Themes dialog box to save changes to your custom Theme. Or, click Save As to save the modified theme as a *new* theme.

6. You can click OK to close the Themes dialog box, or leave the dialog box open to further modify your theme.

Using the Color Wheel to Define Theme Colors

In addition to the set of color schemes that come with FrontPage, you can define your own color scheme for a theme. The Color Wheel tab in the Modify Theme dialog box allows you to generate your own five-color color scheme.

CHAPTER 9
CREATING YOUR OWN THEMES

To Create YOUR OWN COLOR SCHEME:

1 If you aren't already in the Theme dialog box, choose Format | Theme to open the Themes dialog box. Select the theme you are customizing, and click the Modify button.

2 Click the Colors button to display the Modify Themes dialog box.

3 Click the Color Wheel tab of the Modify Theme dialog box.

4 Click in the Color Wheel to choose a base color for your custom five-color set of colors, as shown in Figure 9-3.

5 Use the Brightness slider at the bottom of the dialog box to adjust the brightness of your color scheme.

6 The Normal Colors and Vivid Colors option buttons in the Modify Theme dialog show how your color scheme will look with either option applied.

7 When you have generated a custom color scheme you like, click OK to return to the Themes dialog box.

8 Click the Save button to resave your custom theme with your new color scheme. Or, click Save As and save your changed theme as a new theme.

9 You can click OK to close the Themes dialog box, or leave the dialog box open to further modify your theme.

FIGURE 9-3
Creating a custom color scheme

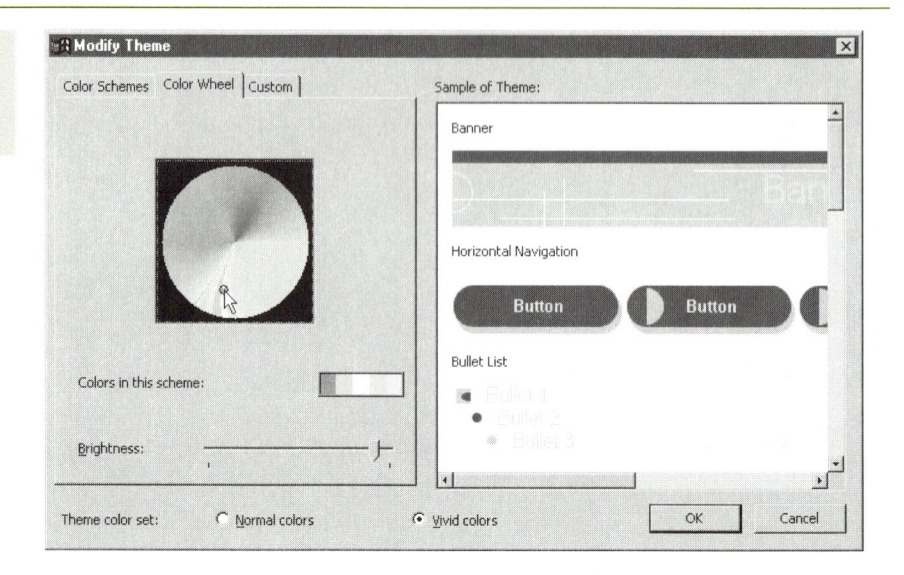

Customizing Theme Colors

If you want *maximum* control over theme colors, you can define specific colors for these elements of your theme:

- ▶ **Page background** The background color for Web pages.
- ▶ **Banner text** The color of text that appears on page banners at the top of pages.
- ▶ **Body** The color of most text on your pages that has the Normal style applied from the Style drop-down list in the Formatting menu.
- ▶ **Heading 1–Heading 6** The color of the six different heading styles available from the Style drop-down list in the Formatting menu.
- ▶ **Hyperlink active, followed, and hyperlinks** Colors for links that are being clicked, have already been clicked, or are unclicked.
- ▶ **Navigation text** Colors for text that appears in generated navigation buttons.
- ▶ **Table border** The color applied by default to table borders.

To Define custom colors for specific theme elements:

1. If you aren't already in the Theme dialog box, choose Format | Theme to open the Themes dialog box. Select the theme you are customizing, and click the Modify button in the Themes dialog box.

2. Click the Colors button to display the Modify Themes dialog box.

3. Click the Custom tab of the Modify Theme dialog box.

4. Use the Item list to select one of the theme elements to which you will assign a color.

5. Use the Color palette to choose a color for the selected theme element.

6. Use the Normal and Vivid Colors options buttons to define separate colors for each option for the selected element.

7. Define colors for additional theme elements, and then click OK.

CHAPTER 9
CREATING YOUR OWN THEMES

8 Use the Save button to resave the modified theme, or use the Resave button to create a new custom theme.

9 You can click OK to close the Themes dialog box, or leave the dialog box open to further modify your theme.

CREATING YOUR OWN THEME GRAPHICS

FrontPage themes supply images for bullets, horizontal lines, page backgrounds, page title banners, and buttons. If you're going to use custom graphics in your theme, the first step is to acquire some Web graphics.

If you are so inclined, you can *create* those pictures using a graphics design program. You can create these images in PhotoShop, PhotoPaint, PaintShop Pro, or even, if you're on a tight budget, the Paint program that comes with Windows. Much as I'd love to digress into a whole exploration of creating Web graphics, I can't. You'll find a large selection of books devoted to creating Web graphics at your favorite computer book store. Or, you can use someone else's Web graphics. A few sources for free, online Web graphics are

- **ABC Graphics** http://www.abcgiant.com/
- **Jelane's Free Web Graphics** http://www.erinet.com/jelane/
- **Free Web Graphics by Lauren** http://www.aureva.com/freegraphics/

Or, do a search for "web graphics" and see what's available on the Web.

Graphics You Need to Create a Complete FrontPage Theme

Depending on whether or not you apply Active Graphics, FrontPage themes use between 20–30 different picture files. Not every site uses every all these picture files. For example you might not use horizontal lines in your site. So you might not need to create or acquire *all* the picture files in the following list. But if you want a *full* set of theme picture files, you'll need all of them.

As you accumulate Web graphics for your custom theme, here are the ones you will need for a full set of theme pictures:

- Background Picture
- Banner
- List Bullet (3)
- Horizontal Navigation Buttons (3)
- Global Navigation
- Horizontal Navigation Buttons (3)
- Horizontal Rule
- Quick Back buttons (3)
- Quick Home buttons (3)
- Quick Next buttons (3)
- Quick Up buttons (3)
- Vertical Navigation buttons (3)

When you create or acquire theme pictures, *don't* use pictures that already have text on them. For example, *don't* get a Home button that says "Home." Instead, choose an image with no text. FrontPage will supply the text for each theme graphic.

Attaching Your Own Images to a Theme

Got a whole set of theme image files stashed away in a folder on your computer? If so, you're ready to assign them to your theme.

To Attach graphics to your theme:

1. If you aren't already in the Theme dialog box, choose Format | Theme to open the Themes dialog box. Select the theme you are customizing, and click the Modify button in the Themes dialog box.

2. Click the Graphics button to display the Modify Themes dialog box.

3. Use the Item drop-down list to choose a theme element.

4. Use the Browse button to open the Open File dialog box. Browse to locate a picture file, and click OK in the Open File dialog box. The new image will display in the Sample of Theme area of the Modify Theme dialog box.

5. Click the Font tab in the Modify Theme dialog box, and define a font, font Style, and alignment, as shown in Figure 9-4.

6. Use the Active Graphics and Normal Graphics options buttons to assign separate, or the same graphics to alternate ways of presenting your theme.

CHAPTER 9
CREATING YOUR OWN THEMES

FIGURE 9-4
Defining a page banner with a custom image, and customized fonts

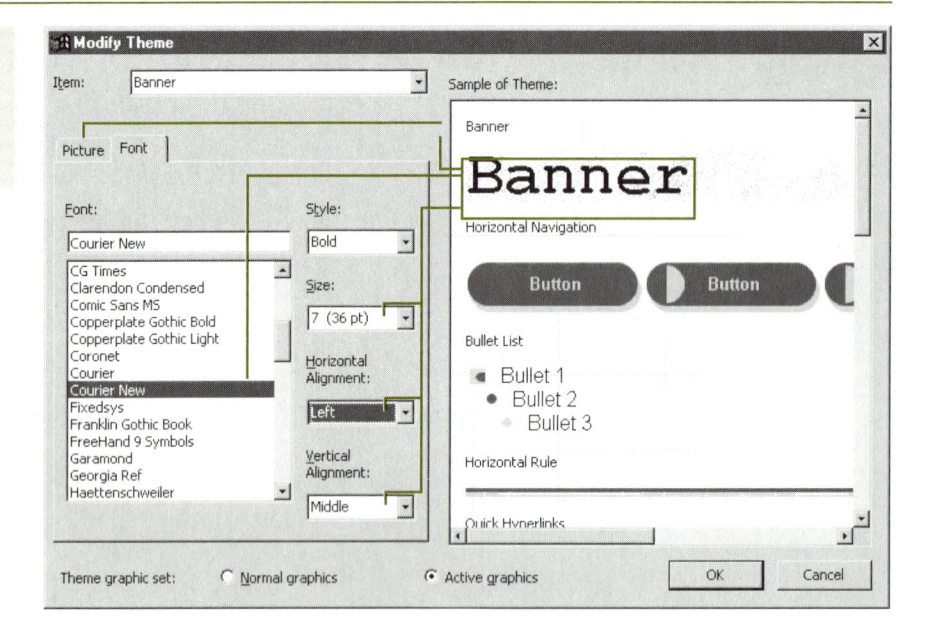

7 Use the Item drop-down list to select additional theme elements. Not all theme graphics have text associated with them, so some elements will have all the options in the Font tab grayed out. Define additional theme elements by assigning image files and (where appropriate) by defining text formatting.

8 After you customize your theme graphics, click the OK button to close the Modify Theme dialog box.

9 Use the Save button to resave your theme, or use the Save As button to create a new theme.

10 You can click OK to close the Themes dialog box, or leave the dialog box open to further modify your theme.

FORMATTING THEME TEXT

Themes control the font size, type, attributes (like boldface), and color for the styles available in the Style drop-down menu in the Formatting toolbar. These *styles*, like Body, Heading 1, Heading 2, and so on, can be applied to any text on a page. In addition, the three Hyperlinks styles are *automatically* applied when you create links. Click the Text button in the Modify area of the Themes dialog box to define text fonts for any HTML style.

To Define TEXT FORMATTING FOR STYLES:

1 If you aren't already in the Theme dialog box, choose Format | Theme to open the Themes dialog box. Select the theme you are customizing, and click the Modify button in the Themes dialog box.

2 Click the Text button to display the Modify Themes dialog box.

3 If all you want to do is change the *font* assigned to either Body text, or a Heading style, choose a style from the Item list, and select a font from the Font list, as shown in Figure 9-5.

4 To assign more text attributes to a style, click the More Text Styles button. The Style dialog box appears.

5 Click the style you are defining in the list in the Style dialog box. In the list in the Style dialog box, h1 = Heading 1, h2 = Heading 2, and so on.

> **NOTE** Fonts display depends on the fonts installed on your *visitor's* system. So avoid fonts that might not be available on other computers. Arial, Courier, and Times Roman are the most widely supported fonts. If you get adventurous and use other fonts, Web browsers will substitute fonts when necessary.

FIGURE 9-5
Assigning Courier New font to the Body style

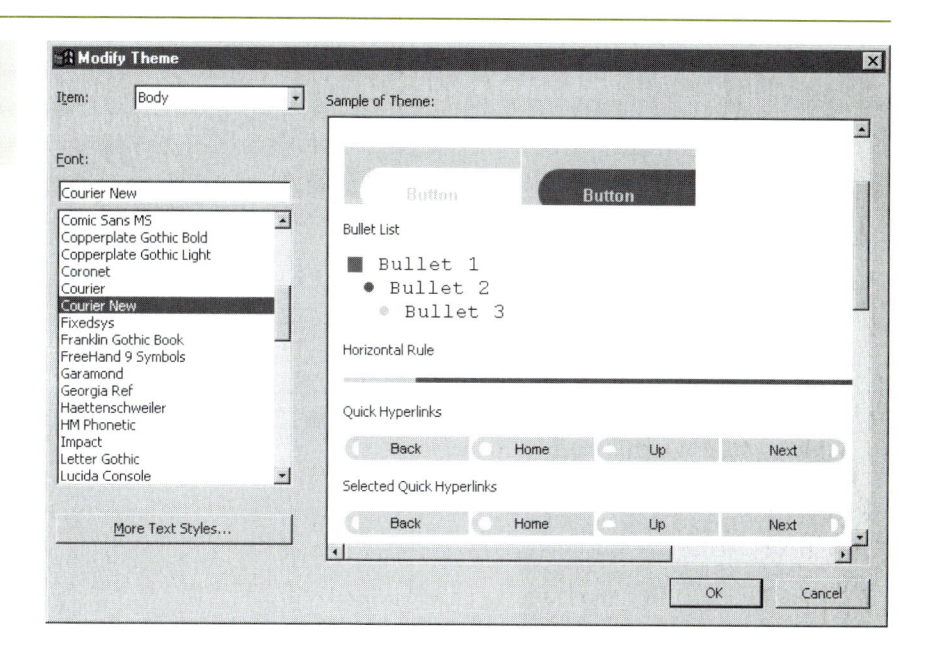

CHAPTER 9
CREATING YOUR OWN THEMES

6 Click the Modify button in the Style dialog box to change the format for the selected style. The Modify Style dialog box appears.

7 Click the Format button. Five options display: Font, Paragraph, Border, Numbering, and Position. Each of these options opens a new dialog box that allows you to define different display elements for the font of your selected style.

8 After you finish applying formatting to your selected style, click OK to close the Modify Style dialog box.

> **NOTE** In addition to defining how these standard styles will appear, it is possible to define additional styles as well. That process is beyond the scope of this book. Normally, there's not much advantage to creating styles beyond the six headings and body style. Defining those styles provides you with seven styles you can apply to page content.

9 Click OK to close the Style dialog box. The new font attributes will be displayed in the Sample of Theme area of the Modify Theme dialog box. You can define additional styles if you want.

10 After you customize your styles, click OK to close the Modify Theme dialog box.

11 Use the Save button to resave your theme, or use the Save As button to create a new theme.

12 You can click OK to close the Themes dialog box, or leave the dialog box open to further modify your theme.

CUSTOM THEMES CREATE UNIQUE SITES

Themes are great for instantly assigning a coherent look to a site. But the drawback to themes is that there are only so many options in FrontPage. Jaded Web browsers will recognize the colors and icons in standard FrontPage themes. Solution: Create your own! In the course of this chapter, you learned to create a theme so unique that it will give your Web site a truly distinctive look and feel. You learned to assign your own color scheme and fonts to a theme and even how to attach a custom set of navigation buttons.

In the next chapter, you'll look at FrontPage Web Components. These are elements of FrontPage that can be used to create interactive and dynamic sites. Components include hover buttons that change colors when rolled over by a visitor's mouse, marquee text that moves around on your page, hit counters, and even news updates from Microsoft-affiliated news providers like MSNBC.

> **ON THE VIRTUAL CLASSROOM CD** In Lesson 7, "Creating Custom Themes," I demonstrate how to design custom Web themes using your own graphics, color scheme, and font selections. The lesson also demonstrates how FrontPage can generate a unique set of navigation icons based on your own pictures.

10

Using Web Components

Many of the best features of FrontPage are found by selecting Insert | Web Components from the menu. Web components range from hit counters (that count visits to a Web page) to embedded news headlines from guess which news networks—Microsoft's MSN, and MSNBC.

Chapter 10
Using Web Components

Web components range from useful and easy to install, to esoteric and confusing. In this book, you'll focus on the useful ones, with a quick introduction to the rest.

An Overview of FrontPage Components

FrontPage components can be thought of as little programs that you can place inside FrontPage Web pages. These hardworking "programmettes" do a variety of tasks. In addition to the previously mentioned hit counters and news modules, other components display photographs, generate an automatically updating table of contents, create dynamic navigation buttons, design rotating pictures, and cause text to scroll back and forth across your page.

How do Components Work?

We won't obsess over the programming behind FrontPage components, but it's helpful to understand generally how they work. Some components use HTML—the basic coding language of Web pages. Others use more complex programming languages like Java and JavaScript to work their magic.

The curious among us can use the HTML tab in Page view to see the coding used with various components. The rest of us will just enjoy being able to include all kinds of animation and interactivity on our pages without worrying about coding.

Many Components Are Scripts

As you examine different components, I'll note what scripting language is used to make them run. Does it matter? Not usually; components that rely on HTML are recognized by any browser. Components that use JavaScript are supported by Netscape Navigator version 2 and newer and Internet Explorer 3 and newer. Components that use Java—Hover Buttons and Banner Ad managers—work on most computers, but they put a lot of stress on a computer's processing capabilities, and can crash older, slower PCs.

FrontPage Extensions

It's also important to be aware that some Web components use files stored on *Web servers* in order to work. Specifically, some Web components require that your Web be published to a Web server with *FrontPage extensions*. These files are beyond your control—they are installed and maintained by the folks who run your server. Many servers do have FrontPage extensions installed, and FrontPage makes these files available free at its Web site to any server administrator.

If you are publishing your site to a Web server without FrontPage extension files, or if you are publishing to a Web on your hard drive, you won't be able to use Web components that require FrontPage extensions. The most useful Web components that require these files are the Web Search and Hit Counter components.

> **NOTE** If you want to include a search box or a hit counter on your site, you can find many free ones by searching the Internet. These free search boxes and hit counters work just fine in FrontPage, and come with instructions for easy installation. At this writing, you can find a good search box at www.freefind.com and a good counter at www.cybercount.com.

SharePoint Extensions

In addition to Web components that require FrontPage extensions, some Web components require servers that have another set of files installed called SharePoint extensions. These files, also provided by Microsoft, are necessary to use the List View and Document Library View components. Those two components are used to customize a special intranet site (used *within* an organization) that is included with Office XP. You'll examine some SharePoint components in Chapter 15.

Inserting Comments and Dates

Comments, timestamps, and position boxes are not exactly Web components—they act pretty much like Web components, so let's look at them here.

Comments are little notes to yourself or others on your development team. They appear visible in FrontPage Page view. Visitors who view your page in a browser will not see the comment unless they look at the source code of your page.

FrontPage's Date and Time codes automatically reflect when a page was last updated. Visitors find them helpful. An message saying that a page was updated recently suggests that there is *fresh* content. Especially if your site is one that caters to repeat visitors, an update message will encourage visitors to stick around.

Chapter 10
Using Web Components

Updating a Page with Timestamps

When I'm Web surfing, I often look for a little message telling me when a page was last updated. This tells me whether the information on the page is current, and, for sites I visit frequently, it tells me whether there's anything new since I visited last.

You can place a component on your pages that *automatically* inserts the date when a page was last updated. You can define this component to change when you hand-edit a page or when the page has been *automatically* updated.

Updating a page automatically means the inserted date will change not only when you open a page in Page view and save it, but also if any included content on the page changes. You'll explore included content components later in this chapter—examples include embedding a Web page within a Web page or a Table of Contents.

To Insert a date and time code:

1. In Page view, with a page open, choose Insert | Date and Time. The Date and Time Properties dialog box appears.

2. Select the Date this Page Was Last Edited radio button to display a new date when the page is opened and saved. Or, choose the Date this Page Was Updated Automatically to change the date when any component on the page changes.

3. Use the Date Format and Time Format drop-down lists to choose how you want to display the date and the time (if at all).

4. Click OK to insert the date and time code into your page.

5. In Page view, select the date and time code, and format it as you would any text.

6. You'll probably want to add some text before the timestamp, like "This page was last updated on...," as shown in Figure 10-1.

FIGURE 10-1
Date codes can be formatted like any text

Date code text is formatted like any other page text

Date code content is generated by the Date and Time dialog box

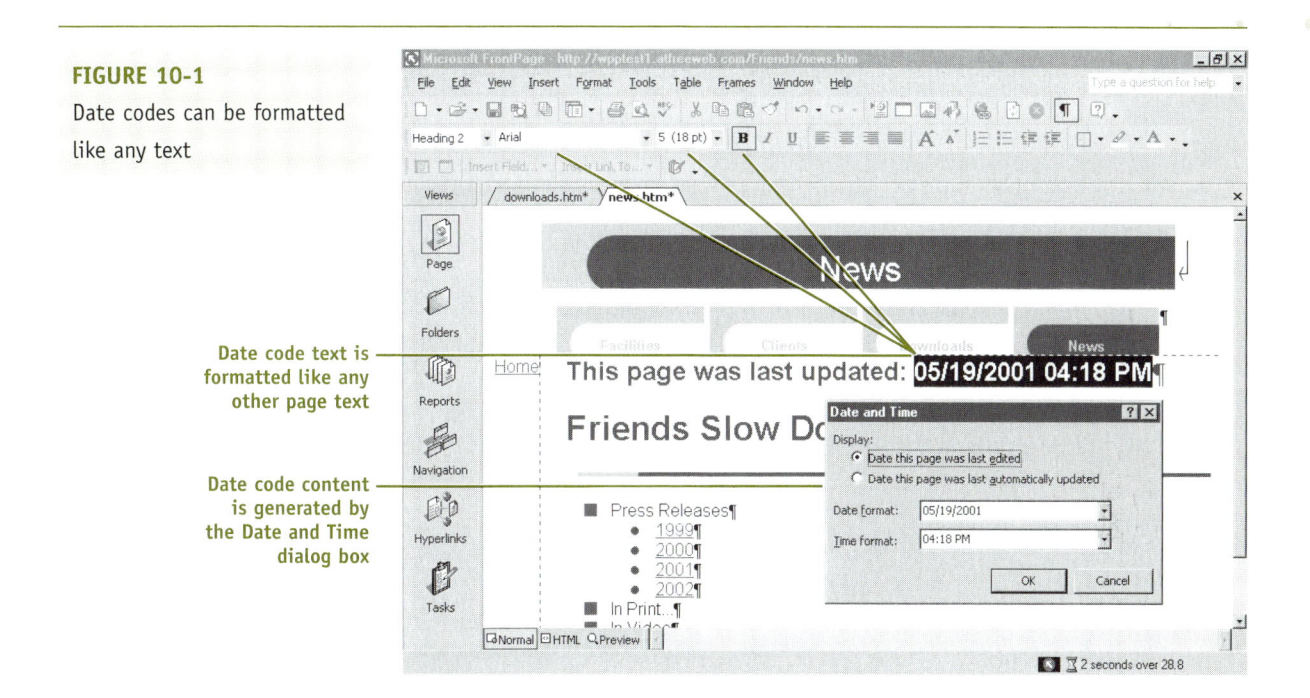

Adding Invisible Comments

Comments are useful for reminding yourself, or your collaborators, about changes you need to make to a Web page. You see them in FrontPage Page view, but not in a Web browser.

Even though comments are not visible in browsers, both Internet Explorer and Netscape Navigator have menu options that allow savvy users to look at the source code (the HTML and other coding languages) used in a page. Comments *are* readable when a visitor looks at your page's source code. So avoid placing information in comments that you don't want the public to see.

To Insert a comment in your page:

1 In Page view, with a Web page open, choose Insert | Comment. The Comment dialog box appears.

2 Type your comment in the Comment dialog box, as shown on the next page.

CHAPTER 10

USING WEB COMPONENTS

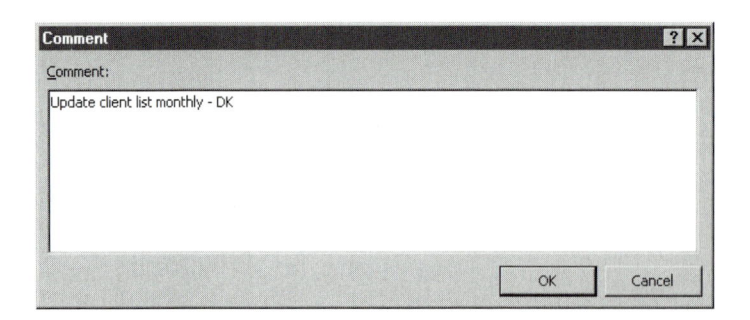

3 Click OK in the Comments dialog box to place your comment on the page. The comment will not be visible in the Preview tab of Page view, or in a browser window.

Dynamic Effects

Dynamic effects make your page more exciting. They add *active* elements to your page—text that moves around, buttons that glow when hovered over, and banners that display several different pictures, one at a time.

Hover buttons change when a visitor *hovers* his or her cursor over them in a browser. Text marquees present text that moves—usually back and forth—across the screen. And Banner Ad Web components rotate several pictures in one display box.

Hover Buttons

A Hover button adds real pizzazz to your site. Visitors who point to a button will see the button *change*. You can define that change using several built-in effects provided by FrontPage.

Hover buttons are controlled by Java programming language programs called *applets*. FrontPage will create these applets for you. The one thing to keep in mind is that Java applets are separate programs that are run on your *visitor's* computer. Too many of them can place untenable demands on a visitor's processor, and cause his or her computer to crash. So, use Hover buttons with restraint, and ask friends with slower, older computers to test your site.

To Place a Hover button on an open page in Page view:

1. Choose Insert | Web Component | Dynamic Effects.

2. In the Insert Web Component dialog box, click Hover Button, and click Finish. The Hover Button Properties dialog box will become visible.

3. In the Button Text area, enter text for the button.

4. Click the Font button to control the font, color, style, and size. After you define the font, click OK to close the Font dialog box and return to the Hover Button Properties dialog box.

5. In the Link To area, enter the Web page or file that that you want to define as the link for your button. You can either type a URL (Web page address) directly in the text box or use the Browse button to find a page.

6. Select a button color from the Button Color list. Here, you are defining the background color for the button before it is *hovered* over.

7. You can also choose a color from the Background Color list. This color is only operative if you assign an image as your button background using the Custom button in the dialog box. It defines a background that shows behind transparent GIF images.

8. Choose one of the effects for your button from the Effect list. These effects occur when a visitor hovers over your button.

9. Define an Effect Color. This is the color that is used to create your chosen effect.

10. In the Width area, define button width (in pixels).

11. In the Height area, define button height in pixels. After you enter text, define colors, and button size, you can click OK to see how your button looks before a visitor hovers over it. You can test the button by previewing your page in a browser (File | Preview in Browser, and choose a browser from the Preview in Browser dialog box).

> **NOTE** You'll want to experiment with different effects. Glow (and its slightly lower contrast Light Glow cousin) are the most frequently used, and work well. With the Glow effect, the middle of the button changes to the effect color. Other effects include Color Fill (the whole button changes color); Color Average (the whole button changes to a color in between the original color and the effect color); Reverse Glow (the middle of the button does not change color, but the outer edges change to the effect color); Bevel Out (adds a 3-D look); and Bevel In (a reverse 3-D effect).

CHAPTER 10
USING WEB COMPONENTS

12 To edit your Hover button, double-click it. The Hover button dialog box reappears, as shown here:

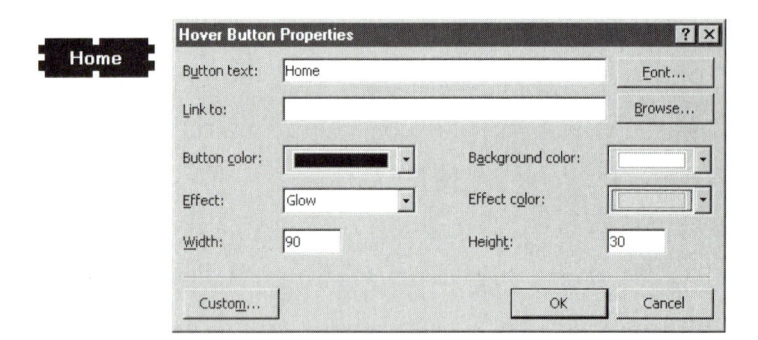

13 You can add background images and sound effects to your Hover button by clicking the Custom button in the Hover Button Properties dialog box. The Custom dialog box appears.

14 To add sound effects, use the browse button to navigate to files you have previously saved on your PC in the On Click and On Hover areas of the Custom dialog box. The On Click sound goes off when a visitor clicks your button, and the On Hover sound plays when the button is hovered over. (Sound files for Hover buttons must be AU sound file format.)

> **NOTE** You can find, download, and save AU file format sound files on the Web by searching for "AU sound files" or "free AU sound files."

15 Use the Button and On Hover areas in the bottom of the Custom dialog box to enter files to display as background images for the button, and the hovered button. Use the Browse buttons to navigate to files. This illustration shows custom sounds and background images defined for a Hover button.

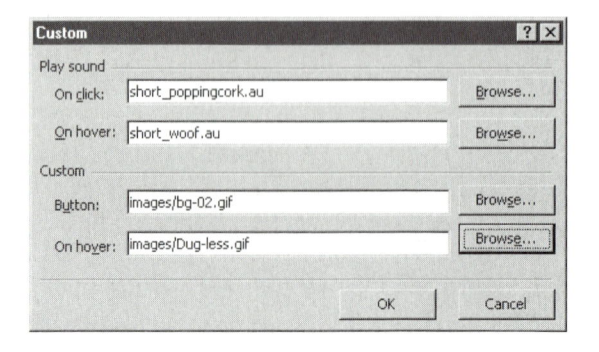

16 After you define custom attributes, click **OK** to close the Custom dialog box, and click **OK** again to close the Hover Button Properties dialog box.

After you define a Hover button, you can edit it by double-clicking it in Page view. You also can resize a Hover button right in Page view by selecting it, and clicking and dragging the side or corner handles.

A quick trick for creating a *set* of Hover buttons is to create *one*—with the effects, fonts, and colors you like, and then copy and paste it. Double-click in the cloned buttons to change the text; this creates a set of Hover buttons like the one in Figure 10-2.

MOVING TEXT IN MARQUEES

Have you had the fun of standing in a long line at the bank or post office lately? Okay, sorry I had to remind you of that experience, but you might have killed time by watching news or information scrolling across a video display sign. You can create scrolling text boxes in FrontPage that work in a similar way, generating boxes that display marquee (moving) text.

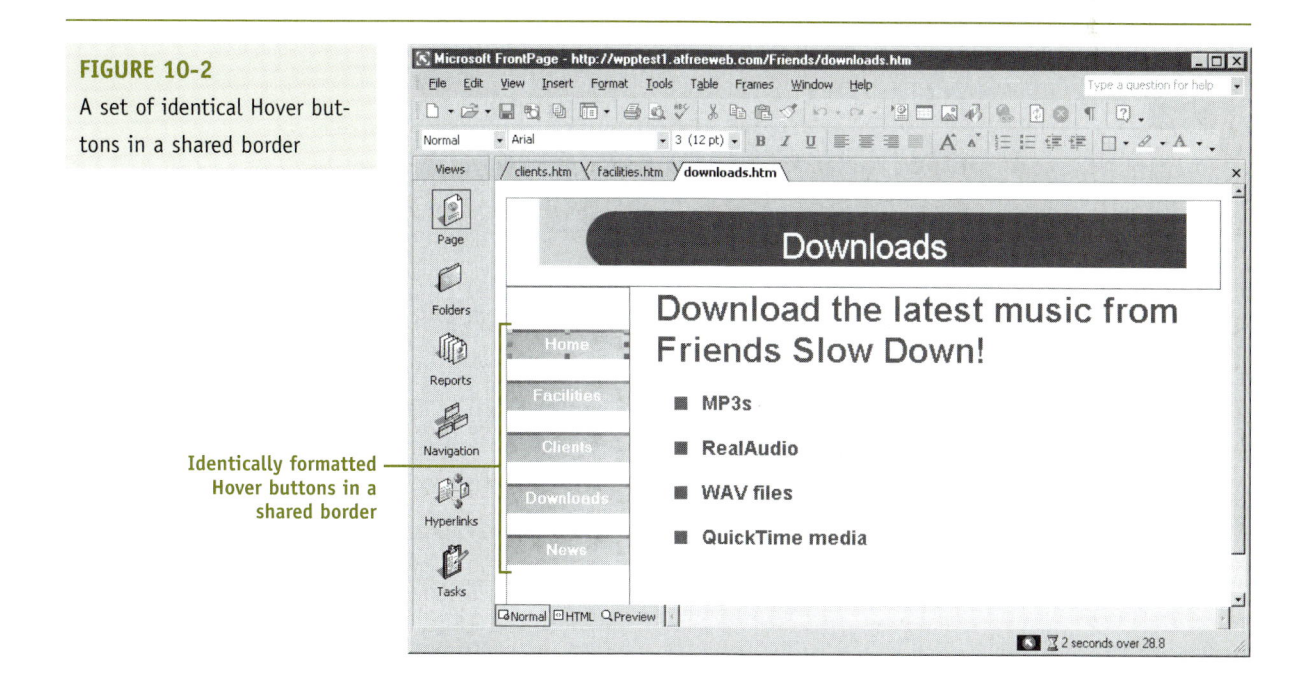

FIGURE 10-2
A set of identical Hover buttons in a shared border

CHAPTER 10
USING WEB COMPONENTS

To Define A MARQUEE:

1 With a page open in Page view choose Insert | Web Component | Dynamic Effects.

2 Click Marquee in right side of the Insert Web Component dialog box, and click Finish. The Marquee Properties dialog box opens.

3 Enter text to display in the Text area of the dialog box.

4 Choose a direction for your text to move in using either the Left or Right option buttons.

5 You can experiment with the Delay and Amount spin boxes in the Speed area of the dialog box. These determine how fast your text moves, and how long it stops before starting to move again.

> **WARNING** Marquee effects do not work in Netscape Navigator 4.7. The text will still display, visitors just won't see it move.

6 Choose one of the Behavior buttons to have your text scroll (as if it was disappearing behind the page, and then reappearing on the side it started from), slide (text *slides* onto the page and stays there), or alternate (the text bounces back and forth within the marquee like a Ping-Pong ball). Use the Continuously check box to make scrolling or alternate display repeat endlessly (sliding happens just once). The following illustration shows a Text Marquee being defined with Alternate style scrolling.

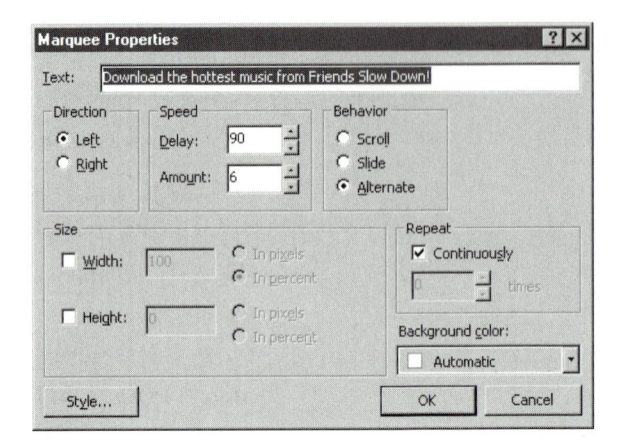

7 After you enter text and define properties, click the OK button to close the Marquee Properties dialog box.

8 You can change the size of the box by clicking and dragging on side or corner handles. You can format font by selecting it in Page view, and using the Formatting toolbar.

Banner Ads

The Banner Ad Web component gets its name, I assume, from the fact that many times rotating image displays are used in ads. You don't have to create an *ad* to use a Banner Ad component. All you need is two or more images that you want to rotate in a single spot on your Web page.

It usually helps if the images you rotate are the same size. Otherwise, your pictures will be distorted when displayed in the Banner Ad box.

To Create a banner ad:

1 With a page open in Page view choose Insert | Web Component | Dynamic Effects.

2 Click Banner Ad on the right side of the Insert Web Component dialog box, and click Finish. The Banner Ad dialog box opens.

3 To associate a link with the banner ad, enter a URL in the Link To area, or use the Browse button to locate a link target.

4 Choose a Transition Effect from the drop-down list. Options include None (image changes, that's it), Blinds Horizontal or Blinds Vertical (like window blinds), Dissolve (pictures fade into each), and Box In or Box Out (the pictures switch either from the outside in or the inside out).

5 Use the Show Each Image For (seconds) area to define how long you want each picture to display before transitioning into the next picture.

6 Use the Height and Width areas to define the size of the banner ad.

> **WARNING** Like Hover buttons, Banner Ad Web components are Java applets. They work with both Internet Explorer and Netscape Navigator. However, because they are Java applets, they draw from the resources of a visitor's computer, and might not work well with, or can even crash, older and slower computers. Even newer, powerful computers may delay in presenting pictures in a banner ad because Java applets place a lot of demand on computer processing capabilities.

CHAPTER 10
USING WEB COMPONENTS

7 Use the Add button in the dialog box to define the pictures that will display in the banner ad. The Add Picture for Banner Ad dialog box appears.

8 In the Add Picture for Banner Ad dialog box, navigate to pictures, select them, and click Open to add them to the list, as shown here. To preview pictures before selecting them, select Views | Preview in the Add Picture for Banner Ad dialog box.

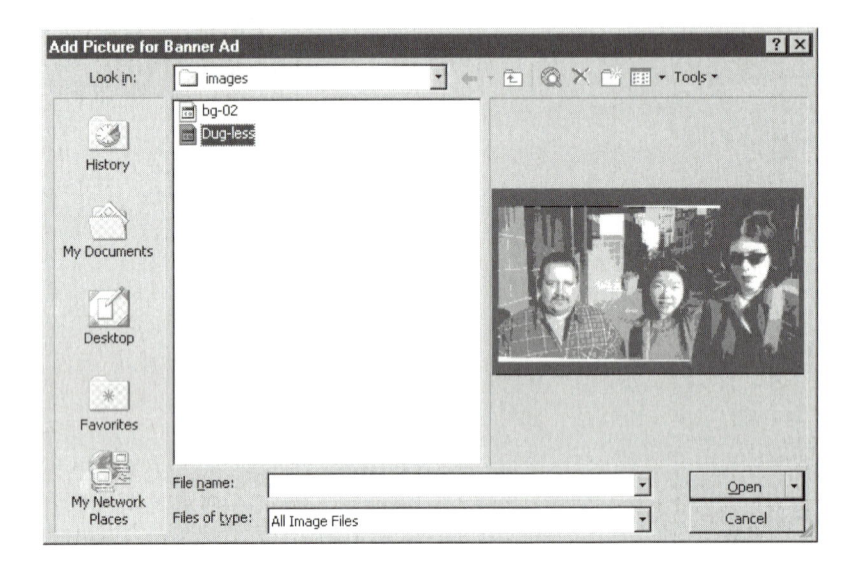

9 Continue to use the Add Picture for Banner Ad dialog box to add pictures to your banner ad. When you've finished, click OK to generate the banner ad.

Banner ads look like regular pictures in Page view, as shown in Figure 10-3. You can resize them in Page view by clicking and dragging on side or corner handles of a selected banner ad. If you use the Left or Right align buttons in the Formatting toolbar, you can configure a banner ad so text wraps around it.

WEB SEARCH

The Web Search component allows visitors to search your Web site. I've found it to be one of the most buggy of the Web components, and one that server providers have a hard time supporting. But if all goes well, it provides an easy way for visitors to find features on your site.

FIGURE 10-3

Resizing a banner ad in Page view; text flows to the right of this banner ad because it is left aligned

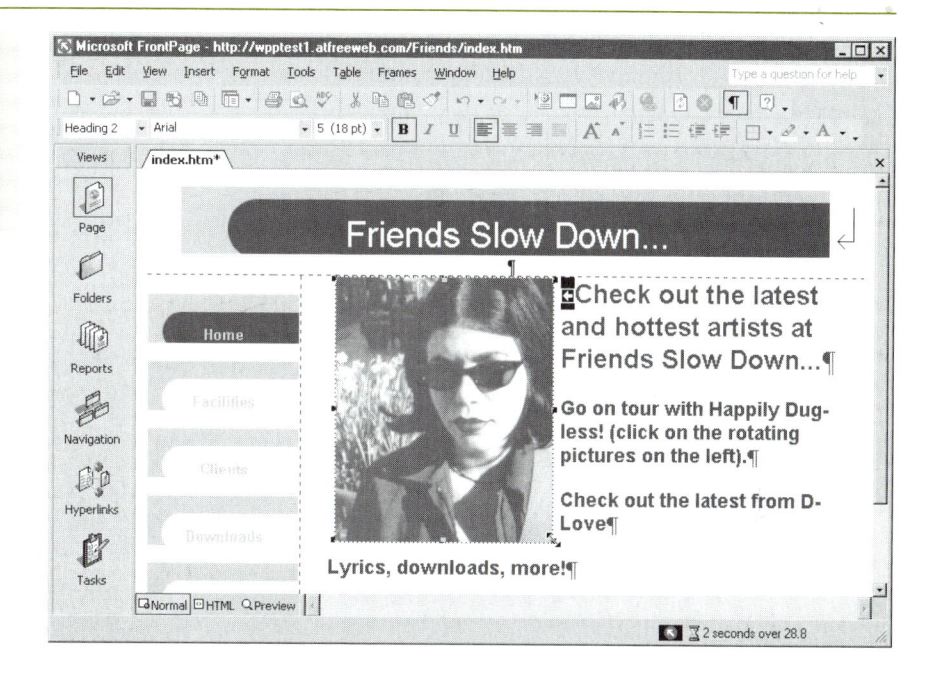

To Insert A WEB SEARCH COMPONENT:

1 With a Web page open in Page view, choose Insert | Web Component | Web Search.

2 Click Finish in the Insert Web Component dialog box to open the Search Form Properties dialog box, as shown here:

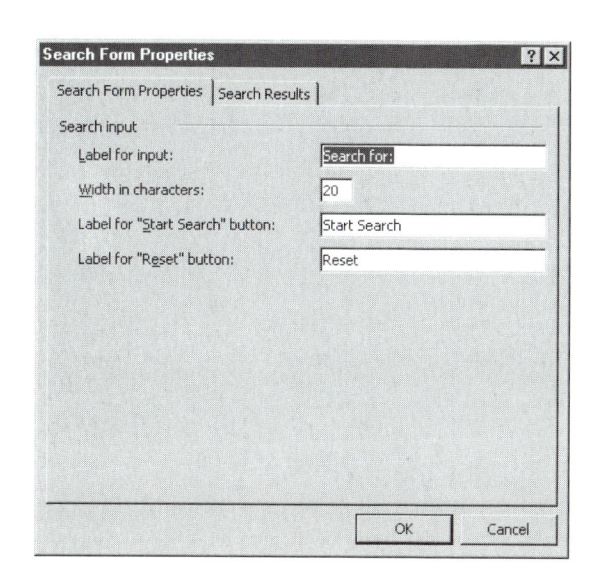

3 You can change your form by entering new text in the Label for Input area, a different width for the box in the Width in Characters area, and new button labels in the Label for Start Search button and Label for Reset button areas. However, most of the time the defaults are fine.

4 Click the Search Results tab in the Search Form Properties dialog box to define how the results of a search will be displayed. If your site has *subwebs* (FrontPage Webs that reside on the same server as another FrontPage Web), or folders, you can use the This Web or Directory options boxes to restrict a search to your subweb or a selected folder.

5 Use the two Maximum Records spin boxes to define how many matching pages to find, and how many to display at one time.

6 Use the check boxes in the Additional Information to Display in the Search Results List to define additional information to display along with search results. In Figure 10-4, I'm selecting *all* the additional information.

Counting Hits

Hit counters display the number of times that a page has been visited. They serve two purposes: They tell *you* how many people have been to your site and they also advertise to the world how popular your site is.

> **TIP** The Web Search component requires that your Web server have FrontPage extensions. Beyond that, many of the features only work if your server provider is using Microsoft's server software. And then, your server provider must set up your site so that the indexing feature—which searches for text on your site—updates properly. If you have trouble with the Web Search component, double-check those three items with your provider.

> **NOTE** As I mentioned earlier, search box options *vary greatly* depending on what server your are publishing to. The options in Figure 10-4 reflect those available when you publish your site to Web server using Microsoft server software and FrontPage 2002 server extensions. If you are publishing to a server without Microsoft server software but with FrontPage 2002 extensions, you will be limited to only three options for presenting results. It seems weird, I know, but that's how the FrontPage folks designed this feature.

If you want to know how many people are coming to your site, but you *don't* want to display this information publicly, the Hit Counter Web Component won't work. Instead, you might want to experiment with the FastCounter component available by choosing Insert | Web Component, bCentral Web Components, and clicking FastCounter in the list of components. FastCounter is more complicated

FIGURE 10-4

This search box will display all possible information about each page

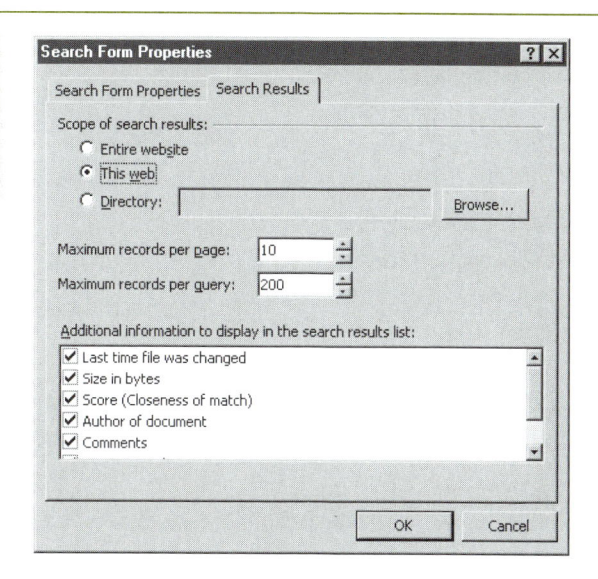

to install and requires that you register at bCentral, but it allows you to track visitors without making the count public.

To Place A HIT COUNTER ON A PAGE:

1 In Page view, with a page open, choose Insert | Web Component.

2 Choose Hit Counter.

3 From the list of counter styles that appears, click one, as shown here:

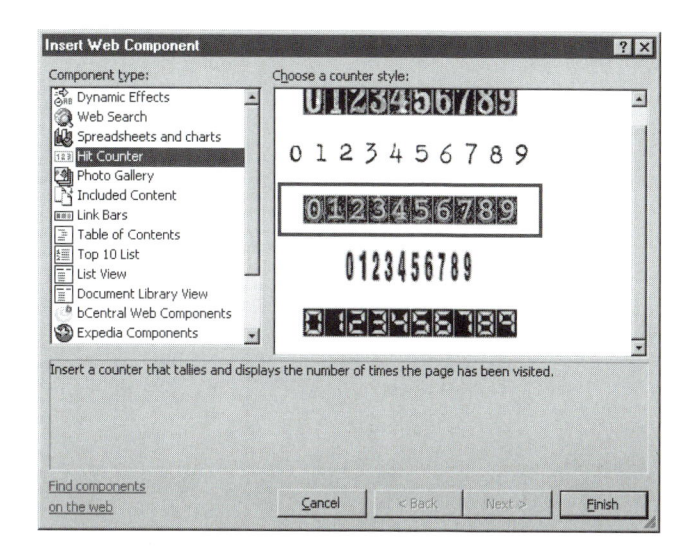

CHAPTER 10
Using Web Components

4 After you settle on a hit counter style, click Finish. The Hit Counter Properties dialog box appears.

5 Use the Reset Counter To check box and area to reset your hit counter to a number other than 0.
For example, if you are adding a hit counter to a page that has already had 10,000 hits, you can make 10,000 the starting number for the counter.

> **NOTE** Hit counters only work if, and when your site is published to a server with FrontPage extensions.

6 Use the Fixed Number of Digits check box and area to define how many digits to display. For example, if you choose four digits, the number 4 will display as 0004.

7 Click OK in the Hit Counter Properties dialog box, and a hit counter appears on your page.

Displaying Pictures in a Photo Gallery

The Photo Gallery Web component allows you to choose from four different ways of presenting many pictures on a page. All the Photo Gallery options involve creating a *thumbnail* (small) version of your photos, linked to a larger, full-size picture. (You explored photo galleries in Chapter 5.) Figure 10-5 shows four photos displayed in a photo gallery on a page.

FIGURE 10-5
Use a Photo Gallery to display pictures

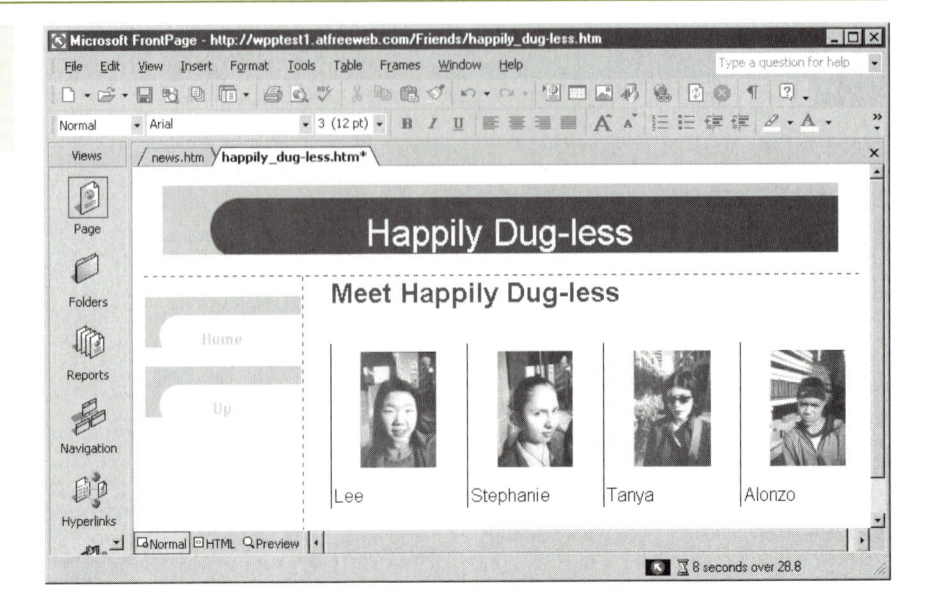

Using Included Content

The group of five different Include Content Web components all embed content of one kind or another in your Web page. The Page component embeds the content of one Web page in another. So, for example, you can have a Web page that contains a brief description of your organization, and embed that page in *many* pages within your Web site. When you update the original page, the content will change for *all* the pages in which that page is embedded. Visitors to your site see one seamless page, but in reality some of the page content comes from *another* Web page. You'll walk through how to include a Page component in this section.

The Page Based on Schedule and Picture Based on schedule both work like the Page component, except that their Properties dialog boxes allow you to define a starting and ending date for the embedded content, as well as substitute material to embed after the page or picture dates expire.

The Page Banner component displays the page title. All themes come with page banner graphics, and themes automatically create page banners in top shared borders.

The Substitution component embeds codes that are associated with values defined in various places in FrontPage and is beyond the scope of this book.

To Include ONE PAGE IN ANOTHER PAGE:

1. In Page view, with a page open, choose Insert | Web Component, Included Content.

2. Click Page.

3. Click Finish and the Include Page Properties dialog box opens.

4. In the Page to Include field in the Include Page Properties dialog box either enter a URL (Web page address), or use the Browse button and navigate to the page you want to embed.

5. Click OK to close the Include Page Properties dialog box and embed the selected page in the open Web page.

The embedded page content will appear on your page in Page view, but you can't edit it there. To change the content of an embedded page, you need to open that

CHAPTER 10
USING WEB COMPONENTS

(embedded) page, and edit it. When you resave the page, the embedded content will change in *every* page in which the page was inserted.

To *change* which page is embedded, double-click the embedded content. The Include Page Properties dialog box appears, and you can change the embedded page, as shown in Figure 10-6.

Even though page banners are automatically generated when you assign a theme and a top shared border, sometimes you can accidentally delete the banner. Other times, you might want to insert a page banner on your own outside a top shared border. In either case, you can put a page banner on a page using the Page Banner Component.

To Place a page banner on a page:

1 Open a page in Page view. If you want your banner on a top shared border, click to place your insertion point in the shared border.

2 Choose Insert | Web Component | Included Content.

3 Click Page Banner.

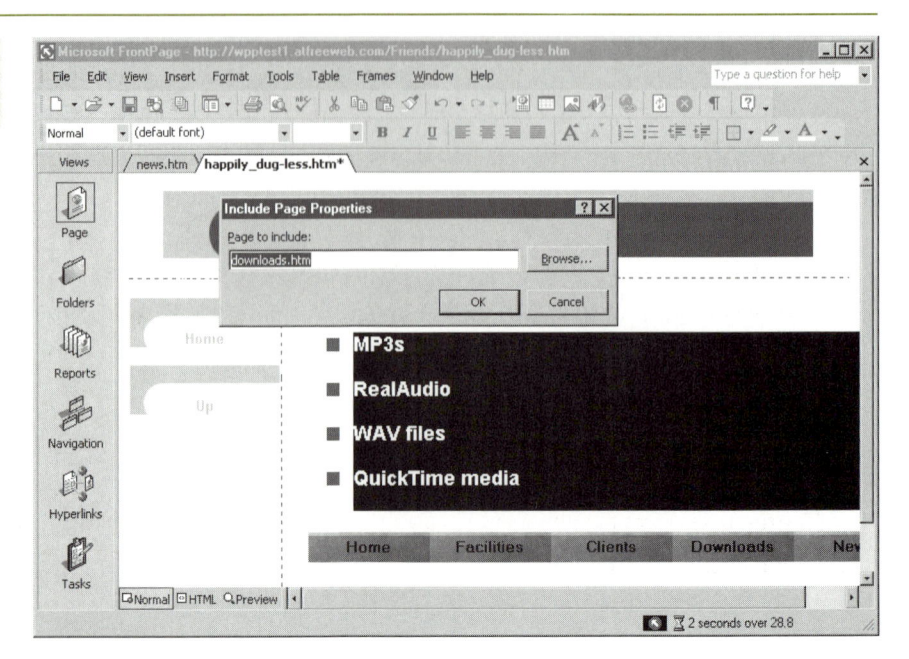

FIGURE 10-6
Changing an embedded page

4 Click Finish and the Page Banner Properties dialog box appears.

5 In the Page Banner dialog box, choose either Text or Picture. If you choose Picture, the image file associated with banners in your theme will be used as the banner background.

6 Click OK. The banner appears on your page.

If you create a text banner, you can format that text using the Formatting toolbar. The content of a page banner is defined by the page title. You can easily change page titles for a page by right-clicking the page in Navigation view and choosing Rename from the options menu. After you type a new name, press ENTER.

INSERTING LINK BARS

Link Bar Web components allow you to insert different kinds of sets of links, based on either your site's navigation structure or on configured groups of pages. Link bars can also be inserted by choosing Insert | Navigation from the menu. For a full exploration of link bars, see Chapter 6.

GENERATING AN AUTOMATIC TABLE OF CONTENTS

FrontPage can generate a table of contents for your site automatically. This generated table of contents is an effective way of providing a way for visitors to see *all* the content of your site. Each table of contents listing is a *link*, so visitors can jump to a page in the table of contents by clicking it.

Tables of contents can be generated based on all the pages in your site or based only on a defined category of pages. Categories are groups of pages you define—for instance pages associated with planning can be assigned to the Planning category. To assign a page to a category, right-click the page and choose Page Properties from the context menu. In the Workgroup tab of the Page Properties dialog box, you can assign one or more categories to a page. Categories of pages are explored in Chapter 6, and you can refer to the instructions there if you want to use categories for your table of contents.

CHAPTER 10
USING WEB COMPONENTS

To Generate A TABLE OF CONTENTS FOR YOUR SITE:

1 In Page view, with an open page, choose Insert | Web Component | Table of Contents.

2 In the Included Content list, click either For This Web Site or Based on Web Category.

3 Click Finish. The Table of Contents dialog box appears.

4 If you are creating a table of contents based on your entire site, the Table of Contents Properties dialog box allows you to define a starting point for your TOC. The default will be your site's home page and will include the entire site. If you enter another page in the Page URL for Starting Point of Table area, your table of contents will only include pages *under* that page in Navigation view.

5 Use the Heading Font Size drop-down list to select the size of the table of contents title.

6 Select the Show Each Page Only Once check box to eliminate duplicate listings of the same page. Choose the Show Pages with No Incoming Hyperlinks check box *only* if you want pages without incoming links to be included in the Table of Contents. Select the Recompute Table of Contents When Any Other Page is Edited to automatically regenerate the table of contents each time any page is changed.

7 Click OK to close the dialog box and place the Table of Contents on your page.

You won't see the real table of contents in Page view, even when you view using the Preview tab. You can only see a generated table of contents in a browser window, as shown in Figure 10-7.

bCentral, Expedia, MSN, and MSNBC Web Components

FrontPage 2002 includes a number of components that are links to other sites. In some cases, the content of these links changes based on information at *other* Web sites. For example, the link to MSNBC's Sports Headlines component will update depending on who beat whom today.

When you embed a Web component from bCentral, Expedia, MSN, or MSNBC, you are placing links to sites *outside your site* on your page. So keep in mind that you are, in effect, sending clients to another Web site when you use these components.

FIGURE 10-7

A generated table of contents

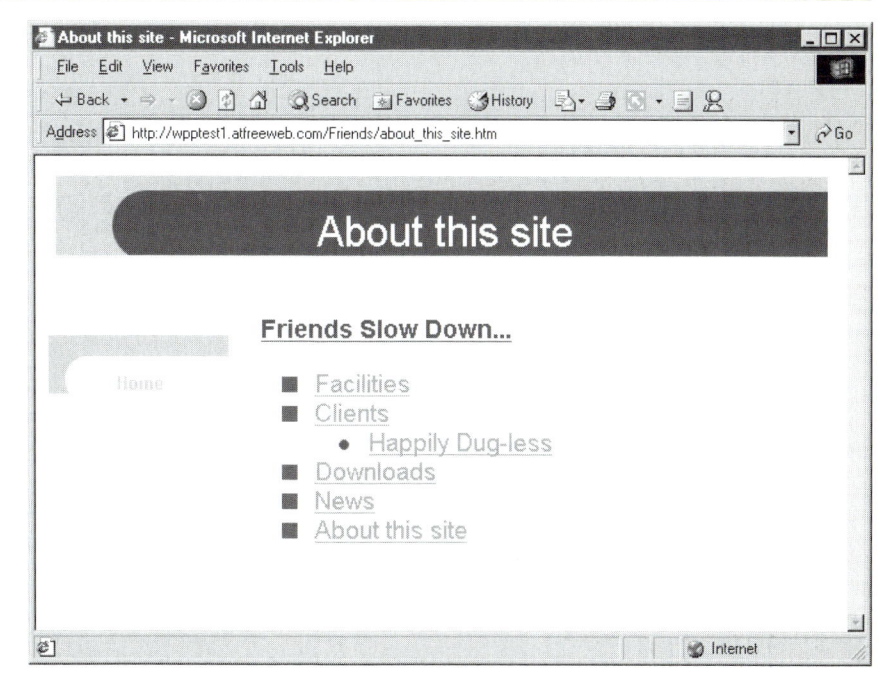

Most components from bCentral, Expedia, MSN, and MSNBC don't have many or any options. You place them on your page, and they appear when visitors come to your site. Because most of them function as *links,* the content associated with these components is at the target site.

bCentral offers a number of useful components that you can download from www.bCentral.com. They include a hit counter that does not display hits on your page (instead you get data by going to bCentral's site), and a banner ad where you get paid if people follow an ad placed on your page.

Expedia components provide maps that you can include in your site.

MSN components provide a search box that links to MSN's Web search engine, and a search box that allows visitors to get stock information from Microsoft's Money Central site.

MSNBC components place updated lists of news headlines on your site. Visitors who click the box of headlines jump to MSNBC's site.

Figure 10-8 shows a page with several of these components.

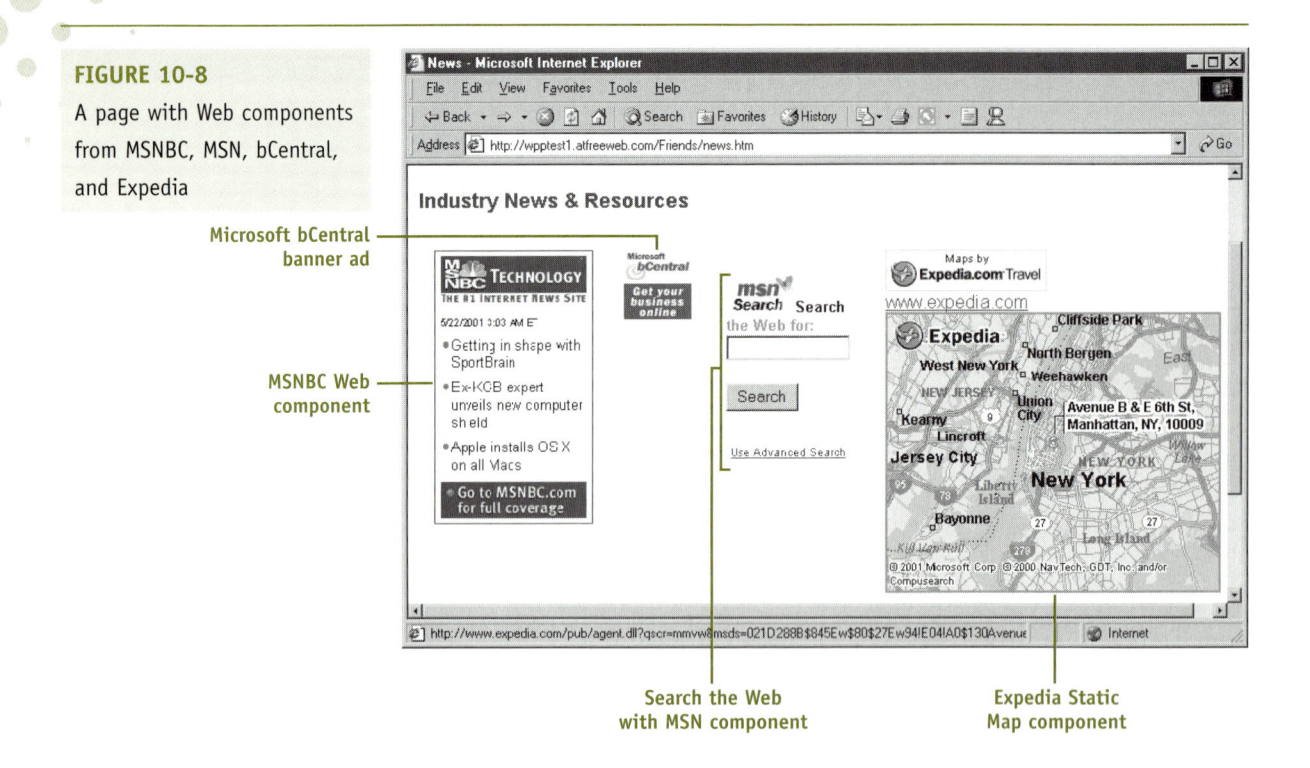

CHAPTER 10
USING WEB COMPONENTS

FIGURE 10-8
A page with Web components from MSNBC, MSN, bCentral, and Expedia

Microsoft bCentral banner ad
MSNBC Web component
Search the Web with MSN component
Expedia Static Map component

ADVANCED CONTROLS

Advanced controls allow you to add your own programming code to your FrontPage Web pages. Because writing code in Java and ActiveX is beyond the scope of this book, ignore those options as well as the Confirmation Field option that is used to customize data entry forms.

You will take a look at the plug-in components in Chapter 14 when you add sound and movies to Web pages.

COMPONENTS ADD DYNAMISM TO YOUR SITE

The FrontPage Web components you've explored in this chapter add action to your site. Hover buttons change as visitors roll over them; marquee text moves back and forth on a page. Banner ads change their picture display.

Other Web components add interactivity. Search boxes *react* to input from visitors to help navigate your site. Hit counters change their display with each visit to your site.

The down side of Web components is that most of them require that your Web be published to a server with FrontPage extensions. You'll learn more about servers and extensions in Chapter 16.

In the next chapter, you'll begin to cover input forms. With input forms, you can collect data from visitors. In Chapter 12 you'll learn to send that data to an e-mail address, capture data to a file, or create an online interactive database.

11

Creating Input Forms

The single most powerful feature of FrontPage—in my humble opinion—is the ability to collect and process data through input forms. With FrontPage 2002's input form-processing features, folks like you and me can manage online mailing lists, feedback forms, and even interactive databases where visitors not only enter, but also view database information.

CHAPTER 11
CREATING INPUT FORMS

Creating input forms and managing input data is a two-step process. First you design the input form, and then you define how data will be managed. In this chapter, you'll focus on how to create input forms. Chapter 12 zeroes in on processing that data.

Before embarking on this two-chapter exploration of collecting online data, you need to know that this whole process requires that your Web site is published to a FrontPage-friendly Web server. You'll look at FrontPage servers in detail in Chapter 16.

CREATING A FORM

There are two parts to a Web page input form: the *form* and the individual *form fields*. The form determines what happens to data that gets collected, and individual form fields collect the data. Figure 11-1 shows an input form with form fields in Page view.

Form fields don't work unless they are in a form. For this reason, I strongly suggest that you create a form first, and then add form fields. Forms also require a *Submit* button, which sends form data to a server. In addition, most forms have a

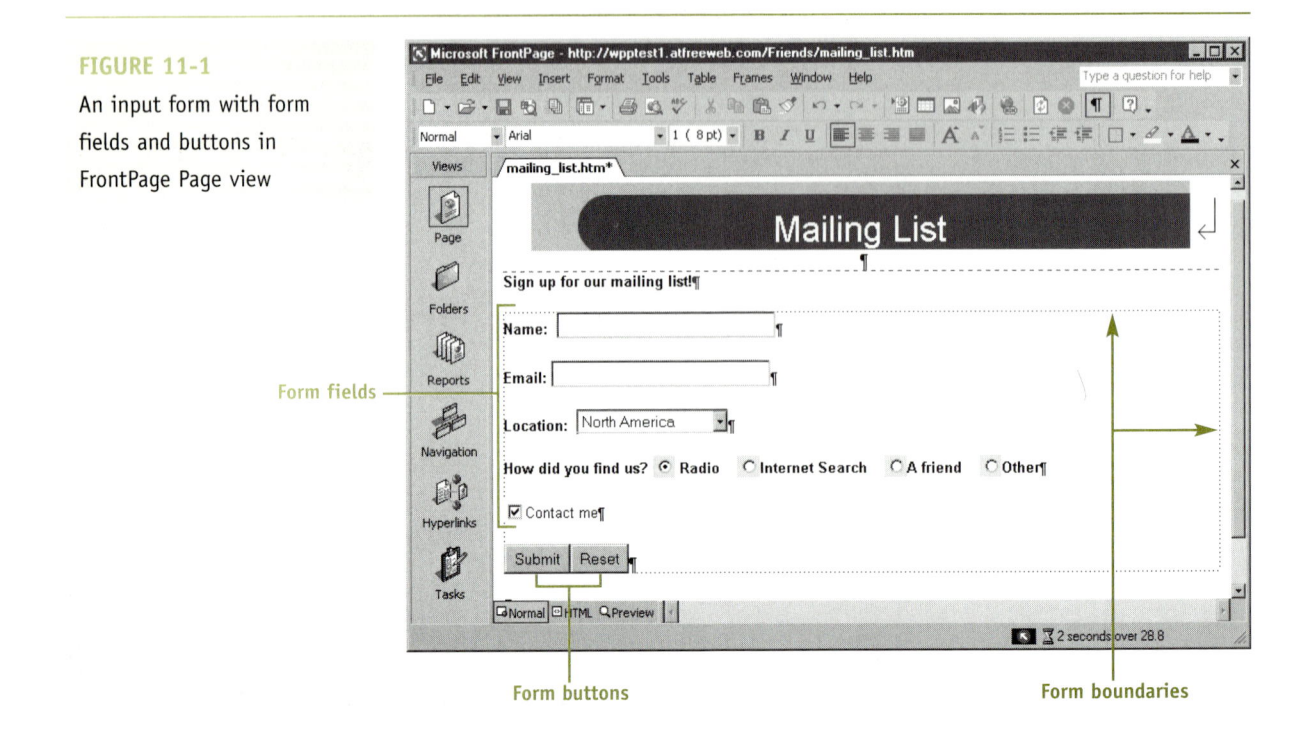

FIGURE 11-1

An input form with form fields and buttons in FrontPage Page view

Form fields

Form buttons

Form boundaries

Reset button that clears all the fields in the form. You'll start creating an input form by generating a form with buttons.

First Step: Define a Form

What happens to information that your visitors enter into a form is defined by the form properties. You'll explore those in depth in the next chapter, but for now it's important to start the process of collecting data by creating a form.

> **NOTE** Can you have more than one form per page? Yes, you can. That would be a relatively complex way of collecting data, but it's possible.

To Create an input form:

1 In Page view, with a page open, you will probably want to start by entering some text to introduce your form, such as "Sign up for our mailing list here," "Share some feedback," or "Place an order." Then press ENTER to create a new line for the form.

2 Choose Insert | Form | Form. A form is generated with a Submit and Reset button. Note that the form is defined by a dotted line.

3 Press ENTER to create a line above the Submit and Reset buttons. You are creating a new line *inside* the form, as shown in Figure 11-2. As you edit the content of your input form, remember that *only objects inside the form* will be processed.

FIGURE 11-2
Input forms are indicated in Page view by dotted lines

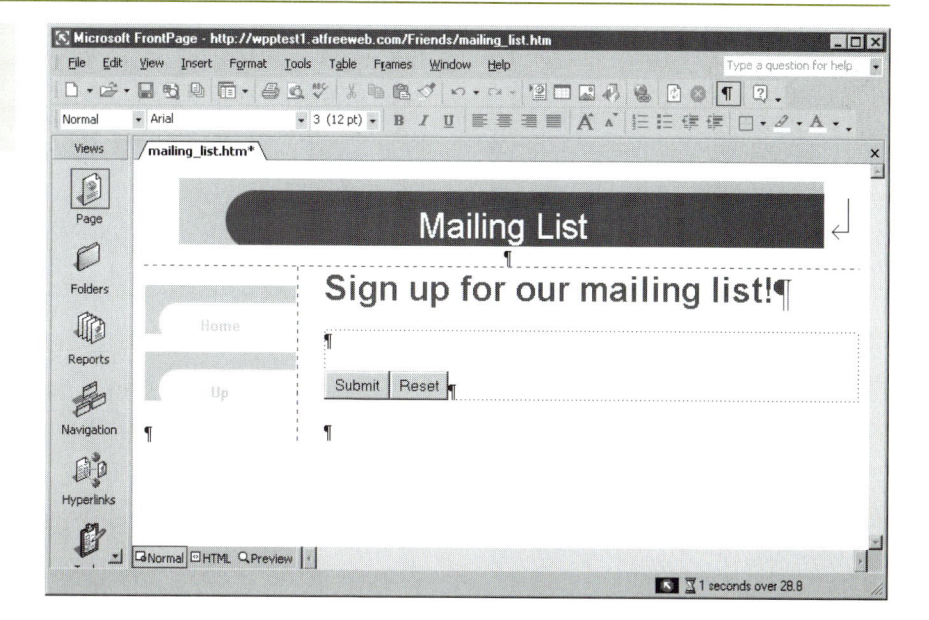

CHAPTER 11
CREATING INPUT FORMS

ADDING BUTTONS

As you saw in the previous set of steps, when you create a Form, FrontPage automatically generates a Submit and a Reset button. The Submit button is essential; it's the button that will make your form work. A Reset button is helpful, though not required. For example, if a visitor wants to enter two sets of information, he or she can enter one set of data, click the Reset button, and have a clean slate to enter a new set of data.

Even though FrontPage automatically generates Submit and Reset buttons, I find many of my students accidentally delete them. If that happens, don't worry. You can add new Submit and Reset buttons inside a form at any time.

To Add A Submit Button to a Form:

1 *Make sure your cursor is inside a form.* If it's not, click inside the dotted lines that define the form.

2 With your cursor inside a form, choose Insert | Form | Push Button. A generic button, with a label of "button" appears, as shown here:

> **NOTE** Don't see any dotted lines on your page in Page view? That means you don't have a form—go back to the previous set of steps and create a form before you add buttons.

3 Double-click the generic button to open the Push Button Properties dialog box.

4 From the Button type options, choose Submit. The button Value/Label automatically becomes Submit, as shown here:

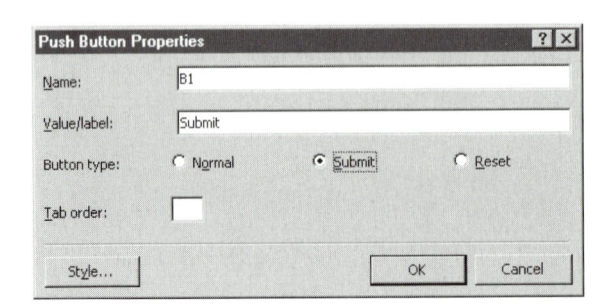

5 Click OK to close the Push Button Properties dialog box, and change the button label.

To Add a Reset button to a form:

1. As always, when editing form content, be sure your cursor is *inside* a form. If it's not, click inside the dotted lines that define a form.

2. With your cursor inside a form, choose Insert | Form | Push Button. A generic button, with a label of "Button" appears.

3. Double-click the generic button to open the Push Button Properties dialog box.

4. From the Button type options, choose Reset. The button Value/Label automatically becomes Reset.

5. Click OK to close the Push Button Properties dialog box, and change the button label.

Adding Form Fields

Once you have a form with a Submit and a Reset button you're ready to create form fields in your form. This is where you define the information that you will get from visitors.

Form design is a science and an art. You want to create forms that invite visitor input and collect the information you need. Often the process of creating a working input form requires some testing to see if your form is easy to use, and if it collects all the data you need.

Here are a few rules you should follow while designing input forms:

▶ **Make it clear what information you want** If you're asking for an address, but will collect the ZIP code later, ask for a street address.

▶ **Make sure your form collects all the information you need** If you need a visitor's phone number to follow up on an urgent service, feedback, or sales inquiry, don't forget a phone number field.

▶ **Indicate which fields are required** Also indicate which fields are optional.

▶ **Keep forms as short as possible** My general rule is that if an input form doesn't fit in a computer screen, it's probably too long and visitors won't have the patience to fill it out.

▶ **Keep in mind that the Web is international** Collect information like country codes for phone numbers, and (if you are in the United States), remember not everyone lives in a "state" or has a "ZIP code."

▶ **Provide a feedback form on your site** This way your visitors will act as volunteer testers, proofreaders, and evaluators for your site.

Okay, that's my two cents worth on form design. Time to add input fields to your form!

Creating Text Boxes

Text boxes collect text... in a box! They're one of the most useful ways of getting information from visitors. Examples include a visitor's name, e-mail address, mailing address, or phone number.

To Insert a text box:

1 With your cursor *inside a form*, type a label for your text box (like "Name:" for example). Press the SPACEBAR to create space between this label and the field you about to insert.

2 Choose Insert | Form | Textbox. A text box appears in your form.

3 Double-click the text box to open the Text Box Properties dialog box.

4 In the Name area of the Text Box dialog box, enter a name for the field. This name should be something that will help you remember what data you are collecting in this field when you receive data through the form. For example, a good name for a field that collects names would be "Name."

> **TIP** Avoid spaces in the Name area of the dialog box—they will cause problems when data is sent to a file or database.

5 Normally, you will leave the Initial Value area blank. This is information that appears before a visitor types anything in the text box. An exception would be, for example, a field where you are collecting URLs (Web site addresses). In that case, you might enter http:// in the Initial Value area so that visitors would not have to type this part of their URL.

6 Use the Width In Characters area to define the *displayed* width of the text box. Visitors can still enter additional information (up to 999 characters)—they just won't *see* all their data in the text box.

7 You can enter a value in the Tab Order area. This defines when a visitor will enter this field if he or she uses the TAB key on his or her keyboard to move from field to field. If you leave this area blank, visitors will move from the top to the bottom of the form automatically—in other words, the default tab order works fine and there is no need to enter a value in this area.

8 Choose Yes in the Password field area only if you want data to display as asterisks. This protects data from being viewed by someone looking over your visitor's shoulders as he or she enters information.

9 The Style button opens the Modify Style dialog box, where you can define formatting for text that visitors enter into the dialog box. You can use the Format button in the Modify Style dialog box to format font, paragraph, border, numbering, or position of text.

10 The Validate button opens the Text Box Validation dialog box. You'll explore validation separately, later in this chapter.

11 After you have defined your text box, as shown here, click OK to close the Text Box Properties dialog box.

> **NOTE** One example of where you might want to manually define tab order is if you place your form fields in table cells, and want to control whether a visitor moves down each column or across each row as they tab from field to field.

> **TIP** Practically speaking, you will only want to modify text font, and in rare cases border formatting for input text. Folks who enter text in your input form fields will be more interested in making sure the text is collected accurately than whether input text displays with a shaded border.

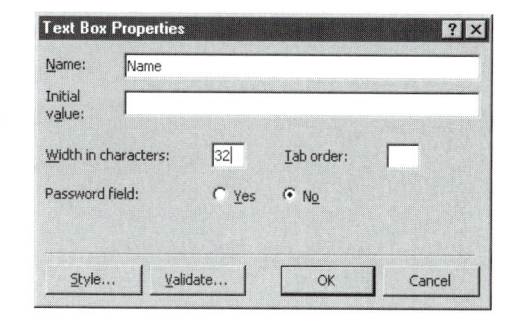

Adding Text Areas

Text areas are like text boxes—they collect information that a visitor types into a box. The difference is text *areas* are not restricted to 999 characters and can be more than one line. For example, a *comments* text box is often a text area, encouraging visitors to enter more than one line of text.

The process for inserting a text area is almost identical to inserting a text box. The only difference is, for a text area, you define the field width and how many lines to display.

This illustration shows the TextArea dialog box. In this example a text area 60 characters wide and 4 lines high is being defined. If visitors enter additional text, scrollbars will allow them to move up and down within the text area.

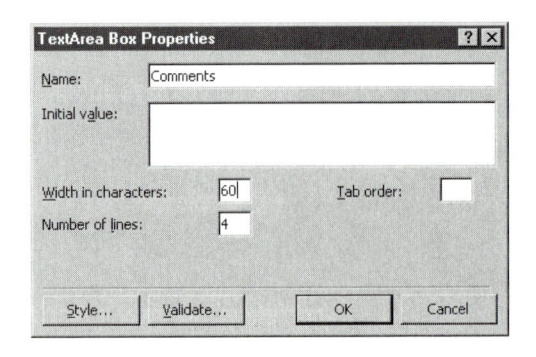

Allowing for File Uploads

A cool new feature to FrontPage 2002—called *File Upload*—allows you to make it easy for visitors to attach a file to their input form. For example, if you want visitors to e-mail you photos, you can include a File Upload button that helps them navigate to the photo file on their local computer, and send it to you.

To Insert a File Upload field:

1 With your cursor *inside* a form, type a label first—something like "Click here to attach a file." Then press the SPACEBAR to create space between the label and the button.

2 Choose Insert | Form | File Upload. An upload file area, along with a Browse button, will appear in your form, as shown here:

3 Double-click the Browse button to open the File Upload Properties dialog box.

4 In the Name area, enter a name for this field—something like "Photo." This will help you identify the collected file.

5 You are unlikely to want an initial value for this field, as visitors will either enter file names or use the Browse button to locate files.

6 You can define the display width of the field in the Width in Characters area.

7 If you are assigning tab order to your input form, you can enter a value in the Tab Order area.

8 Use the Style button to define formatting for text that displays in the field area.

9 Click OK to close the File Upload Properties dialog box and change the field properties.

Including Check Boxes

Check boxes are a simple way to collect data from a visitor. He or she can either check the box... or not. Check boxes are often used to offer options, like "Contact me," "Add me to the mailing list," or "I agree to the terms of this offer."

To Add a check box to a form:

1 Check boxes are often displayed *to the left* of an associated label. So, even before you type a label for the check box, make sure your cursor is inside your form and choose Insert | Form | Check box.

2 Press your SPACEBAR, and type a label first—something like "Contact me."

3 Double-click the check box to open the Check Box Properties dialog box.

4 In the Name area, enter a name for this field, for example, "Contact." This will help you evaluate the data you collect in this field.

5 Leave the value for this field at *on*, or substitute another value that indicates the box was selected (something like "Yes").

6 Choose an initial state for the check box by clicking either the Checked or Unchecked option button.

7 You can enter a tab order in the Tab Order area if you want to change the default order by which visitors "tab through" your form.

8 Use the Style box if you want to define the font and/or border formatting for the check that appears in the check box.

CHAPTER 11
CREATING INPUT FORMS

9 When you have completed the Text Box Properties dialog box, as shown here, click OK.

ADDING OPTION BUTTONS

Option buttons are helpful when you need to restrict a visitor to making one choice from a group of options. For example, if you want a visitor to choose *one* form of payment—MasterCard, Visa, or American Express Card—you could provide option buttons like the ones shown here:

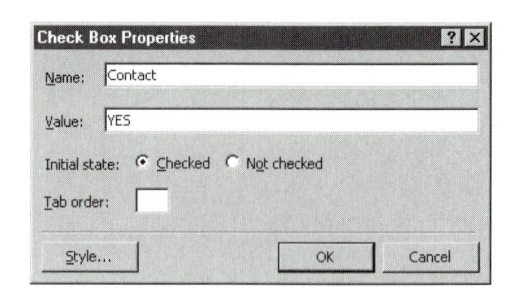

Form of payment:

○ Visa   ○ American Express   ○ MasterCard

To Create A GROUP OF OPTION BUTTONS:

1 Normally, you will want to introduce your set of option buttons with some kind of question or explanation, like "Please rate our site," "Choose a payment option," or "How did you hear about us?" So, start by typing an introduction to your set of option buttons.

2 Option buttons are usually displayed *to the left* of an associated label. So, before you type a label for your first option button, make sure your cursor is inside your form and choose Insert | Form | Option button.

3 Press the SPACEBAR, and type a label for the option button.

4 Double-click the option button to open the Option Button Properties dialog box.

5 In the Group Name area, enter a group name for *all* the buttons in the set of options. For example, this might be "Rating," "Payment," or "Source."

6 In the Value area, enter a *unique* field value for this *specific* option button, as shown here. In this

TIP Option buttons, also known as *radio buttons*, come in groups. They always present a visitor with a *choice* of options, and a visitor is always restricted to choosing *one* of these options. Is that too restrictive? Then use check boxes to collect information.

WARNING It is important to define the option button properties for your *first* button before you add additional buttons. The reason is that each button in your group will have the *same* group name, and it's easier to copy your first button to ensure that each button in the group has the exact same group name.

example, the *group* name for this *set* of option buttons is Source, and the specific value for *this option* is Radio Ad.

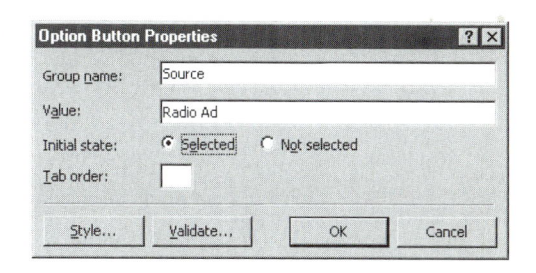

7 Choose an initial state for the radio button by clicking either the Selected or Not Selected option button.

8 You can enter a tab order in the Tab Order area if you want to change the default order by which visitors "tab through" your form.

9 Use the Style box if you want to define the font and/or border (or shading) formatting for the bullet that appears in the check box.

NOTE Only *one* button in a set of radio buttons can be selected by default. However, you don't *have to* assign selected status to *any* button.

10 Click OK to create the *first* of your *set* of option buttons.

11 Copy and paste to create additional radio buttons and add new labels.

12 Double-click each of your radio buttons and assign a unique value.

NOTE Technically, drop-down boxes can be configured to allow visitors to make more than one choice, but this is an awkward setup that most visitors will find unintuitive, and one that we won't explore.

Adding Drop-Down Boxes

Drop-down boxes are similar to option buttons in that they provide a list of choices, and visitors choose one option. Drop-down boxes (sometimes called drop-down lists or drop-down menus) just look different from option buttons. This illustration on the right shows a drop-down list in action.

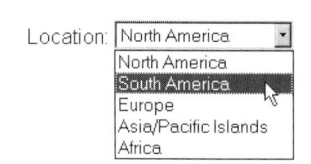

To Create a drop-down box:

1 Start by typing an introductory comment that tells visitors what options are provided in the drop-down box, like "Choose a product," or "Select a location."

2 With your cursor inside a form, choose Insert | Form, Drop-Down Box. A (too small) drop-down box is inserted in your form.

3 Double-click the drop-down box to open the Drop-Down Box Properties dialog box.

4 In the Name area, enter a description of the options—this is just for *your* benefit when you see the collected data. Avoid spaces in the name.

5 Click Add to open the Add Choice dialog box.

6 In the Choice area of the Add Choice dialog box, enter a description of the choice that will appear in the drop-down box.

> **WARNING** Avoid having a value of more than 1 in the Height area, and avoid selecting Yes in the Allow Multiple Selections area. These options create a confusing drop-down box that allows visitors to choose multiple options from your drop-down list.

7 The text you enter in the Choice area automatically becomes the value of the data you collect. If for some reason you need to have the collected data be *different* from the choice, click the Specify Value check box and enter different information in the Specify Value area.

8 Choose one of the two initial state dialog boxes. Normally, you will want to leave this set to Not Selected for all options in your drop-down box.

9 Click OK in the Add Choice dialog box to add the choice to the Drop-Down Box list.

10 Click Add to create additional menu options.

11 After you have added choices to your list, use the Move Up and Move Down buttons to change the order of a selected choice.

> **TIP** If you want to create a drop-down button that works as a jump navigation menu, FrontPage does not have a built-in menu option for this. Your choices are to look for jump menus in online collections of free JavaScripts, or use the FrontPage add-in J-Bots, which do have a built-in jump menu feature. You can find out more about these and other FrontPage resources at www.ppinet.com.

12 Click the Remove button in the Drop-Down Box Properties dialog box to delete a selected choice.

13 Use the Modify button to change a choice.

14 You can use the Tab Order area to override default tab order scrolling in your form.

15 Use the Style button to define text formatting for text in the list.

16 After you define your drop-down box choices, click OK to generate the drop-down box.

Drop-down boxes make it easy for visitors to provide you with data—and you don't have to worry about people making spelling errors because you've done the spelling for them.

Adding Form Extras

In addition to form buttons and form fields, FrontPage offers some more complex options for form content.

Labels are assigned by clicking and dragging to select both a radio button and its associated text label, or a check box and its associated label, and then choosing Insert | Form | Label. When you do this, visitors using Internet Explorer can click either the field (radio button or check box) or the associated text to make a selection.

Picture fields are clickable fields in a form that let visitors choose an option by clicking a picture. These pictures also function as Submit buttons, making their use quite complex and potentially confusing—leave them to advanced form designers.

Group boxes are used to create subgroups of data. They're a bit too advanced for the scope of this book and are used in connection with grouped database results.

Formatting Forms

You can use any text-formatting feature (like boldface, fonts, and text colors) inside a form. To format labels and other text in the form, simply select the text, and apply formatting as you would if the text was outside a form.

To format how text that is entered in a text field appears, use the Style button in the Text, TextArea, Drop-Down, Option Button, or Check Box Properties dialog boxes.

The biggest challenge in designing forms is keeping fields aligned. For this, most sophisticated form designers use tables. You can create and format tables *inside* forms, and use them to align fields. Figure 11-3 shows a form with table rows and columns used to align labels and form fields.

You can refer to Chapter 5 for a full discussion of creating and formatting tables.

CHAPTER 11
CREATING INPUT FORMS

FIGURE 11-3
Table properties have been used to align fields horizontally and vertically and create cell and table background colors for this input form

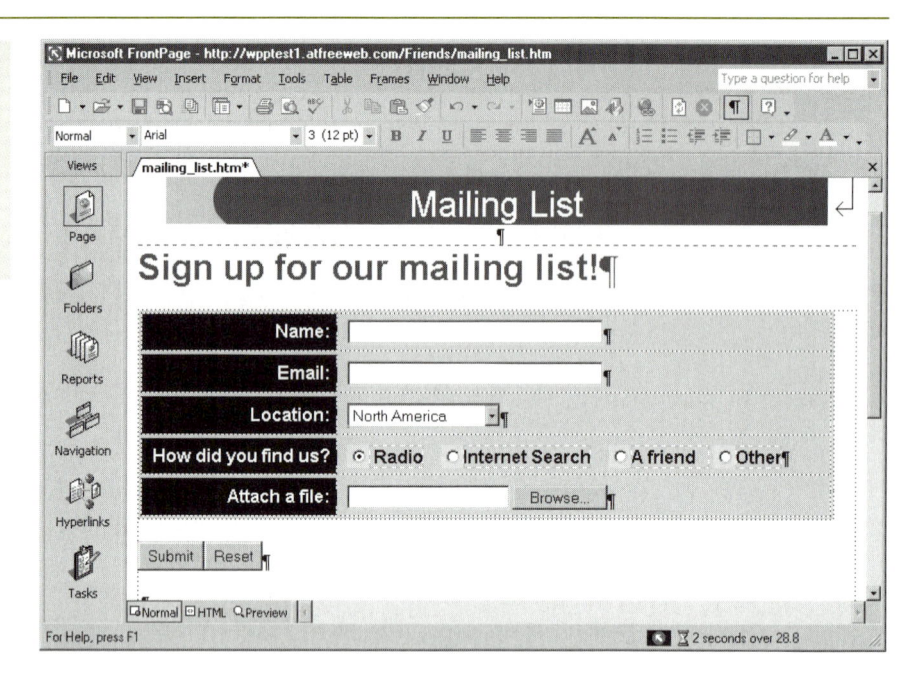

Validating Input Data

Even before a visitor submits data to a database, it can be tested in his or her browser to see if the data is *valid*. Valid data is data that meets criteria that you define.

Validation can be quite complex or fairly easy to apply The most common, useful, and accessible type of data validation is to create *required* fields in a form. These are fields that *must* be filled in, or the form will be rejected even before the data is sent to the database.

To Create A REQUIRED FIELD:

1 Double-click any field to open the form field's properties dialog box.

2 Click the Validate button in the properties dialog box. The appropriate validation dialog box opens.

3 Each validation dialog box includes a Required check box. Select the Required check box.

4 Some fields (like text boxes) also have Minimum Length and Maximum Length areas. You can use these areas to define a minimum, and/or a maximum number of characters for each field. For example, you might want to require at least 10 characters in an e-mail field, as shown here:

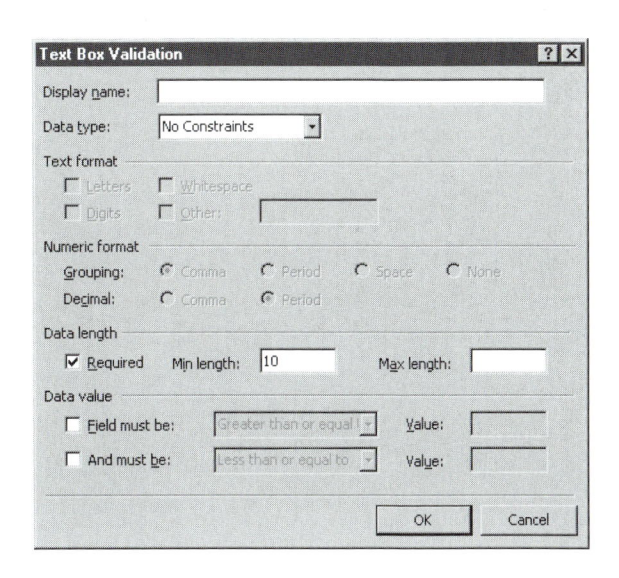

5 Click OK to close all dialog boxes. If a visitor attempts to submit a form without a required field, he or she will see a message like the one in Figure 11-4.

FIGURE 11-4
Oops! Someone didn't enter an e-mail address

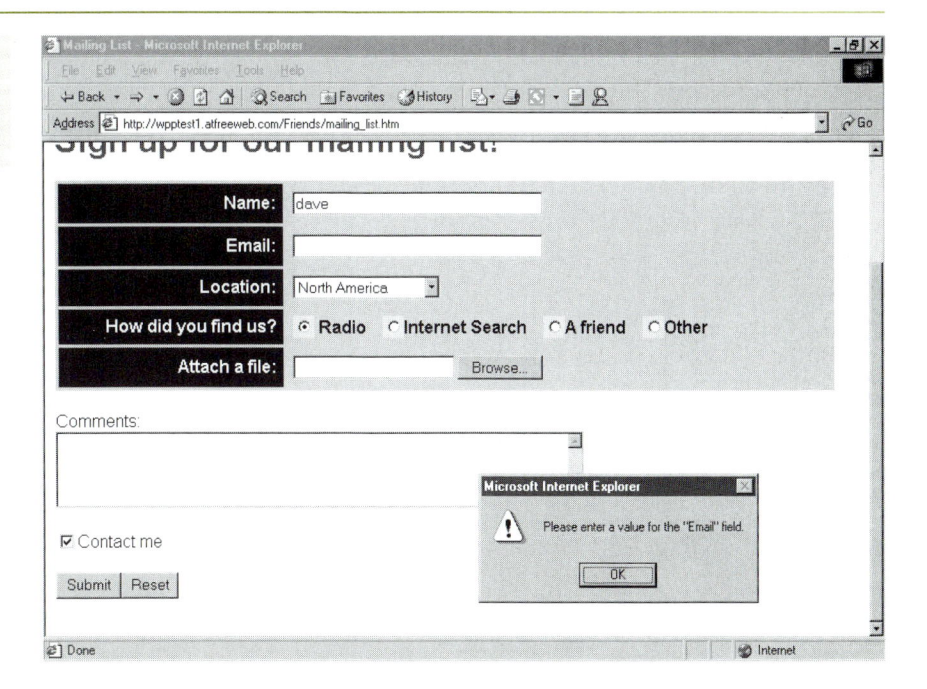

Testing Input Forms

As I noted at the beginning of this chapter, input forms only work when your site is published (uploaded) to a Web server that has FrontPage extension files. These files enable a server to collect the data in a form and send it to a database. You can enter data in your form in the Preview tab of Page view. But you can't test your form until you publish your Web to a FrontPage server.

Moving On to Collect Data

In this chapter, you learned to create input forms to collect data. And, you learned to place form fields, including text boxes, option buttons, check boxes, drop-down menus, and file submit buttons inside forms. If you publish your Web site to a Web server with FrontPage extensions, you can easily collect this data at your server. You can have the collected information e-mailed to you or saved to a file. You can even connect your input forms with an interactive, online database that can be viewed by visitors. In the next chapter, you'll learn to do all that.

> **ON THE VIRTUAL CLASSROOM CD** In Lesson 8, "Designing Input Forms," I demonstrate how to design forms to collect data using text boxes, option buttons, check boxes, and drop-down menus. The lesson demonstrates how to organize input form fields into a form with submit and rest buttons.

12

Managing Form Data

Perhaps the single most valuable thing about working with FrontPage is the ability to not only design Web forms, but to *collect* data. Without FrontPage, you need to connect to something called *Common Gateway Interface* (CGI) scripts—programs that are custom written for your site and reside in a folder at your Web server.

CHAPTER 12
Managing Form Data

FrontPage eliminates the need for messing with complicated CGI scripting by connecting with *FrontPage extension* files that are included with FrontPage Web servers. If you're going to be collecting data, *you will need to publish your site to a server with FrontPage extensions*. Web server providers who support these features are listed at the Microsoft Web site. At this writing, the exact URL is http://www.microsoftwpp.com/.

Provided you are hooked up with a Web server host who supports FrontPage 2002, you have several options for collecting and managing the data that visitors enter into input forms. You can send the data you collect to an e-mail address. You can post the data you collect on a Web page. You can save the data you collect in a file that can be opened (and sorted, filtered, etc.) in a database. Finally, you can create an interactive, online database where visitors can both enter data into a form, and access that data through a Web page.

Four Ways to Collect Form Data

When you collect information through an input form, you can send that information to an e-mail address. This is a simple way to collect information and see that data right away. For example, you might have a "feedback" form on your site, and direct the information collected in it to your e-mail address. That way, whenever someone finds a mistake at, or makes a suggestion about improving your site, you can be notified immediately. Couldn't you just put a link to your e-mail address at your site and get visitor feedback that way? Yes, you can, but with an input form, *you can control* the information you get by asking for things like specific page URLs that have problems, contact information for the person e-mailing you, and so on.

Another easy way to manage input form data is to send that data to a file that can be opened by a database program (such as Excel or Access). For example, you can maintain a mailing list in a file that can be opened in Microsoft Excel. That list can be sorted or filtered for specific mailings, or e-mailing.

Another way to manage input form data is to share the collected information with visitors by posting it on a Web page. For example, you might want to allow visitors to post comments on a Web page and share those comments with each other.

This is especially helpful for intranets. And yes, you can edit or censor those comments after they're posted if you want.

Finally, FrontPage can serve as a front end for complex database applications. For example, you can send data from a form to a Microsoft Access database. That data can be stored, manipulated, used to generate reports, and queried by a database administrator. You can also make that data available *online* at your Web site. Connecting input forms to databases is an advanced application of FrontPage, but you'll walk through one example in this chapter, using the wizard provided with FrontPage 2002.

How Data Gets Managed

In keeping with the overall non-techie tone of this book, I won't delve too deeply into how data is managed online. But it will be helpful for you to have a basic understanding of what happens when a visitor clicks the Submit button on a form.

Data entered into an online form can be processed in two fundamental ways. These two ways of managing data are sometimes referred to as *client-side* and *server-side* data management. Client-side data management processes data right in the Web browser software—such as Internet Explorer or Netscape Navigator. Data processed by a browser (client-side data) is *lost* as soon as a visitor closes his or her browser window. The most popular example of using client-side data processing is using JavaScript to do things like respond to data a visitor enters in a browser window.

The advantage of processing data *at your server* is that the data is saved permanently to a file. Server side data management is better for collecting information you want to keep.

You explored an example of client side data processing in Chapter 11, when you assigned validation tests to forms. The validation testing (such as determining whether a visitor has filled in a required field) takes place right in the Web browser. Programming scripts written in languages such as VBScript or JavaScript tell the browser what to test for, and what to do if the form passes of fails a test.

CHAPTER 12
MANAGING FORM DATA

If you use FrontPage 2002, and publish your site to a server provider that supports FrontPage extensions, you can manage data *without* worrying about server files at all.

COLLECTING FORM DATA THROUGH E-MAILS

When you send input form data to an e-mail address, the data that is entered into the form gets sent to whatever e-mail address you assign to the form. That data comes with form fields displayed, as shown in Figure 12-1.

To Assign AN E-MAIL LINK AS THE TARGET FOR AN INPUT FORM:

1 Right-click an existing form, and choose Form Properties from the context menu.

2 The Form Properties dialog box displays a target file for data in the File Name area. The Send To option button should be selected, if not, click it.

3 You'll explore file targets for data in the next section of this chapter. If you want to send your data *only* to an e-mail address, delete the information in the File Name Area. Otherwise, leave the default setting as it is.

FIGURE 12-1
This data was collected in an input form

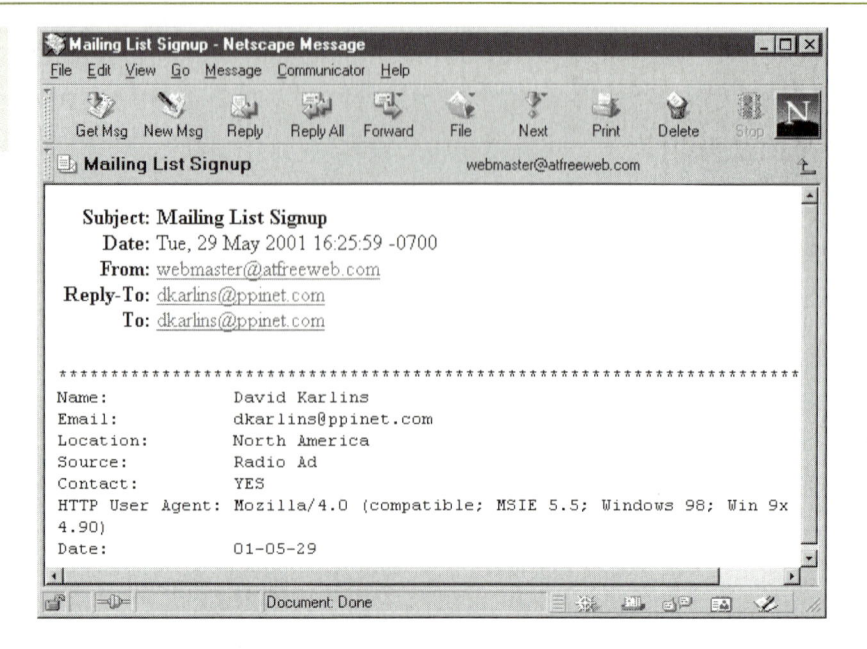

4 In the E-mail Address area, enter the e-mail address to which you want to send the collected data.

5 In the Form Name area, enter a name that will help you remember what information is being sent to you, as shown here:

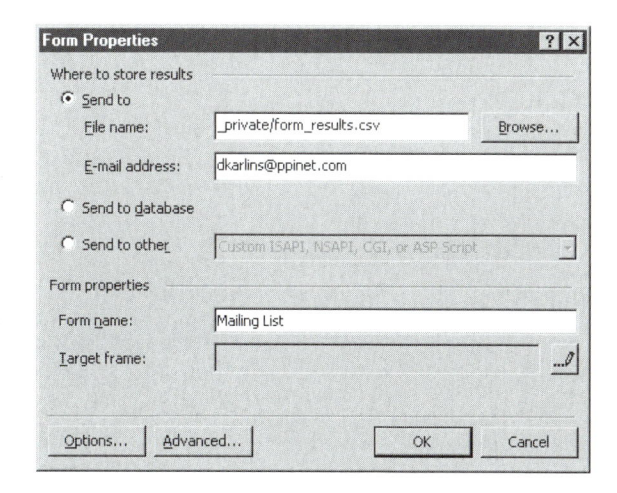

6 Click the Options button in the Form Properties dialog box. The Saving Results dialog box appears. Click the E-Mail Results tab.

7 The E-Mail Address to Receive Results area displays the e-mail address you already chose as the target for your data. You can change this address here if you want.

8 You can select a text format from the E-Mail Format drop-down menu. If you have an e-mail reader program that interprets HTML (and not all do, for instance AOL does not), you can choose one of the HTML options. However the default choice of Formatted Text will work well for anyone.

9 Check the Include Field Names to display the field names that go with collected data. This is usually helpful in understanding the information as you read it in an e-mail.

10 In the Subject Line area, deselect the Form Field Name check box, and type some text that will appear in the subject line of e-mails. For example, "Feedback Form Data," or "Sign-Up List Form Data." Visitors will not see this information, but it will help you identify incoming form input.

CHAPTER 12
Managing Form Data

11 The Reply-To Line automatically allows you to reply to an e-mail address you collect in a form. For example, if your form has a form field called *E-mail*, you would check the Form Field Name check box, and enter E-mail in this area, as shown here:

By entering the form field name "Email" in the Reply-to Line area, you are making it possible to reply to input form data simply by clicking the Reply button in an e-mail program.

12 One more thing before you okay the form: Click the Saved Fields tab in the Saving Results dialog box. You'll see a list of all the fields that will be collected when a form is submitted. Here, you can delete fields you don't want to collect and add invisible fields that will provide data not entered by a visitor.

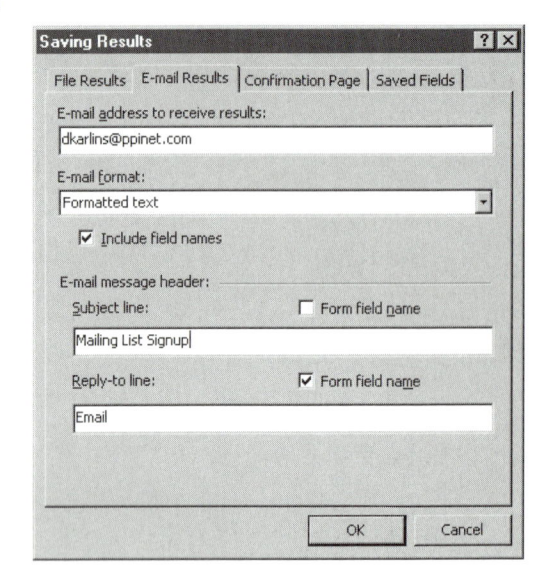

13 In the Form Fields to Save area, delete fields like "B1" (which just represents the Submit button) that you don't want sent to you.

14 Use the Date and Time area to collect the time and/or date that a form was submitted.

15 Use the Additional Information check boxes to collect the remote computer name, the user name, and/or the browser type used by the person submitting data. This information will be collected through the visitor's browser.

16 Click OK twice to close the open dialog boxes, and then save your page. You can test your form by filling out a form in a browser and collecting the data through an e-mail.

When you publish your form and test it in a browser, you should see a confirmation page each time you submit data. Then, open your e-mail program and look for e-mails with input form data.

Collecting Form Data in Text Files

When you collect data in a text files, that data is saved to files that are stored in your server. You can open these files using applications on your own computer. My favorite trick in working with data in text files is to save the data with filenames that prompt Windows to open the file in the application I want to use to work with the information. For example, I might use a DOC filename extension for data I want to work with in Microsoft Word, or I can use an XLS filename extension for data I want to work with in Excel. The *Comma Separated Values* (CSV) filename extension that is assigned by default also opens well in Excel.

FrontPage provides you with several text formatting options for saving input form data to text files. I find that most applications, including Word and Excel, open the data files best if I save data to text files using tabs to separate each field. In the following steps, I'll show you how I do that.

To Collect INPUT FORM DATA IN A TEXT FILE:

1. Right-click in an existing form, and choose Form Properties from the context menu.

2. The Form Properties dialog box appears. The Send To option button should be selected—if not, click it.

3. The default setting is _private/form_results.csv. This filename might be different if you have already generated a form results file. Or, you might have deleted it. Note that FrontPage is generating this text file in a folder named _private. This folder is not normally visible in FrontPage's Folders view, so you'll have to make it visible later in this set of steps.

4. You can leave the target text filename as it is, or you can change it. I recommend not changing the target folder—_private. This folder is not accessible to Web searches, and is a good place to save input data. This is where you can create a filename with an extension that will prompt windows to open your file in a specified application. For example, you can name this file _private/list.xls, as shown here:

5. In the Form Name area, enter a name that will help you remember what information is being sent to you.

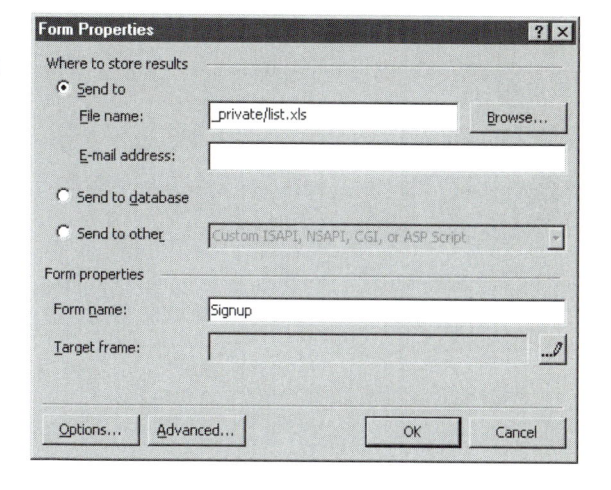

6. Click the Options button in the Form Properties dialog box and the Saving Results dialog box appears.

CHAPTER 12
MANAGING FORM DATA

7 Open the Saved Fields tab in the Saving Results dialog box. You'll see a list of all the fields that will be collected when a form is submitted. Here, you can delete fields you don't want to collect and add invisible fields that will provide data not entered by a visitor.

8 In the Form Fields to Save area, delete fields like "B1" (which just represents the Submit button) that you don't want sent to you.

9 Use the Date and Time area to collect the time and/or date that a form was submitted.

10 Use the Additional Information check boxes to collect the remote computer name, the user name, and/or the browser type used by the person submitting data. This information will be collected through the visitor's browser.

11 Open the File Results tab of the Saving Results dialog box.

12 From the File Format drop-down menu, choose Text Database Using Tab as Separator. This is the best format for importing data into programs like Word or Excel.

13 Select the Include Field Names check box. This enables your form to collect field names along with the data that is entered into the form fields and will make it easier to interpret the data later.

14 Click OK twice to close the open dialog boxes, and then save your page.

15 Test your form by filling out a form in a browser. Enter several sample sets of data to test your form. You should see a confirmation page each time you enter data.

After you have tested your input form by publishing the form and submitting several test data sets, you can open the text file that holds the data.

To View A TEXT FILE WITH COLLECTED DATA:

1 With your Web site open, switch to Folders view in FrontPage

2 Because, by default, the folder that holds input data is hidden, you have to reveal it. To do this, choose Tools | Web Settings, and click the Advanced tab in the Web Settings dialog box. Click the Shown Hidden Files and Folders check box if it is not already selected, and then click OK.

3 Double-click the _private folder in the Folder List area of Folders view. The files and folders in the _private folder are displayed in the Contents of _private area on the right side of Folders view. You'll see the file with your saved data, as shown here:

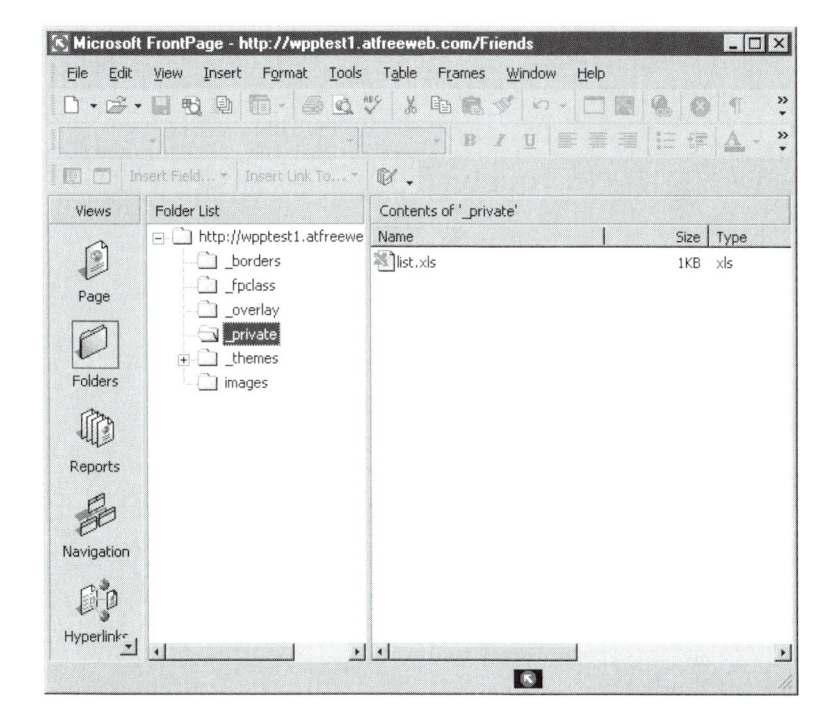

4 Since you saved your data file with a filename extension of XLS, you can open it automatically in Microsoft Excel by double-clicking the file.

5 If you want to save the file to a *local* computer, choose File | Save As, and save the Excel file to your local computer. You can format, sort, filter, or print the local file in Excel.

Keep in mind that if you save a file to your local computer, that file will not reflect *new* data that is entered into forms. Only the *online* version of your file will reflect the latest data. I generally organize my information by periodically opening my online data file and saving it to a new local file.

Results will not be posted to your text file instantly—the delay will depend on how fast your server processes the data. And, you might have to choose View | Refresh to update the content of your text file.

CHAPTER 12
MANAGING FORM DATA

SENDING FORM DATA TO A WEB PAGE

You can create an interactive Web site, where visitors instantly publish content to the site, by collecting data in a form and sending it to a Web page. For example, you can create an online bulletin board for your site, allow visitors to advertise products for sale, contribute comments about topics of interest, or provide an online "sign-in sheet" for visitors.

There are two parts to displaying form data on a Web page. The first is to create a page that will present the collected data. The second is to direct your form data to that page.

CREATING A WEB PAGE TO DISPLAY FORM DATA

When you create a page to display input form data, you will generally want to start with a blank page. After you've directed a form to send input data to this page, content will be posted whenever someone fills out an online form.

The page you create to display form data can be edited—just like any Web page. But, before you send input form data to a Web page, that page *does* have to exist. So, for this part of the process, just create a new Web page and save it. Remember the name of this page—you'll need it when you define a target for input data.

POSTING FORM DATA TO A WEB PAGE

Form data can be displayed on a Web page either by placing the newest entries on the top or bottom of the page. Normally, I find visitors like to see the latest postings first, so I usually choose that option.

To Post INPUT FORM DATA TO A WEB PAGE:

1 Right-click in an existing form, and choose Form Properties from the context menu.

2 The Form Properties dialog box appears. The Send To option button should be selected—if not, click it.

3 In the File Name area, use the Browse button to navigate to the Web page you created in the previous set of steps. This is the file that will display the contents of submitted forms.

4 In the Form Name area, you can enter a name that will help you remember what information is being collected.

5 Click the Options button, and select the Saved Fields tab in the Saving Results dialog box. You'll see a list of all the fields that will be collected when a form is submitted. Here, you can delete fields you don't want to collect and add invisible fields that will provide data not entered by a visitor.

6 In the Form Fields to Save area, delete fields such as "B1" (which just represents the Submit button) that you don't want sent to you.

7 Use the Date and Time area to collect the time and/or date that a form was submitted.

8 Use the Additional Information check boxes to collect the remote computer name, the user name, and/or the browser type used by the person submitting data. This information will be collected through the visitor's browser.

> **NOTE** Collect this additional information *only* if you want to *display* it on the Web page where the results will be posted.

9 Open the File Results tab of the Saving Results dialog box.

10 From the File Format drop-down menu, choose HTML Definition List. This is the best format for displaying collected data, along with the field name for that data. This illustration shows the Saving Results dialog box configure to post data in HTML format.

11 Select the Include Field Names check box. This enables your form to collect and present field names along with the data that is entered into the form fields.

12 Click OK twice to close open dialog boxes; then save your page.

13 Test your form by publishing your form and filling it out in a browser. Enter several sample sets of data to test your form. You should see a confirmation page each time you enter data.

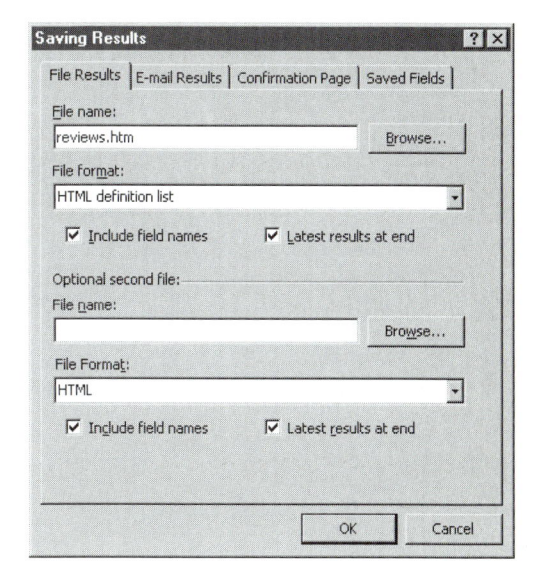

CHAPTER 12
MANAGING FORM DATA

After you have submitted some test forms, open the page where you sent the form data. You should see your data on the page, as shown in Figure 12-2.

You can open, and edit this page just as you would any Web page in FrontPage. That comes in handy because it allows you to manage the content that appears on the page. You can delete objectionable or out of date content.

USING THE DATABASE INTERFACE WIZARD TO CREATE A LIVE DATABASE CONNECTION

The difference between collecting data in a *text* file (as you did earlier in this chapter), and sending data to a *database* is that when you send information to a database, you can allow *visitors* to *query* that data right in the database. For example, if you create a directory of organization employees, you can let anyone look up an employee to find out how to contact that person. Or, users can look up *all* employees in a certain department. You also can create an online "want-ad"

FIGURE 12-2
Data collected in input forms is displayed on this Web page

operation, where visitors can post items for sale and later delete them after they are sold. In short, online databases not only allow you to *collect* data, you can also *share* that data online.

As I warned you at the beginning of this chapter, online databases can be quite complex. However, FrontPage provides a Web template that allows you to generate one by filling in the blanks in a wizard. That template—the Database Interface Wizard—creates a database that collects information, displays it, allows visitors to *query* (look up) data, and even allows visitors to edit or delete records in the database. This template is very good for creating an updateable online employee directory. The adventurous among you may try editing the template to customize it for your own database needs. If you want to go beyond that point, you might want to study the discussion of FrontPage databases in the most advanced FrontPage books available, including *FrontPage 2002: The Complete Reference* (ISBN 072132221) and *Microsoft FrontPage 2002 Bible* (ISBN 076453582X).

Because the Database Interface Wizard pushes the envelope in terms of what FrontPage can do, you will need to make sure that your Web server provider allows you to create *subwebs* in your Web site. An e-mail to a reliable and friendly FrontPage Web provider should prompt a quick confirmation that you can create subwebs at your site, or you should find out from your server provider how to upgrade to a site that does allow subwebs.

To Generate AN ONLINE DATABASE USING THE WIZARD:

1 With your Web site open, choose File | New | Page or Web.

2 In the New Page or Web pane (on the right of your screen), click the Web Site Templates link. The Web Site Templates dialog box opens.

3 Click the Database Interface Wizard icon in the Web Site Templates dialog box.

4 Click the Add to Current Web check box to make this a subweb of your open Web site.

5 Click OK to close the Web Site Templates dialog box.

6 In the first wizard dialog box, the option Create a New Access Database Within Your Web should be selected. Use this option to create your own database for your input form. Click Next. (Your other option, if this is just a learning experiment, is to use the sample database provided by FrontPage.)

7 Enter a name for your database in the Enter a Name for Your Database Connection area. Click Next.

8 FrontPage will automatically create an input form for your database. In the next wizard dialog box, use the Add, Modify, and/or Delete buttons to edit the default field names for the database. For example, in this illustration, the fields have been modified to create an input form that collects name, e-mail address, and department. After you modify the form fields, click Next. You'll see an animated graphic as FrontPage generates your database and input form pages.

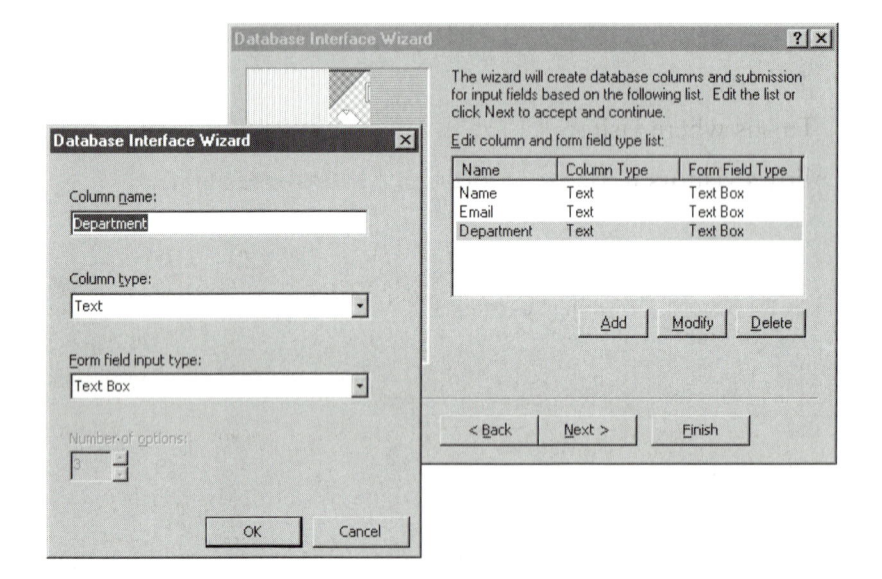

9 When the wizard window appears that says "Database Connection Established," click Next. The next wizard window has check boxes that allow you to generate any or all of three pages—a results page that displays input data, a submission form that collects data, and a database editor. The submission form is necessary—without it you can't collect data. The Results page is necessary if you want to display the data that is entered online. The Database Editor page is only necessary *if you want to allow visitors to edit data in the database*. For example, if you want to let employees update their own contact information online. After you select check boxes in this wizard window, click Next.

10 If you elected to create a database editor in the previous step, the next wizard window will prompt you to define a password and user name to restrict access to the online database. You can enter a user name and password, or you can select the Don't Protect

My Database Editor with a Username and Password check box. If you select this check box, anyone can make changes to the online database. After defining a user name and password, click Next.

11. The final wizard dialog box will inform you of where your database files will be stored on your server. That's useful information if you decide to experiment with or investigate more about online databases. When you've noted this information, click Finish to generate the subweb with your online database.

Depending on which options you selected in the wizard, FrontPage will generate up to four Web pages and open them in Page view. Those pages are

- **Index (home)** Has navigation links to the pages in the online database.
- **Results** Displays database information, and allows visitors to query (get filtered information from) the database.
- **Submission Form** This is where visitors enter data.
- **Database Editor** Allows visitors to delete records in the database online.

Each of these generated files can be edited and formatted. Some of the objects on the pages—like the Database Results Region in the Results page—are database regions that will look a little alien to you, as shown in Figure 12-3.

FIGURE 12-3
The database results region is a table that has codes embedded in cells that display data from a database

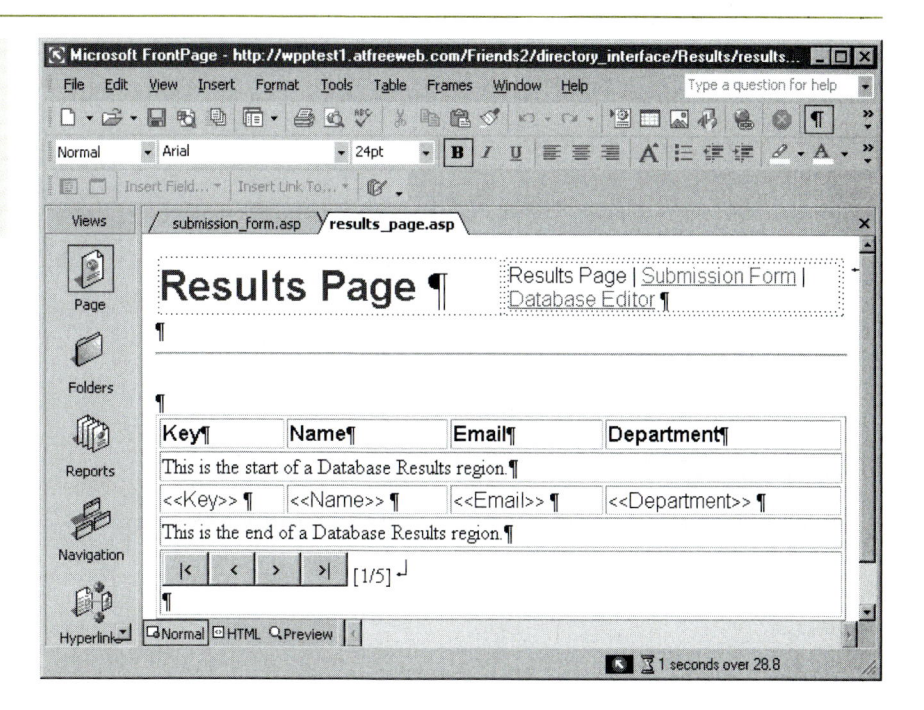

CHAPTER 12
MANAGING FORM DATA

This is a FrontPage component that displays data from a database. These weird-looking objects will make much more sense when you view the generated pages in a Web browser. The Results page is shown in a browser in Figure 12-4.

Unless you elect to delve more deeply into how online databases function, you will probably want to restrict your editing to changing the content of the page, and avoid changing the input forms or database display areas.

Do, however, feel free to *format* anything in the generated pages. You can format the tables that are generated to display the database content. You can format text, and you can format page colors and other attributes. You'll see *comment* text—invisible in browsers—which alerts you to elements of the generated pages that you should *not* edit.

Unlike a text file, online databases can be viewed, printed, and edited right in a Web browser. And, if you elected to include the Database Editor in the wizard, you can delete records from the database online, as shown in Figure 12-5.

MANY OPTIONS FOR COLLECTING DATA

In this chapter, you explored several very different options for collecting and managing the data visitors enter into your input forms. You can send that information to yourself (or anyone else) in the form of an e-mail message. You can collect that data in a file. And, you can publish the data to a Web page, which is useful for

FIGURE 12-4
The Results page displays data input in the Submission Form page; in a browser, visitors see the data in the database

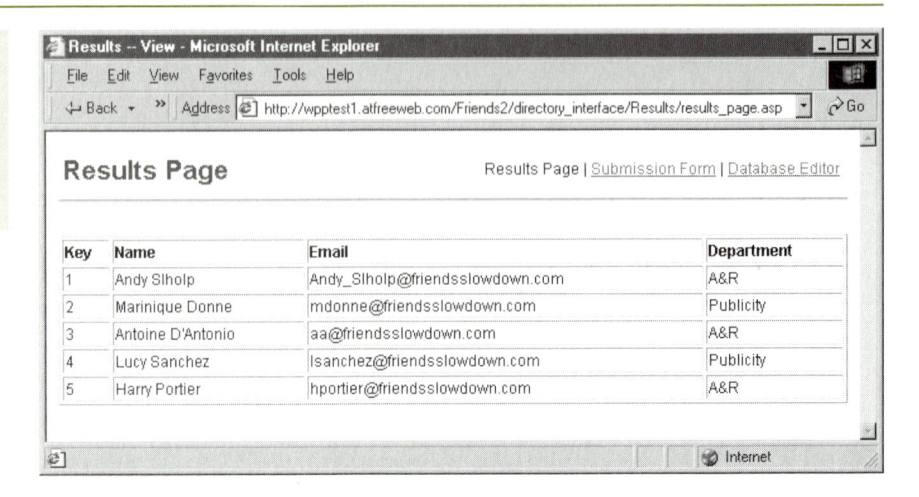

Key	Name	Email	Department
1	Andy Slholp	Andy_Slholp@friendsslowdown.com	A&R
2	Marinique Donne	mdonne@friendsslowdown.com	Publicity
3	Antoine D'Antonio	aa@friendsslowdown.com	A&R
4	Lucy Sanchez	lsanchez@friendsslowdown.com	Publicity
5	Harry Portier	hportier@friendsslowdown.com	A&R

FIGURE 12-5

Marking records for deletion in the online database

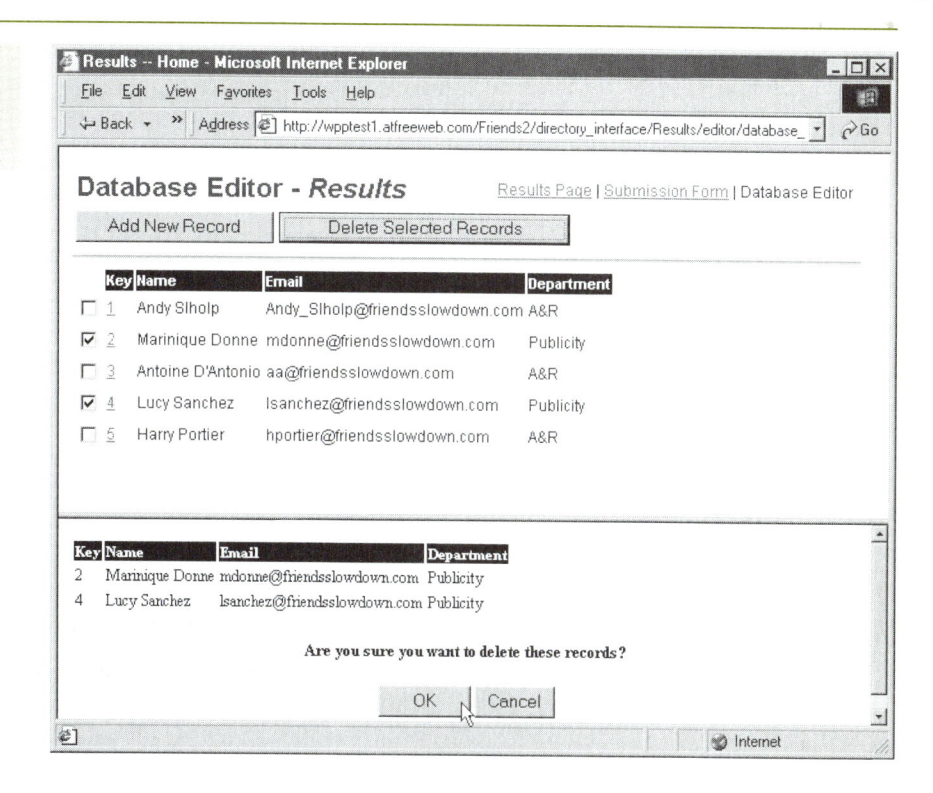

things such as community forums or intranet discussions groups where visitors both submit, and read data.

In this chapter, you also took a brief look at FrontPage's capability to connect with an interactive, online database. That process can become quite complex, but anyone can create a simple database that collects information and posts it online by using the wizard that has been added to FrontPage 2002.

> **ON THE VIRTUAL CLASSROOM CD** In Lesson 9, "Collecting Data Online," I demonstrate how to direct data collected by input forms to e-mail addresses. The lesson also demonstrates how to collect form data in online files for use as mailing lists.

13

Animating with Dynamic HTML

Normal Web page content just sort of... well, *sits there*. It doesn't move; it doesn't react to things visitors do. That's because of the limitations of the HTML (HyperText Markup Language)—the code that is used by Web browsers to interpret the text and picture formatting you assign to Web pages.

Chapter 13
Animating with Dynamic HTML

Recently, an enhanced version of HTML called DHTML—*Dynamic* HTML—has become more widely recognized by Web browsers. DHTML allows you to format pictures that change when a visitor rolls his or her cursor over them, objects that move around on your Web page, and to create pictures that display different effects—like glowing or changing color.

Before you Use DHTML.... Read This!

DHTML can be used to format text that bounces around a page, pictures that change when rolled-over, and pages that fade in and out. But DHTML can be flakey. Not all effects work in all browsers. And some effects are so unpredictable that they look downright ugly in browsers.

In general, the effects you apply using the DHTML tools covered in this chapter work in Internet Explorer 5.5. However, some of them will work in Netscape Navigator 4.7. That's because Netscape Navigator 4.7 does not implement the latest Web industry standards for DHTML.

The other (negative) consideration in using DHTML effects is that, when over-used, they make a Web site awfully distracting. A whole bunch of text flying around on the page, or weird fade-ins between page displays might keep visitors entertained and energized, or it might drive them away.

If you decide, after these warnings, to stay away from DHTML effects, you can turn off DHTML features in FrontPage.

To Turn off DHTML:

1 With a page open in Page view, select Tools | Page Options.

2 Click the Compatibility tab in the Page Options dialog box.

3 Deselect the Dynamic HTML check box, as shown on the following page.

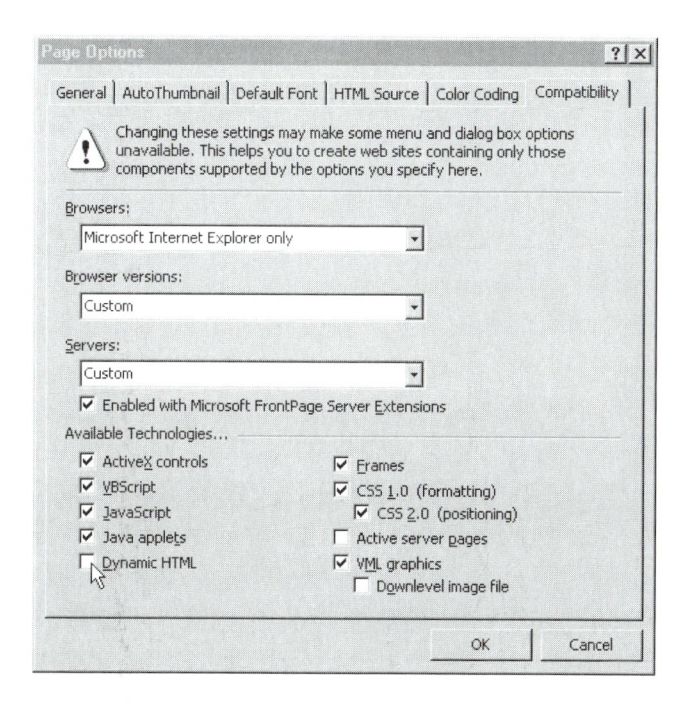

CREATING PAGE AND SITE TRANSITIONS

Page or site transitions are special effects that change the way a page first appears in a browser. There are more than two dozen different transition effects available in FrontPage, and you can experiment with them to see which one you like. What all transition effects have in common is that they display your page *in pieces*, bit by bit, until the entire content is displayed. For example, the Blend In effect transitions from transparency to opacity (from a very light looking page to one with full color). The Box In effect starts out by displaying the *outside* (sides) of the page, and finally displaying the middle of the page.

You can't see transition effects if you simply refresh a page in your browser window. To actually *see* how a transition works, you will need to preview your page in a Web browser (File | Preview in Browser). You can activate the transition by opening a page for the first time or by navigating away from the page (for example with your browser's Back button), and then returning to the page.

> **WARNING** Netscape Navigator 4.7 does not display page transitions; they are only visible in Internet Explorer. Visitors who view your page in Netscape will not see the page transition effect.

Chapter 13
Animating with Dynamic HTML

Transitions assigned to a page can be activated when the page is first opened or exited. Alternatively, the transition effect can be set to activate only if the page is accessed when your site is first opened, or exited, in a browser.

Page transitions can take effect when a *site* or a *page* is opened, or exited. If you assign a transition effect to your *site*, that effect displays only when a visitor comes to your site's home page. If you assign an effect to a *page*, that effect takes place when a visitor comes to the open page.

To Apply a transition effect to a page or site:

1. With a page open in Page view, select Format | Page Transition. The Page Transitions dialog box opens.

2. Choose an event that you want to start the transition effect from the Event drop-down menu. The choices are Page Enter, Page Exit, Site Enter, or Site Exit.

3. In the Durations area, enter an amount of time in seconds. This defines *how long* your transition effect will take.

4. In the Transition Effect area, select an effect, as shown here:

5. Click OK.

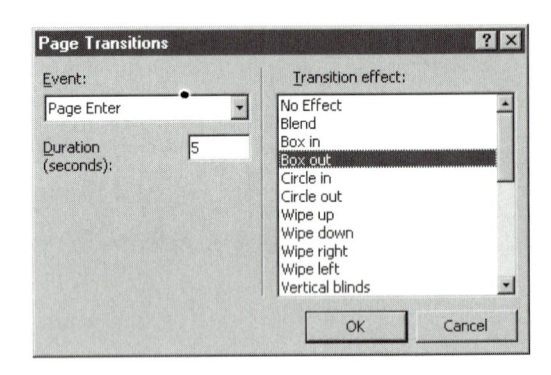

Applying DHTML to Pictures and Text

In addition to transitions that effect an entire page, DHTML effects can be applied to selected pictures or text. When DHTML is applied to pictures or text, you define two things: an *event* and an *effect*. The event is the action that triggers the effect. For example, if a visitor rolls his or her mouse cursor over text or a picture, that is an event. Another example is a visitor *clicking* text or a picture. The first step in defining a DHTML effect for text or a picture is to define the event that will trigger the effect.

Depending on whether your are formatting text or a picture, FrontPage offers a variety of effects. The most popular DHTML effect for pictures is the *rollover* effect.

FrontPage calls this effect swapped pictures. Whatever they're called, rollovers cause a picture to change when a visitor rolls his or her cursor over a picture.

DHTML effects are applied using the DHTML toolbar. Figure 13-1 shows that toolbar. The DHTML Effects toolbar assigns events and effects to selected objects, and is shown in the following illustration.

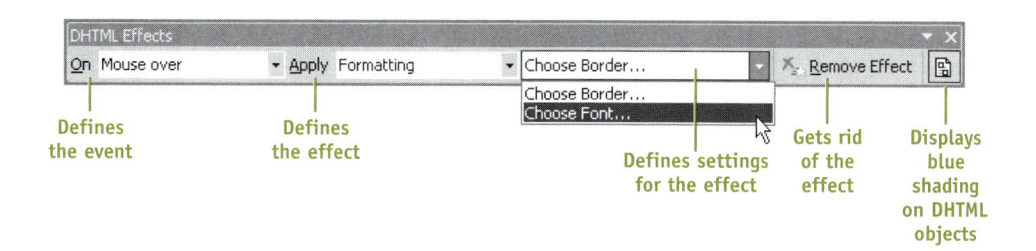

DHTML Effects toolbar with labels: Defines the event | Defines the effect | Defines settings for the effect | Gets rid of the effect | Displays blue shading on DHTML objects

Swapping Pictures

You can use rollovers to liven up your Web site, surprise visitors, and pack two pictures into the place of one. One trick I use sometimes is to use an *animated* GIF image as the "swapped for" picture, so that when a visitor hovers over a picture with his or her cursor, the original photo appears to animate.

> **NOTE** Animated GIFs are GIF format image files that have animation embedded in them. You'll find resources and tutorials for creating animated GIFs at www.ppinet.com.

Normally, you will want both the original picture, and the second picture (that displays when a visitor rolls over the picture) to be the *same size*. If you don't use two pictures of the same size, FrontPage will distort one of them (stretching it up and down, or sideways) to create a rather ugly effect—as if you were looking at the picture in a funhouse mirror.

> **NOTE** You can crop or resize pictures right in FrontPage—for advice on this check out Chapter 4.

To Create a rollover picture:

1 Choose Insert | Picture | From File to open the Picture dialog box.

2 Navigate to the folder with your pictures, and click the picture that will display *before* a visitor "rolls over" the picture. If you choose Preview from the Views menu in the Picture dialog box, you can preview pictures before you select them, as shown next.

Chapter 13
Animating with Dynamic HTML

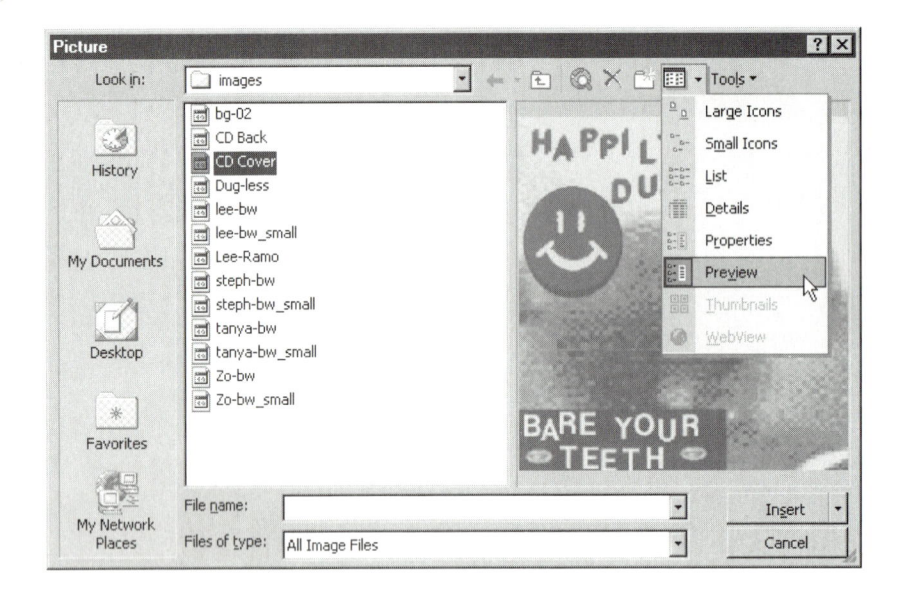

3 Click Insert in the Picture dialog box to insert the first picture.

4 Display the DHTML toolbar by choosing View | Toolbars, and selecting the DHTML Effects toolbar if it is not already selected.

5 Click your picture. Only the On / < Choose an Event > area of the DHTML toolbar will be active.

6 Use the drop-down menu in the On area of the DHTML Effects toolbar to select Mouse Over from the effects options, as shown in Figure 13-1.

7 From the Apply area drop-down list, choose Swap Picture. It's the only option available.

8 In the Choose Settings area, select Choose Picture. The Picture dialog box opens.

9 Navigate to, and select a picture that will display when the original picture is rolled over. Click the substitute picture, and click Open in the Picture dialog box.

10 Save your page, and test your picture in a browser. The "swap" picture will appear when a visitor rolls over your picture, as shown in Figure 13-2.

> **NOTE** You can also create a rollover using scanned pictures or clip art.

> **NOTE** The other options, Click, Double-Click, and Page Load aren't very much fun so don't worry about them.

FIGURE 13-1

Defining a rollover picture—the image will "swap" when a visitor rolls his or her cursor over the picture

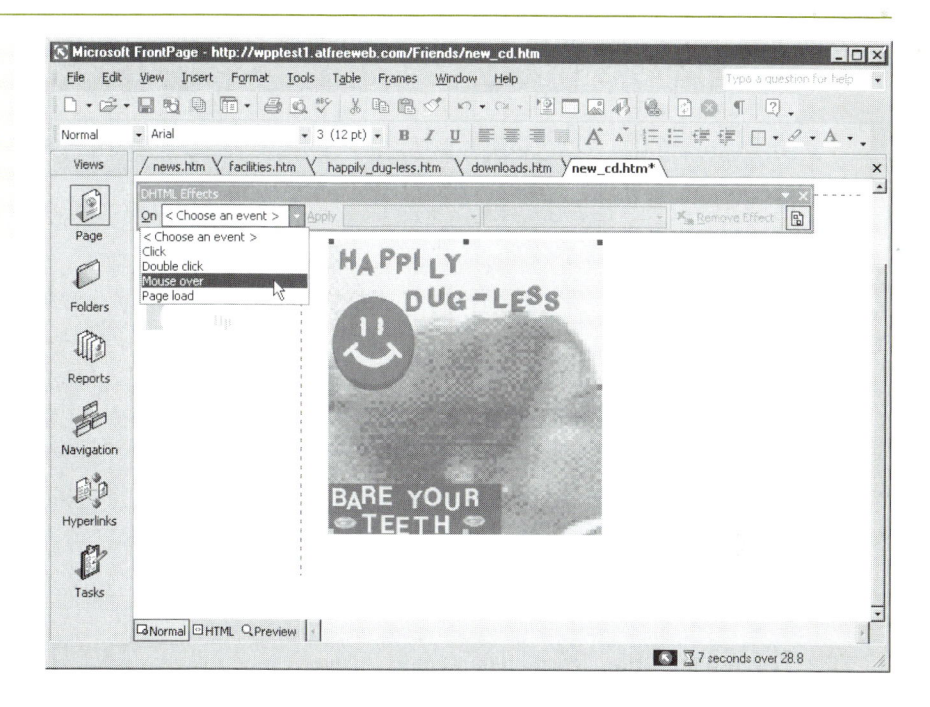

FIGURE 13-2

Testing a rollover picture in a browser

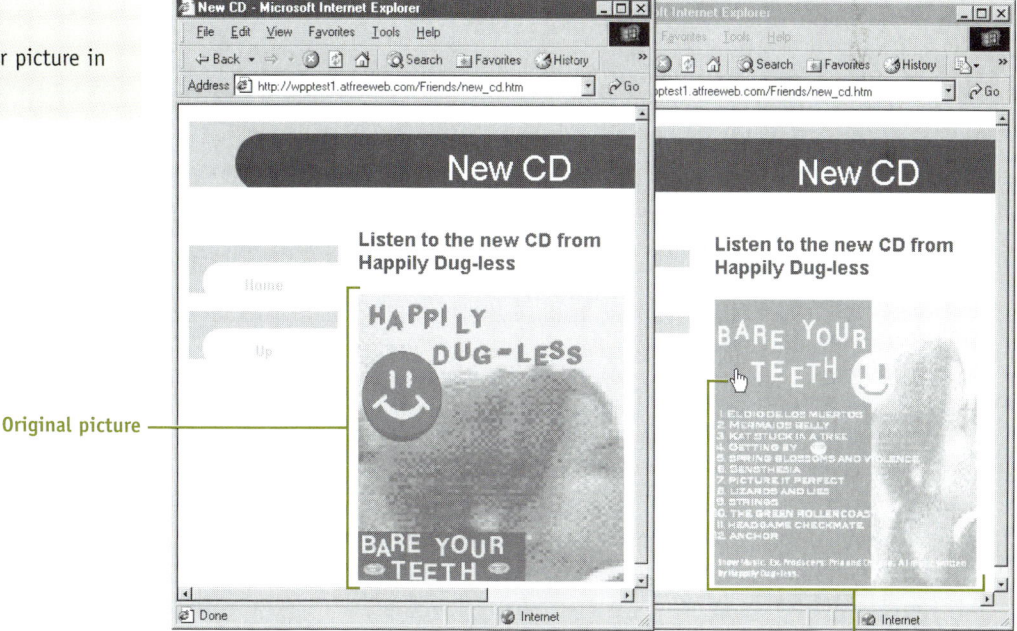

Original picture

Swapped picture—triggered by rollover

Chapter 13
Animating with Dynamic HTML

Not all DHTML effects work in Netscape Navigator 4.7, but swapped pictures work just fine. So feel unfettered as you pepper your pages with these dynamic displays!

Adding DHTML to Text

You can use DHTML effects to make text change as a visitor rolls over it with his or her cursor. For example, some Web sites now use DHTML effects—such as text changing color or displaying in boldface—in place of underlining to denote a link.

The problem with that trick is that browsers that don't support DHTML won't activate the effect, and the link might not be obvious to visitors. On the other hand, juicing up text with DHTML makes a site more active and entertaining.

To solve the dilemma posed by the fact that not all browsers support DHTML, my advice is to use DHTML to *supplement* site content, without making the content *dependent* on a visitor having a browser that supports DHTML. In the example I just mentioned, you could use *both* DHTML *and* conventional underlining to identify link text.

Using Rollover Effects on Text

As with pictures, FrontPage provides four options for triggering events that can be assigned to rollover text. Besides Mouse Over, you can define other event triggers: Click, Double-Click, or Page Load. It's unlikely that anyone is going to be double-clicking text on your page, so forget that effect. You *might* want to make link text dynamic by assigning an effect to click. The effect won't last long—just for the instant that a visitor clicks text. Mostly, you'll use the Mouse Over event to trigger dynamic text effects.

There are two different effects that can be applied to rollover or clicked (or double-clicked) text. Formatting effects can be used to change *text font* formatting. For example, you assign an effect so that rolled-over text will turn red, and become boldface. You can also define *border* effects. When you do, you can choose from border or shading effects. For example, you could display a yellow border with blue shading around hovered-over text.

Using Page Load Effects on Text

If you elect to trigger a text effect by having a page load, you can choose a rather wild set of dynamic effects for the text that cause words to fly onto the page from corners of the screen, bounce around, or zip around your page in spirals before landing in place.

Use these Page Load text effects judiciously. Dynamic text can wake up and shake up visitors, and add some fun and action to your page. On the other hand, too much text racing around your page might induce vertigo or nausea among sensitive Web surfers. And yes, these effects *will* display in Netscape Navigator 4.

Here's a quick survey of the DHTML text formatting available when you use Page Open as a triggering event:

TABLE 13-1   DHTML Available for Page Open Triggered Text Effects

DHTML Effect	What It Does	Additional Effect Settings
Drop In By Word	Selected words "drop" from the top of the page, one at a time.	None
Elastic	Text flies in and bounces up and down as it moves to its normal location.	Text can bounce from the bottom of the page or in from the right.
Fly In	Text moves onto the page and into position.	You can define the direction from which the text flies into the page, and elect to have text move word-by-word, or all at once.
Spiral	Text zooms around the page in smaller and smaller circles until it reaches its location.	None
Wave	Words move over each other into place in a wave-like pattern.	None
Wipe	Text fades in one line at a time.	Text can appear from left to right, from top to bottom of the page, or "unfold" from the middle of the page.
Zoom	Text expands or contracts, and ends up at the defined font size. This only works if you assign Normal size to selected font, and use the Heading styles in the Style drop-down list to increase text size.	Settings are "in," in which case the element starts small and grows to its final size, and "out," which causes the element to start large and shrink down to its final size.

CHAPTER 13
ANIMATING WITH DYNAMIC HTML

ASSIGNING DHTML TO TEXT

Whether you are assigning DHTML text effects that will be triggered when a page loads, or by mouse actions, the basic process is the same. Just remember that the specific effects that are available for text will differ, depending on whether you are using a page load triggered event, or a mouse triggered event. Page load triggered events make text fly all over the page, while mouse event triggered effects cause text to change color, size, font, border, or shading.

To Assign DHTML effects to selected text:

1. Select the text in Page view.

2. Choose View | Toolbars, and make sure the DHTML Effects toolbar is selected.

3. From the On drop-down menu, choose an event to trigger your text effect.

4. From the Apply drop-down menu, choose an effect to apply to the text.

5. Some effects have additional, definable features. If so, the Effect area becomes active in the DHTML Effects toolbar. Choose additional effect parameters from the Effects drop-down menu, as shown in Figure 13-3.

FIGURE 13-3
Some, but not all effects have additional parameters that are defined in the Effects area of the DHTML Effects toolbar

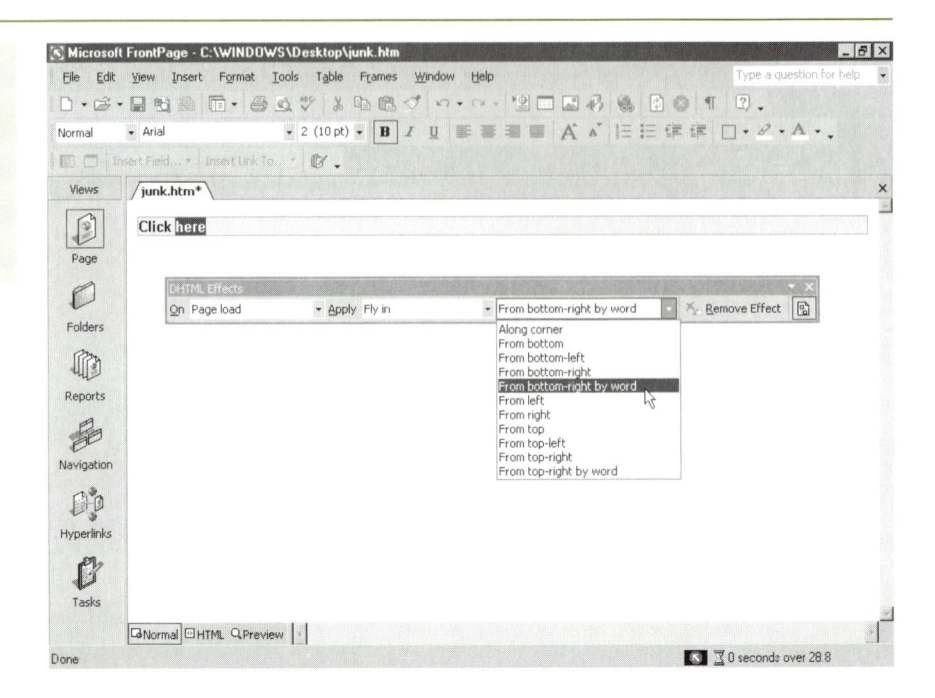

6 Save your page. You can examine the effect in the Preview tab of Page view or by previewing your page in a Web browser.

Removing DHTML Effects

If you want to remove a DHTML effect from a picture or text, you can do so. Sometimes it's not so easy to find text to which DHTML effects have been applied. To make that task easier, you can highlight DHTML effects.

To Highlight and/or delete DHTML effects:

1 Choose View | Toolbars, and make sure the DHTML Effects toolbar is selected.

2 Click the Highlight Dynamic HTML Effects button on the far right side of the DHTML Effects toolbar to toggle back and forth between displaying and hiding blue highlighting on text with DHTML effects.

3 Click text to which DHTML effects have been applied—it's easier to see with highlighting on.

4 Click the Remove Effect button in the DHTML Effects toolbar to remove the DHTML effect, as shown here:

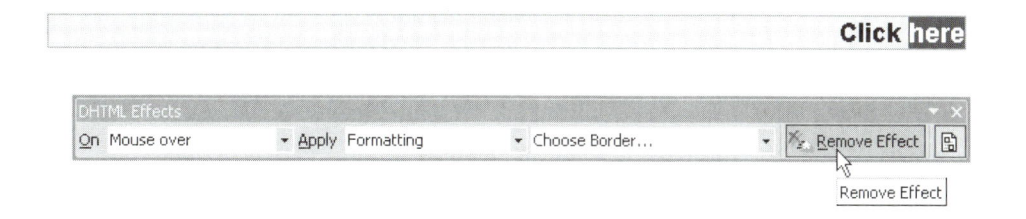

5 Save your page. The effect is removed.

DHTML Everywhere...

In addition to the effects you explored in this chapter, DHTML technology is used to create other dynamic objects in FrontPage. In Chapter 3, you learned to create collapsible outlines. In Chapter 5, you learned to position pictures in exact locations on a page, and even more absolutely positioned objects in front of, or behind each other. Both absolutely positioned pictures, and collapsible outlines employ DHTML tools. And, like all DHTML effects, they only work when viewed in a browser that supports the specific DHTML code that makes any object work.

DHTML—Techie Stuff

Early in this chapter, I cautioned that DHTML can be flakey. Why is that? DHTML effects are created by a combination of JavaScript and a feature called Cascading Style Sheets (CSS). All recent versions of Web browsers, including Netscape Navigator 4.7, detect and interpret JavaScript. Therefore, DHTML effects that rely completely on JavaScript work well in most browsers.

Other DHTML effects require that browsers *also* support a recent version of Cascading Style Sheet (called CSS-2) that allows for absolute positioning of elements on a page. Not only does Netscape Navigator not fully support this enhanced version of CSS, but my experience is that even Internet Explorer 5.5 does not always interpret CSS generated by FrontPage in a reliable way. Therefore, some FrontPage-generated DHTML effects will display unpredictably in *all* browsers. For an authoritative discussion of CSS versions and compatibility, you can visit the online Style Master site at http://www.westciv.com/style_master/academy/css_tutorial/introduction/index.html.

What to do about the unreliability of DHTML? The solution is to *test* your DHTML effects in both Internet Explorer and Netscape Navigator and see how they look on a page. Most will work well, some will not, but only testing will tell.

Interactivity, Animation... and Media

In this chapter, you learned to use Dynamic HTML to make elements of your Web site *interactive* and *animated*. Interactive elements *react* to *events*—like a visitor rolling over a picture or text with his or her mouse. In response to these events, DHTML generates *effects*—such as changed text formatting or swapped pictures.

In the next chapter, you'll investigate how to incorporate even more complex animation by using media files, like Flash movies, sound files, and animated GIF pictures.

> **ON THE VIRTUAL CLASSROOM CD?** In Lesson 10, "Using Dynamic HTML Effects," I demonstrate how to assign Dynamic HTML effects to page transitions, and to text. And, I'll demonstrate how to trigger effects with actions like loading a page and scrolling over text.

14

Adding Sound and Video

FrontPage makes it easy to include sound and video in your Web pages. FrontPage can handle almost any kind of media file, not just Windows Media files (such as AVI or MPEG), but also animated GIF video, QuickTime movies, and Macromedia Flash (SWF) files.

CHAPTER 14
Adding Sound and Video

FrontPage also handles a long list of audio files, including MP3, Macintosh AIFF files, and WAV format. In this chapter, you'll learn to integrate audio and video into your FrontPage Web.

Sound and Video—the Coming Wave

Sound and video add a whole new dimension to Web sites. It's one thing to read text and see a picture, and something else—much more interactive and exciting— to listen to music and watch a video.

Over the past couple years, two developments have combined to make sound and video broadly accessible. One is the advance of technology for compressing and *streaming* media files—reducing file size and allowing them to start playing a visitor's browser even before they are completely downloaded. The other development is the availability, in many cities and countries, of high-speed (*high bandwidth*) Internet connections.

In fact, as I write this chapter, probably the biggest roadblock to widespread media accessibility is figuring out how someone will get *paid* for all the sound files (and increasingly video) that we are downloading.

NOTE It is becoming increasingly necessary for those of us who put content on the Web to document permission to use that material. While the laws governing the use of media content on Web sites are complex, confusing, and contradictory, I rely on one basic rule: My clients or I get written permission from the owner of a media file before I put it on a Web site. I find that *most* folks *want* their media exposed to the world and are happy to cooperate.

How Do Visitors See and Hear Media Files?

Sound and video files require *players* to be seen and heard. Internet Explorer 5.5 includes player software that automatically detects and plays most popular media files. Other media formats, notably RealMedia files, require proprietary player software. In that case, folks have to download a viewer or player to see the video or hear the music.

While most people have some form of media player (and sound card hardware) on their computers, you—as a Web developer—don't really know *which* media player software will be available to visitors to your Web site. This means that *how* visitors see your movie or hear your sound file is beyond your control. To be safe, you'll want to include media file types that are supported by *most* media players, and also include *links* at your site so that visitors can easily download a free player to see and hear your media content.

FrontPage developers have two main options in presenting online media: You can allow visitors to view or hear media in an independent media player, or you can embed media in a FrontPage Web page using a plug-in. Figure 14-1 shows a media file embedded in a FrontPage Web site.

In this chapter, you'll survey the kinds of media files you can include in your FrontPage Web site and walk through how to add them to your Web pages.

A Quick Survey of Media File Types

Surveying the current batch of media file types is kind of like reporting on the latest successor to Britney Spears or NSYNC—by the time this book gets into your hands, there will have been changes in the way folks download and watch or listen to media files.

FIGURE 14-1
The player controls in this embedded video file are integrated right into the FrontPage Web page

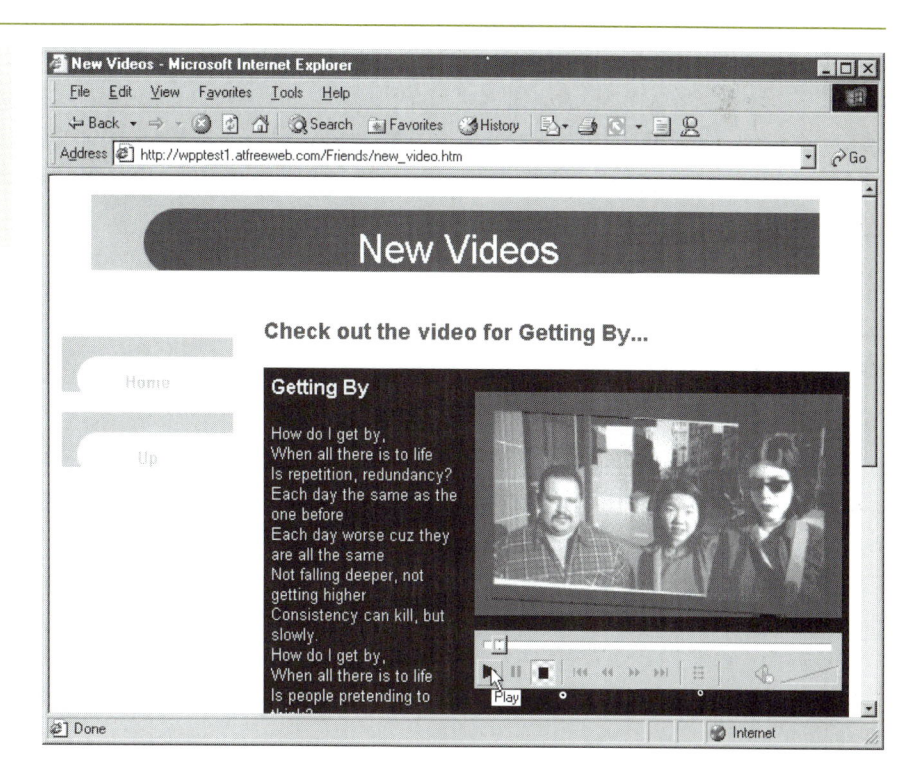

CHAPTER 14
ADDING SOUND AND VIDEO

Still, at this point, available media file types have begun to sort themselves out, and it will be helpful to briefly identify and discuss different ways you can provide media at your Web site.

MICROSOFT MEDIA FORMATS

Microsoft's favored media file types include Wave sound files (WAV), MPEG movie files, AVI video files, and ASF media files. These formats are most uniformly supported by Microsoft applications, and will generally play on Windows systems. In addition, the Windows Media Player—downloadable from Microsoft—plays these files formats. Here, Windows Media Player is shown playing an AVI video:

FrontPage handles WAV, MPEG, AVI, and ASF files easily, and provides quite a bit of control over how these media files are presented in FrontPage Web pages.

REALMEDIA VIDEO AND AUDIO FILES

RealMedia (RM) and RealAudio (RA) files can be viewed by people who download the RealPlayer or get a copy on CD. The CD that accompanies my colleague Laurie Ann Ulrich's book *Web Design Virtual Classroom* (ISBN 007213111-X) includes RealMedia video files like the one shown on the next page.

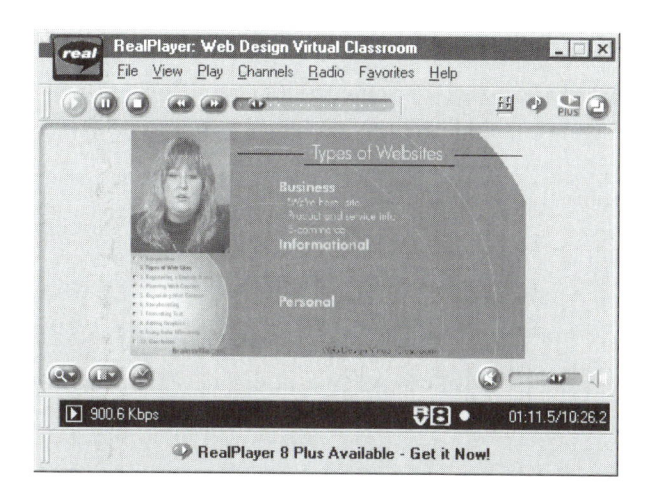

RealMedia files download fast and are available for all kinds of movies and even live broadcasts. Unlike other media distributors, RealMedia makes money from selling players and online content, not from selling media development software. Time will tell whether that, or another business model, works for distributing online media content. But because RealMedia is in the business of selling players, visitors have to fight their way through a maze at real.com to find and download the free version of the RealPlayer.

On the positive side, RealPlayer *is* available free if you look hard enough at the real.com Web site. And RealMedia files download faster than other streaming media files, allowing visitors to start watching movies quickly.

> **WARNING** A final negative: FrontPage and RealMedia don't mesh well—it's not possible to integrate RealPlayer into FrontPage Web pages as a plug-in. I'll explain how plug-ins work with FrontPage later in this chapter.

QuickTime Media

QuickTime is the video format included with Macintosh computers. The main reason to use this format is to provide seamless video for people viewing your Web site on a Mac. QuickTime movies are viewed using the QuickTime Player. The player is free and easily accessible to both Windows and Macintosh users. The pay-to-play version of QuickTime provides a video viewer and a video editor. QuickTime format is reliable, and even though it's associated with Macs QuickTime movies play nicely in Windows, as shown here:

Flash Movies

Macromedia Flash movies—and their cousins Shockwave movies—require the Flash (or Shockwave) player. IE 5.5 has built-in Flash movie support. For Web surfers without IE 5.5, Macromedia makes the Flash player easily accessible at www.macromedia.com.

FrontPage supports Flash's movie format particularly well. Later in this chapter I'll walk through how to integrate Flash movies into your FrontPage Web site.

MIDI Sound Files

MIDI Sequencer sound files are very compact (small) in size and widely supported by media player software: MIDI files are limited in sound quality. In the days when 28.8kps modem connections typified how people connected to the Internet, MIDI files were widely used because they are so small. They are still useful for sites that will be accessed by visitors in areas of the world where higher speed Internet connections are not available. And sometimes the tinny, "techie" sound of MIDI files is an appropriate effect for a site.

MP3 Audio

Made famous by the Napster controversy, MP3 format delivers quality sound from files that are compressed to download quickly. Many media players including the QuickTime player and Windows Media player handle MP3 format sound files. And, MP3 files can be transferred to portable players for easy access away from a computer.

AIFF Audio Files

AIFF is the audio format associated with Macintosh computers. AIFF files play in Windows as well, using the Windows Media player. FrontPage developers are unlikely to work with AIFF files much, because FrontPage is a "windows-only" application. However, if you are provided with AIFF files by a client, FrontPage will be happy to import those files, and they will play just fine with the Windows Media Player.

AU Sound Files

AU sound files are associated with the UNIX operating system. Their main relevance here is that they are used to present sound files with Java applets, including with FrontPage's Hover Button Web component. (See Chapter 10 for a discussion of adding AU sound files to Hover buttons.)

How Do You Get Video and Sound Files?

In many cases, your Web design clients, or your company or organization, will provide you with media files for their Web site. Internet searches, as well, will turn up many sources of free and royalty-free (you pay just once to use them) media files.

In addition, video production shops are springing up in many places. For example, the folks at Brainsville.com, invited me into their studios to create the video files that accompany this book.

Another source of media files are CDs. If you search the Web for "ripper software," you'll find dozens of free and trial-version software that extracts media files from CDs. A number of my clients in the music and entertainment industries have provided me with CDs and authorized me to "rip" tracks or excerpts of media files for inclusion in their Web sites.

We're getting a bit beyond the scope of the book here, but there are many ways to *create your own* sound and video files. Windows ME comes with the Sound Recorder program and a new program called Windows Movie Maker. These programs allow you to input sound and video (from a microphone or digital video camera), and edit media files. Explanations for how to use these programs are found in advanced level Windows ME books.

> **NOTE** If you've got the book *Windows Millennium Edition: The Complete Reference* (ISBN 0072127511), jump to page 374 for an easy-to-follow explanation of the process of creating and editing movies in Windows ME.

Importing Media Files into FrontPage

The first step in presenting a media file at your Web site is to *import* it into your site. Once you have the media file at your site, you can either embed that media file in an integrated plug-in, or you can allow visitors to see or hear the file in their own media player software.

Either way, you will want to upload the media file to your site first. This takes time, because most media files—especially video files—are *large*. Keep in mind that a video file stores hundreds or thousands of frames—maybe more. And many video files have embedded sound tracks as well. So if you've got a minute, a handy cup of coffee, soda, or bottle of beer, you're all set to upload a media file.

To Import a media file into your Web site:

1. With your Web site open in FrontPage, select File | Import. The Import dialog box opens.

2. Click the Add File button to open the Add File to Import List dialog box.

3. In the Add File to Import List dialog box, navigate to find the media file you want to import into FrontPage, as shown here:

4. Click the Open button to add the file to the list of files to import in the Import dialog box.

5. Use the Add File button again, as needed, to add additional media files to your import list.

6. Click OK in the Import dialog box to upload the selected media files to your Web site.

> **TIP** If you want to import your media file into a specific folder, select that folder in the File List before you open the Import dialog box.

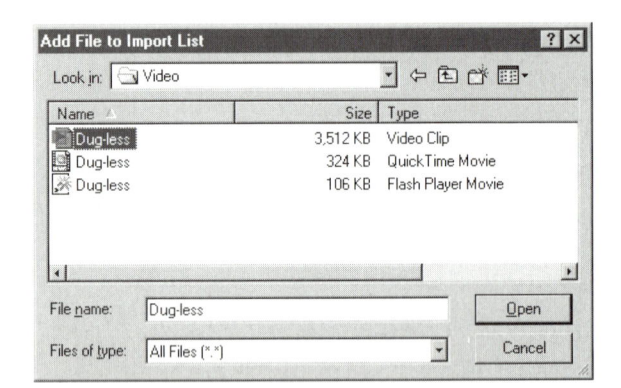

Once you have uploaded media to your FrontPage Web, you can make it available to visitors to your site. Just remember, it took you time to *upload* these media files, and it will take some time (not as much probably) for visitors to download the files. However, many media file formats have *streaming* properties so that the video (or sound) file *begins* to play even before the entire file is downloaded.

The Easy way to Embed Sound and Video

Okay, assuming that you *have* a media file or more at your FrontPage site, how do you make that file accessible to visitors? There's really nothing to it. All you have to do is include a link to that file in a Web page.

When visitors follow a link to a media file, their system automatically launches whatever media player software is associated with that media file. So, for example, if you include a link to a WAV sound file, Windows users will automatically hear that file in the Windows Media Player—unless they have configured Windows to substitute a different default media player. On the other hand, Macintosh users will hear the file via the QuickTime player, which is the default media player for Macs.

The drawback of providing media files by simply linking to them is that a media player will open independently of the Web site, and viewers will leave the Web site to see or hear the sound or movie. If you want to integrate a media player right into your Web page, you'll need to use a plug-in, something you'll explore in the next section of this chapter.

To Link TO A MEDIA FILE:

1 Open a Web page from which you will link to one of your media files.

2 Enter text (or insert a picture) that will serve as a link to the media file, as shown here:

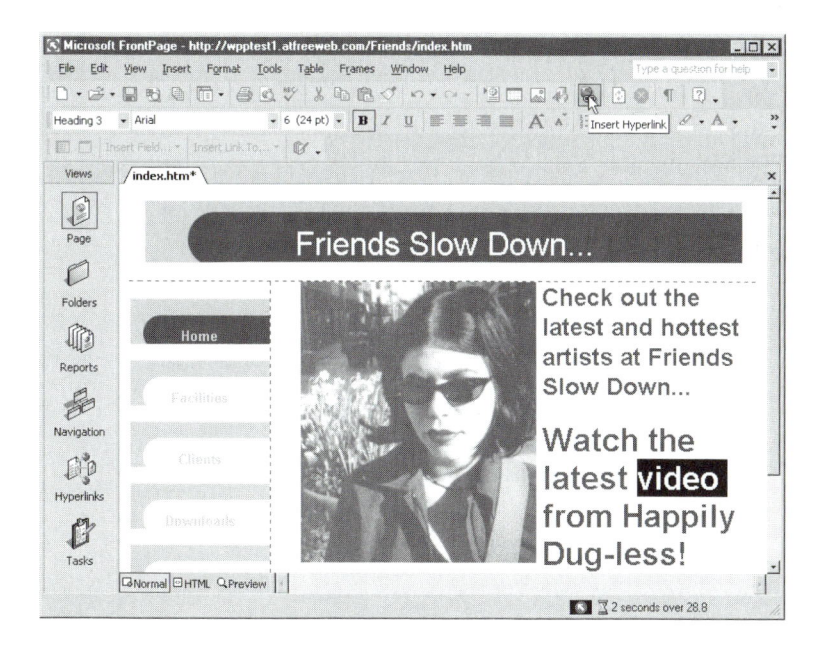

3 Click the Insert Hyperlink button to open the Insert Hyperlink dialog box.

4 In the Insert Hyperlink dialog box, navigate to the folder with your video file. This can be a file of any video format—you are depending on media player software *at your visitor's computer* to detect and play this file.

5 Select a video file, and click OK to close the Insert Hyperlink dialog box.

6 Save your page, and test the link in a Web browser.

If *your* computer has software that will detect and play the embedded video, the video will play on *your* computer. If you want to ensure that *visitors* can play the video, include a note on the page that reads "This link opens a file that requires the Windows Media Player," or another appropriate media player. And, to be nice, you can include a link so visitors can easily download the required player if they don't have it.

Embedding Media Files in Your Page

As I explained earlier, when you *link* to a media file, you simply allow visitors to your site to *download* that file, and you rely on their local system settings to determine what media player will play that file, and what settings will be applied to that media player.

A more integrated way to present media files is to embed them as plug-ins in FrontPage. This way, the controls for the media file are right in the Web page. And, you can define the size of the media object on the page, as well as having some freedom to define player controls.

In addition to using the plug-in component, some media files can also be embedded in a page as pictures. Videos embedded as pictures have somewhat different options and controls than videos embedded as plug-ins, so you might want to experiment with both options before deciding how best to present your video.

Adding a Plug-In

You can embed a plug-in in FrontPage for Flash movies, QuickTime movies, AVI, MPEG, and other video formats, as well as many sound formats. Of the video file formats surveyed earlier in this chapter, only RealMedia files cannot be easily incorporated into a FrontPage Web page as a plug-in. Until Microsoft and RealMedia come to terms, the best way to include RealMedia files at your site is to use the linked-file approach explained in the previous section of this chapter.

To Embed PLUG-IN TO PRESENT VIDEO IN A WEB PAGE:

1 Assuming you have imported (uploaded) a media file into your Web site, open the page that will display the embedded media file in Page view.

2 Choose Insert | Web Component, and click Advanced Controls (at the bottom of the list of Web Components).

3 In the Choose a Control area of the Insert Web Component dialog box, click Plug-In.

4 Click the Finish button to open the Plug-In Properties dialog box, as shown here:

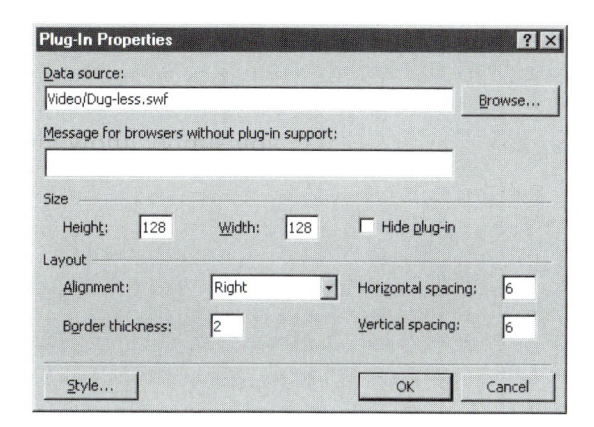

5 Use the Browse button in the Plug-In Properties dialog box to select a media file to embed.

6 In the Message for Browsers Without Plug-In Support area, type a message, such as "Your browser does not support Plug-Ins. Sorry, you're missing the video."

7 In the Height and Width areas, you can define a size for the plug-in display.

8 Don't select the Hide Plug-In check box—this hides your embedded media.

> **NOTE** Avoid options other than Left, Right, or Center in the Alignment drop-down menu. Those options are for tiny graphic objects occasionally used by advanced page designers for layout and spacing purposes and are not helpful in aligning video or sound plug-ins.

CHAPTER 14
ADDING SOUND AND VIDEO

9 You can use the Alignment drop-down menu to select Left or Right. Either of those options will flow text *around* your plug-in.

10 You can define border thickness in pixels by entering a value in the Border Thickness area.

11 Use the Horizontal Spacing and Vertical Spacing areas to define a buffer between your media plug-in and text that is adjacent to the plug-in.

12 When you have finished defining plug-in properties, click **OK** to embed the plug-in on your page.

Plug-ins display as icons in the Normal tab of Page view. You can test them in the Preview tab of Page view.

Different plug-ins have different properties. For example, AVI plug-ins display a player like the one shown in Figure 14-1. Figure 14-2 shows the different plug-in displays that result when you embed a QuickTime movie and a Flash movie. The QuickTime movie plug-in displays a Control Panel under the movie, whereas the Flash movie controls are visible when a viewer right-clicks the movie.

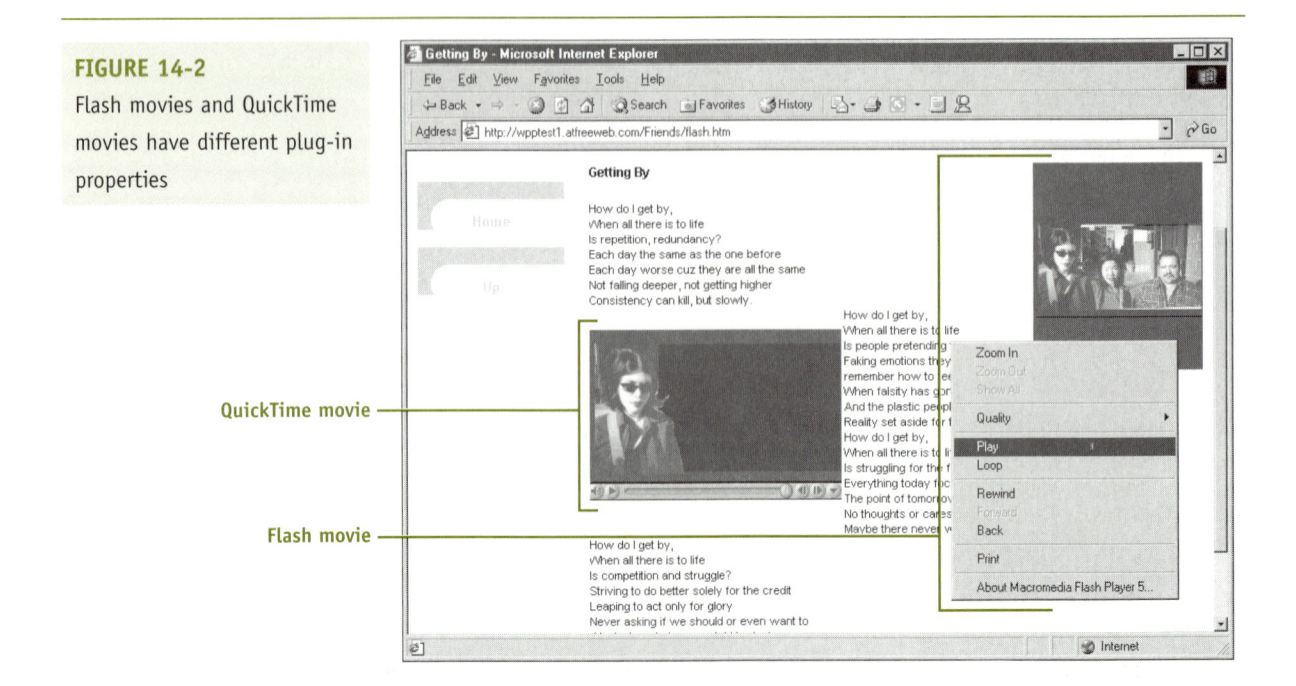

FIGURE 14-2
Flash movies and QuickTime movies have different plug-in properties

Embedding Video as Pictures

In addition to using the Plug-In Web Component to display video on your Web page, FrontPage also provides the option of embedding videos as pictures. Embedding videos as pictures works for AVI video format, and for animated GIF files, but not for Flash or QuickTime movies.

When you embed a video as a picture, you can define whether a movie should loop continuously or play once. And you can define how you want the movie to start—when the page is opened or when a visitor rolls over the video with their mouse cursor.

To Embed a video as a picture:

1. Assuming you have imported the video file into your FrontPage Web, open the page in which you will embed the video file.

2. Choose Insert | Picture | Video. The Video dialog box opens.

3. Navigate to a video file in the Video dialog box. Select the file, and click Open. The video file is placed on your Web page.

You can test embedded picture/video in the Preview tab of Page view, or in a Web browser. After you embed a picture/video, you can define how the video will play. You can also change the video file to a different movie without completely deleting the video area in your Web page.

To Define properties for an embedded picture/video:

1. Click to select the video.

2. Right-click the video, and choose Properties. The Video tab of the Picture Properties dialog box appears.

3. Use the Loop spin box to define how many times a movie will play. Check the Forever check box to make the movie repeat endlessly.

4. Use the Loop Delay spin box to define a waiting period before the movie repeats after it is finished playing.

CHAPTER 14
Adding Sound and Video

5 Select either the On File Open or the On Mouse Over options button to define when a movie will start playing.

6 Click OK to close the dialog box. Save and test your movie.

Videos embedded as pictures (again, this works for animated GIF files and AVI files, but not for Flash or QuickTime movies) can be formatted like pictures. To do that, right-click a picture/movie and choose Picture Properties from the context menu.

Use available options in the General and Appearance tabs to define wrapping style, alignment, border thickness, horizontal and vertical spacing, and movie size in the Appearance tab. In the General tab, define alternate text, and a link for your video.

ALIGNING, SIZING, AND CREATING SPACE FOR EMBEDDED VIDEOS

You can easily resize and align embedded videos—whether they are plug-ins or embedded picture/videos. To resize a video, simply click a handle and drag to make the video area larger or smaller. If you are resizing a *plug-in* video, the size of the plug-in area *may* determine what kinds of controls are displayed. You'll have to switch back and forth between FrontPage Page view and your Web browser to see exactly how the plug-in will look at different sizes.

To align a video—and make text flow around it—you can select the video and use the Align Left or Align Right tools in the FrontPage Formatting toolbar.

To change the *spacing* around a video, right-click the video. Choose either Picture Properties or Plug-In Properties, depending on which option is available in the context menu.

If you opened the Picture Properties dialog box, select the Appearance tab and enter values in the Horizontal Spacing or Vertical Spacing areas to create buffer space between the video and adjacent text. Here, you can also use the Border Thickness area to define a border (in pixels) for your video. Click OK to close the dialog box.

> **WARNING** Borders don't mesh well with many video plug-in formats. Experiment, and if the border doesn't align well with the video, remove it.

If you opened the Plug-In Properties dialog box, you can use the Vertical Spacing and Horizontal Spacing areas to change spacing around the video. Use the Border Thickness area to define a border around the video. Click OK to close the dialog box.

Adding Background Audio to Pages

Page background sounds work differently than embedded media files. They are not visible to visitors, and visitors cannot use controls to modify the background sound files. For these reasons, background sound files can be annoying, and you should consider embedded sound files as an option that gives visitors more control over the audio they experience at your site. If you do elect to add background sounds, be aware that they will increase page download time.

To Assign a background sound to a Web page:

1 Open the Web page in FrontPage Page view.

2 Select File | Properties. The Page Properties dialog box appears with the General tab selected.

3 In the Background Sound Location area of the General tab, click the Browse button to locate an audio file to play when the page is loaded. The Background Sound dialog box opens.

4 Navigate to a sound file in your Web, or in your local computer, and click Open to close the Background Sound dialog box.

5 To repeat the sound a defined number of times, deselect the Forever check box, and enter a value in the Loop spin box.

6 To loop the sound over and over—without end—select the Forever check box.

7 Click OK to close the Page Properties dialog box.

Save the Web page. You are prompted to add the sound file to your Web, if it is not already uploaded. Preview the page in your Web browser to test the background sound file.

You can reopen the Page Properties dialog box and use the General tab to change settings for your background sound file. To delete the background sound, delete the information in the location area, and click OK in the Page Properties dialog box.

Have Fun with Media

In this chapter, you learned to embed both sound and video files in your Web site. Sound, and especially video files are large; they take time to upload *to* a Web site, and also take time for visitors to download *from* a Web site. At the same time, faster Internet connections and increasingly polished media tools are making it more and more possible for many people to download and appreciate sound and video over the Internet.

FrontPage can easily present AVI and animated GIF format video as pictures. You can present additional video formats (as well as AVI files) as plug-ins. Depending on the file format of your video, different video plug-ins display different player controls for embedded video.

Some video file formats require additional software to play—software not included in Windows or Macintosh systems. If you embed video that requires these players, you can include links to Web sites where visitors can obtain the necessary players to appreciate your video files.

As with any complex element of a FrontPage Web site, be prepared to test, test, and test again to make sure your media files are available to visitors. You might want to create an easy e-mail link or a link to your site's feedback page so that you can learn about any difficulties visitors have downloading your media files.

In the next chapter, you'll explore something quite different from video, but still a way for visitors to interact with your Web site. You'll look at FrontPage options for generating online discussions groups.

ON THE VIRTUAL CLASSROOM CD? In Lesson 11, "Embedding Media in Your Web Site," I demonstrate how to include different kinds of sound and video files in your Web site. The lesson explores background sound files, links to sound and media files, and presenting video with plug-ins.

15

Creating Complex Webs with Web Templates

FrontPage Web templates can be used to save time by instantly generating a Web site structure. Other FrontPage templates allow you to add powerful features to your site that are not normally accessible to FrontPage developers—such as discussion forums or Web site portals that allow visitors to post and download documents.

Chapter 15
Creating Complex Webs with Web Templates

While some Web templates are best used to save time, others create complex Webs with features not readily accessible in FrontPage 2002. You explored one example in Chapter 12, where you used the Database Interface Wizard to create a Web site with an interactive database that can be viewed or edited (a little bit) by visitors in their browser window. In this chapter, you'll look briefly at how to use templates that save time, and in more detail at Web templates that generate discussion forums and SharePoint Web portals.

Saving Time with Web Templates

Templates save development time by creating Web structure and generating Web pages with generic content. Of course, you have to *replace* that generic content with *real* information by editing each generated page.

FrontPage 2002's Corporate Presence and Consumer Support Webs have the advantage of creating a basic structure for Web sites, including page content, input forms, and navigation links. You can use them when you need to throw up a functional site overnight. Or, you can use these templates as "starters" to create a basic framework for a site, and then you can edit, delete, and expand on the pre-fab content.

The customer support Web includes a pre-made feedback form that will save you time if you don't want to design your own. On the other hand, I found it took more work to convert the FAQ page to real content than it did to create an FAQ page from scratch. Bottom line: Create a site using this template to get ideas, but you'll probably end up designing your own support site from scratch.

The Corporate Presence Web Wizard generates a site that has some useful features for designers of sites for small business and organizations. The wizard creates a site that can include pages to tell visitors what's new, tell them about your products or services, and provide them with a table of contents page, feedback form, and search form. Figure 15-1 shows a navigation structure generated by the Corporate Presence Web Wizard.

The generated home page can provide spaces for an introduction, a mission statement, a company profile, and contact information. The formatting and design of the site generated by the Corporate Presence Web Wizard is nothing to write home about, but it provides a respectable, professional-looking interface for your business, as shown next.

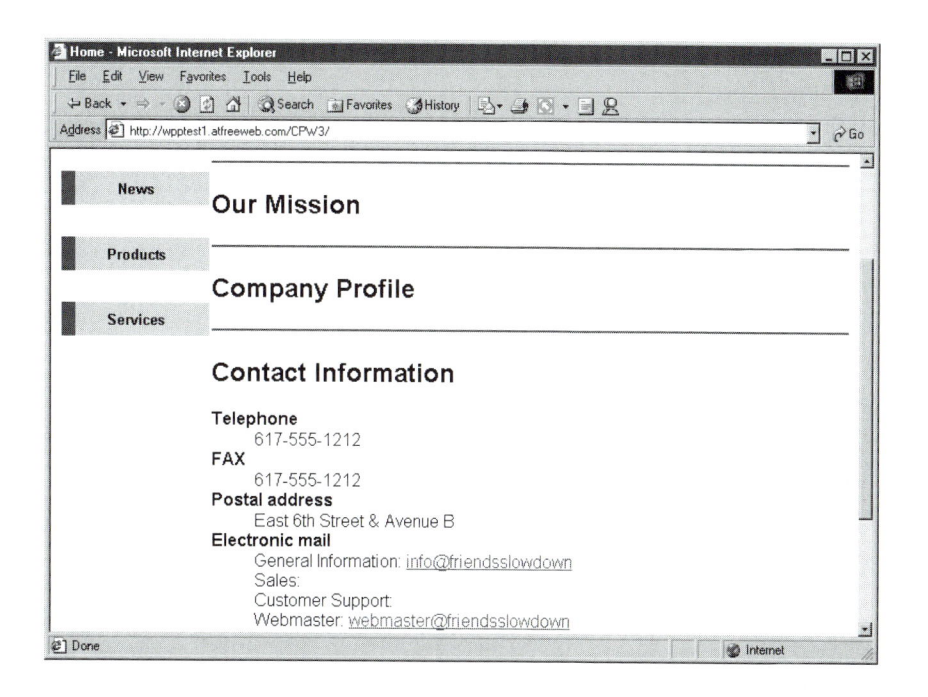

FIGURE 15-1

The Corporate Presence Web Wizard creates a site with News, Products, and Services areas

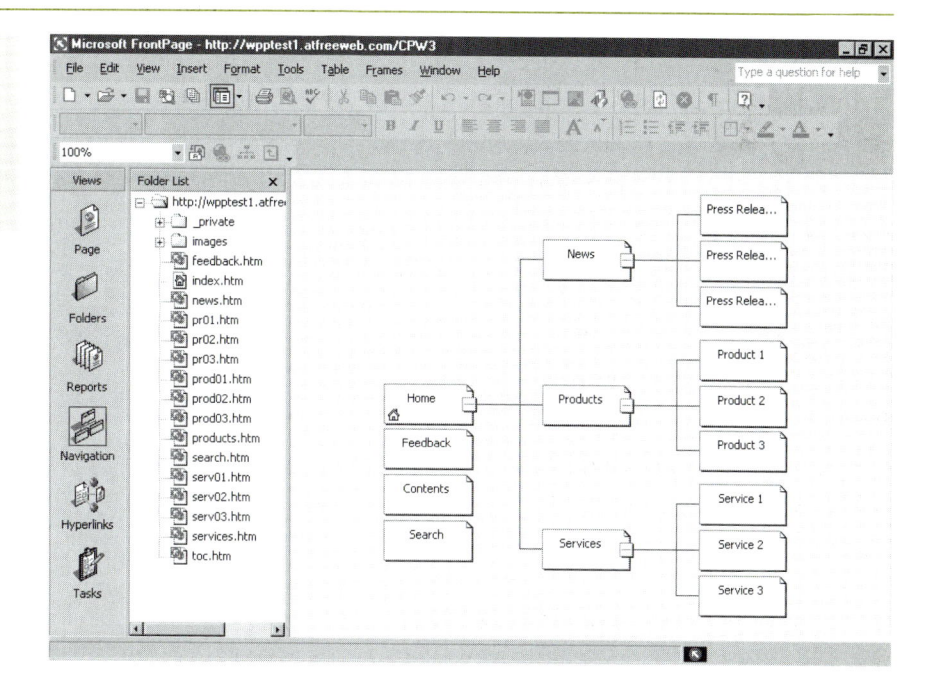

Chapter 15
Creating Complex Webs with Web Templates

After your corporate site is created, FrontPage lists pages that need editing for custom content in Tasks view.

> **NOTE** You'll explore using Tasks view to manage ongoing work in Chapter 17.

Other Web templates, like the Personal Web, create fairly simple sites that can get you going quickly, or serve as sources of ideas for your own site structure.

The Project Web creates a fairly esoteric Web site that looks like someone adapted it from a Microsoft development team site. Project management experts may find a few time-saving elements in this site template.

In addition to sites that save time by generating site layout and page content, the Discussion Forum and SharePoint Team Services Web templates generate Webs with features that would be very difficult to create from scratch in FrontPage.

To Create a new site using a Web template:

1. Select File | New, Page or Web to open the New Page or Web pane on the right side of the FrontPage window.

2. To generate a new site using a Web template, click the Web Site Templates link. The Web Site Templates dialog box appears.

3. Click various Web templates to display a description of the template in the lower-right corner of the dialog box.

> **NOTE** You'll explore SharePoint-based Team Web sites later in this chapter.

4. In the Specify the Location of the New Web area, enter a file folder or Web server location. If you want to create your new Web in a subfolder of a currently open Web, add a / (slash) at the end of the displayed location and type a name for the new folder.

> **NOTE** Available templates will vary depending on whether you have installed add-in products. For a survey of available FrontPage add-ins, see Appendix B.

5. Click OK to generate the new Web.

6. After the new Web is created, explore and edit the generated content.

One drawback to generating Web sites from templates is that FrontPage will place quite a bit of generic content on the pages. Be sure to look for e-mail addresses and other content that *must be changed* to reflect the actual content you want to display on your site.

Including a Discussion Forum

Discussion forums are a great way to create an interactive element at your Web site. Visitors can post questions, opinions, or information, and other visitors can join in the discussion. These discussion forums can be edited if inappropriate content is posted.

FrontPage allows you to generate a *threaded* discussion forum. A threaded forum is one where visitors can engage in ongoing discussion of a selected topic. For example, at my FrontPage forum (www.ppinet.com), readers of my FrontPage books post questions, and other readers (or myself) respond. Each set of responses is a *thread* in the discussion forum. Figure 15-2 shows a few threads at my forum.

Setting Up a Discussion Forum

Creating a threaded discussion forum goes beyond what can be realistically created from scratch in FrontPage 2002. But the Discussion Form Web template makes it relatively simple to set up your own threaded discussion forum.

FIGURE 15-2
This forum includes many discussion threads

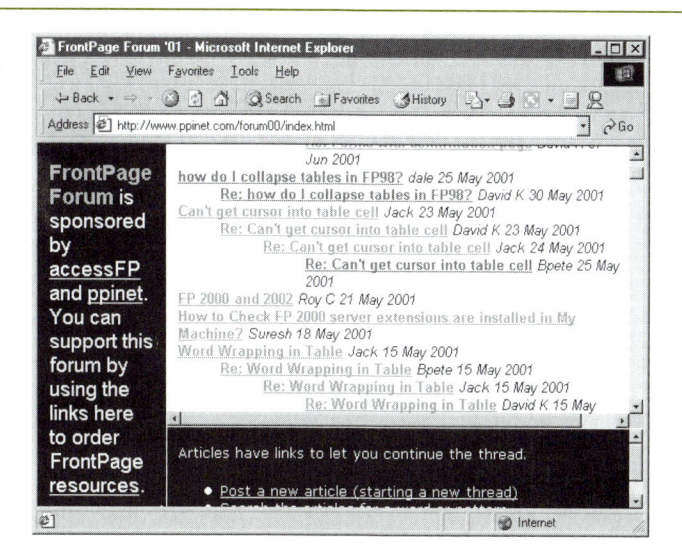

CHAPTER 15
CREATING COMPLEX WEBS WITH WEB TEMPLATES

Discussion forums can include

▶ **Submission form** This is how visitors post comments to the discussion, and it is required for your forum to work. Each posting is referred to as an *article*.

▶ **Table of contents** This is the page that displays the content of the discussion forum, with links to *articles*. Along with a submission form, a table of contents is essential for a working discussion forum.

▶ **Search form** This page allows visitors to search your forum for text.

▶ **Threaded replies** This option organizes submitted articles into threads, and allows visitors to reply to an existing thread or start a new thread when they post articles.

▶ **Confirmation page** This page confirms the content of posted articles and provides a link to a refreshed table of contents page.

All the options provided for discussion Webs are helpful in making your discussion forum easy to contribute to, and easy to use to locate information.

To Generate A NEW DISCUSSION WEB:

1 Select File | New, Page or Web to activate the New Page or Web pane in FrontPage.

2 Double-click the Discussion Web Wizard icon in the Web Site Templates dialog box. In a moment, the first discussion Web Wizard dialog box appears, describing how the wizard works. Click Next.

3 The second wizard dialog box has five check boxes. Use these to select (or deselect) elements to include in your discussion forum. Click Next.

4 The next wizard dialog box allows you to name your discussion forum and define the folder in which the files are saved. FrontPage generates a default folder name that will work, and there's no need to change that. However, you can enter any title you want for your forum, as shown here. Then, click Next.

> **TIP** My advice is to include all the optional elements of a discussion forum, they make it easier for visitors to post and find information. The remaining steps assume you selected all of the optional elements to include in your discussion forum. If you elect to deselect some options, skip the steps that don't apply to your wizard choices.

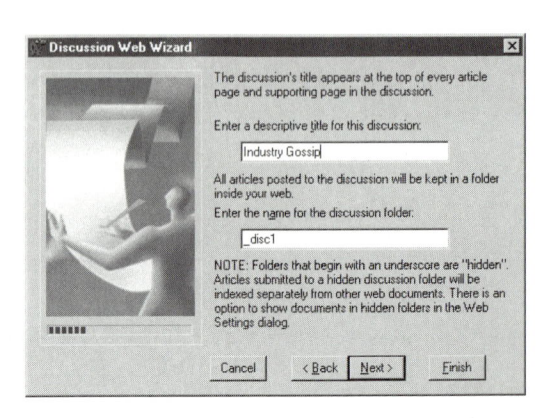

5 In the next wizard dialog box, use the option buttons to select input fields for visitors who are posting articles. Normally, subject and comment are all you need, as shown here. Then, click Next.

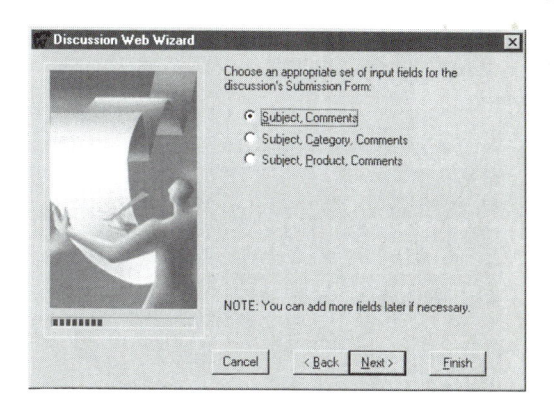

6 The next wizard dialog box offers you the option of making your discussion available to anyone or only to registered users. Choose the No, Anyone Can Post Articles option to allow open access to the forum, and click Next.

7 The next wizard dialog box allows you to post new articles two ways: Oldest to Newest (default) or Newest to Oldest. Beats me why they made Oldest to Newest the default choice—normally you will want to post the newest articles at the *top* of your forum. To do that, choose the Newest to Oldest option, and click Next.

NOTE If you want to confine participation in your forum to registered users, you must have permission to define registered users at your server. For a discussion of registered users, see Chapter 16.

8 The next wizard dialog box asks if you want the Table of Contents to become the Web home page. Because you are creating a *new* Web, you most likely *do* want the table of contents to be the home page for this discussion forum. Choose Yes, and click Next.

9 The next wizard dialog box allows you to choose what content to report for visitors who use your generated search box. The Subject, Size, and Date option provides all the information most visitors will want. Choose this option, and click Next.

10 The next wizard dialog box allows you to choose a Web theme. You can apply a theme at any time once you create your site, so for now simply click Next in this dialog box.

11 The next wizard dialog box presents different frame options for displaying your table of contents along with articles. If you expect your visitors will have browsers that support frames (a fair supposition these days), choose one of the three framed options for displaying content and articles together, as shown here. Click Next.

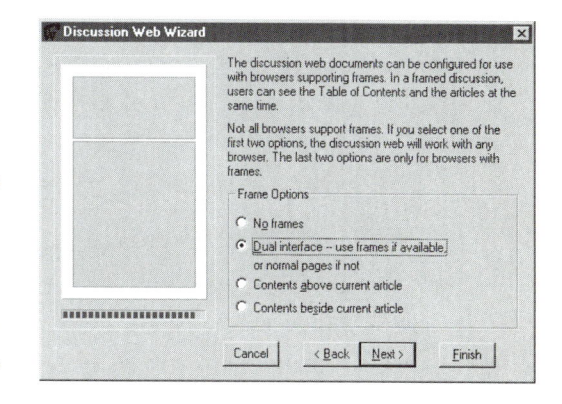

12 The final wizard dialog box explains how the discussion forum works. Read it, and click Finish to generate your discussion forum.

After you generate a discussion forum Web, you can format page text or change themes the same as you would for any site. Feel free to add your own content to the index.htm page that explains the purpose of your forum or provides links to other sites.

> **WARNING** While it's fine to *format* page content, and change wording, be very careful not to edit or delete any *links* in the generated site. These links are essential to the functioning of the forum.

Using a Discussion Forum

Once you generate a discussion forum, visitors can post articles or engage in threaded discussions by responding to already existing articles. If you accepted all the options for a discussion forum, your home page will offer visitors the option of posting a new article (starting a new thread) or searching your forum for text. Figure 15-3 shows a typical discussion forum with those options.

Visitors who want to *read* an existing article can click the article in one frame (the location will vary depending on the frame options you select in the wizard), and read the article in another frame, as shown in Figure 15-4.

Viewed articles include links to allow visitors to return to the contents page, search the forum, post a *new* article, reply to an article (continuing a thread),

FIGURE 15-3
Visitors can click on the Post a New Article link to start a new discussion thread

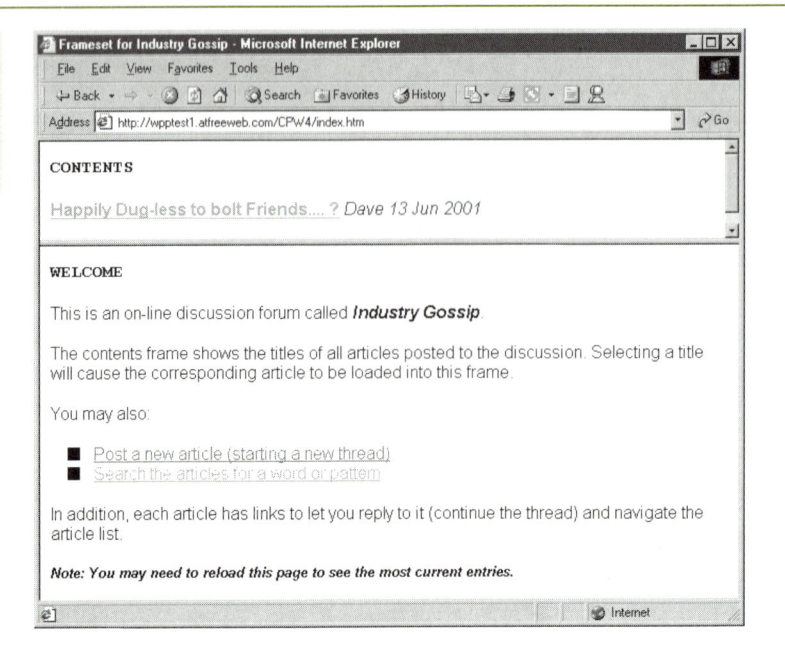

FIGURE 15-4

Visitors can read posted articles by clicking them in the list of contents; they can reply by clicking the Reply link in the article

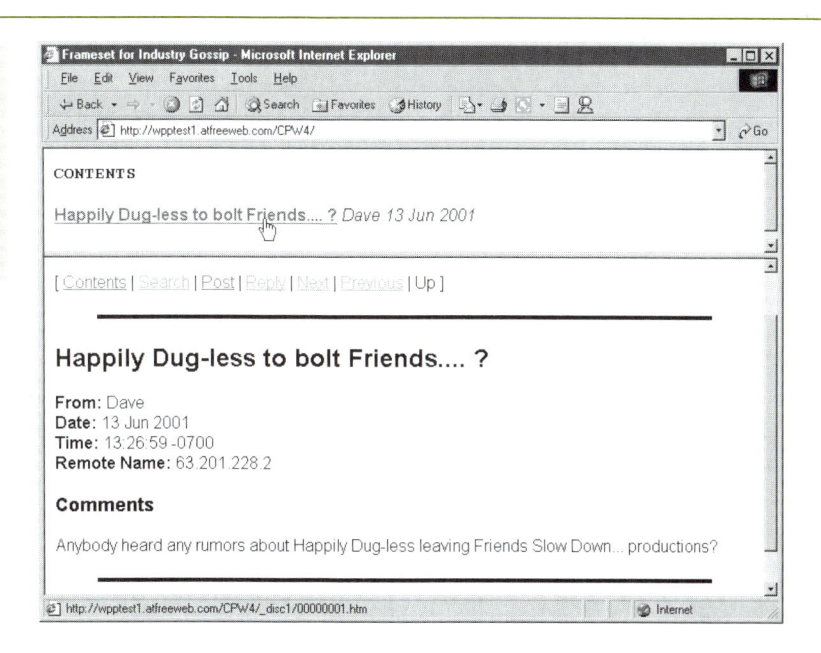

or go to the next or previous article in the forum. These options provide all the links needed for a lively and interactive discussion forum.

Editing a Discussion Forum

Sometimes it may be necessary to delete or edit articles posted to a discussion forum. You might want to perform periodic "housekeeping" by deleting old articles. Or, some article content might not be appropriate.

Articles are saved in a *hidden* folder in FrontPage. So, the first step in editing them is to reveal the hidden folder. Do this by selecting Tools | Web Settings, and clicking the Advanced tab in the Web Settings dialog box. Select the Show Hidden Files and Folders check box if it is not already selected, and click OK. Your Folder list will be regenerated to reveal hidden folders.

Articles will be saved in a folder called something like _disc1. This folder name will vary if you have more than one discussion forum at your site, or if you renamed this folder during the wizard setup process. If you look at the contents of this folder in either the Folder list or Folders view, you'll see a list of posted articles with filenames like 00000001.htm, 00000002.htm, and so on, as shown in Figure 15-5.

FIGURE 15-5

Posted articles can be seen in Folders view—they can be deleted or edited if necessary

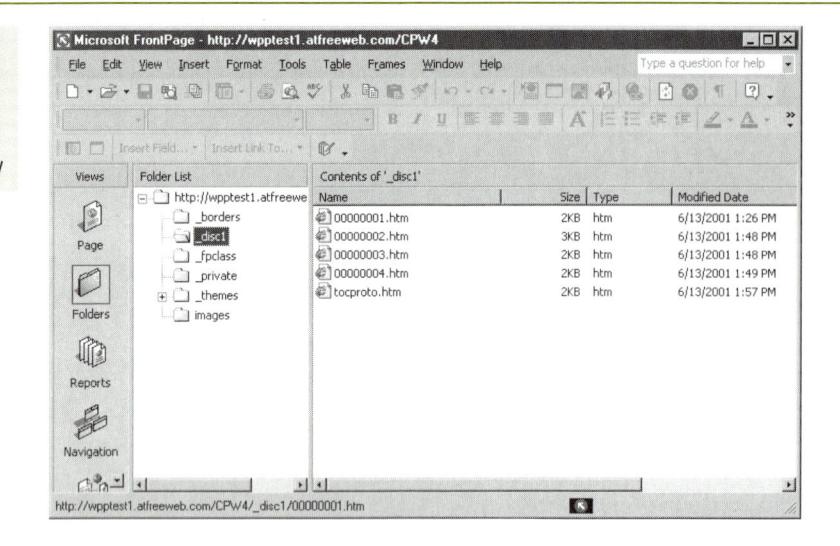

You can see the contents of an article by opening it in page view and double-clicking it. Once opened, you can edit the content of an article just as you would edit any FrontPage page content. To delete an article in Folders view, simply select it and press the DELETE key. Deleted articles will be removed from the table of contents.

Using the SharePoint-based Team Web Site

The SharePoint-based Team Web Site is included with Office XP. It is a pre-configured Web site that facilitates visitors uploading and downloading files, posting announcements, and conversing on an online bulletin board. The connection to FrontPage is that you can both generate a SharePoint portal in FrontPage 2002, and you can, to some extent, edit and format that portal in FrontPage.

SharePoint—Do You Need It?

Who can benefit from using the SharePoint-based Team Web Site? If you and your organization fit any of the following criteria, you might find SharePoint a productivity and communications aid:

▶ You are collaborating on a common project with many people and need a place to share announcements and information.

▶ You need to share a frequently changing schedule with your team.

▶ You need to keep libraries of easily downloadable documents (or other files, like images) at a central server.

If your organization and project fit one or more of the preceding criteria, you might find the SharePoint portal handy. But there's one more catch: The SharePoint portal requires that your Web server provider not only support FrontPage extensions, but *also* have an available set of files called SharePoint Team Services files.

These SharePoint Team Services files are available to administrator of Windows' networking software, so if you want to set up a SharePoint portal on your local network, ask your server administrator to install the necessary SharePoint files.

You can set up a SharePoint portal on the Internet as long as your server provider supports SharePoint. Low cost SharePoint sites are available from discount server providers such as atfreeweb.com, or you can shop for a site provider that supports SharePoint at http://www.microsoftwpp.com/default.asp. Scroll around until you find a search area that allows you to look for providers that support SharePoint, as shown in Figure 15-6.

NOTE Because the SharePoint-based Team Web Site serves as a *portal*—an entry way—into a Web server, it is sometimes referred to as a SharePoint portal or a SharePoint site.

SharePoint Portals—Edited by Visitors

The fundamental difference between a SharePoint Web site and other FrontPage sites is that SharePoint sites are *edited mainly by users*. Yes, you can open these sites in FrontPage and edit them. But they are mainly designed so that a group of people can upload content right in a Web browser such as Internet Explorer, *without* using FrontPage or any file transfer program to upload files.

How does this work? Every page in a SharePoint site has links that allow visitors to *add* content. For example, in Figure 15-7, clicking the Add a New Announcement link in the SharePoint page opens an input form where a visitor can add an announcement to the list.

CHAPTER 15
CREATING COMPLEX WEBS WITH WEB TEMPLATES

FIGURE 15-6
Searching for Web presence providers that support SharePoint features

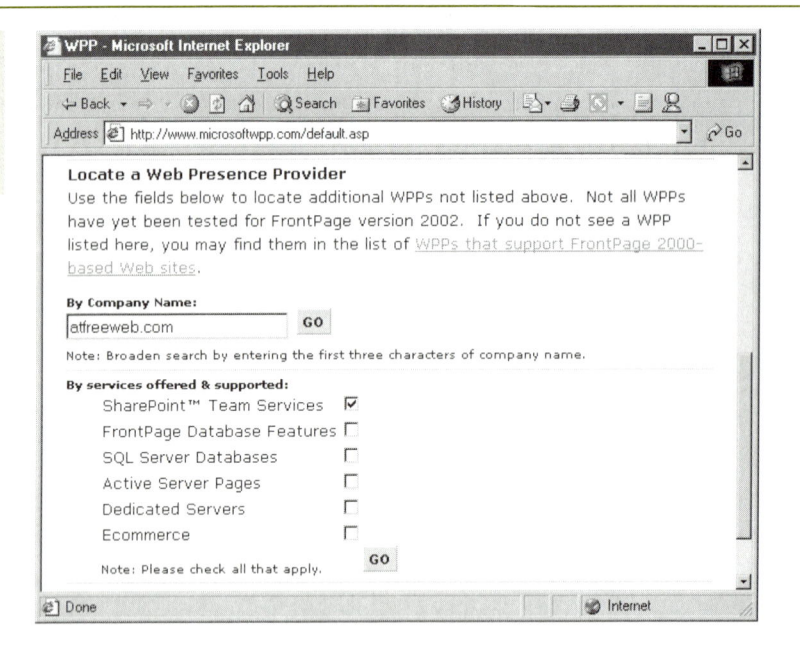

FIGURE 15-7
With SharePoint sites, most site content is posted through a browser

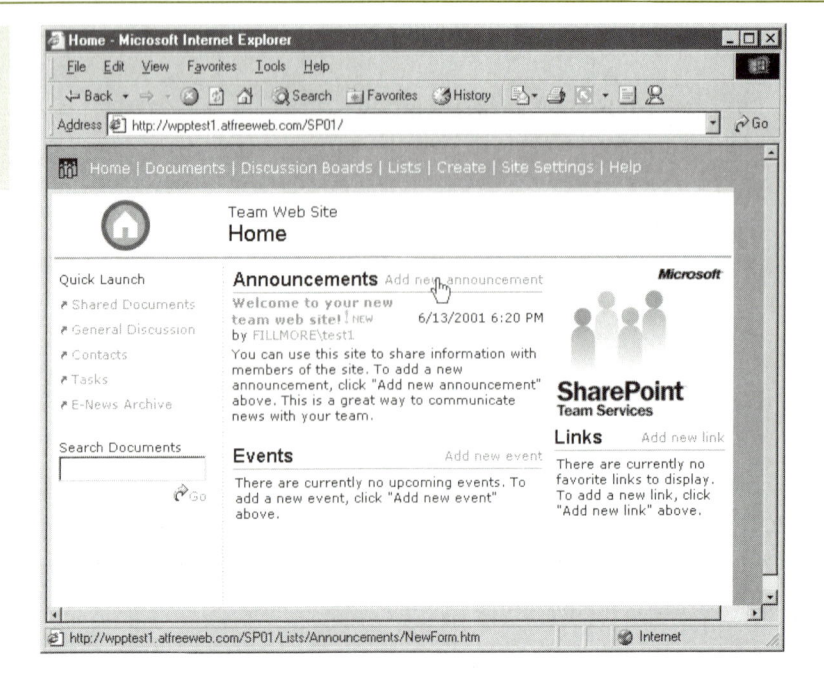

Access to the input forms to add content to the Web site is protected by passwords distributed by the server administrator. So, just as you have to log on to your site to edit it in FrontPage, visitors need logon information to add site content through their browsers.

Assuming you've hooked up with a server that supports SharePoint, you're ready to create and use a SharePoint portal.

Creating a SharePoint Portal

You can generate a SharePoint-based Team Web Site using a FrontPage Web template. There are not a whole lot of options in this process—no set of wizards or dialog boxes, just click and you've got a portal. Remember: Most of your "site editing" is actually done through a browser once the site is generated.

To Create a SharePoint Team Services Web portal:

1 Select File | New | Page or Web to activate the New Page or Web pane in FrontPage.

2 Click the link to Web Site Templates.

3 In the Web Site Templates dialog box, click once on the icon for SharePoint-based Team Web Site.

4 In the Specify the Location of the New Web area of the Web Site Templates dialog box, enter the URL (Web address or intranet address) for your site. This information is provided by your server administrator.

5 After a little delay—for files to upload—the SharePoint Web site opens in FrontPage.

At this point, you can edit and format your SharePoint-based Team Web Site in FrontPage, or you can open it in a browser and add content through the browser.

Formatting and Editing a SharePoint Portal

While most *files* are uploaded to SharePoint-based Team Web sites through a browser, you can't edit existing page content or tweak the formatting without opening pages in FrontPage.

Chapter 15
Creating Complex Webs with Web Templates

One way to add your own style touch to a SharePoint-based Team Web site is to change the theme. You can apply a theme of your own choosing to an open SharePoint site by selecting Format | Theme. Choose a theme from the Themes dialog box, and click OK to apply your own colors and fonts to the site. For a nice clean, business-like look, I generally replace the default SharePoint theme with the Blank theme.

You can also open pages in a SharePoint site and edit content. As with other complex, template-generated sites, it's a good idea to be cautious when editing content. It's fine to add your own text, but most of the *links* in a SharePoint site are essential to the functioning of the site. Many of them allow visitors to upload files, and without those links the site won't work.

Apply your own formatting to text and graphics in the SharePoint site—change color, font, picture size, or even picture content. In Figure 15-8, for example, I've substituted my own picture for one supplied by the template.

List and Library Web Components

Much of the interactivity of SharePoint sites comes from two rather complex Web components: Lists and Libraries. An exploration of these Web components is

FIGURE 15-8
Feel free to edit text and pictures in SharePoint sites—just avoid messing with the links

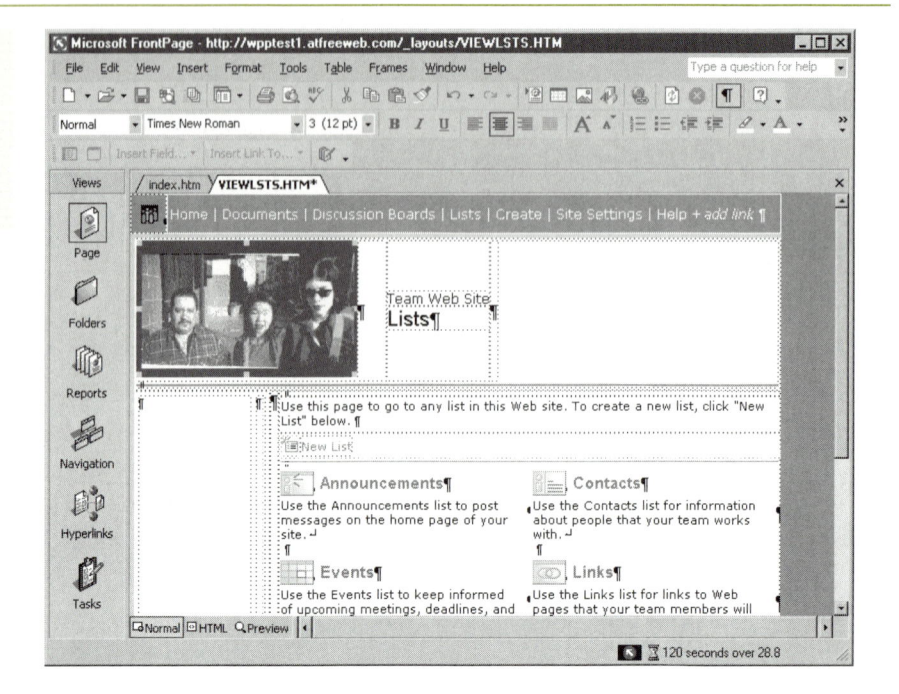

beyond the scope of this book, but a brief explanation will help demystify how SharePoint sites work.

- **Lists** Interactive lists. FrontPage can create preformatted lists for discussion boards, links, announcements, contacts, events and tasks.
- **Libraries** Collections of uploaded files. Libraries can be defined to display various fields—like a document name, size, and when it was created. You can also sort and filter libraries.

SharePoint sites are chock full of lists and libraries, and chances are you'll find what you need already created as part of the template. If you want to experiment with creating and adding your own lists and libraries, you can do so.

To Create A NEW LIST OR LIBRARY:

1 Choose File | New | List or File | New Document Library to open the New List or the New Document Library dialog box.

2 Choose one of the template lists or libraries. Descriptions on the right-hand side of both dialog boxes explain the type of list or document library you are creating. In Figure 15-9, I'm creating a new document library.

3 Click OK to create the list or document library

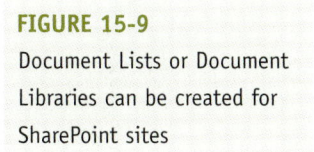

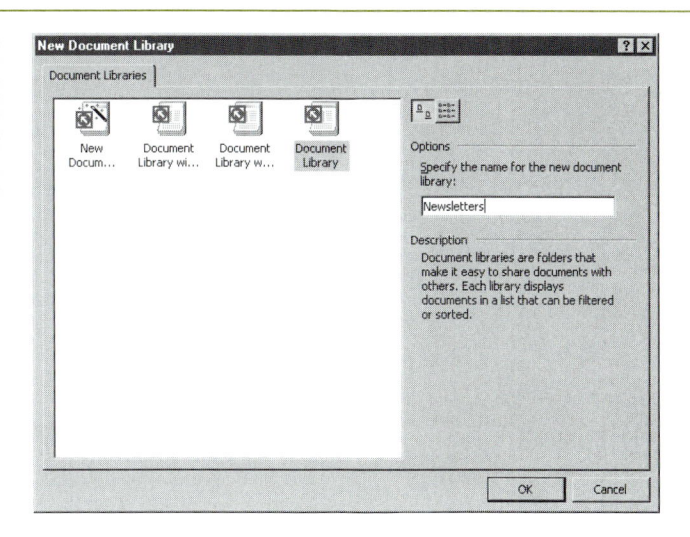

FIGURE 15-9
Document Lists or Document Libraries can be created for SharePoint sites

CHAPTER 15
CREATING COMPLEX WEBS WITH WEB TEMPLATES

Once you create a new list or document library, you can insert that object anywhere on a page in a SharePoint site. These lists, or library document *views*, allow visitors to upload and share files at the SharePoint site.

To Insert A LIST OR DOCUMENT LIBRARY:

1 With a page open in a SharePoint site, choose Insert | Web Component to open the Web Components dialog box.

2 Select List View or Document Library View from the Component Type list in the Web Components dialog box.

3 From the options on the right side of the dialog box, choose a view for your list or document library, as shown here:

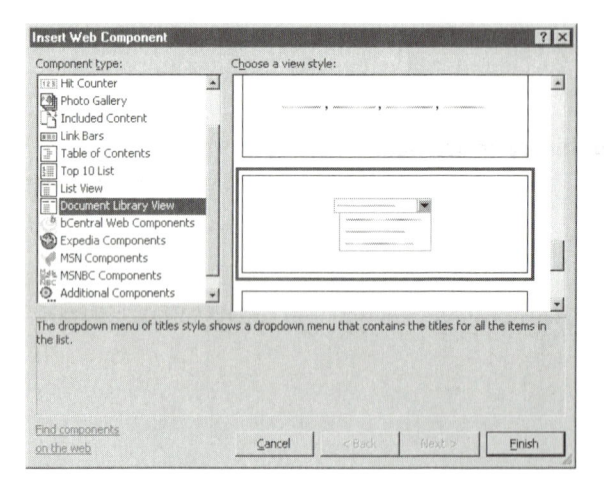

4 Click Finish to exit the Web Component dialog box. The Choose Document Library or Choose List dialog box opens.

5 Select one of your existing lists or document libraries, as shown here:

6 Click OK to close the dialog box. A new dialog box appears—either Document Library View Properties, or List View Properties.

7 You can use the Library or List button in the dialog box to substitute a different list or library.

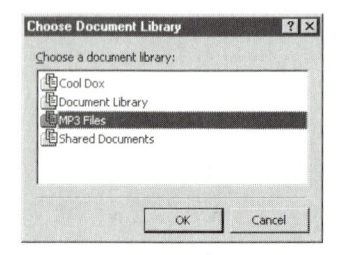

8 Depending on list or document library style, the Fields button allows you to define which fields are displayed. If there are no documents in a library or list from which to generate fields, this is grayed out.

9 Use the Sort button open the Sort dialog box. Here you can define the order in which files will be displayed. In this illustration, files will be sorted first by date, and then (if dates are the same) by filename.

10 You can use the Filter button to filter (restrict) files to only those that match a criteria for date, title, or other matching information.

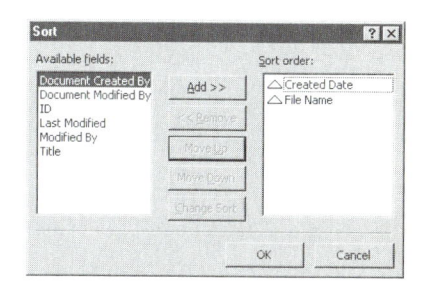

11 The Options button opens the View Options dialog box. Here you can change the display of the list or document library, and add other features to the display. Choose Full Toolbar from the Toolbar Type drop-down list to provide visitors with links to upload, filter, or revise the layout of the list or document library.

12 After you've defined your library or list view, click OK.

Once you have defined a custom list or document library, visitors to your site can use the associated toolbar to add, sort, filter, or open documents, or add to lists. Figure 15-10 shows a custom-defined document library.

> **WARNING** As I've emphasized before, lists and document libraries *only work* if you publish your site to a server that supports SharePoint features. If your site is *not* published to a SharePoint-enabled server, lists and document libraries will not be available options.

Using a SharePoint Portal

As I've emphasized, much of the work of adding content to a SharePoint site happens not in FrontPage, but in the *browser*. Visitors using Internet Explorer or Netscape Navigator can open and upload files to and from the SharePoint server portal.

Much of the interface of a SharePoint site is very self-explanatory. Links that say "Upload Document" allow visitors to browse their local system and send files to the site. Visitors who want to *read* or see a file simply click a link to open the file in their browser window.

FIGURE 15-10

New, custom document libraries can be created in FrontPage 2002

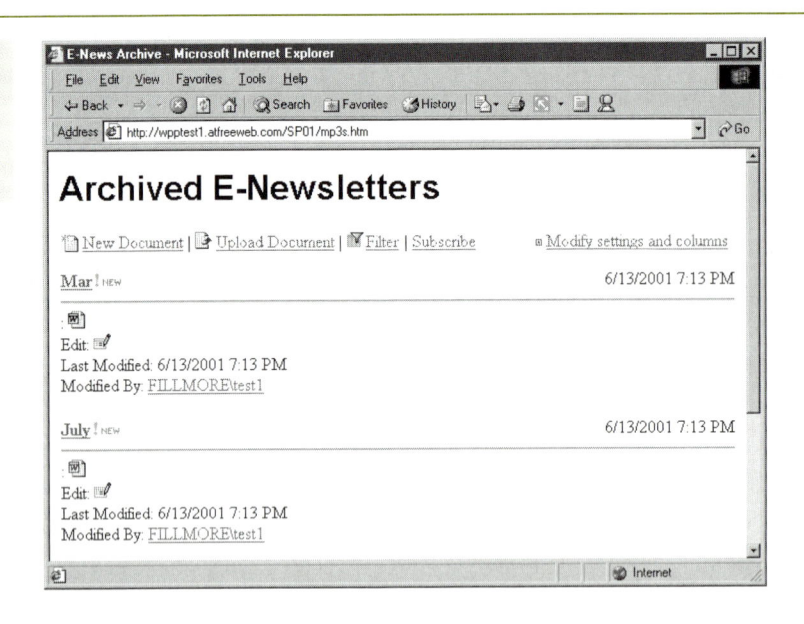

Discussion lists have links such as "Add New Link," to add links to a list or "Add New Announcement" to add to a list of announcements. Links that say "New Discussion" start a new discussion list topic; posted messages can be opened by clicking links. Links that say "Reply" allow visitors to reply to a link at a discussion, as shown here:

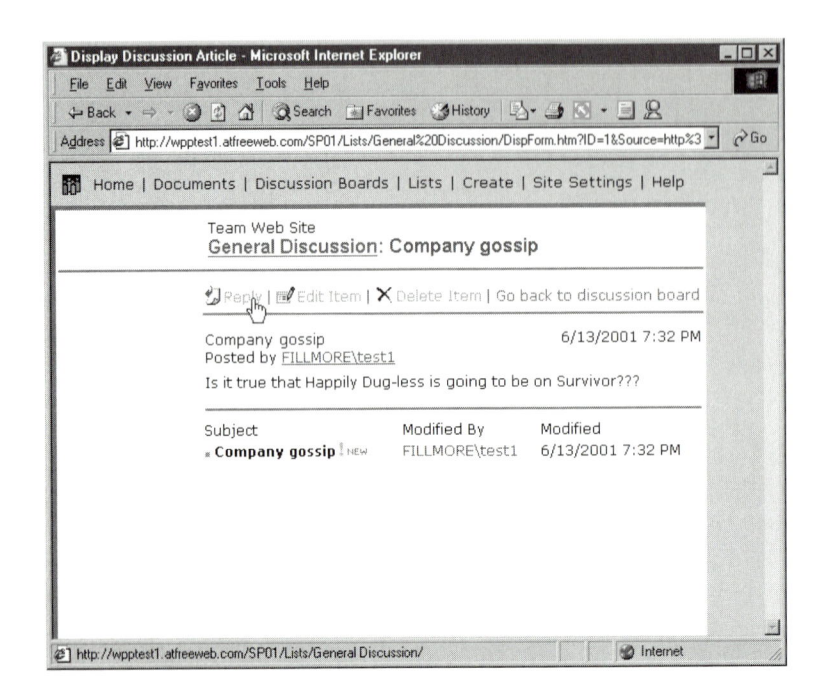

SharePoint portals are very well documented and designed, so, non-developers can freely add and download content and files.

Working with Servers

You've seen throughout this book that many features of FrontPage depend on the configuration of the Web server to which you publish your Web site. You *can* publish your FrontPage Web site to your local hard drive. But sooner or later, you'll want the world, or at least the folks on your local network, to be able to *access* your server.

Server administration itself is the subject of many thick books and requires a high level of technical expertise. But in the next chapter, you'll briefly look at some aspects of server administration that are accessible to developers using Microsoft 2000 or Microsoft XP.

16

FrontPage and Web Servers

You can create a FrontPage Web site in a folder on your own local computer hard drive. However, these *disk-based Webs* don't allow you to apply or test many important elements of FrontPage (like collecting input data, for example). In order to create a fully functional FrontPage Web site, you need to publish that site to a Web server. When it comes time to do that, you have two basic (realistic) options: You can contract with a commercial FrontPage-friendly Web server provider to hook you up with a remote server. Or, or you can install and manage your own server software on your intranet or local computer. In this chapter, I'll explain how and when to use both of these options.

CHAPTER 16
FrontPage and Web Servers

Remote Web Sites—Let Someone Else Sweat the Server Stuff

Server administration is a science and an art in itself and well beyond the scope of this book. Most FrontPage users will be publishing sites to a server administered by someone else. In that case, it's important that you form a partnership with your server administrator.

If you want to publish your site to a remote server, the easiest option is to purchase server space from one of hundreds of competing providers. You only need to be sure that your provider supports FrontPage 2002 server extensions. When you publish your site to a server with FrontPage 2002 extensions, you can use features like input form management, online databases, and Web components, all of which require FrontPage extensions.

To publish your site to a *remote* Web server, you will of course need an Internet connection, such as a phone modem or preferably a faster connection like DSL or a T1 line.

If you follow the link in the Publish Destination dialog box, you'll jump to Microsoft's Locate a *Web Presence Provider* (WPP) site. Here you'll find links to hundreds of FrontPage-friendly server providers. You can go directly to this site with a browser; it's located at http://www.microsoftwpp.com/default.asp.

Shopping for a Web Presence Provider

At Microsoft's Locate a Web Presence Provider site, you can learn what kinds of FrontPage features are supported by various site providers. For instance, all the listed providers will support FrontPage extensions, but if you need to use the additional features in FrontPage that require SharePoint Team Services, you can identify providers that will support those features as well. Figure 16-1 shows the FrontPage Web Presence Provider page.

When you find a Web presence provider that fits your budget and needs, you can contract with them—usually immediately—to set up a site. They'll take your payment over the Internet in almost all cases.

> **NOTE** SharePoint Team Services are a set of FrontPage features used to construct intranet sites for organizations and companies. SharePoint features are covered in Chapter 15.

FIGURE 16-1

The FrontPage Web Presence Provider site lets you shop for a Web server that fits your budget

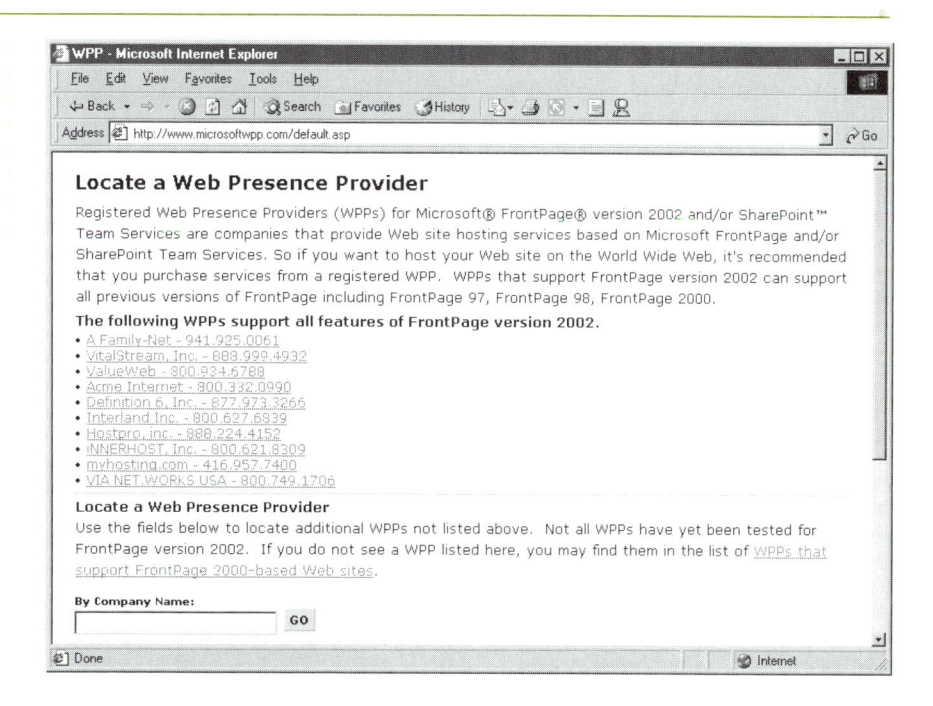

Look for Web server providers that respond quickly and in a helpful way to your initial inquires about service. If they're slow and mean when you're shopping, they won't get any friendlier or faster after you pay them.

Connecting to a Remote Server

Once you have selected a provider and have arranged for an account, carefully note (and store) the login information your provider sends you. You'll need this information when you attempt to publish (upload) your site to a remote Web server.

To Publish your site from a local drive to a remote server:

1. Start FrontPage 2002 and open the Web you intend to publish.

2. Make all changes that you want to any pages that might need adjustments. Use the File | Save All command to render all changes to disk.

3. Select File | Publish Web to open the Publish Destination dialog. Enter the URL for your Web site (provided by your Web Presence Provider).

CHAPTER 16
FrontPage and Web Servers

4 If the server is valid *and* the site does not already have a root directory defined for it, FrontPage will ask you if you would like the server to create the directory for your Web. Normally your Web Presence Provider server administrator will have configured this directory for you in advance.

5 Next, you will be asked to provide a valid user name, password, and domain, as you can see in this illustration. Entering a domain is optional, but you will need to enter one if you have more than one domain accessible to the target server or an active FrontPage administrator or author account.

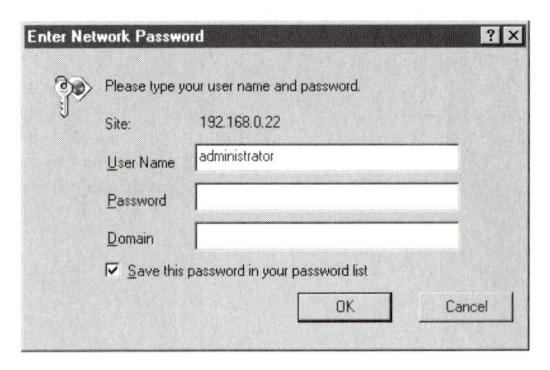

After you connect to your remote server, you can open your site from FrontPage at any time to make changes in the site. Just remember to keep your password and user name handy.

Renting server space from a Web Presence Provider allows you to take full advantage of FrontPage server features without having to configure your own site.

Publishing Your Site to a Local Server

There are two reasons why you might want to install and configure your own Web server on your local computer. One is that you want to fully test your Web site, including features like the Hit Counter, Web Search, and Top 10 List components that require server connections. The second reason for installing a Web server on your local computer is if you want to host a Web site for your local intranet.

Here are the basic requirements for adding Web server software that will support FrontPage extensions on your local computer:

> **NOTE** Technically, there is a third possible use for a server on your local computer. You *can* host a Web site connected to the Internet, but that option is well beyond the scope of this book.

▶ You need to be running either the Windows 2000 or Windows XP operating system. Windows 98 will not support FrontPage 2002 extensions, and Windows ME will not support *any* server software that connects with FrontPage. (We're not happy about that either—Microsoft listened, but wouldn't budge on allowing ME users to host FrontPage sites).

- You will need to install extra software, called Internet Information Server, from your Windows 2000 or Windows XP CD.
- You will need to download the latest version of FrontPage 2002 extensions.

> **NOTE** The FrontPage server extensions are also available for Windows NT and various UNIX operating systems, but they are beyond the scope of this book. More details regarding the UNIX versions can be found at http://msdn. microsoft.com/workshop/languages/fp/ 2002/fpse02unix.asp.

Installing Internet Information Server (IIS) 6.0

Internet Information Services—more commonly known as IIS—is Microsoft's Web services suite. IIS is *not* automatically included when you install Windows 2000 or Windows XP. IIS *is* included on the Windows 2000 and Windows XP CD's, but you need to install it separately.

> **A NOTE ABOUT WINDOWS XP PROFESSIONAL** Fortunately, setting up IIS and the FrontPage server extensions on Windows XP Professional is exactly the same as on Windows 2000. Of course, the interface in XP is slightly different than what you expect in earlier versions of Windows. One difference between Windows XP Professional and earlier versions of Windows is that the My Computer icon does not appear on the desktop. Instead, the My Computer settings appear in the newly renovated Start menu. Click the Start button, navigate to the My Computer item on the right, and then right-click it, as if it were on the desktop. From the context menu, select the familiar Manage item. From there on, everything that works in Windows 2000 works the same in XP.

To Install IIS on any Windows 2000 or Windows XP:

1 You have two paths to start from. If AutoPlay is active in your Windows settings (this automatically starts programs on a CD), you can insert the Windows installation CD and select Install Add-On Components item when the Installer window appears. If AutoPlay is disabled (if your CD program doesn't start automatically), you will need to go to Start | Settings | Control Panel (Start | Control Panel in XP) and select the

Add/Remove Programs item. Click the Add/Remove Windows Components button on the left. Both of these paths will lead to the same destination.

2 In the Windows Components Wizard, check the box next to Internet Information Services (IIS).

3 Next, click Details or double-click the IIS item to show a dialog that lists all the subcomponents of IIS. Make sure that the Visual InterDev RA—Remote Deployment Support—item is *unchecked*. The remainder of the items should be checked.

4 After the Installation Wizard completes the installation process, restart your computer.

> **TIP** I'm advising you to deselect Visual InterDev RA (Remote Deployment Support) because Windows experts tell me it opens up all kinds of possibilities for problems running IIS, as well as creating security issues for your computer.

You now have IIS, the server software that will host your local Web site. You might assume (wish!) that Microsoft would include FrontPage 2002 server extensions with IIS. However, because FrontPage extensions evolve more quickly than IIS, there is still one more step before your local server can host your FrontPage site: You need to add FrontPage server extensions to your IIS software.

Adding FrontPage 2002 Extensions to IIS 6.0

The next task in creating a FrontPage server on your computer is to install the latest FrontPage server extensions from Microsoft. You can find the latest versions of these extensions at the following address: http://msdn.microsoft.com/workshop/languages/fp/default.asp.

These files should be regularly updated, so check back often. The site contains helpful information, and security-related issues are posted to this Web site that are not made available through the extensions upgrade utility.

Click the Download link at the Web site to copy the FrontPage extension installation file to your computer. When the file has been downloaded, double-click it. The file is an executable (program) file that automatically detects your IIS server and adds the required FrontPage 2002 extension files.

That's it! Now, you can publish FrontPage Web sites to your own computer or network, and utilize all the features in FrontPage. You can do this because you installed server software, with FrontPage 2002 extensions on your system. When IIS and FrontPage 2002 files are installed on your system, the installation process automatically creates and names a Web server on your computer. This server is given a name—actually a bunch of letters and numbers that don't spell anything—during the installation process. When you publish a FrontPage site, the location of the local server will be available when you click the Browse button in the Publish Destination dialog box.

To publish (save) Webs to your local server, you will create *subwebs* as you publish. So, for example, if your local server is named http://net-iukuzmtgub0, you will add a backslash (/) and a Web name to create new Webs. In this case you could name Webs http://net-iukuzmtgub0/myweb, http://net-iukuzmtgub0/myweb2, http://net-iukuzmtgub0/myweb3, and so on.

Administering Your Server

Some FrontPage features require that you jump into the role of server administrator and make changes to your IIS settings. For example, if you want to create authorized administrators, you might need to change some of the settings in your server.

If you installed IIS on your own computer, you are an administrator and you can define server properties. If you are using a remote Web server, your server administrator *may* give you permission to make these changes to your site. Or, you might need to ask the server administrator to make these changes for you.

To configure server settings *for an open Web* or subweb, you choose Tools | Server | Administration Home to access the Web site Administration window. This window looks like (and is) a Web page—with links to various options for administering your site.

The available options will apply to the Web or subweb you have open. For your purposes, you'll focus on those options available if you are working with an open subweb—created under your own IIS parent Web. This is the most likely option for developers working on a local IIS site or remote site. The available administration options for such a subweb are listed on the following page.

- ▶ **Users and Roles** Here you can modify anonymous access to the server; manage, add, or remove user accounts; and send an invitation to someone to become a member.

- ▶ **Server Health** These options allow you to modify health settings, check on server health at will, and what is called *recalculate* the server extensions. What that means is that you can reinstall them to the particular virtual server if they are having problems. The FrontPage 2000 server extensions were known to become corrupt if you accessed the FrontPage server using an FTP client and not FrontPage itself. If this happens often, your Web can become corrupted and not work properly.

- ▶ **Version Control** Enabling this allows for greater control over documents slated for the Web when working with a number of people. This is off by default.

- ▶ **Subwebs** Depending on how you want to configure your server, you can allow authors to create subwebs to the root webs. A subweb, as you're likely already well aware from earlier in the book, is an independent site that is subordinate to another Web, even while it retains wholly different characteristics than its progenitor.

The most important element of administering your Web site is deciding who can do what to it. You don't want to allow just anyone to open your Web site and change it! In the next section, you'll focus on how to control who can change your site.

Defining Server Permissions

FrontPage protects your site by requiring a user name and password to change the site. There are various levels of *permission* that can be assigned to people who work on or use your site. FrontPage 2002 allows you to define many levels of what it calls "users"—assigning different permissions to change your site. For example, you can define a role of "Page Editor," and only give people assigned to that role permission to change page content. You can define another role of "Theme Designer" or "Border Designer," and give people assigned to those roles permission to change themes or page borders. In short, FrontPage 2002 extensions allow you to define a vast hierarchy of designers at your site, each with their own set of permissions.

The permission settings discussed in the rest of this chapter apply to sites hosted by IIS with FrontPage 2002 extensions. *Different* types of permissions are available for FrontPage sites hosted on different servers. One real limitation of the permission features in IIS with FrontPage 2002 extensions is the lack of an accessible way to restrict *visitor access* to your site. That feature can be implemented easily if your site is being hosted on a UNIX server, but not easily at all with IIS.

> **NOTE** Just to be clear, when FrontPage (and I) refer to "users" and "permissions" in the remainder of this chapter, we're talking about people with various levels of permission to *edit* a FrontPage site. We're *not* talking about controlling access to the site by *visitors* who simply view the site in their browser. If your site is hosted by a Web Presence Provider (WPP) on a UNIX platform, you can ask them about restricting access to your site to only registered users.

Assigning Unique Permissions for Your Site

Most of the time, server administrators will set up sites in what are technically subwebs of a server root folder. This is different than a subweb *within* a Web site. Subwebs can have their own domain names, so unless you are concerned with server administration issues, the fact that your Web site is a subweb of a server site usually isn't that important or relevant.

However, if you want to define features like restricting visitor access to your site, you will need to "get beneath the hood" of your site and change server settings. Here, you will run into the fact that your default server settings are *inherited from the root server*. And, if you want to control the settings for your own site, you'll technically be defining settings for a *subweb*.

Before you can define your own administrators, and define who can visit your site, you need to enable your site's subweb with unique permissions. This way, if your site is hosted by a Web server that hosts many sites, you can define your own access rules.

To Assign unique permission rules to your site (if it is a subweb on a server):

1. With your Web site open in FrontPage, choose Tools | Server | Permissions from the menu. This opens the Permission Administration page in your Web browser.

CHAPTER 16
FrontPage and Web Servers

2 In the Permission Administration page, click the Change Permissions link. The Change Subweb Permissions page opens.

3 Select the Use Unique Permissions for This Web Site option button, and click Submit.

4 You can close the Change Subweb Permissions browser window, and begin to define unique permissions for your Web site that are different than those of the server root Web.

Once you've established that your own site will have unique permission settings, you can begin to change those settings.

Adding Roles

If you want to assign someone else authority to edit the content of your site (or share administrative privileges), you can do that. The first step is to define one or more *roles* for these developers. Each role is allowed a set of editing permissions.

For example, you could create a role of "Page Designer," and choose to allow folks assigned to that role to edit pages, but not change themes. The Permissions Administration feature provides many options for how much control to allow a group of developers to have over a site.

To Define a new administrator for an open Web site:

1 Choose Tools | Server | Permissions. The Permissions Administration page opens in your browser.

2 Click the Manage Roles link. The Manage Roles page opens.

3 Click the Add a Role link. The Add a Role page opens. Here you can use the list of check boxes to define new administrators, and choose from a variety of options that determine what authority to assign to the new administrator.

4 After you define the new role, click the Submit button.

You can create as many roles as you want. A very large Web site project in a large organization might have dozens of roles. A more flexible environment might only have one or two roles—for instance, an administrator and a designer.

Defining Users

After you create and define roles, you can assign different people to these roles. For example, you can assign several people to "Page Design" role, if that was a role you defined in the Permissions Administration window (this process is described in the previous section).

To Assign users to roles:

1. With your Web open, choose Tools | Server | Permissions. The Permissions Administration page opens in your browser.

2. Click the Manage Users link. The Manage Users page opens in your browser.

3. Click Add a User. The Add a User page opens.

4. Enter a user name and password for the user, and choose one of your defined roles for the user in the User Role area.

5. Click the Add User button at the bottom of the page.

Server Administration and Site Management

In this chapter, you've walked through the basic routine for both contracting for a Web presence provider, and for setting up your own local FrontPage server. For most small business, organizations, and institutions, a good way to develop a site is to contract with a *Web Presence Provider* (WPP). Your WPP will provide you with the size and type of server resources you need for your FrontPage site. Just make sure they support FrontPage 2002 extensions. The server administrators at your WPP will take responsibility for maintaining your server at their location

Chapter 16
FrontPage and Web Servers

and will give you the information you need to connect your local FrontPage installation to their server.

In some cases, you might want to install a FrontPage server on your own local computer or network. Doing this involves installing both server software and FrontPage 2002 extensions on your local computer. You might want to do this for two possible scenarios: to test your site before uploading to an Internet server, or to use your Web as an intranet site available only to other computers connected to your Web server.

If you do elect to set up your own local server, you'll find the process much easier if your operating system is Windows 2000 or Windows XP. As mentioned earlier, unfortunately, Microsoft elected to *not* make the current set of FrontPage extensions available for users of Windows ME, and therefore the option of using a server on your own PC is not available to Windows ME users.

In the next chapter, you'll explore FrontPage features for managing your Web site. These include accessing reports (like usage reports) that must be enabled by a server administrator.

17

Managing Your Web Site

As your Web site grows, you'll find that it accumulates huge numbers of files. The small "Friends Slow Down..." site I've used as a model for this book contains over 200 files, while my PPINET site has over 900 files.

Where do all these files come from? Some, of course, are the HTML and Web graphic files that you added to, or created in your FrontPage Web, other files are generated by FrontPage—often without you realizing it. For example, themes can generate image files, as well as CSS (cascading style sheet) files. If you place a counter on your site, you'll find a CNT file that keeps track of how many hits your site has received. If you used Java applets (for example, with a Hover button), look for CLASS files on your site. Form results may be saved to TXT (text) files on your site. And background sounds on your pages will take up their share of server space as well.

As the number of files at your site grows, you will want to use FrontPage's reporting tools to find, keep track of, and manage all these files. It's not the sexiest part of Web design, but maintaining your site files is vital to keeping your server space requirements under control and identifying and weeding out bad files and links.

Looking at Files

Taking a close look at your site files can be quite eye opening. You'll likely find old files that should be deleted, files that are hogging a lot of server space without being used in your site, and files with no incoming links. Beyond that, FrontPage's file reports are helpful for *finding* files. Say, for example, you know you uploaded a logo file to your site, but you don't remember the filename. You can sort and filter your file listings in FrontPage to find that file.

Analyzing Your Site Summary Report

The Site Summary Report in FrontPage presents a very comprehensive picture of your Web site. It tells you how large your site is (in *kilobytes*—KB), how many files are on your site, how many pictures, how many linked pages, and how many linked files (such as embedded image or sound files).

The Site Summary Report also lists potential problem files at your site, such as pages with broken links, unused themes, and Web components that don't work. You'll explore the problem file rows in the Site Summary Report later in this chapter. First, let's focus on summarizing your site and finding files.

To view the Site Summary Report, click Reports in the Views bar, or choose View | Reports, Site Summary from the menu. The Site Summary Report appears, as shown in Figure 17-1.

FIGURE 17-1

The Site Summary Report

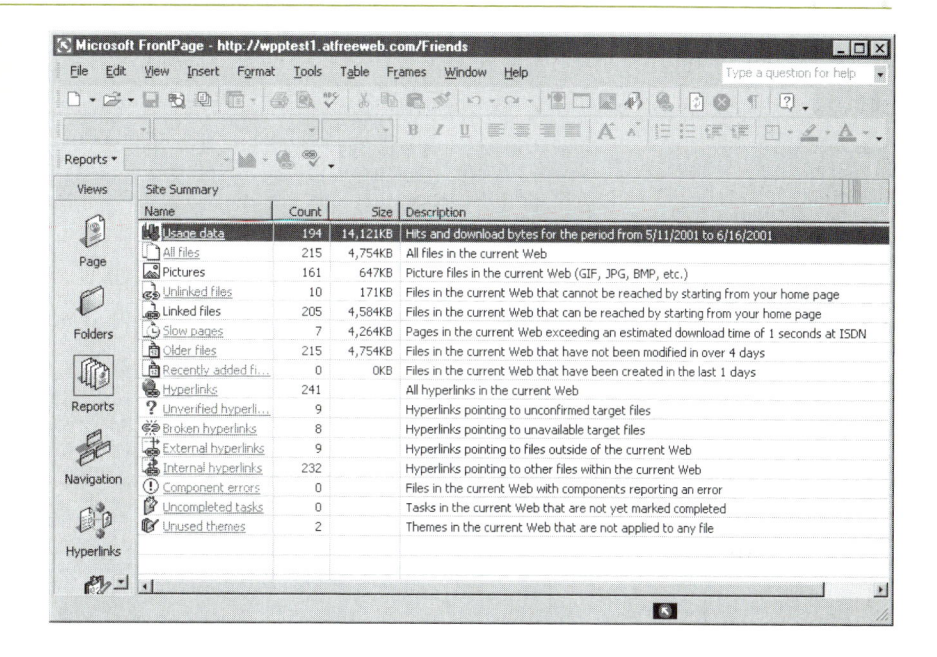

The exact configuration of your Site Summary Report will vary depending on what FrontPage features are installed on your site, and which features are available from your server provider. The Usage Data row summarizes how many visits your site has received. If you click the Usage Data link, the Usage Summary Report opens, displaying more a detailed breakdown of hits to your site, downloaded files, and other information on who is visiting your site.

The All Files row in the report tells you the total number of files at your site and the total size of those files in kilobytes. Many of the remaining rows in the Site Summary Report list problems or potential problem files. Those rows have links to additional reports that you'll explore later in this chapter. You can go to a detailed report from the Site Summary Report by following a link in the report or by using the Reports drop-down menu, as shown here:

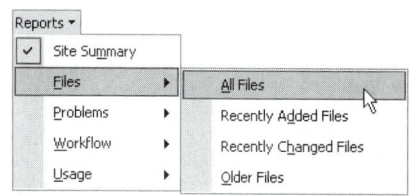

FINDING FILES

The All Files report lists every single file in your Web site. This is where you go when you *know* you have a sound file somewhere in your site, but you have no idea in which of your 86 folders the file is hiding.

The All Files Report, like other detail reports, can be sorted or filtered. This is helpful both in finding lost files, and in creating summary reports for large site development projects that list files by developer, by file type, or by date.

You can also use the All Files report to sort your files by hits, identifying which pages in your site are the most popular with visitors. You can sort files in the All Files Report by any of the following criteria:

- ▶ **Name** Sorts by the name of the file (not the page title), alphabetically.
- ▶ **Title** Sorts by the page title. Because only HTML Web pages have titles, this is more useful if you first filter by file type. (You'll explore filtering in the next section of this chapter.)
- ▶ **In Folder** Sorts the report by folders.
- ▶ **Size** Sorts the report by file size.
- ▶ **Type** Sorts the report by file type.
- ▶ **Modified Date** Sorts the report by the date the file was last saved.
- ▶ **Modified By** Sorts by the developer who modified the file. This information is assigned automatically based on who logs in to the server to work on a file.
- ▶ **Total Hits** Sorts the report by how many hits.
- ▶ **Comments** Comments can be added by right-clicking a file and choosing Properties form the context menu. The Comments area in the Summary tab defines file comments. It's unlikely you'll sort using this field unless you set up a standardized system of comments for your site.

You can sort files by *any* of these criteria by clicking the column title. As you point to a column title in All Files view, the title turns blue. Clicking once sorts alphabetically A–Z; clicking a second time resorts Z–A.

In addition to sorting files, you can filter files using any of the column headings, and defining criteria for your search. For example, if you want to see only GIF files, you can filter the Type column for GIFs. Or, if you know you have a file somewhere in your site that begins with Z, you can filter for only those files. Yet another use for filtering the All Files Report is to produce a list of files larger than a certain size.

> **NOTE** If you're looking for new or old files, special Report views can assist you in doing that. You'll examine them later in this chapter.

To Filter FOR A FILE FROM THE ALL FILES REPORT USING LISTED CRITERIA:

1 With the All Files Report open, decide on a column heading that you want to use as a filter. Click the blue triangle to the right of the column name to open a drop-down list of filter options, as shown here:

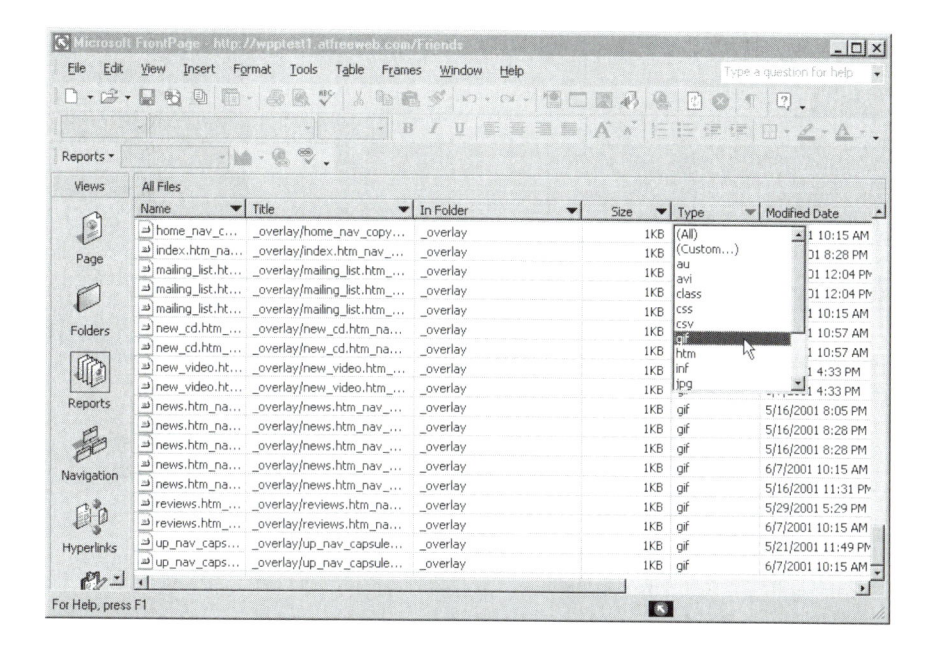

2 If you see the criteria you want to filter for listed (like GIF in the preceding illustration), click that criteria. The All Files Report will display only files that fit the matching criteria.

3 You can filter *additional* columns to further restrict your report. Filtered columns will be identified with a blue triangle.

4 To view all files, choose All from the filter list in all columns.

If you don't see matching criteria that will filter for the files you want to list, you can define a custom filter. Custom filters for any column require that you define an *operator* and *criteria*. An operator is a math equation term, like "equals," or "greater than." Text operators include "begins with" and "contains." Operators in custom filters are matched with criteria. So, for example, if you are searching for files that begin with the word "new," your operator would be "begins with" and

CHAPTER 17
Managing Your Web Site

your criteria would be "new." Or, if you are searching for files larger than 100KB, your operator would be "greater than," and your criteria would be "100KB."

To Apply A CUSTOM FILTER TO AN ALL FILES REPORT:

1 With the All Files Report open, decide on a column heading that you want to use as a filter. Click the blue triangle to the right of the column name to open a drop-down list of filter options.

2 Choose the Custom option in the filter drop-down list. The Custom AutoFilter dialog box opens.

3 The Custom Filter dialog box will differ depending on what column you are filtering for, but each filter dialog box will offer a list of operators. In Figure 17-2, I'm filtering the Size column for files over 100KB.

4 Click OK in the Custom dialog box to apply the filter criteria.

5 You can apply more than one filter or custom filter. To remove filters, choose All from the filters list in every column.

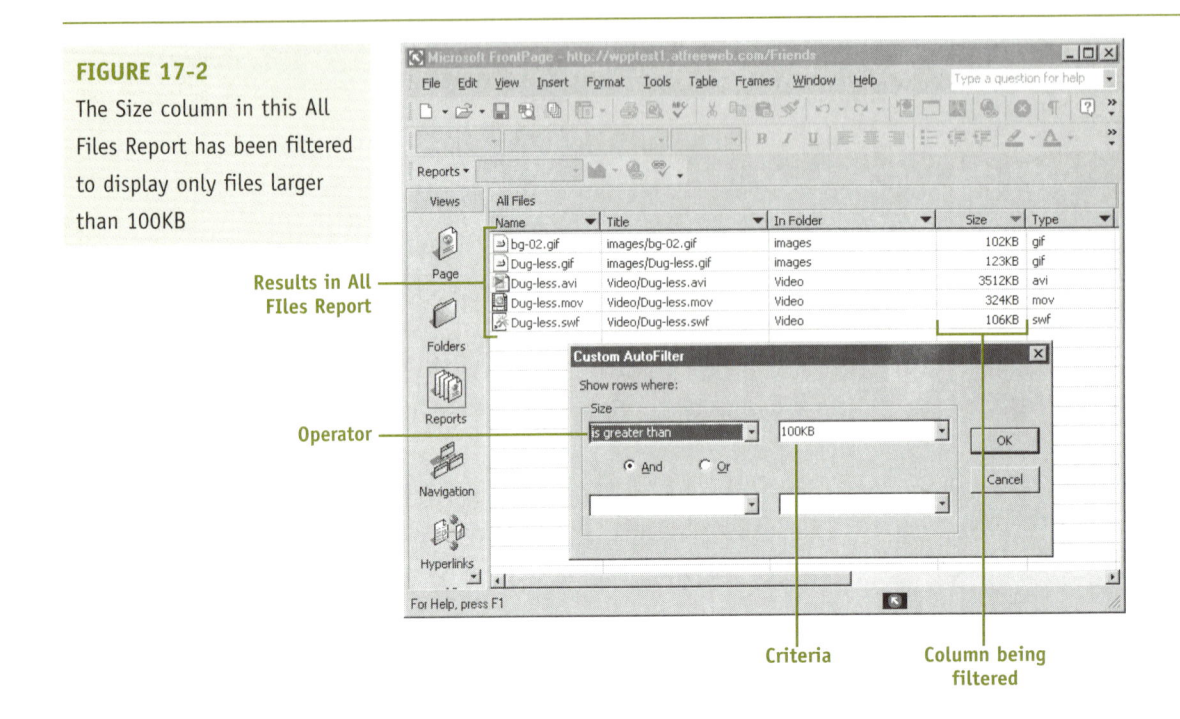

FIGURE 17-2
The Size column in this All Files Report has been filtered to display only files larger than 100KB

Results in All FIles Report

Operator

Criteria

Column being filtered

Listing Old Files

As you accumulate files in your Web site, some become outdated. You'll find that you delink some Web pages from your navigation structure. You will remove pictures from pages, and you will generate files with Web components that you later don't use.

All these files pile up. They waste server space, and they make it difficult for you to manage your site, and find the files you *do* want to find.

FrontPage dates files by when they were last *saved*. So, a file that hasn't been opened and saved for a year is considered a year old, while a file that was opened, not changed, and *resaved* yesterday is considered a day old.

FrontPage allows you to define a time period, such as a week, a month, or a year, and then look for "older files" that are older than that time period. If you update your site daily, "older" files might be 30 days old. With other sites, you might only begin to worry about files if they are older than a year.

To See a list of old files:

1 Choose View | Reports | Files | Older files from the FrontPage menu.

2 From the Report Setting drop-down menu, choose a time period, as shown here:

Viewing Recently Added or Recently Changed Files

Let's say you've edited 20 pages today, and you know that on *one* of them you subconsciously inserted a nasty joke making fun of the large corporation that is about to acquire your company. Oops! How do you find that page?

FrontPage will generate a report that shows all the files you've edited within a defined time period. This can be a day, a week, 30 days, or any time period up to a year.

You can also generate a report of recently *added* files to look at files that you imported into your site within a set time period.

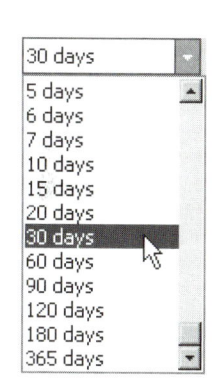

To See a list of recently added or recently changed files:

1 Choose View | Reports | Files, and then select either Recently Added Files or Recently Changed Files from the FrontPage menu.

2 From the Report Settings drop-down list, choose a time period. The displayed files will be those that were added or changed within the selected time frame.

Identifying Problems in Your Site

Bad links. Slow downloads. Big files hogging server space that nobody goes to. These are three of the most annoying problems you can have at your Web site.

Bad links send your visitors off into cyberspace, meaning you miss connecting them with the intended target, and they get a bad impression of your site. Slow downloads are, according to many experts, the single biggest reason why visitors will abandon your site. And, big files sitting on your site that nobody can get to can either mean that you need to change your navigation structure, or that you're wasting server space with files nobody wants. FrontPage 2002 makes it easy to identify and fix all these problems.

Finding and Fixing Unlinked Files

Usually when you have files on your site that have no incoming links, it means that these files are taking up server space but not really part of your Web site. For example, you might have uploaded a set of pictures to your server that are no longer used on your site. Many of us, myself included, find the tedious task of looking for and deleting these files one of the least fun parts of Web management.

Not to worry. FrontPage can search your site for files that have no link connection to other files in your site. Most likely, these are files you can delete. In some cases, however, you might *want* files at your server that don't have any incoming links. Perhaps you are planning to use them soon. Or, you might be using your server as an online storage locker. Maybe you have a deal for server space that allows you to stash large graphics, movies. Or, you might have online databases that collect data from input forms, but are not linked to any Web page. In those cases, of course, you should be careful *not* to delete unlinked files that you *want* at your site.

To Identify AND FIX FILES WITH NO INCOMING LINKS:

1 Choose View | Reports | Problems | Unlinked Files from the FrontPage menu.

2 Use SHIFT+click to select contiguous rows, or use CTRL+click to select non-contiguous rows.

3 Press DELETE to delete the selected files. A dialog box will prompt you to confirm that you want to delete the files, as shown here:

4 Click Yes or Yes to All in the Confirm Delete dialog box to delete the selected file(s).

> **NOTE** Reports view now lists only files that have no incoming links. You should *not* automatically delete all these files. Look them over carefully, and note—among other things—the Modified Date. Recently modified files are likely to be ones you want to keep on your server.

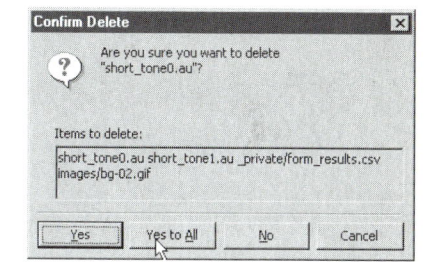

IDENTIFYING SLOW PAGES

The temptation in Web design is to create pages that upload fast enough for *your own* Internet connection. Many a Web designer who has upgraded his or her connection from a 56K modem to a T1 line suddenly decides that mega-sized movie files and large sized sound files are just fine for their site, forgetting that perhaps their *visitors* have not upgraded simultaneously.

DEFINING AN ASSUMED CONNECTION SPEED

FrontPage allows you to define a standard Internet connection speed, and then filter your site to locate pages that download too slowly. So, the first step in finding slow pages is to tell FrontPage what connection speed you expect your visitors to use.

The right way to assess how much is too much when it comes to page download time is to do your best to survey your actual visitors. For example, one of my sites is aimed at visitors from areas of the world where slow phone modems are still the only way to access the Internet. Another site I manage is aimed at visitors from rural and suburban areas of the United States that still don't have access to DSL or high-speed cable Internet connections. For those sites, I use a 56kps modem as the standard for how long a page can take to download.

CHAPTER 17
Managing Your Web Site

To Set AN ASSUMED CONNECTION SPEED FOR YOUR USERS:

1 Choose Tools | Options from the FrontPage menu, and click the Reports View tab in the Options dialog box.

2 In the Assume Connection Speed Of drop-down list, choose an assumed download speed for visitors, as shown here:

3 Click OK to close the Options dialog box.

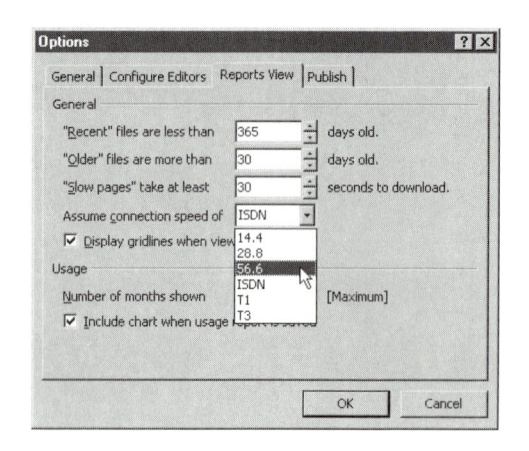

Telling FrontPage How Long Is Too Long

After you define an assumed connection speed, you can tell FrontPage how long is too long for pages to download. If visitors are coming to your site expecting to see a video, they might be comfortable with waiting 30 seconds or more for page content to download. But even if they expect to wait for media content, will your visitors wait seven *minutes* for a page to download? Not in most cases.

And, if visitors are simply following a link from another page or a search engine, many will give up and go away after much less than seven minutes.

At any rate, you should be conscious of how long your pages will take visitors to download. To do this, you can first define how long you consider too long for a page to download, and then examine the list of slow pages.

To See A LIST OF SLOW PAGES:

1 Choose View | Reports | Problems | Slow Pages from the FrontPage menu.

2 From the Report Settings drop-down list, select a time to filter for pages that download too long.

3 To sort pages in order of download time, click the Download Time column heading. Click a second time to see the slowest pages at the top of your list, as shown in Figure 17-3.

FIGURE 17-3

By sorting slow pages in order of download time, you can identify pages that slow down visitors at your site

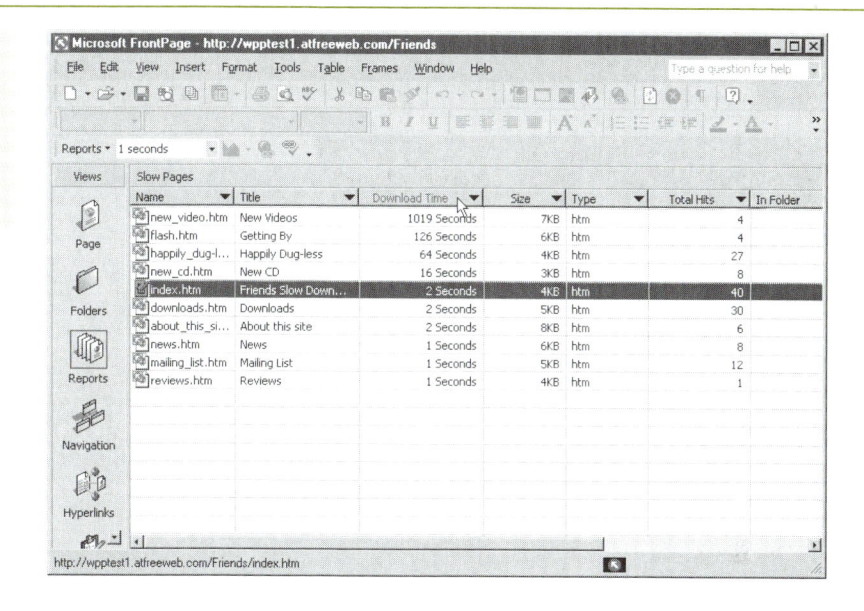

Speeding Up Page Download

If you end up discovering that some of your page download times are too long, you can consider changing your page and site to either speed up the pages, or make the wait less annoying.

The most universal way to speed up page download time is to reduce the size of pictures. Consider using thumbnails to display icons that link to large pictures, instead of making visitors wait to download the picture. Or, consider using progressive passes for JPEG images to make the download time less frustrating for visitors. These techniques are discussed in Chapter 4.

For media, experiment with reducing file size using newer, more compressed audio and video file formats. Chapter 14 surveys currently available formats, but they are constantly changing. The new MP3 format, being released at this writing, promises to provide faster downloading sound files with good sound quality.

The other alternative is to provide links that tell visitors in advance how long they should expect to wait to download a file. For example, if you find that a video takes seven minutes to download over an ISDN line, you can include that information in your page content before a visitor follows a link. By *changing* the connection setting in the Options dialog box, and then toggling back to the slow files report, you can calculate several download times, as shown in Figure 17-4.

CHAPTER 17
Managing Your Web Site

FIGURE 17-4
You can use FrontPage to calculate estimated download times

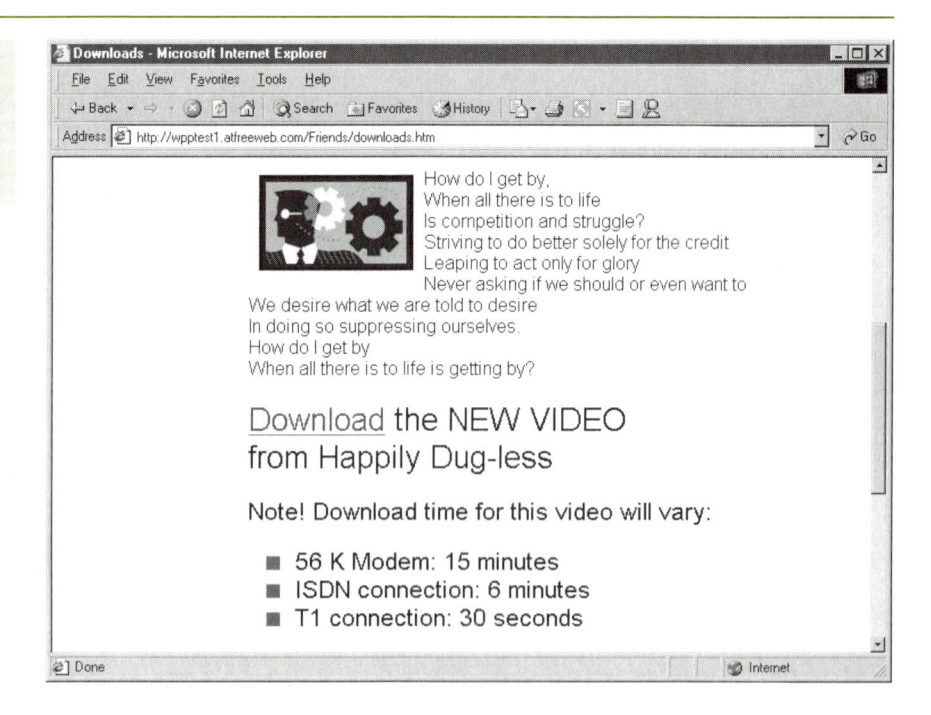

Finding and Fixing Broken Links

Your site probably has many links to pages *within* your site, and *outside* of your site. Links inside your site are usually called *internal* links, while links outside your site are usually called *external* links. These links can go bad. Bad internal links are not so common in FrontPage, because every time you change or delete a page that affects links on another page, FrontPage will automatically change the path to the linked file.

Still, there are a variety of reasons why internal links can go bad, including that you uploaded a file without uploading all files that link to the uploaded file. Or, a file could be corrupted. I've found that a frequent source of bad internal links is when I create files outside of FrontPage, and then import them into my Web. These files aren't tested for link errors the same way that files created completely in FrontPage are.

More frequently, external links go bad. The Internet changes so often that today's link to a valuable site is tomorrow's link to a defunct or changed site. FrontPage will test all your links and identify those that don't work. And, FrontPage makes it easy to fix broken links.

To Test FOR AND FIX BROKEN LINKS:

1 Save any open Web pages so that the links on those pages will be checked.

2 Choose View | Reports | Problems | Broken Hyperlinks from the FrontPage menu.

3 The Broken Hyperlinks report shows both internal links that are broken and external links that need to be tested. To test the external links, click the Verified Hyperlinks in the Current Web button in the Reports toolbar. To test your entire site, select the Verify All Hyperlinks options button, as shown here:

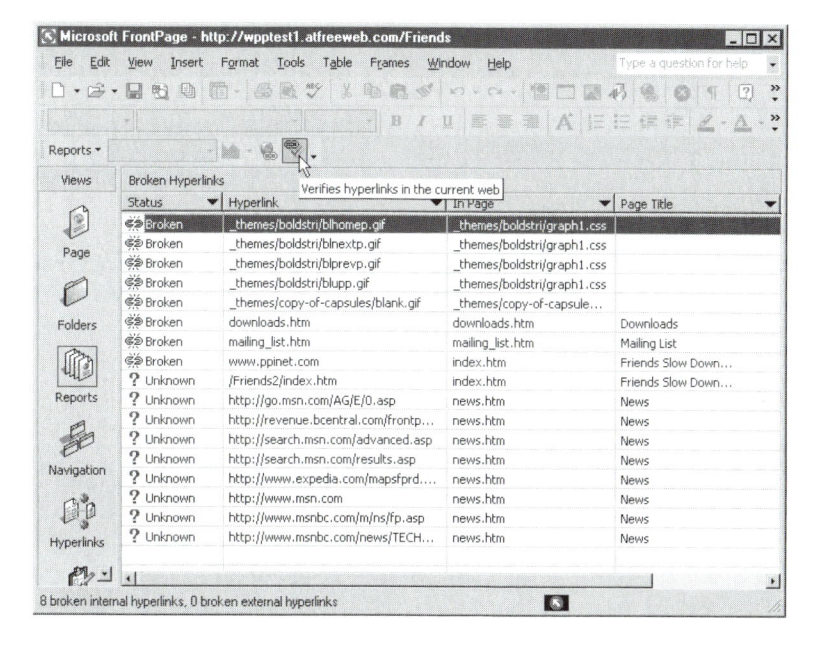

4 In the Verify Hyperlinks dialog box, choose the Verify All Hyperlinks options button to test all your site's links.

5 Click Start in the Verify Hyperlinks dialog box.

FrontPage will test all the links in your site, and produce an updated list of bad links. Tested links that worked will be marked with a check, while bad links will display a bad link icon. You can sort by Status to list all your bad links together, as shown in Figure 17-5.

CHAPTER 17
Managing Your Web Site

FIGURE 17-5
Creating a list of broken links

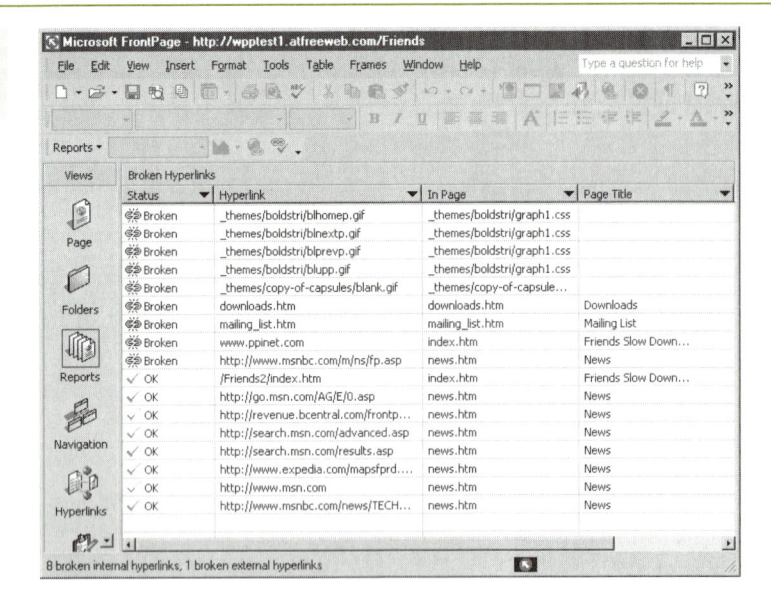

The FrontPage Broken Hyperlinks Report lists the *pages* in which bad links are found. You can either edit links by opening the page with the bad link and making changes, or you can do a kind of "search and replace" for bad links right from the Broken Hyperlinks Reports.

To Fix broken links throughout your site:

1 Double-click a bad link page in the Broken Hyperlinks Report. The Edit Hyperlink dialog box opens.

2 If you know the correct link, type that corrected link in the Replace Hyperlink With area of the Edit Hyperlink dialog box, as shown here:

3 After you type the corrected link address, you can choose the Change in All Pages options button to change that link *everywhere in your site*. Or, use the Change in Selected Pages options button to fix the link only on the selected page(s).

4 Click the Replace button.

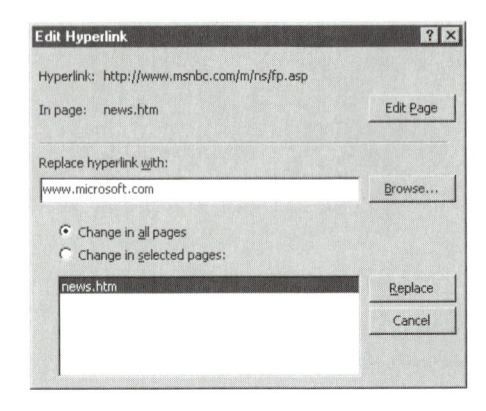

If you don't know the corrected Web or site link for a bad link, you can open the page with the bad link, and edit that page. This can be done directly from the Broken Hyperlinks Report.

To Edit a page with a bad link from the Broken Hyperlinks Report:

1 Double-click a bad link page in the Broken Hyperlinks Report. The Edit Hyperlink dialog box opens.

2 Click the Edit Page button in the Edit Hyperlink dialog box.

3 After you edit the page to fix the broken link, save the page. The link status will be marked as "? Edited" in the Broken Hyperlinks Report, as shown here:

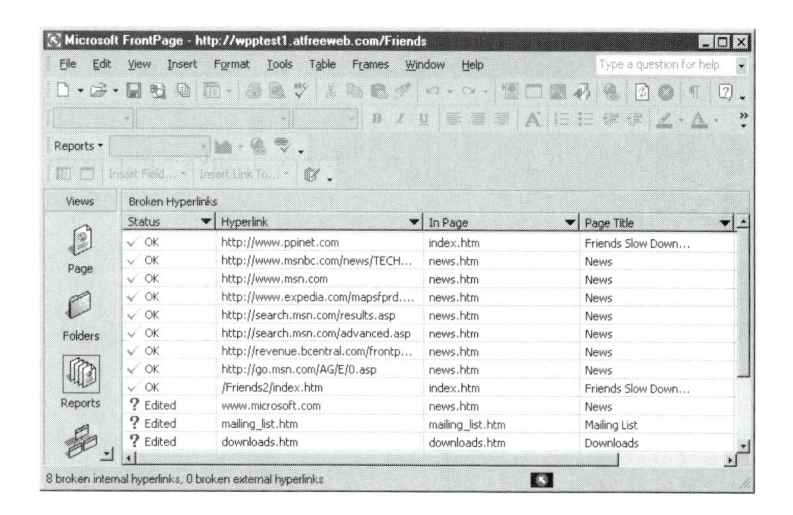

4 After you fix your broken links, you can—again—click the Verifies Hyperlinks in Current Web button. Your report will be refreshed, and if your links are fixed, they will not appear in the report.

Finding and Fixing Component Errors

FrontPage Web components use generated HTML code, JavaScript, Java, and other programming languages to do their magic. Hover buttons, for example, require relatively complex Java applets that contain references to images and other

CHAPTER 17
MANAGING YOUR WEB SITE

files used to make the buttons glow when a visitor rolls over them. A moved or deleted image file can throw a monkey wrench into the applet, causing the buttons not to work.

You can test your site to see if there are problems with any of your Web components. Then, when you locate these problems, you can fix them—sometimes by changing the component properties, and sometimes by deleting the bad component and creating a new one from scratch.

To Find AND FIX WEB COMPONENTS ERRORS:

1 Choose View | Reports | Problems | Component Errors from the FrontPage menu to display a list of components that don't work.

2 The Errors column of the Component Errors Report displays detailed explanations for why any listed Web components won't work. To read the entire explanation, right-click the error description in the report, and choose Properties. The page properties dialog box opens, with the Errors tab selected, as shown here:

3 Read the description of the error, and click OK to close the Properties dialog box.

4 Either delete the offending component, or fix it.

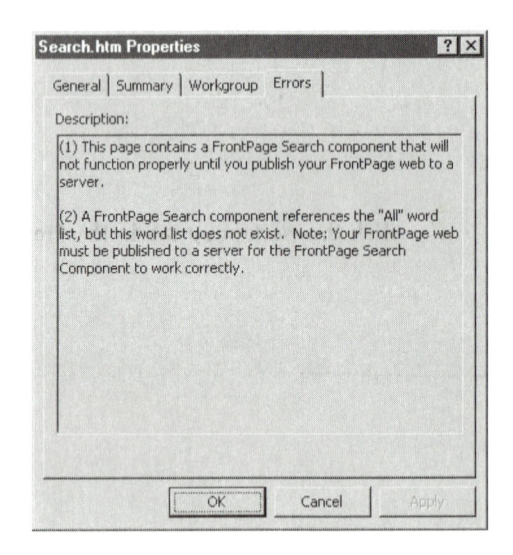

MANAGING WORKGROUPS

If you are working on a Web site with other members of a development team, FrontPage has special features to allow you to coordinate the work of the entire *workgroup*. You can assign pages to individuals or groups of people. You can also organize pages into *categories*—such as artwork, input forms, or other custom areas of work.

Finally, you can attach a review status note to each file in your project. With a review status assigned to pages, you can produce lists of pages that have been approved, pages that are waiting for approval, and pages that have been denied approval. Or, you can create your own review status options.

Assigning Work

Personnel assignments, category assignments, and review status are all defined in the Properties dialog box for selected pages. You will want to make these assignments in conjunction with an overall project management plan for your site. So, for instance, you might want to define categories that correspond to departments in your Web design division—such as graphical design, database development, and page design. For review status, you might want to define options like finished, 50% done, or not started. Once you assign personnel, categories, and/or review status to pages, that information will be displayed in FrontPage's set of workflow reports that can be distributed to management, or to team members.

To Assign PERSONNEL ASSIGNMENTS, CATEGORY ASSIGNMENTS, AND REVIEW STATUS:

1. Right-click a page in Folders view, or any report view, and choose Properties from the context menu to open the Properties dialog box for the selected page.

2. Click the Workgroup tab in the Properties dialog box for the selected page.

3. To add new categories, click the Categories button, and type a new category in the New Category area, as shown here:

4. After you enter a new category in the New Category area, click the Add button to include this new item in your categories list. Continue to add new categories as needed. After you add categories, click OK to return to the page Properties dialog box.

5. In the Categories area of the dialog box, click check boxes to assign a page to one or more existing categories.

6. Click the Names button. The Usernames Master List dialog box opens. Enter names of people, groups, or departments in the New Username area. Click Add to add the new name to the list of resources. Use the Add button to add additional resources, then click OK to return to the page Properties dialog box.

7. Use the Assigned To drop-down list to choose resources to attach to the selected page.

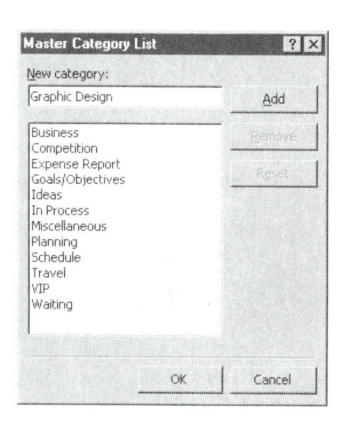

> **NOTE** A page can only be assigned to one person or group.

CHAPTER 17
Managing Your Web Site

8 Click the Statuses button to open the Review Status Master List dialog box.

9 If you want to add to the default options for review status, enter a new status name in the New Review Status area of the Review Status Master List dialog box. Click Add.

10 Add additional review statuses as needed, and click OK to return to the page Properties dialog box.

11 Use the Review Status drop-down list to define a review status for the selected page, as shown here:

12 After you have assigned categories, personnel (in the Assigned to area), and review status, click OK to apply the work status to the page, and close the page Properties dialog box.

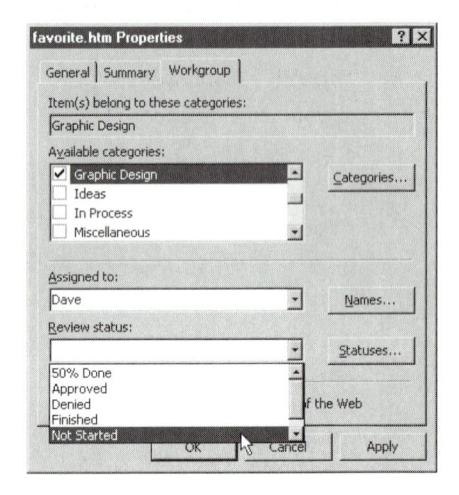

Tracking Work

Once you have assigned people, categories, and completion status to pages, you can use FrontPage 2002's report views to generate site workflow reports. To view a workflow report, choose View | Reports | Workflow, and either Review Status, Assigned To, or Categories.

Workflow reports can be sorted by clicking the column heading for any column in the report, or filtered by clicking on the triangle in the top row of the report next to the column for which you want to sort,

Checking In and Checking Out

FrontPage allows several users to check out files for editing, and then check them back in after they are edited. In order to avoid confusion when two people are editing the same file, you can establish policies that ensure only one developer has a file checked out at a time.

The Check In and Check Out features require both that your Web server has FrontPage extension files, *and* that your server administrator has enabled *Version Control* features.

To Enable Version Control on your Web Server:

1 Choose Tools | Server | Administration Home from the FrontPage menu.

2 You will be prompted to log in as a server administrator, and only allowed to continue if you are authorized a server administrator. After logging in, the server administration page for your server appears.

3 Locate the Configure Version Control link or area in your server administration page, and open the Configure Version Control area of your server administration site.

4 Choose the Use Built-In Version Control radio button, and click the Submit button to enable version control, as shown here:

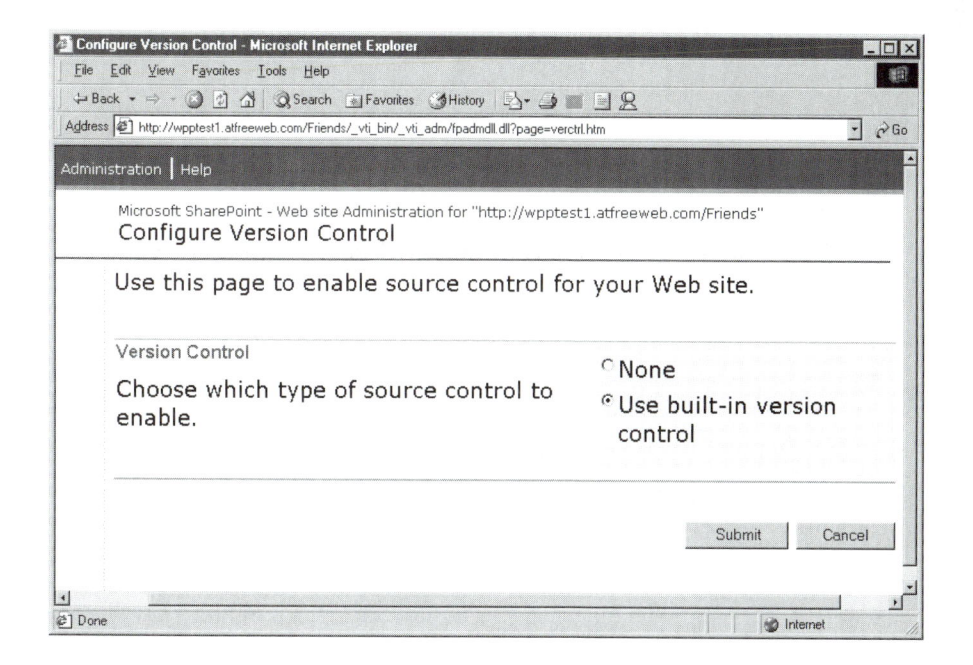

5 Exit your server administration site. Version control is now enabled in your site, and users can check files in and out.

If you are administering your own server, or if you can get your server administrator to enable version control (try bribing him or her with a 2-liter bottle of cola), you and other developers can check pages in and out, and see the check-out status of pages in a workflow report.

CHAPTER 17
Managing Your Web Site

To Check PAGES IN AND OUT:

1 In Folders view, right-click an HTML Web page file, and choose Check Out from the context menu as shown in Figure 17-6.

2 Open the page, and edit it.

3 Save changes, and close the page.

4 Right-click the page in Folders view, and choose Check In from the context menu.

If many developers are working together on a site, they can note which pages are checked out by looking at the Checkout Status Workflow Report. To view that report, choose View | Reports | Workflow | Checkout Status.

The Checkout Status Report includes a Checked Out By column that identifies who has a file currently checked out. If there is more than one version of a file checked out (and it's probably a good idea to avoid that to prevent two developers from stepping on each other's work), additional versions are listed in the Version column.

Figure 17-7 shows a Checkout Status Report, with several files checked out.

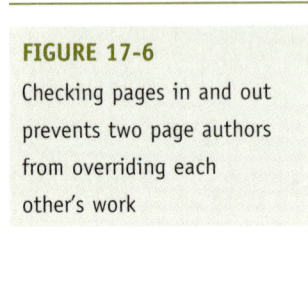

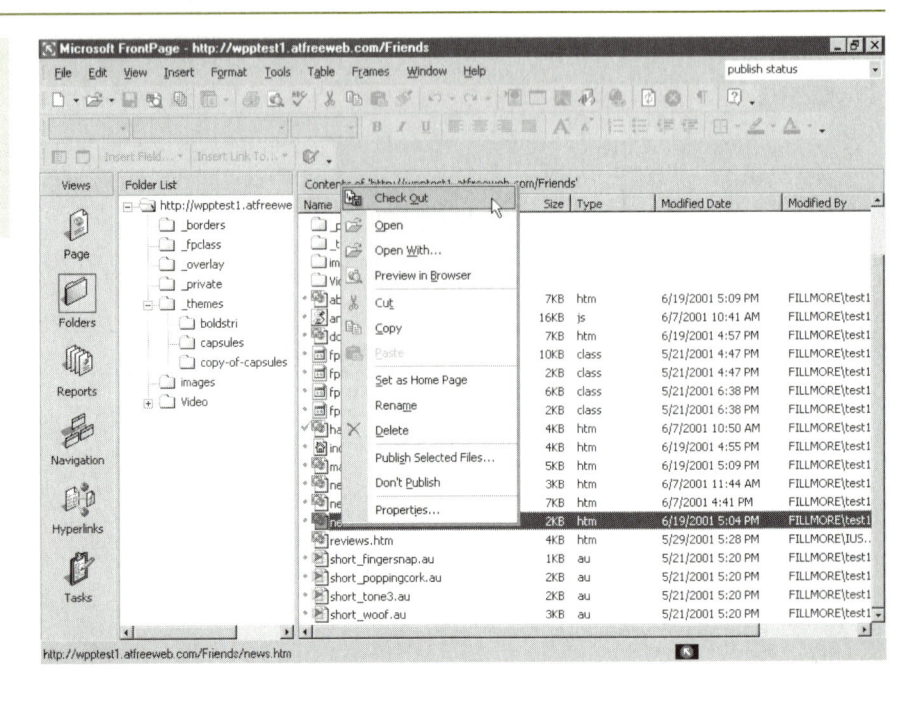

FIGURE 17-6

Checking pages in and out prevents two page authors from overriding each other's work

FIGURE 17-7
Checked out status means a developer is currently working on the file

Checked out status is indicated with check marks

The Checkout Status report lists whom has what file checked out

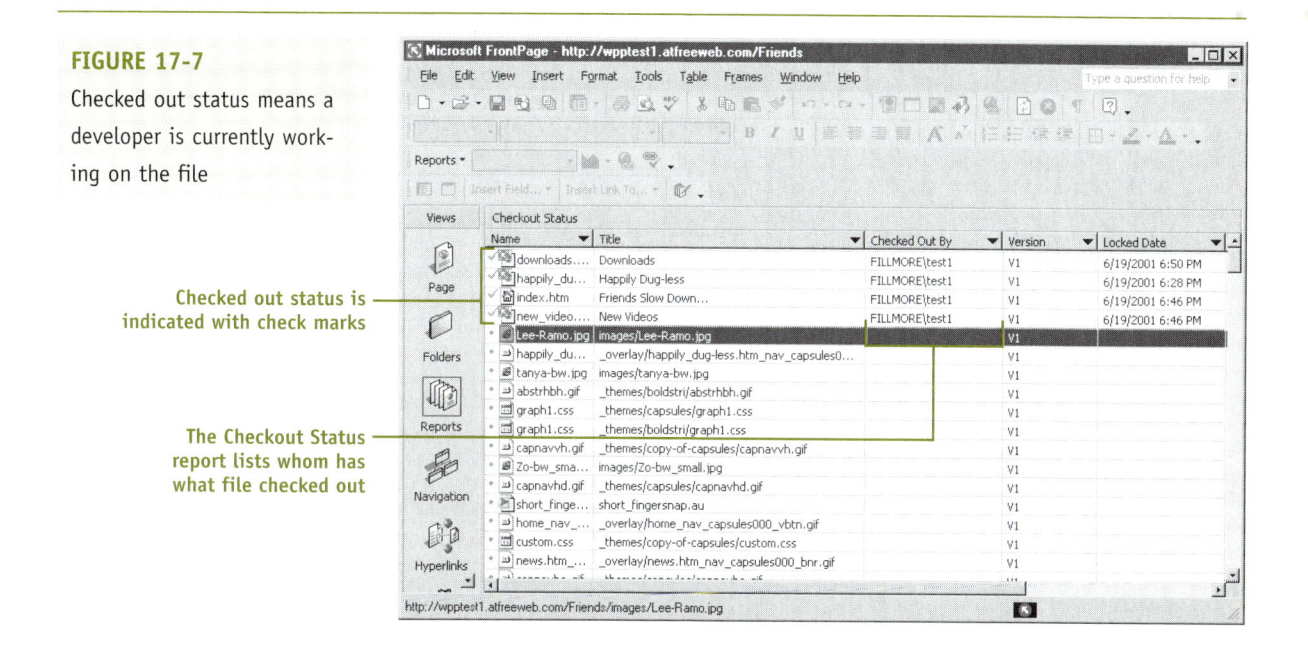

THE PUBLISH STATUS REPORT

The Publish Status Report doesn't really belong in the Workflow Reports category, but FrontPage stuck it there on the menu, and I figure you might be looking here for an explanation of how to use it.

Publish status determines whether a file will be uploaded to your server when you publish your site. Assigning Don't Publish status to a page essentially makes the page function like a Read-Only file. It can be opened but not saved to a server until the Don't Publish status has been removed. If the file is on a local computer, and the site is published to a remote site, files with Don't Publish status won't be uploaded.

To assign Don't Publish status to a file, right-click the file and select Don't Publish from the context menu. To remove Don't Publish status, repeat the process to deselect Don't Publish status.

You can view files and their Publish status by choosing View | Reports | Workflow | Publish Status. Here you can sort or filter to display only Publish or Don't Publish files.

CHAPTER 17
Managing Your Web Site

Tracking Site Usage

One of the most powerful new features in FrontPage 2002 is the ability to easily see detailed reports on who is coming to your site. The FrontPage counter Web component tells you the total number of visitors that come to your site. But for those of you who need to monitor closely how many visitors you get, and when, that's not enough. Further, a counter is a *public* display of how many people have visited your site, whereas FrontPage usage reports make this information available *in FrontPage*—so that it is not accessible to the public.

Summarizing Site Hits

FrontPage usage reports allow you to see how many visitors came to your site over a period of a month, a week, or a day. Beyond counting the total number visits to your *site*, FrontPage 2002 can also count how many times *individual pages* and even images have been opened by visitors. This allows you to analyze in great detail where folks are going *once they get to your site*.

All this information can be a little too much. For example, at my site, the background image used in all my pages is the single most viewed file. That's not very helpful—what I want to know is what *pages* visitors are going to. Fortunately, FrontPage 2002 makes it possible to filter usage reports. This way, for example, you can restrict a report to only HTML Web page files.

To view a usage report, choose View | Reports | Usage, and select one of the available usage reports. The Monthly and Weekly Summary Reports total hits to your site. The Monthly, Weekly, and Daily Page Hits Reports detail how many hits *each page* in your Web site got over the selected period. You can sort these reports by the Total Hits column by clicking the column heading to sort pages by how popular they are with visitors. If you filter for only HTM files in the Type column (click the triangle, and select HTM from the list), you can restrict the hits report to just Web pages, as shown in Figure 17-8.

Who Is Coming to Your Site?

In addition to *counting* hits to your site, and your site pages, FrontPage can collect information about visitors to your site and display this information in usage reports. These usage reports can summarize the following information about your visitors:

FIGURE 17-8
The Monthly, Weekly, and Daily Page Hits Reports provide a breakdown of what pages are being visited at your site

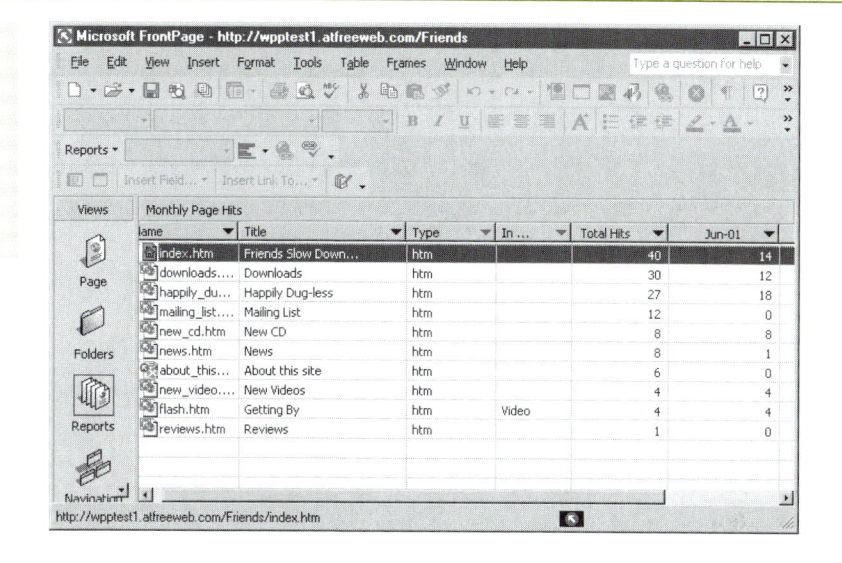

- ▶ **Visiting Users** Displays user name collected from a visitor's system.
- ▶ **Operating Systems** Counts the number of visitors using different operating systems (like Windows 95, Windows 98, Windows 2000, and so on).
- ▶ **Browsers** Counts the number of visitors using different browsers and browser versions.
- ▶ **Referring Domains** Counts the number of visitors who come to your site from different domains—this option displays only the domain name of the referring site.
- ▶ **Referring URLs** Counts the number of visitors who come to your site from different URLs—this option displays a complete URL with the domain name, folder, and page of referring site).
- ▶ **Search Strings** Counts the number of hits generated by different search entries.

In order to collect and view this information in FrontPage, your server administrator must enable Usage Analysis settings. This can only be done for an *entire* Web, not for individual subwebs.

To view one of the usage reports that tracks who is coming to your site, and from where, choose View | Reports | Usage, and select one of the usage reports.

Assigning and Managing Tasks

For large Web site projects, you can create a task list to keep track of work that needs to be done, and monitor the status of various tasks. Tasks are listed in Task view. You can create them yourself. Additionally, Tasks are automatically generated when you use some Web templates, like the Corporate Presence Web template.

Adding Tasks

A task can be anything you want it to be. For example, you can create a task called "Test site," "Create logo artwork," or "Add text to home page." You can associate a Web page with a task, but this isn't required.

To Create a task not associated with a page:

1 Select Tasks view from the FrontPage Views bar.

2 Right-click anywhere in Tasks view, and choose Add Task from the context menu. The New Task dialog box appears.

3 In the Task Name area, name your task with a descriptive title.

4 In the Priority area, select the High, Medium, or Low option button.

5 In the Description area, enter additional comments about the job, as shown here:

6 Click OK to add the task to the Task List.

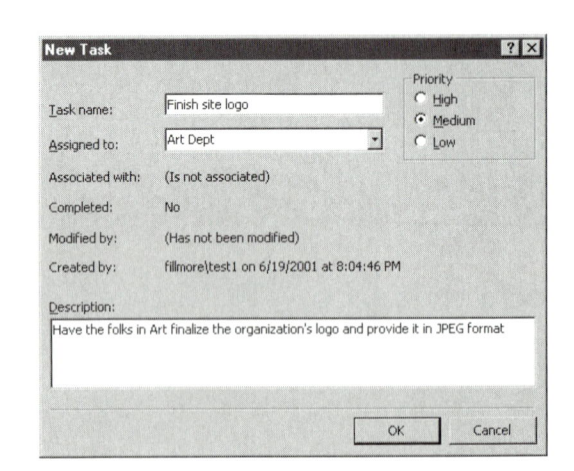

If you want to associate a task with a specific page, the routine is the same *except that you first open the page in Page view*. Then, choose File | New Task to open the New Task dialog box. The page that you had open will be assigned as the Associated With page.

Editing Tasks

Once you accumulate a list of tasks in Task view, you can edit them, sort them, filter them, and mark them completed when they are finished. You can edit a task, start a task, mark a task complete, or delete a task, by right-clicking it in Task view and choosing an option from the context menu, as shown here:

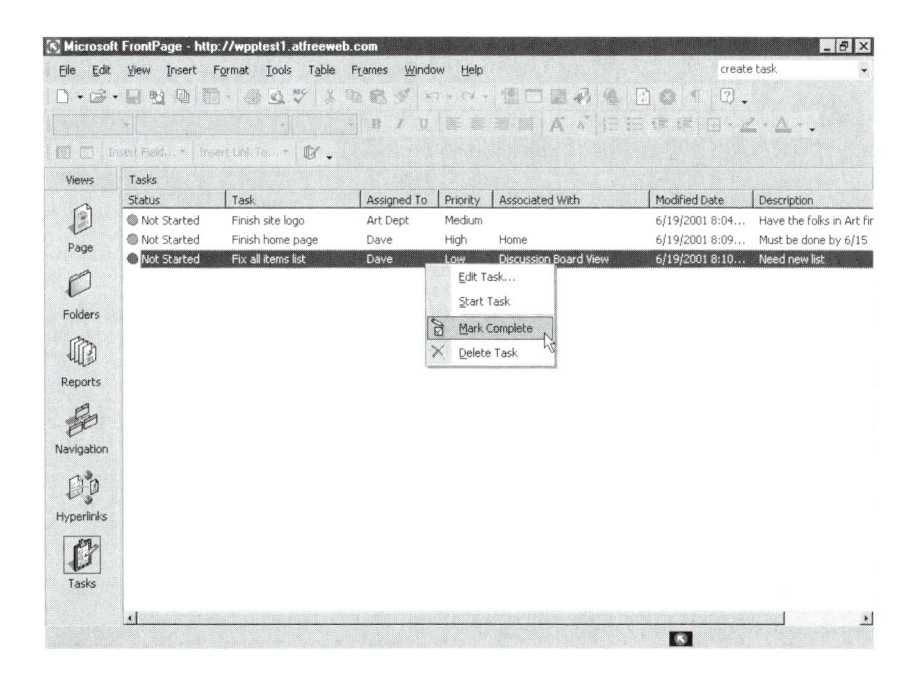

To sort the task list, click a column heading—such as Assigned To, or Status. To filter the list—for example to display only tasks assigned to a single resource—use the triangle filter icons next to each column heading.

NOTE The Start Task option is only available if a task has an associated page.

As you mark tasks complete, you can elect to hide or show these finished tasks. To display finished tasks, right-click in a blank area of the Task list and choose Show History from the context menu, as shown here:

Where to From Here?

In this chapter, you learned to maintain and troubleshoot your site using FrontPage's Problem Reports. You also

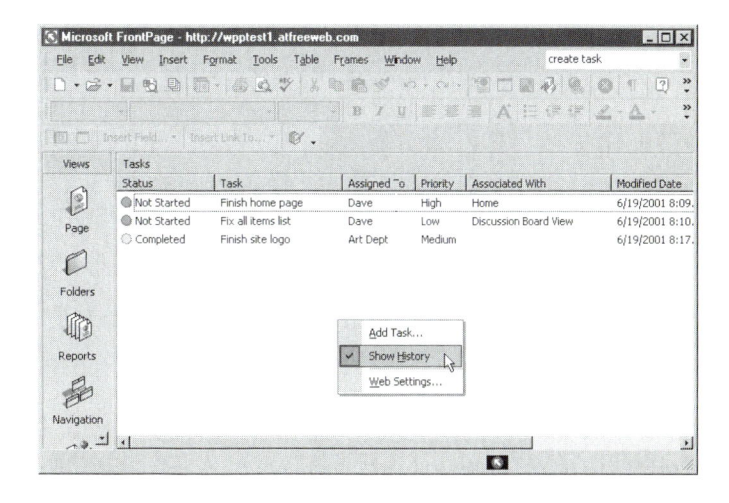

CHAPTER 17
MANAGING YOUR WEB SITE

explored FrontPage's usage reports to track how many visitors are coming to your site, and from where.

If you are working on your Web site as part of a development team, you can use the Task features to organize and track your team's progress. Tasks are also covered in this chapter.

This is the final chapter in this *Virtual Classroom* book. But it's not the end of the story. On the CD that accompanies this book you'll find many additional insights and demonstrations that will help you create your FrontPage Web site. In addition, I invite you to visit www.ppinet.com and explore additional FrontPage resources I maintain for readers, including a discussion forum and links to useful add-ins.

And last but not least, have fun creating your FrontPage Web site!

Appendix A

Installing FrontPage 2002

The exact routine for installing FrontPage 2002 will depend on whether you are installing FrontPage 2002 as part of Office XP, or as a stand-alone product, as well as what operating system you are using to run FrontPage 2002. The installation guide that comes with FrontPage is more clear than most installation documentation and provides a helpful explanation of the main installable features. While the installation routine will vary, the basic installation options are the same. In this appendix, I'll alert you to issues you will want to pay attention to as you install FrontPage 2002 on your own system.

Appendix A
Installing FrontPage 2002

Which Operating System Is Best for FrontPage 2002?

FrontPage 2002 will run on Windows 98, Windows 98SE, Windows ME, Windows NT 4 with Service Pack 6 or later, Windows 2000, and Windows XP. So, if you already have one of those operating systems working reliably and safely, you probably won't want or need to change operating systems to run FrontPage.

The main difference between these operating systems with regard to FrontPage is that *some* of them allow you to install FrontPage server software.

> **WARNING** FrontPage 2002 *cannot* be installed on Windows 95.

Do You Need to Install Server Extensions?

FrontPage actually works as a combination of programs. The regular FrontPage program runs on your PC, while additional files called *server extensions* are installed on the computer that hosts your Web site.

Many FrontPage features require that you publish (upload) your site to a Web server with FrontPage extensions before they will work. However, just because your operating system doesn't support all (or any) FrontPage server options doesn't mean your Web site can't include every FrontPage feature. It only means that to get these features to work, you'll need to publish your site to a remote server that does support FrontPage extensions.

My package of FrontPage 2002 came with special deals allowing me to publish my site to a FrontPage server for three months for free. And, when you publish a site in FrontPage (see Chapters 16 and 17) to a remote server, FrontPage provides a link to many Web server providers who support FrontPage extensions.

In short, if your operating system doesn't support server extensions, this might not be a problem at all. For rates starting around $8/month, you can contract with a remote server provider who will supply you with a location for your site that supports all FrontPage features, and you won't even need to worry about what operating system they are using. If you won't be managing your own server, skip to the section "Installing FrontPage," later in this appendix.

Different Server Extensions Are Available for Different Operating Systems

If you are determined to configure your own PC as a Web server—either to host real live Web sites or test FrontPage Webs before you publish them—it does matter which operating system you use to run FrontPage. Microsoft has set things up so that different operating systems are capable of handling different variations and versions of FrontPage extensions. Some operating systems will support FrontPage extensions, but not the *latest* FrontPage 2002 extensions. Others will support FrontPage 2002 extensions, but not the additional *SharePoint Team Services* server software that is used for building special intranet portals.

The following table outlines which operating systems are capable of hosting which versions of FrontPage Web servers:

OPERATING SYSTEM	SERVER EXTENSIONS SUPPORTED	FEATURES SUPPORTED
Windows 98	FrontPage 2000	Most components, most database tools
Windows ME	None	Windows ME cannot support a FrontPage Web server
Windows NT Workstation 4	FrontPage 2002	All FrontPage database and component features, but not SharePoint portal features
Windows 2000 and Windows XP	FrontPage 2002 and SharePoint Team Services	All FrontPage 2002 features including SharePoint intranet portal features

Installing FrontPage

When you install FrontPage, you'll be prompted to select which features of FrontPage you want to include in your installation. As with other Office XP applications, you have the option of making features available on your PC or dependent on the program CD. If you think you'll use a feature often, you'll want to install it on your PC. If not, making features accessible from your CD saves disk space.

Appendix A
Installing FrontPage 2002

When you insert the FrontPage 2002 or Office XP in your CD drive, the Installation Wizard will begin automatically. The first step is to enter your user information and Product Key, which is available on the back of the CD case.

After you and your legal team scrutinize and accept the license agreement (or, just decide you have to accept it no matter what it says), you'll be presented with three or four installation options—depending on whether you are upgrading from an earlier version of FrontPage.

Which Installation Is Best?

If you want to upgrade, while keeping the settings of your previously installed version in tact, choose the Upgrade Now option, as shown here:

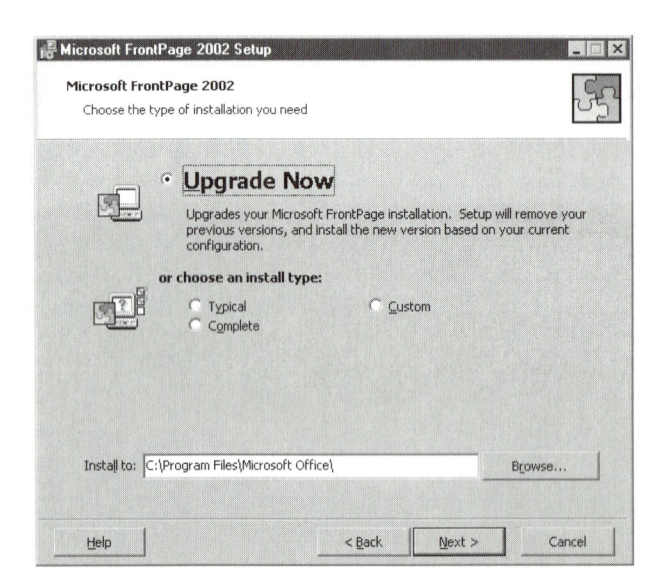

If you are installing FrontPage for the first time, choose Typical, Complete, or Custom options. Typical will install features Microsoft thinks most users want, whereas Complete installs all features. For the most control over your installation, choose Custom.

You can accept the Default Installation folder or define a new one in the Install To area of the setup dialog box. Then, click Next.

Choosing Features to Install

If you chose Custom as your installation option, you can select which features to install and how to install them. The default settings are typical settings, but you can change them.

To select a feature to install or uninstall, expand one of the three categories of features—Microsoft FrontPage for Windows, Office Tools, or Office Shared Features. Here, I've expanded FrontPage options:

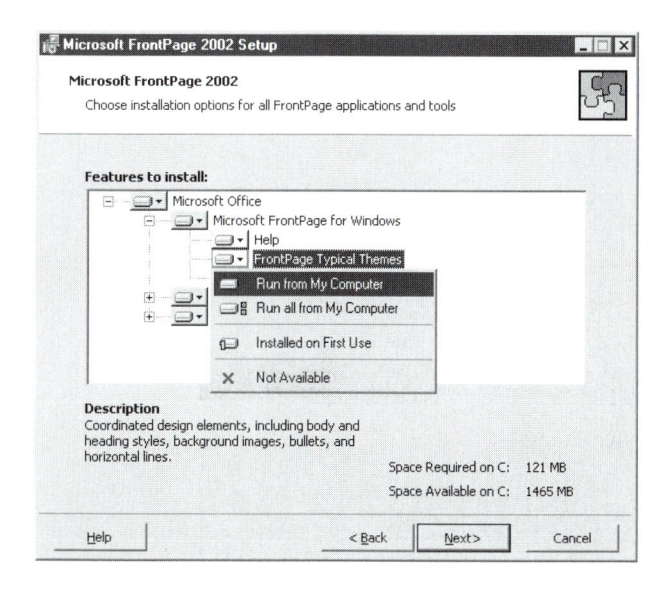

You can elect to run a feature from your computer by choosing Run from My Computer from the drop-down menu associated with that feature. Groups of features can be enabled all at once by choosing the Run All From My Computer option. Choose Installed on First Use to install a selected feature from the CD the first time the feature is used. Or, you can elect to not make a feature available at all by choosing Not Available.

You will definitely want to make FrontPage available from your computer. As for other options, you can elect to install them on first use if you're not sure you'll use them. For example, additional themes take up a lot of disk space because they are graphic intensive—you might want to wait to see if you'll need them before adding them to your computer.

Appendix B

FrontPage Add-In Programs

With so many folks using FrontPage to create their own Web sites, a large satellite industry has sprung up of companies who make add-ins that complement the features in FrontPage.

Appendix B
FrontPage Add-In Programs

I've been experimenting with these add-in programs since well before most of you were born. Okay, since FrontPage 97. I've come to rely on two of these add-ins so much that I consider them an integral part of FrontPage. FrontLook provides access to dozens of frequently updated sets of additional themes for your site, plus tools to edit existing themes. J-Bots adds a JavaScript-generator menu that creates components FrontPage forgot—like drop-down navigation bars.

In addition to these two useful add-ins, FrontPage e-commerce developers will want to check out StoreFront 5.0. This program requires a good working knowledge of online Access database management, so you will want an advanced-level reference book on Microsoft Access 2002 on your bookshelf if you decide to create your own e-commerce site with FrontPage and StoreFront.

> **NOTE** You can find a frequently updated set of links to FrontPage add-ins on the Resources page at www.ppinet.com. Many add-ins offer trial versions.

Installing FrontPage Add-Ins

Most FrontPage add-ins install invisibly and automatically. After you follow the Installation Wizard for programs such as FrontLook or J-Bots, these programs work within FrontPage and simply provide additional options in FrontPage menus. For example, my FrontPage screen in Figure B-1 includes the Super Themes option in the Format menu. That's only because I installed the Super Themes package that is distributed by FrontLook.

Add-in manufacturers like FrontLook and J-Bots know FrontPage better than Microsoft, and they work hard to make their programs install seamlessly. Microsoft has a strategy of creating generic add-in programs that will work with FrontPage as well as other programs. Therefore, these add-in packages do not install seamlessly, but require additional steps to activate in FrontPage.

Installing Microsoft Add-Ins

Among the add-ins available from Microsoft is the bCentral Commerce Manager. If you want to install this, or other Microsoft add-ins, you will need to first follow the installation instructions that come with the add-in software, and then configure FrontPage to recognize them.

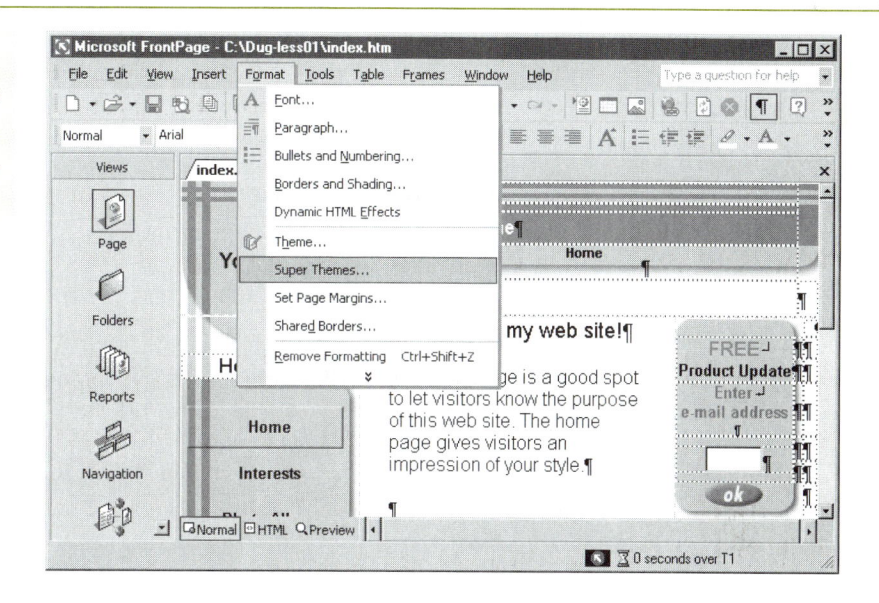

FIGURE B-1

Add-ins change the FrontPage interface by adding new menu options—like the Super Themes option here

To Install FRONTPAGE ADD-INS THAT DON'T INSTALL AUTOMATICALLY:

1 Install the Add-in (download or purchase the product and follow the installation instructions).

2 Choose Tools | Add Ins.

3 Click the Add button. Available tools are listed in the Add Add-In dialog box, as shown here:

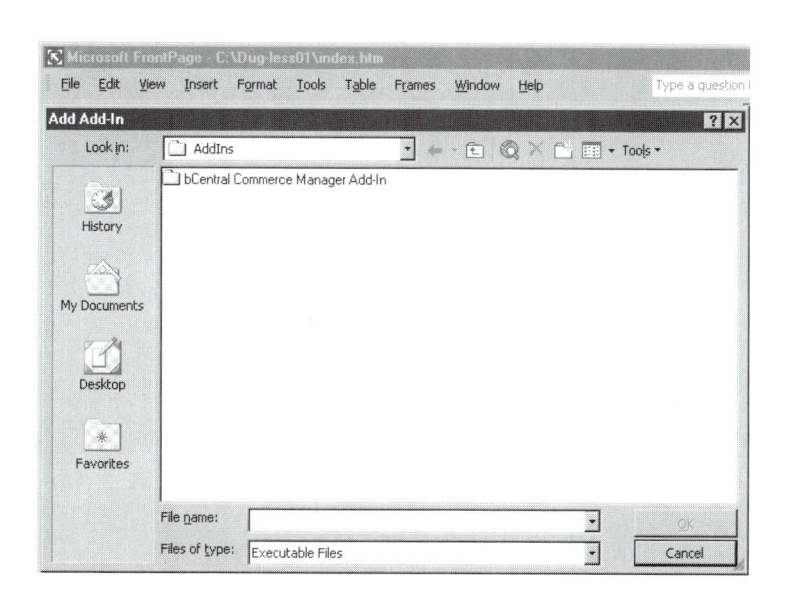

Appendix B
FrontPage Add-In Programs

4 Navigate to the folder with your add-in program.

5 Select the *.DLL file in the application folder, and click OK to add the add-in to FrontPage.

> **NOTE** Microsoft add-ins are in C:\Windows\Application Data\Microsoft\AddIns\.

Removing Add-ins

If, for any reason, you need to delete a FrontPage Add-In program, you can do so. For example, if you are sharing a FrontPage installation with a co-worker or a collaborator, he or she might be disoriented or confused by all the additional menu options that come with add-in programs.

To Remove an add-in:

1 From the FrontPage menu, choose Tools, | Add-ins.

2 Select (with a check box) *only* those program you want to *delete*, as shown here:

3 Click OK.

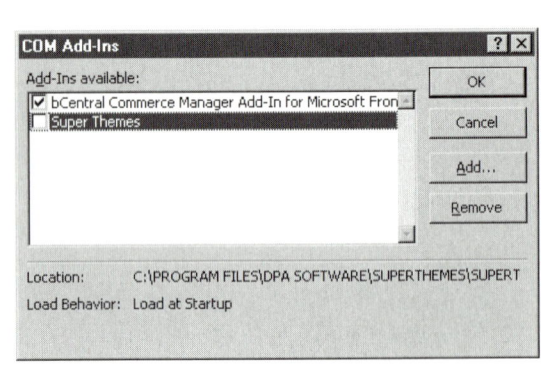

After you remove add-ins, you can easily install them again using the Tools | Add-in menu option. It isn't necessary to reinstall an add-in from the original application—removed add-ins can be reinstalled simply by adding them in the Add-In dialog box.

A Quick Look at FrontLook

FrontPage has never been accused of being on the cutting edge of Web design. While its powerful features allow you to easily set up a database that Dreamweaver users can only envy, FrontPage's page design tools per se are not competitive with other page design packages.

Consider FrontLook the equalizer. Available in three versions (S1, S2, and S3), FrontLook provides page layout features and theme customization that opens up new realms of Web design.

FrontLook Series 3 comes with 30 new themes and more than 300 pieces of Web art. In addition, a Scroller applet supports multiple columns with different fonts, text styles, colors, linking, and sound triggers. The presentation applet supports banners and image presentations, eye-candy image transitions, linking, and status bar support.

The latest version of FrontLook comes with Theme Chameleon. In a nutshell the Chameleon. With this tool, you can change the color scheme of a theme quickly. And, you don't need to mess around with your own graphics.

As this book goes to press, FrontLook is finalizing a new feature that automatically creates wrap-around page themes, like the one in Figure B-2.

JavaScripting with J-Bots Plus 2002

J-Bots Plus 2002 includes dozens of helpful JavaScript applets. J-Bots features are available from the Insert | Web Components dialog box. J-Bot tools include Image

FIGURE B-2
FrontLook's new Super Themes component generates themes with complex wrap-around formatting

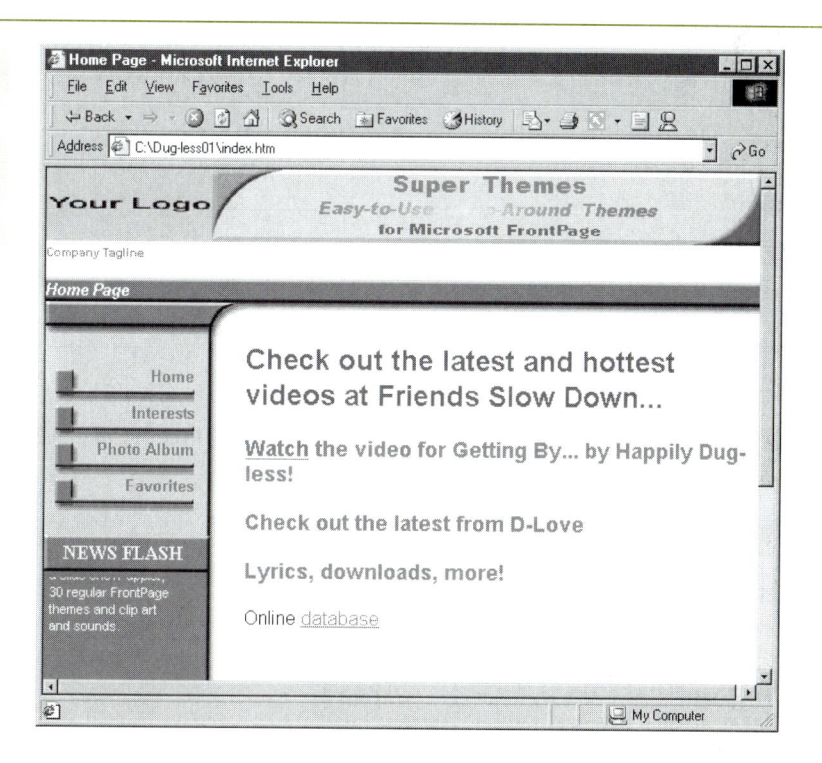

APPENDIX B
FrontPage Add-In Programs

Components that apply effects to images, the Mouse Over Image component that creates JavaScript-based rollovers, Form Components that supplement form tools with features such as telephone number and credit card number validation, and a navigation drop-down menu.

To Insert a J-Bots component:

1 In Page view (Normal), choose Insert | Web Component.

2 Scroll down the Component type list, and click Additional Components. A list of installed additional components will display, with J-Bots indicated, as shown here:

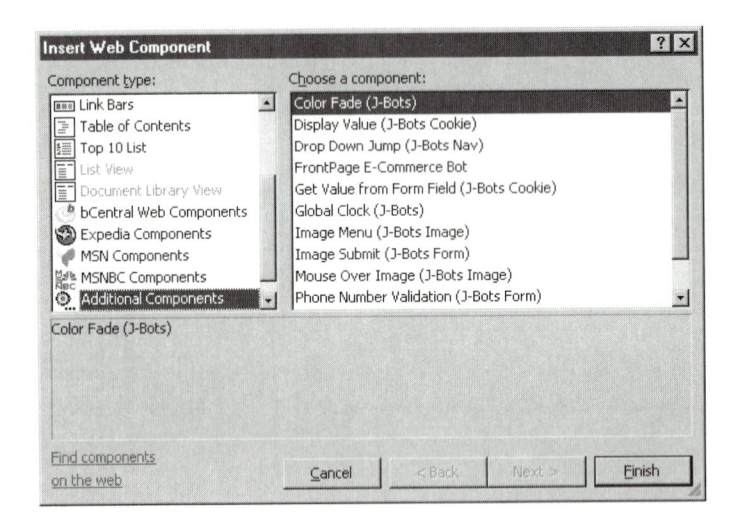

Other Add-Ins

StoreFront 5 provides a powerful e-commerce package for FrontPage. As I mentioned earlier, you should be very comfortable with managing online databases with Microsoft Access before considering this tool. That said, if you take the plunge, you can configure StoreFront 5.0 to sell an unlimited number of products, set up a convenient shopping cart interface, calculate taxes on orders, connect with UPS, FedEx, and USPS shipping rates, take credit cards, and track inventory.

HiSoftware distributes add-ins for FrontPage as well as non-FrontPage versions of its software. HiSoftware products automate submission to Web search engines and provide other tools to increase Web traffic. As I test and review other add-in packages, I'll make links available at www.ppinet.com.

Index

A

Absolute button, 65
absolute positioning, 64–66, 89–91
Absolutely Positioned button, 66
Access database, 205, 316
Active Graphics option, 8, 151, 156
Add button, 34, 36, 37, 87
add-in programs, 315–320
administrator, system, 280–282, 301
AIFF audio files, 240
AIFF format, 51, 60
Align Bottom button, 85
Align Center button, 36, 37
Align Left button, 36, 37, 63
Align Right button, 36, 37, 63
Align Top button, 85
alignment
    form fields, 199–200
    paragraphs, 37, 44
    pictures, 60, 62–65, 70
    table cells, 82
    tables, 78
    text, 37, 44
    video, 248
All Files report, 27, 285–289
All Pages option, 9, 148
alternative representation, 70
animation
    animated GIFs, 225, 247, 250
    with DHTML, 221–233
Appearance tab, 70, 248
applets, 60–241, 168, 173, 319–320

applications
    add-in programs, 315–320
    assigning to files, 24
    pasting tables from, 79
arrow buttons, 38
ASF files, 238
.asp extension, 25
AU format, 51, 60–241, 170
AU sound files, 170, 240–241
audio. *See* sound
auto formats, 85
Auto Thumbnail button, 66
AutoFit to Contents button, 85
Automatic option, 67
AVI files, 238
AVI format, 247, 250
AVI plug-ins, 246

B

Background drop-down list, 50, 51
Background Picture option, 50, 151
Background tab, 49–51
backgrounds
    adding sound, 51–52, 249–250
    cell backgrounds, 83, 84
    color in, 48, 49, 51, 120–121, 155
    defining, 49–51
    pictures as, 83, 84
    pictures in, 50, 151
    shared border, 118, 120–121
    showing through, 67, 73
    text background color, 37

324 INDEX

Banner Ad Web component, 173–174
banner ads, 173–174, 175, 183
banner text, 155, 181
banners, 124, 158, 180–181
bCentral component, 182–184
Bevel button, 66, 67
bevels, 67
Black and White option, 67
Bold button, 36, 37, 43
bold text, 37, 43, 44
bookmarks, 41–42
Border Properties dialog box, 120–121
borders. *See also* shared borders
    borderless tables, 81–82
    color of, 48, 68, 118
    deleting, 71, 72
    formatting, 8–9, 46–48
    links and, 68, 71
    paragraphs, 47–49
    pictures, 70, 71–72
    plug-ins and, 248
    removing, 71, 72
    shared, 8–9
    size of, 70
    spacing, 48
    support for, 46
    thickness of, 78
Borders and Shading dialog box, 47–48
_borders folder, 122
brightness
    color schemes, 154
    pictures, 66

brightness buttons, 66
Bring Forward button, 66
Broken Hyperlinks report, 295–297
Browse button, 50
browsers. *See* Web browsers
bulleted lists, 37, 44, 45–46
Bullets button, 36, 37, 44
bullets, image, 45
buttons. *See also specific buttons*
    arrow buttons, 38
    brightness buttons, 66
    changing on toolbars, 36, 37
    contrast buttons, 66
    on forms, 188–191, 196–197, 199
    hover buttons, 168–171
    navigation buttons, 8, 9
    option buttons, 196–197, 199
    radio buttons, 196–197, 199

C

captions, 66, 88
Cascading Style Sheets (CSS), 150, 151, 232
categories, 107–108, 181, 298
Categories Properties dialog box, 108
CDs, media files from, 241
Cell Properties dialog box, 82–83
cells, table
    alignment, 82
    background color, 83, 85
    breaking apart, 85
    copying contents of, 86
    deleting, 85

entering data in, 79
formatting, 82–84
merging, 85
moving text within, 85
navigating between, 79
properties, 82
resizing, 82
spacing, 78
Center Vertically button, 85
CGI (Common Gateway Interface), 203, 204
Change Folder button, 59
Character Spacing tab, 44
Check Box Properties dialog box, 195–196
check boxes, 150–151, 195–196, 199
Check In feature, 300–303
Check Out feature, 300–303
Checkout Status report, 302–303
Child Level option, 99
child pages, 10, 97, 99
Circular Hotspot button, 66, 67, 68, 69
client-side data processing, 205
clip art, 57–58
Clipboard, 35
color
    backgrounds, 48, 49, 51, 120–121, 155
    banner text, 155
    body text, 155
    borders, 48, 68, 118, 120–121, 125
    faded, 67

headings, 155
highlights, 37, 43
hyperlinks, 51, 155
making invisible, 67, 73
navigation text, 155
options for, 67
    shared borders, 118, 120–121, 125
    table cells, 83, 85
    text, 37, 43, 49, 50, 51, 155
    in themes, 151, 152–156
Color button, 66, 67
Color palette, 155
Color Wheel tab, 153–154
columns, table
    adding, 79
    changing width of, 82
    deleting, 85
    displaying data in, 80
    inserting, 85
    making same size, 85
    specifying number of, 78
Comment dialog box, 167–168
comments
    adding to files, 23, 286
    adding to pages, 107, 165, 167–168
    described, 165
    on forms, 193
    intranets and, 205
    invisible comments, 167–168
    posting to pages, 204–205
Comments area, 286
comments text box, 193
Common Gateway Interface (CGI), 203, 204

components. *See* Web components
Consumer Support Web
    template, 5, 252
content
    adding to frames, 132–137
    creating from scratch, 134–135
    defining, 12
    editing in framed pages, 137
    shared, 115–116
    updating in Web pages, 114–115
    using included content, 179–181
contrast, 66, 154
contrast buttons, 66
contrast, pictures, 66
Copy button, 34, 35
Copy command, 56
copying items, 35, 38, 56
Corporate Presence Web template,
    5, 252–254
Corporate Presence Web Wizard,
    252–254
Create Hyperlinks button, 68
Create New drop-down list, 35
Create New Page button, 34, 35
cropping pictures, 66
CSS (Cascading Style Sheets), 150,
    151, 232
.css extension, 150
cursor, 85
Custom tab, 53–54
Cut button, 34, 35
cutting items, 35

D

data
    forms, 199, 200–201, 203–219
    tables, 79–80
Database Editor page, 217
Database Interface Web template, 5
Database Interface Wizard, 214–218
databases
    Access database, 205, 316
    forms and, 5, 204, 214–218
    live connection, 214–218
    online, 214–218
    subwebs and, 215
    template for, 5
    wizard for, 214–218
date codes, 165–167
Decrease Font Size button, 36
Decrease Indent button, 36, 37
default.htm page, 6
Delete Cells button, 85
deleting
    borders, 71, 72
    commands from toolbars, 36, 37
    frames, 141
    photos, 88
    shared borders, 123, 124
    table cells, 85
    table columns, 85
    table rows, 85
    toolbar commands, 36
description meta tags, 53, 54
DHTML (Dynamic HTML), 221–233

digital cameras, 87–88
directories, 6, 7
Discussion Forum Web template, 255–256
discussion forums, 254, 255–260
Discussion Web Wizard, 6, 256–257
Distribute Columns Evenly button, 85
Distribute Rows Evenly button, 85
document libraries, 35, 265–267, 268
domains, 305
downloading
   GIF images, 73
   media files, 244
   speed of, 293–294
   Web pages, 51, 290, 291–294
drag-and-drop feature, 10, 11, 58, 98, 99
Draw Table button, 85
Drawing button, 34, 36
Drawing toolbar, 36
drawing tools, 67, 74–75
drives, transferring files to, 35
drop-down boxes, 197–199
Drop-Down Properties dialog box, 198
dynamic effects, 168–174, 184–185
Dynamic HTML (DHTML), 221–233
dynamic links, 115

E

Edit Paste command, 56
editing
   discussion forums, 259–260
   framed page content, 137
   HTML code, 29–30
   link bars, 103
   photos, 88
   pictures, 65–67
   shared borders, 118–123
   SharePoint portals, 263–264
   tasks, 306–307
   text, 37–38
   Web pages, 28–32
effects, 224, 232
e-mail
   collecting form data through, 204, 206–208
   links to, 38, 39, 204, 206–208
Empty Web template, 6
Enable Collapsible Outlines option, 45
Enable Hyperlink Rollover Effects option, 50
Eraser button, 85
eraser cursor, 67
events, 224, 232
Expedia component, 182–184
Extensible Markup Language. *See* XML
extensions, file, 25, 38, 209. *See also specific extensions*

F

FastCounter feature, 176–177
fields, form, 191–201
   adding, 188, 191–200
   alignment, 199–200

clearing, 189
file upload fields, 194–195
length of, 201
picture fields, 199
required fields, 200–201
file formats. *See also specific formats*
changing settings, 59
graphics files, 56
sound files, 51
File Upload button, 194
File Upload Properties dialog box, 194–195
files
AIFF files, 240
analyzing, 284–290
ASF files, 238
assigning applications to, 24
assigning comments to, 23, 286
AU files, 170, 240–241
AVI files, 238
checking in/out, 300–303
collecting form data in, 208–211
displaying information about, 23–24
displaying list of, 22
document libraries, 35, 265–267, 268
downloading, 244
extensions for, 25, 38, 209
filtering, 267, 286
fixing broken links, 291–297
formats. *See* file formats
GIF files, 56, 73, 247
inserting pictures from, 36
JPEG files, 56
links to, 242–244, 267
media files. *See* media files
MIDI files, 60, 240
MPEG files, 238
old, 289
opening, 28–29
organizing, 2–4, 24–25
picture files, 56–60, 67, 87–88
placing on Web page, 57
publishing, 35
RealMedia video/audio files, 238–239, 244–245
recently added/changed, 289–290
reducing size of, 67
renaming, 25–26
searching for, 35, 284, 285–289
SharePoint Team Services files, 261
size of, 60, 288
sorting through, 267, 286
sound files, 51, 52, 241
theme files, 149–150
TIFF files, 56
tracking, 22
unlinked, 28–29
uploading, 18, 194–195
video files, 241–242
viewing, 6, 23–24
WAV files, 243
Fill Color button, 85
Fill Down button, 85, 86
Fill Right button, 85, 86

filters, 267, 286–288
Flash movie controls, 246
Flash movies, 240, 246, 247
Flash player, 240
Flip Horizontal button, 66
Flip Vertical button, 66
Folder view, 122
folders. *See also* FrontPage Webs
   _borders folder, 122
   changing default picture folder, 59
   creating, 24–25, 35
   displaying, 121–122, 149–150, 210
   hidden, 87, 121–122, 149–150, 210, 259
   Images folder, 22
   organizing files in, 24–25
   pictures, 59
   _private folder, 22, 211
   renaming, 25
   searching, 176
   _themes folder, 149, 150
   viewing, 6, 7, 23–24, 122
Folders view, 6, 22, 23–26
Font Color button, 36, 37
Font dialog box, 43–44
Font drop-down list, 36, 37
Font Size drop-down list, 36, 37
Font tab, 44
fonts, 36, 37, 43–44, 158–160.
     See also text
Form Properties dialog box, 206–210, 212–213
Format Painter button, 34, 35

Format Picture button, 66, 67
formats. *See* file formats
formatting
   borders, 8–9, 46–48, 120–123
   choosing styles, 37
   forms, 199–200
   global, 7–14
   link bars, 9–14
   lookup boxes, 110
   paragraphs, 44–46
   shared borders, 8–9, 120–123
   SharePoint portals, 263–264
   showing elements, 36
   tables, 80–86
   text, 42–46, 54, 158–160
   themes, 7–8, 158–160
   Web pages, 48–54
Formatting toolbar, 36–37
forms, 187–203
   buttons on, 188–191, 196–197, 199
   check boxes, 195–196
   collecting data in, 203–219
   creating, 188–191
   databases and, 5, 204, 214–218
   defining, 189
   designing, 191–192
   drop-down boxes, 197–199
   e-mail and, 204, 206–208
   fields in, 191–201
   file uploads and, 194–195
   formatting, 199–200
   group boxes, 199
   labels, 199

Index

managing data in, 205–206
sending data to Web page, 204, 212–214
templates and, 5
testing, 202
text areas, 193–194
text boxes, 192–193
validating input data, 200–201
forums, discussion, 254, 255–260
Frame Properties dialog box, 138–143
framed pages
  building, 130–137
  creating, 131–132
  creating from template, 134–135
  editing content, 137
  making resizable, 140–141
  margins, 140
  resizing, 139–141
  titles and, 137
frames, 127–144
  adding content, 132–137
  around pictures, 67
  deleting, 141
  display frames, 128–129
  displaying different pages in, 134
  HTML pages and, 130
  inline frames, 143–144
  link target frames, 40
  links and, 142–143
  navigation frames, 128
  as navigation tools, 128–129
  "no frames" options, 141–142
  properties, 138–141
  resizing, 138–139
  scrollbars and, 129–130
  splitting, 141
  support for, 141–142
  target frames, 142–143
  using in Web sites, 128–130, 144
  vs. shared borders, 115, 125
framesets
  adding existing pages to, 133–134
  creating from templates, 131–132
  deleting frames from, 141
  margins, 139–140
  saving, 135–136
  shared borders and, 134
  titles for, 137
FrontLook, 152, 319
FrontPage 2002
  add-in programs, 315–320
  adding pictures to, 56–58
  getting around in, 21–32
  installing, 309–313
  installing add-ins, 316–318
  operating system guidelines, 310
  removing add-ins, 318
  resources for, 152, 198, 308
  server extensions. *See* FrontPage server extensions
  Windows 95 and, 310
FrontPage components. *See* Web components
FrontPage Forum, 255

FrontPage server extensions
   adding to IIS 6.0, 276–277
   data collection and, 204
   described, 18–19
   installation of, 310–311
   provider support of, 204, 272
   PWS and, 19
   Web components and, 164–165, 176
   Web servers and, 18–19, 164, 274–277
FrontPage Web site providers, 17, 204
FrontPage Webs. *See also* subwebs; Web sites
   choosing location for, 3–5
   complex, 251–269
   configuring server settings for, 277–278
   creating, 4–5
   creating pages for, 9–10
   described, 2
   disk-based, 4, 17
   previewing, 14–16
   publishing, 3–4, 17–18
   testing, 14–16

G

General tab, 53, 72–73
Get Background and Colors from Page option, 50, 51
.gif extension, 150
GIF files, 56, 73, 247
GIF format, 56, 58, 73, 250
GIF images, 70, 73
GIFs, animated, 225, 247, 250
Glow effect, 169
graphics. *See also* photographs; pictures
   graphic link properties, 94–96
   sources for, 156
   in themes, 156–158
   Web design and, 3
Grayscale option, 67
group boxes, 199

H

handles, image, 60, 61
hard drive, transferring files to, 35
headings, 155
help feature, 34, 36
hidden items. *See* invisible items
Highlight Color button, 36, 37, 43
Highlight Hotspots button, 66, 67
highlights, 67
HiSoftware products, 320
Hit Counter Web component, 176–178
hit counters, 174–178, 183, 304
hits, Web site, 27, 176–178, 183, 286, 304
home page, 6, 217
horizontal orientation, 101
horizontal spacing, 70, 248
hotspots, 67, 68–69

hover buttons, 168–171
.htm extension, 25
HTML code, 14, 15, 29–30, 53
HTML Page view, 29–30
HTML pages, 130
HTML tab, 15, 164
HTML tags, 29–30
HTML view, 15, 29, 30
Hyperlink drop-down boxes, 50, 51
hyperlinks
    adding to link bar, 103–105
    assigning to text, 38–41
    automatic, 38
    back/next sequence, 103–105
    to bookmarks, 41, 42
    borders and, 68, 71
    broken, 23, 26–27
    checking, 16, 26–27
    to child pages, 99
    color of, 51, 155
    defining, 38–41, 42, 95–96
    described, 39
    discussion forums and, 258, 268
    dynamic, 115
    e-mail, 38, 39, 204, 206–208
    external, 26, 39, 40, 95–96, 294
    to files, 267
    fixing broken, 290–297
    frames and, 142–143
    inserting, 36
    internal, 294
    link bars. *See* link bars
    link targets, 38
    to media files, 242–244
    navigation links, 7, 8
    opening in new window, 40, 95–96
    to parent pages, 99
    to pictures, 67–69, 72, 143
    properties, 94–96
    rollover effects, 50
    ScreenTips, 38, 40–41, 94–95
    shared navigation and, 115
    in SharePoint Web sites, 264, 267–268
    within site, 39, 40
    to table of contents, 181–182
    testing, 16, 26–27
    to text, 143
    unlinked files, 28–29
    uploading documents, 267
    viewing, 23
    vs. link bars, 97
    to Web sites, 182
Hyperlinks view, 23

I

IIS (Internet Information Server), 275–277
image bullets, 45
image maps, 67, 68–69
Images folder, 22
Import dialog box, 242
Import Web Wizard, 6
importing media files, 241–242
Include Content Web components, 179
Include Navigation Buttons checkbox, 9
Increase Font Size button, 36
Increase Indent button, 36, 37

indenting
  paragraphs, 37, 45
  text, 46
Index page, 217
index.htm page, 6, 18
inline frames, 143–144
inline pictures, 72
Insert Clip Art window pane, 58
Insert Hyperlink button, 34, 36
Insert Hyperlink dialog box, 39, 69
Insert Picture From File button, 66
Insert Picture from File button, 34, 36
Insert Table button, 34, 36
Insert Table dialog box, 78–79
Insert Web Component dialog box, 87
Inset Columns button, 85
Inset Rows button, 85
installing
  FrontPage 2002, 309–313
  FrontPage add-ins, 316–318
  FrontPage server extensions, 310–311
  Internet Information Server (IIS), 275–276
Interlaced attribute, 73
interlacing, 70, 73
Internet connection, 291–292
Internet Explorer, 14
Internet Information Server (IIS), 275–277
Internet search boxes, 108–110
intranets, 6, 19, 205

invisible items
  comments, 167–168
  folders, 87, 121–122, 149–150, 210, 259
  making color invisible, 67, 73
IP addresses, 3, 17, 18
Italic button, 36, 37, 43
italic text, 37, 43, 44

J

Java applets, 60–241, 168, 173, 319–320
Java language, 164
JavaScript, 164, 205
JavaScript applets, 60–241, 168, 173, 319–320
JavaScripting, 319–320
J-Bots Plus 2002, 319–320
JPEG files, 56
JPEG format, 56, 58–59, 73
JPEG images, 70, 73, 293
.jpg extension, 150
jump menu feature, 198
Justify button, 36, 37

K

keywords, 53

L

labels, 199
Less Brightness button, 66
Less Contrast button, 66
libraries, interactive, 264–267, 268

Index

Library component, 264–267, 268
Line Style button, 66, 67
Link Bar Properties dialog box, 13, 101–103
Link Bar Web components, 181
link bars
    adding links to, 103–105
    back/next links, 103–105
    creating, 97–105
    custom, 101–103
    defining, 11–12, 101–103
    described, 97
    formatting, 9–14
    inserting, 181
    in shared borders, 97, 118, 123
    strategies for, 14
    vs. links, 97
link target frames, 40
links. *See* hyperlinks
List component, 264–267
List Properties dialog box, 45
lists
    bulleted lists, 37, 44, 45–46
    creating, 35
    interactive lists, 264–267
    numbered, 37, 44, 45–46
lookup boxes, 110
looping
    movies, 247
    sound, 52, 249

M

Macintosh computers, 60, 239, 243
Macromedia Flash movies, 240

margins, 52–53, 139–140
Margins tab, 52–53
marquees, 171–173
media files
    downloading, 244
    embedding in Web pages, 244–249
    file types, 236–241
    importing into Web sites, 241–242
    links to, 242–244
    overview, 236–241
    size of, 241–242
    sources of, 241
    working with, 250
media players, 236–240, 243, 244
Merge Cells button, 85
meta tags, 53–54
Microsoft Access database, 205, 316
Microsoft FrontPage 2002. *See* FrontPage 2002
Microsoft FrontPage Help button, 34, 36
Microsoft media formats, 237
MIDI files, 60, 240
MIDI format, 51
mini-toolbar, 88
Modify Theme dialog box, 153–160
Money Central site, 183
More Brightness button, 66
More Contrast button, 66
movies. *See also* video
    Flash movies, 240, 246, 247
    looping, 247
    QuickTime movies, 246, 247
    Shockwave movies, 240
    Windows Movie Maker, 241

MP3 format, 60, 240
MPEG files, 238
MSN component, 182–184
MSN Web search engine, 183
MSNBC component, 182–184

N

navigation, 93–111. *See also*
    hyperlinks
  arrow buttons, 38
  frames and, 128–129
  link bars, 9–14
  links and, 7, 8, 143
  shared borders. *See* shared borders
  structure for, 10, 11–12, 97–101
  viewing links between pages, 23
navigation buttons, 8, 9
Navigation view, 9–12
  adding Web pages, 97–101
  changing page titles, 26
  described, 23
  dragging pages into, 99
  flowchart, 98
  opening files from, 28–29
navigational links. *See* hyperlinks
Netscape Navigator, 14, 223, 228, 232
Netscape Navigator (version 4.7), 46, 94, 172
New button, 34
New Page button, 133
No Frames tab, 142
Normal Color option, 154, 155
Normal Page view, 29, 31

numbered lists, 37, 44, 45–46
Numbering button, 36, 37, 44
Numbers tab, 45

O

Office XP, 6, 260
One Page Web template, 5
Open button, 34, 35
Open Web button, 34
operating systems, 305, 310, 311
operators, 287
option buttons, 196–197, 199
Option Properties dialog box, 196–198
outlines, 45–46, 47
Outside Borders button, 36, 37

P

padding, 78, 83
Page Banner component, 179
page banners, 124, 158
Page Based on Schedule component, 179
Page Properties dialog box, 49–54, 107, 249–250
Page Templates dialog box, 82, 131–132
page transitions, 223–224
Page view
  described, 22
  HTML, 29–30
  navigation and, 11–12
  normal, 29

previewing in, 14–15, 31
text editing in, 37–38
pages. *See* Web pages
panes, 35
paragraphs
   alignment of, 37, 44
   borders, 47–49
   formatting, 44–46
   indenting, 37, 45
   shading, 47–49
Parent Level option, 99
parent pages, 10, 97, 99
passwords, 3, 17
Paste button, 34, 35, 37
Paste Special menu, 37
pasting items, 35, 37
permissions, 5, 278–281
Personal Web Server (PWS), 19
Personal Web template, 6, 254
Photo Album Wizard, 6
Photo Gallery, 86–89, 178
Photo Gallery Properties dialog box, 87–89
photographs. *See also* graphics
   captions for, 88
   deleting, 88
   description, 88
   editing, 88
   JPEG format, 59, 73
   Photo Album Wizard, 6
   Photo Gallery, 86–89, 178
   thumbnails, 86–87, 178
Picture Based on Schedule component, 179

Picture Bullets tab, 45
Picture dialog box, 57
picture fields, 199
picture files, 56–60, 67, 87–88
picture links, 67–68
Picture Option button, 59
Picture Properties dialog box, 70–74, 248–249
Picture toolbar, 66–67
pictures, 6, 55–75. *See also* graphics; photographs
   absolute positioning, 64–65, 66, 89, 91
   adding to Web sites, 56–58
   alignment, 60, 62–65, 70
   alternative representations, 72
   applying DHTML to, 224–225
   assigning links to, 36
   background pictures, 50, 151
   bevels, 67
   borders, 70, 71–72
   buffer space, 60
   as cell background, 83, 84
   changing default folder for, 59
   changing settings for, 59
   clip art, 57–58
   copying, 56
   cropping, 66
   from digital camera, 87–88
   disk space for, 28
   displaying in Photo Gallery, 86–87, 178
   displaying information about, 28

download time, 61, 73
drawing tools, 74–75
editing, 65–67
embedding video as, 247–248
fading in, 70
flowing text around, 60, 62–63, 74
frames around, 67
inline, 72
inserting, 66
inserting image files, 36, 56–57
interlacing, 73
links to, 67–69, 72, 143
low-res alternatives, 72
moving forward/backward, 66
number of, 28
outlines for, 67
overwriting picture file, 67
progressive passes, 73, 74
properties, 59, 69–74
renaming, 59
resizing, 60–61, 70
resolution, 72
rollover effects, 224–228
rotating, 66
saving, 58–60
saving with Web pages, 59
from scanners, 87–88
selecting, 88
in shared borders, 119
size of, 293
spacing, 70, 71
swapping, 225–228
thumbnails, 61–62, 66
ToolTips for, 70
watermarks, 50
Pictures report, 28
pixels, 52, 70, 138
player controls, 250
players, 236–240, 243, 244
Plug-In Properties dialog box, 245–246
plug-ins
  AVI plug-ins, 246
  borders and, 248
  embedding in Web pages, 244–246
  properties, 245–246
  QuickTime movie plug-in, 246
  RealPlayer as, 239
  video plug-ins, 248, 250
Polygonal Hotspot button, 66, 67, 68
Position dialog box, 65
Preview in Browser button, 34, 35
Preview in Browser dialog box, 31
Preview mode, 14–15, 31
Preview Page view, 31
Preview tab, 14–15, 31
Print button, 34, 35
printing Web pages, 35
_private folder, 22, 211
Problem reports, 290–298
progressive passes, 70, 73, 74
Project Web template, 6, 254
properties
  embedded pictures/video, 247–248
  frames, 138–141
  graphic links, 94–96

links, 94–96
pictures, 59, 69–74
plug-ins, 245–246
scrollbars, 141
table cells, 82
tables, 82, 84
text links, 94–96
Web pages, 48–54
Publish Destination dialog box, 17–18
Publish Status report, 303
Publish Web button, 34, 35
Publish Web dialog box, 18
publishing Web sites
    to local server, 274–277
    to remote server, 272, 273–274
    to Web server, 3–4, 17–18
Push Button Properties dialog box, 190
PWS (Personal Web Server), 19

Q

Quality setting, 73
QuickTime format, 239
QuickTime movie plug-in, 246
QuickTime movies, 246, 247
QuickTime player, 60, 243

R

RA format, 51
RA (RealAudio) files, 238
radio buttons, 196–197, 199
RAM format, 51

Real Audio, 51
RealAudio (RA) files, 238
RealMedia (RM) files, 238–239, 244–245
RealMedia video/audio files, 238–239
RealPlayer, 238, 239
Rectangular Hotspot button, 66, 67, 68, 69
Redo button, 34, 35
Refresh button, 34, 36
Remove button, 34, 36, 37
Rename button, 59
reports, 27–28
    All Files report, 285–289
    Broken Hyperlinks report, 295–297
    displaying, 22
    Problem reports, 290–298
    Publish Status report, 303
    Site Summary report, 284–285
    usage reports, 27, 304–305
    Workflow reports, 300
Reports view, 22, 27–28
Resample button, 66, 67
Reset button, 189, 190, 191
resolution, 72
Restore button, 66, 67
Results page, 217
ripper software, 241
RM (RealMedia) files, 238–239, 244–245
roles, 280–281

rollover effects
   hyperlinks, 50
   pictures, 224–228, 230–231
   text, 228–231
Rotate Left button, 66
Rotate Right button, 66
rotating pictures, 66
rows, table
   adding, 79
   changing width of, 82
   deleting, 85
   displaying data in, 80
   inserting, 85
   making same size, 85
   specifying number of, 78

S

Save As dialog box, 135–136
Save button, 34, 35, 135, 136
Save Embedded Files dialog box, 59
saving framesets, 135–136
Saving Results dialog box, 213
scanners, 87–88
ScreenTip button, 40
ScreenTip text, 40–41
ScreenTips, 38, 94–95
scripts, 164
scrollbars, 129–130, 141
Search button, 34, 35
search engines, 53–54, 108, 183
search features
   Internet search boxes, 108–110
   stock lookup boxes, 109–110
   Web Search component, 174–176

Search Results tab, 175–176
search strings, 305
searching
   for files, 35, 284, 285–289
   for sound files, 51
   Web site, 174–176
Select button, 66, 67
Send Backward button, 66
server administration, 281–282, 301
server extensions. *See* FrontPage server extensions
servers. *See* Web servers
server-side data processing, 205
Set Action button, 59
Set Initial Page button, 133, 134
Set Transparent Color button, 66, 67
shading text, 46–48
shared borders, 113–125
   applying, 9
   color, 120–121, 125
   creating, 116–118
   customizing, 123–124
   described, 7, 114
   design tips, 124–125
   editing, 118–123
   formatting, 8–9, 120–123
   framesets and, 134
   hidden folders and, 121–122
   for individual pages, 123–124
   link bars in, 97, 118, 123
   marquees and, 171
   navigation links and, 115
   page design with, 113–125

pictures in, 119
problems with, 115–116
removing, 123, 124
shared content, 115–116
using, 114–116
vs. frames, 115, 125
width of, 119–120
Shared Borders dialog box, 117–118, 124
SharePoint extensions, 165
SharePoint portals, 261–269
SharePoint Team Services files, 261
SharePoint Team Web Services, 311
SharePoint Team Web template, 6, 254
SharePoint Web sites, 260–269
Shockwave movies, 240
Shockwave player, 240
Show All button, 34, 36
.shtml extension, 25
Site Summary report, 284–285
site transitions, 223–224
SND format, 51
sound, 235–250
   AIFF format, 60
   AU format, 60–241
   audio formats, 293
   background sound, 51–52, 249–250
   embedding into Web pages, 242–244
   file formats, 51
   file types, 236–241
   looping, 52, 249
   Microsoft media formats, 238
   MIDI format, 60

MP3 format, 60
overview, 236–241
RealAudio format, 238–239
sound files, 51, 52, 241
Sound Recorder program, 241
spacing
   borders, 48
   between cells, 78
   horizontal, 70, 248
   pictures, 70, 71
   table cells, 78
   text, 44, 45
   vertical, 70, 248
   video, 248
spell checking, 35
Spelling button, 34, 35
Split Cells button, 85
Standard toolbar, 34–36
stock information, 183
stock lookup boxes, 109–110
Stop button, 34, 36
StoreFront 5.0, 316
streaming properties, 242
Style drop-down list, 36, 37
Style tab, 101
styles, 37, 159–160
Styles list, 43
Submission Form page, 217
Submit button, 188, 190, 199, 205
Substitution component, 179
subwebs. *See also* FrontPage Webs
   configuring server settings for, 277–278
   creation of, 278

databases and, 215
described, 5, 278
local servers and, 277
permissions, 279–280
searching, 176
support for, 215
surveys, creating, 35
swapped pictures, 224–228

T

Table AutoFormat button, 85, 86
Table AutoFormat Combo button, 85
Table AutoFormat dialog box, 80, 85, 86
Table menu, 78–79
table of contents, 105–108, 181–182
Table toolbar, 84–86
tables, 78–86
   alignment, 78
   AutoFormat option, 80
   borderless, 81–82
   cells. *See* cells, table
   columns. *See* columns, table
   creating, 36
   entering data in, 79–81
   formats, 80–86
   formatting cells in, 82–84
   inserting, 78–79
   layout options, 81–86
   pasting, 79
   properties, 82, 84
   resizing, 85
   rows. *See* rows, table
   setting defaults, 79
   width of, 79
target frame, 96
Target Frame dialog box, 96
target frames, 142–143
targets
   e-mail links as, 206–208
   for picture links, 68
task list, 306–307
tasks
   associating with specific page, 306
   creating, 35, 306
   editing, 306–307
Tasks view, 23
templates, 251–269
   choosing, 4–6
   creating framed pages from, 134–135
   creating framesets from, 131–132
   creating new site with, 254–255
   types of, 5–6
   viewing, 81
   working with, 5–7
text
   absolute positioning of, 89–91
   alignment of, 37, 44
   applying DHTML to, 224–225, 228–230
   assigning links to, 36, 38–41
   attributes, 37, 43–44
   banner text, 155, 181
   body text, 155

buffer space, 60
captions, 66
color of, 37, 43, 49, 50, 51, 155
copying, 35, 38
cutting to Clipboard, 35
defining alternate text, 72
defining for ToolTips, 70
editing, 37–38
flowing around images, 60, 62–63, 74
flowing around video, 248
fonts, 36, 37, 43–44, 158–160
formatting, 42–46, 54, 158–160
highlight color, 37, 43
highlighting, 43
indenting, 37, 45, 46
links to, 143
in marquees, 171–173
moving, 38, 90
moving within cells, 85
page load effects, 229
pasting, 35, 37
pop-up, 40–41
resizing, 90
rollover effects, 228–231
ScreenTip text, 40–41, 94–95
selecting, 43
shading, 46–48
spacing, 44, 45
subscript, 44
superscript, 44
text link properties, 94–96
in themes, 158–160

text areas, 193–194
text blocks, 83, 90
text boxes, 192–193
Text button, 66
Text drop-down list, 50, 51
text operators, 287
Text Properties dialog box, 192–193
TextArea dialog box, 194
Theme Chameleon, 152, 319
theme files, 149–150
themes, 145–161
  applying to selected pages, 148–149
  applying to Web site, 8, 147–148
  changing, 150–151
  check boxes for, 150–151
  color in, 151, 152–156
  creating, 151–160
  custom, 160
  described, 7, 146–147
  fonts and, 158–160
  formatting with, 7–8
  graphics in, 156–158
  hidden folders and, 149–150
  previewing, 8
  removing, 49, 149
  SharePoint Web sites, 264
  text formatting in, 158–160
  using, 146–150
Themes dialog box, 49, 147–160
_themes folder, 149, 150
thumbnails
  described, 60
  displaying in Photo Gallery, 86–87, 178

download speed and, 293
photos, 86–87, 178
pictures, 61–62, 66
TIFF files, 56
time codes, 165–167
timestamps, 165–167
titles, Web pages, 124, 137, 179
Toggle Pane button, 34, 35
toolbars, 34–37
    adding commands to, 36, 37
    customizing, 36, 37
    deleting commands from, 36, 37
    detached, 34
    displaying, 34
    Drawing toolbar, 36
    Formatting toolbar, 36–37
    mini-toolbar, 88
    Picture toolbar, 66–67
    Standard toolbar, 34–36
    Table toolbar, 84–86
tools, deselecting, 67
ToolTips, 70
transition effects, 223–224
Transparent attribute, 73
troubleshooting, 290–298
tutorial, 6
Type option, 73–74

U

Underline button, 36, 37, 43
underlined text, 37, 43, 44
Undo button, 34, 35

UNIX operating system, 60, 275
Unlinked Files report, 28
uploading files, 194–195
URLs, 3, 5, 17, 18, 39, 305
Usage Analysis reports, 27
Usage Data report, 27
usage reports, 27, 304–305. *See also* hit counters; hits, Web site
user name, 3, 17
users, assigning to roles, 281

V

validation dialog boxes, 200–201
version control, 301–303
vertical orientation, 101
vertical spacing, 70, 248
video, 235–250. *See also* movies
    alignment, 248
    embedding as pictures, 247–248
    embedding into Web pages, 237, 242–244
    file types, 236–241
    Flash movies, 240
    flowing text around, 248
    Microsoft media formats, 238
    overview, 236–241
    QuickTime format, 239
    RealMedia format, 238–239
    resizing, 248
    Shockwave movies, 240
    sources of, 241
    spacing in, 248

video files, 241–242
video formats, 293
video plug-ins, 248, 250
Views bar, 9, 22
Visual InterDev RA, 276
Vivid Colors option, 151, 154, 155

W

Washout option, 67
Watermark option, 50
watermarks, 50
WAV files, 243
WAV format, 51, 238
Web browsers
   adding, 16, 31
   borders and, 46
   choosing between, 16
   compatibility issues, 46
   described, 14
   DHTML and, 222, 232
   frame support, 141–142
   information about, 305
   inline pictures, 72
   opening links in new window, 40, 95–96
   paragraph formatting, 44, 45
   previewing pages in, 14, 16, 31–32, 35
   resizing frames in, 138, 140–141
   shading and, 46
   window sizes of, 31–32
Web Component button, 34, 35
Web Component dialog box, 35
Web components, 163–185
   FrontPage extensions and, 164–165, 176
   overview, 164–165
   scripts and, 164
   SharePoint extensions and, 165
   troubleshooting, 297–298
Web design, 2–3, 12
Web pages
   adding background sound, 51–52, 249–250
   adding comments to, 107, 165, 167–168
   adding pictures to, 56–58
   adding timestamps to, 165–167
   adding to framesets, 133–134
   advanced controls, 184
   applying themes to, 148–149
   assigning to individuals/groups, 298–300
   bookmarks. *See* bookmarks
   child pages, 10, 97, 99
   creating, 9–10, 35
   Database Editor page, 217
   defining backgrounds, 49–51
   defining content for, 12
   displaying in different frames, 134
   download time, 51, 290, 291–294
   drag-and-drop feature, 10, 11, 99
   dynamic effects, 168–174
   editing, 28–32
   embedding media files into, 244–249

embedding plug-ins into, 244–246
embedding sound into, 242–244
embedding video into, 237, 242–244
filenames, 137
formatting, 48–54
hit counters, 177–178, 183, 304
home page, 6, 217
Index page, 217
margins, 52–53
opening, 28–29, 35
parent pages, 10, 97, 99
placing files on, 57
posting comments to, 204–205
previewing in browser, 14–16, 31–32, 35
printing, 35
properties, 48–54
refreshing, 36
removing themes from, 49
renaming, 25–26
Results page, 217, 218
reverting to last saved version, 36
saving images with, 59
sending form data to, 204, 212–214
showing formatting elements, 36
slow, 290, 291–294
spell checking, 35
stopping connection to, 36
Submission Form page, 217
titles for, 10, 25–26, 124, 137, 179
unlinked, 28–29

updating content in, 114–115
viewing links between, 23
within Web pages, 179–180
Web Presence Providers (WPPs)
    server administration and, 281–282
    SharePoint support, 261, 262
    shopping for, 204, 272–273
    subweb support, 215
Web Search component, 174–176
Web servers, 271–282
    administration of, 272, 277–278, 301
    connecting to remote server, 273–274
    creation of, 19
    data processing and, 205, 206
    FrontPage extensions and, 18–19, 164, 274–277
    Internet Information Server (IIS), 275–276
    operating systems and, 311
    permissions, 278–281
    publishing sites to local server, 274–277
    publishing sites to remote server, 272, 273–274
    publishing Web sites to, 3–4, 17–18
    requirements for adding software, 274–275
    setting up local server, 282
    space required for, 27
    transferring files to, 35

version control, 301–303
Web components and, 164–165
Windows ME and, 274–275, 282
working with, 269
Web Settings dialog box, 122, 149–150
Web sites. *See also* FrontPage Webs
adding pictures to, 56–58
animated GIFs, 225, 247, 250
assigning themes to, 147–148
broken links, 291–297
choosing location for, 3–5
corporate, 5
creating, 4–5, 35
creating with templates, 254–255
CSS, 232
defining administrator for, 280–281
designing, 2–3
discussion forums, 255–260
disk-based, 4, 17
dynamic effects, 168–174, 184–185
file extensions, 38
FrontPage resources, 152, 198, 308
FrontPage Web site providers, 17
global formatting, 7–14
graphics sources, 156
hits received, 27, 176–178, 183, 286, 304
importing media files into, 241–242
interactive, 212–214
intranets, 6, 19, 205
links. *See* hyperlinks
links to, 182
managing, 22–28, 281–282, 283–308
Money Central site, 183
opening, 35
permissions, 279–280
personal, 6
planning, 2–3
publishing to local servers, 274–277
publishing to remote servers, 272, 273–274
publishing to Web servers, 3–4, 17–18
remote, 272–274
search feature for, 174–176
searching for files in, 35
SharePoint Web sites, 260–269
size of, 22, 27, 284
Style Master site, 232
table of contents, 105–108, 181–182
tracking files associated with, 22
tracking usage, 27, 304–305
troubleshooting, 284, 290–298
types of, 5–6
viewing, 22–23
viewing folders/files, 6, 7, 23–24, 122
Web templates. *See* templates
Webs. *See* FrontPage Webs
Window XP Professional, 275
Windows 95, 310
Windows 98, 274
Windows 2000, 19

Windows ME, 241, 274–275, 282
Windows Media Player, 60, 238, 243
Windows Metafile Format (WMF), 56
Windows Movie Maker, 241
Windows NT, 19, 275
wizards
   Corporate Presence Web Wizard, 252–254
   Database Interface Wizard, 214–218
   Discussion Web Wizard, 6, 256–257
   Import Web Wizard, 6
   Photo Album Wizard, 6
WMF (Windows Metafile Format), 56

Workflow reports, 300
workgroups, 298–303
WPPs. *See* Web Presence Providers
WYSIWYG editors, 29

X–Y

XML (Extensible Markup Language), 29
XML rules, 29

Z

Z values, 65, 90
Z-Order spin box, 65, 90

INTERNATIONAL CONTACT INFORMATION

AUSTRALIA
McGraw-Hill Book Company Australia Pty. Ltd.
TEL +61-2-9417-9899
FAX +61-2-9417-5687
http://www.mcgraw-hill.com.au
books-it_sydney@mcgraw-hill.com

CANADA
McGraw-Hill Ryerson Ltd.
TEL +905-430-5000
FAX +905-430-5020
http://www.mcgrawhill.ca

GREECE, MIDDLE EAST, NORTHERN AFRICA
McGraw-Hill Hellas
TEL +30-1-656-0990-3-4
FAX +30-1-654-5525

MEXICO (Also serving Latin America)
McGraw-Hill Interamericana Editores S.A. de C.V.
TEL +525-117-1583
FAX +525-117-1589
http://www.mcgraw-hill.com.mx
fernando_castellanos@mcgraw-hill.com

SINGAPORE (Serving Asia)
McGraw-Hill Book Company
TEL +65-863-1580
FAX +65-862-3354
http://www.mcgraw-hill.com.sg
mghasia@mcgraw-hill.com

SOUTH AFRICA
McGraw-Hill South Africa
TEL +27-11-622-7512
FAX +27-11-622-9045
robyn_swanepoel@mcgraw-hill.com

UNITED KINGDOM & EUROPE (Excluding Southern Europe)
McGraw-Hill Publishing Company
TEL +44-1-628-502500
FAX +44-1-628-770224
http://www.mcgraw-hill.co.uk
computing_neurope@mcgraw-hill.com

ALL OTHER INQUIRIES Contact:
Osborne/McGraw-Hill
TEL +1-510-549-6600
FAX +1-510-883-7600
http://www.osborne.com
omg_international@mcgraw-hill.com

LEARN WEB SITE DESIGN!
VIDEO LESSONS FROM LAURIE ULRICH AND BRAINSVILLE.COM

FrontPage is a useful tool to create Web sites quickly and easily. But you need to decide for yourself how you want your site to look, feel, and act. I'm Laurie Ulrich, author of *Web Design Virtual Classroom*, and I've created a video CD showing you the vital information you need to create sharp-looking sites. It's called the **Web Design CD Extra**, and it covers key areas like these:

Graphics and Design Tools
Photoshop, Flash, and Dreamweaver help speed development and produce better-looking images faster

Web Site Critiques
Frank opinions about other people's mistakes—plus simple principles for sharp-looking sites

HTML Basics
Learn the language of the web to make your sites work the way you want

Structuring Pages
See how tables and frames let you control text and image placement

Creative Page Balancing
Eye-pleasing colors, layouts, and designs to keep your site visitors coming back

...And more! The complete contents are listed at www.Brainsville.com.

The lessons on the **Web Design CD Extra** use the same easy-to-follow video presentation style as the CD included with this book. I'm right there on your screen, talking to you about Web design in the same practical, understandable way.

The **Web Design CD Extra** is an essential tool for learning Web design. Check it out at www.Brainsville.com.

Best Wishes,

Laurie Ulrich

Laurie Ulrich

Name: Laurie Ulrich
Project: Web Design

ORDER THE WEB DESIGN CD EXTRA AT
Brainsville.com™
The better way to learn.™